Luciano L'Abate
Editor

Using Workbooks in Mental Health
Resources in Prevention, Psychotherapy, and Rehabilitation for Clinicians and Researchers

Pre-publication
REVIEWS,
COMMENTARIES,
EVALUATIONS . . .

More pre-publication
REVIEWS, COMMENTARIES, EVALUATIONS . . .

"Luciano L'Abate's latest book follows his tradition of excellence in writing about therapy. It identifies several major shortcomings of how therapy is currently practiced, based both on current literature and clinical experience, and identifies a number of ways to correct the problems, one of which is the use of workbooks in therapy. *Using Workbooks in Mental Health* explains why the workbook model has not been previously adopted, and describes the extensive support for the use of the materials, including the emerging role of evidence-based treatments that are replicable and available to be disseminated. L'Abate presents chapters prepared by respected clinicians and researchers who have applied his recommended applications of distance writing to use with specific populations. These groups include those with dementia, depression, gambling problems, substance abuse, and marital and other issues. The chapters include sound theoretical principles, relevant clinical examples, and supportive documentation of the applications.

L'Abate does not oversell the model—he presents it as a work in progress, but a work that has substantial theoretical, practical, clinical, and evaluative support. This will be a very beneficial contribution to practitioners looking for increased effectiveness in their work, for students learning how to enter the field and be impactful and effective in their work, and for program developers and managers looking for the efficient methods of delivering services to an ever-expanding population of individuals in need of more effective mental health services."

Arthur M. Horne, PhD
Distinguished Research Professor,
The University of Georgia, Athens

THRP

The Haworth Reference Press
An Imprint of The Haworth Press, Inc.
New York • London • Oxford

Using Workbooks in Mental Health

Resources in Prevention, Psychotherapy, and Rehabilitation for Clinicians and Researchers

HAWORTH Practical Practice in Mental Health Guidebooks for In-Patient, Out-Patient, and Independent Practice

Lorna L. Hecker, PhD
Senior Editor

101 Interventions in Family Therapy edited by Thorana S. Nelson and Terry S. Trepper

101 More Interventions in Family Therapy edited by Thorana S. Nelson and Terry S. Trepper

The Practical Practice of Marriage and Family Therapy: Things My Training Supervisor Never Told Me by Mark Odell and Charles E. Campbell

The Therapist's Notebook for Families: Solution-Oriented Exercises for Working with Parents, Children, and Adolescents by Bob Bertolino and Gary Schultheis

The Therapist's Notebook for Children and Adolescents: Homework, Handouts, and Activities for Use in Psychotherapy edited by Catherine Ford Sori and Lorna L. Hecker

The Therapist's Notebook for Lesbian, Gay, and Bisexual Clients: Homework, Handouts, and Activities for Use in Psychotherapy edited by Joy S. Whitman and Cynthia J. Boyd

Collaborative Practice in Psychology and Therapy edited by David A. Paré and Glenn Larner

A Guide to Self-Help Workbooks for Mental Health Clinicians and Researchers by Luciano L' Abate

Using Workbooks in Mental Health Resources in Prevention, Psychotherapy, and Rehabilitation for Clinicians and Researchers edited by Luciano L'Abate

The Psychotherapist As Parent Coordinator in High-Conflict Divorce: Strategies and Techniques by Susan M. Boyan and Ann Marie Termini

Using Workbooks in Mental Health

Resources in Prevention, Psychotherapy, and Rehabilitation for Clinicians and Researchers

Luciano L'Abate
Editor

The Haworth Reference Press
An Imprint of The Haworth Press, Inc.
New York • London • Oxford

Published by

The Haworth Reference Press, an imprint of The Haworth Press, Inc., 10 Alice Street, Binghamton, NY 13904-1580.

The poem "Autobiography in Five Chapters" is ©1993 by Portia Nelson from the book *There's a Hole In My Sidewalk*, Beyond Words Publishing, Hillsboro, OR.

PUBLISHER'S NOTE
Identities and circumstances of individuals discussed in this book have been changed to protect confidentiality.

Cover design by Marylouise E. Doyle.

Library of Congress Cataloging-in-Publication Data

Using workbooks in mental health : resources in prevention, psychotherapy, and rehabilitation for clinicians and researchers / Luciano L'Abate, editor.
    p. cm.
  Includes bibliographical references and index.
  ISBN 0-7890-1593-5 (case: alk. paper)—ISBN 0-7890-1594-3 (soft : alk. paper)
   1. Mental health—Study and teaching. 2. Mental health—Programmed instruction. 3. Mental health—Computer-assisted instruction. 4. Written communication—Therapeutic use. 5. Internet in psychotherapy. I. L'Abate, Luciano, 1928 -.
RA790.8.U856 2004
616.89'0071'1—dc22

                                               2003021894

CONTENTS

About the Editor   xiii

Contributors   xv

Foreword   xix
   James W. Pennebaker

Preface   xxiii

SECTION I: INTRODUCTION

**Chapter 1. The Role of Workbooks in the Delivery
of Mental Health Services in Prevention, Psychotherapy,
and Rehabilitation**   3
   Luciano L'Abate

   The Status of Mental Health Needs in the United States   7
   The Status of Individual Psychotherapy   9
   Toward an Increasing Formalization of Psychological
      Interventions   12
   Implications of an Increasing Trend in Formalization   19
   Differences Between Clinical Practice and Research   21
   Workbooks in Current Psychological Literature   27
   Overview of Workbook Administration   31
   Toward a Classification of Writing   33
   Toward a Classification of Workbooks   35
   Advantages of Workbooks   39
   Metafunctions of Workbooks   45
   Disadvantages and Dangers of Workbook Administration   46
   Testing Theories Through Workbooks   47
   On the Nature of Evidence to Support Workbook
      and Structured Computer-Assisted Interventions   49
   Importance of Evaluation and Informed Consent
      for Workbook Administration   50

Successive Sieves and Stepped Treatment
    in the Delivery of Mental Health Services   51
Conclusion   52

**Chapter 2. Systematically Written Homework
Assignments: The Case for Homework-Based
Treatment**   **65**
    Luciano L'Abate

Professional Antecedents of Systematically Written
    Homework Assignments   65
Workbooks As Extensions of Existing Knowledge   69
Bridging the Semantic Gap   72
Research with SWHAs   75
A Meta-Analysis of Workbook Effectiveness   92
Professional Implications   93
Conclusion   96

SECTION II: INDIVIDUALS

**Chapter 3. Dementia, Depression, and Workbooks:
A Personal Odyssey**   **105**
    Everett Gorman

The Problem of Depression   106
Completing Personal Assignments for Depression   109
Conclusion   113

Chapter 4. Life-Challenging Conditions and Helpers   **115**
    Rubin Battino

Description of Workbooks   116
Workbook for People Who Have a Life-Challenging
    Disease   117
Workbook for Caregivers   120
Workbook for Grieving   123
Results from a Brief Survey   124
Susan and Bill: A Case Study   126
Implications and Conclusions   127

Chapter 5. Schema-Focused Cognitive Therapy:
A Stage-Specific Workbook Approach   **129**
Demián F. Goldstein

Rationale and Background for the Creation
     and Development of the Workbook   129
Description of the Workbook   131
Administering the Workbook   131
The Stage-Specific Schema Inventory   132
Implications for the Role of Workbooks
     in Cognitive-Behavioral Therapy   133
Implications of the Present and Future Use
     of Workbooks in Mental Health Interventions   134
Appendix: A Sample Assignment from the 3S
     Workbook—Crisis Three, Initiative versus Guilt   135

Chapter 6. Healing the Trauma of Abuse:
A Women's Workbook   **141**
Ellen Arledge
Joselyn Y. Barsfield
Caroline L. Mitchell
Emily Moody
Carolina J. Quesada

Description of Workbook   141
Results of Workbook Administration   146
Clients' Comments Concerning Workbook Utilization   147
The Role of Workbooks in Prevention   151
Implications for Using the Workbook in Practice   156
Conclusion   156

Chapter 7. Workbooks for Individuals with Gambling
Problems: Promoting the Natural Recovery Process
Through Brief Intervention   **159**
David C. Hodgins

Recovery from Problem Gambling   160
Natural versus Treatment-Assisted Recovery   161
Applying the Stepped Care Model to Problem Gambling   162

Self-Help Workbooks in Addictions 164
Developing a Self-Help Workbook for Problem Gamblers 164
Clinical Trial 166
Conclusion 170

Chapter 8. The Wheel of Wisdom with Depressed Inpatients **173**

Piero De Giacomo   Giovanni Carrieri
Marco Storelli   Odilia Mele
Andrea De Giacomo   Massimiliano Morreale
Caterina Tarquinio   Francesco Vaira

Objectives and Research Hypothesis 174
Scriptotherapy 174
The Technique 175
Method and Experimental Procedure 176
Analysis and Description of the Sample 177
Analysis of Results 178
Discussion and Conclusions 186

**Chapter 9. Substance Abuse in Women:
An Empirical Evaluation of a Manualized
Cognitive-Behavioral Protocol** **191**

Terry Michael McClanahan

Description of the Manualized Cognitive-Behavioral
  Protocol 192
Clinical Efficacy of CBT Workbooks with Female
  Substance Abusers 194
Conclusion 202

**Chapter 10. Workbooks and Psychotherapy
with Incarcerated Felons: Replication of Research
in Progress** **205**

Oliver McMahan
John Arias

Benefits of Writing in Interventions with Felons 205
Felon Writers and Emotionality 206

Continuing Research in Progress: Rehabilitation Program
    Using Programmed Distance Writing   208
Conclusion   212

SECTION III: COUPLES

Chapter 11. Marriage Preparation and Maintenance   217
    Mario Cusinato

Historical and Cultural Context for Marriage
    Preparation and Maintenance   217
Strategies for Intervention   219
A Program of Marriage Preparation and Maintenance   222
Workbooks for Marriage Preparation   228
Workbooks for Marriage Maintenance   231
Evaluation of the Educational Process   232
Conclusion   239

Chapter 12. Homework in Couple Therapy:
A Review and Evaluation of Available Workbooks   247
    Krista S. Gattis
    Mia Sevier
    Andrew Christensen

Defining Homework   247
Clinical Issues in Homework with Couples   248
Research Basis of Homework with Couples   250
Workbooks for Use with Couples   251
Special Considerations   261

Chapter 13. Intimacy in Couples: Evaluating
a Workbook   265
    Eleonora Maino

Contextual Considerations   266
The Early Couple Relationship   266
Research with Structured Interventions   268
Intervention: An Intimacy Workbook   272
Discussion and Summary   276

SECTION IV: FAMILIES

Chapter 14. Manualized Treatment for School-Refusal Behavior in Youth   283
> *Christopher A. Kearney*
> *Krisann M. Alvarez*

Rationale for the Creation and Development
   of a Therapist Guide and Parent Workbook   284
Description of the Therapist Guide and Parent Workbook   285
Research Evidence   293
Case Studies   294
Predictions About the Future of Manuals
   and Workbooks in Mental Health Interventions   298
Conclusion   299

Chapter 15. A Review of Workbooks and Related Literature on Eating Disorders   301
> *Katherine J. Miller*

Introduction   301
Descriptions of Workbooks and Related Research   307
Conclusion   319

Chapter 16. Couples with a Handicapped Child: Experiencing Intimacy   327
> *Eleonora Maino*
> *Silvia Pasinato*
> *Donatella Fara*
> *Umberto Talpone*
> *Massimo Molteni*

Contextual Considerations   328
Clinical Considerations: Family Resources
   and the Impact of Disability   328
Intervention Modality: Psychoeducational Counseling
   and Workbooks   329
Research with Structured Interventions   332
Intervention: An Intimacy Workbook   334

Representative Case Studies   336
Discussion and Summary   343

SECTION V: CONCLUSION

**Chapter 17. The Status and Future of Workbooks
in Mental Health: Concluding Commentary**   **351**
  Luciano L'Abate
  Lorna L. Hecker

Introduction   351
Unstructured versus Structured Interventions   354
Questions About Programmed Distance Writing   355
Epidemiological Implications of Workbooks   357
A Research Agenda for Workbooks   359
Psychotherapy and Workbook-Based Interventions   365
Conclusion   369

**Appendix. Survey Questionnaire: Participant
Satisfaction with Workbooks**   **375**

Index   **381**

ABOUT THE EDITOR

Luciano L'Abate, PhD, is a retired professor emeritus of psychology at Georgia State University in Atlanta, where he founded the first in the world PhD program in Family Psychology. He has produced over 100 self-help workbooks for clinicians and researchers. Eight workbooks are available in Spanish. He has authored or co-authored over 200 papers, chapters, and book reviews in professional journals. He is also author, co-author, editor, or co-editor of more than thirty books, including *A Guide to Self-Help Workbooks for Mental Health Clinicians and Researchers* (The Haworth Press). His work has been translated into Chinese, Japanese, Finnish, Spanish, French, Polish, and German, and five of his books have been translated and published in his native Italy.

Dr. L'Abate is a diplomate and former examiner of the American Board of Professional Psychology, and a fellow and approved supervisor of the American Association for Marriage and Family Therapy, fellow of Divisions 12 and 43 of the American Psychological Association, life member of the American Orthopsychiatric Association, charter member of the American Family Therapy Academy, member of the National Council on Family Relations, co-founder and past-president of the International Academy of Family Psychology, charter member of the American Association for the Advancement of Preventative Psychology, and member of the Society for Prevention Research.

Dr. L'Abate was awarded the 1983 GSU Alumni Distinguished Professorship in the School of Arts and Sciences, named "Outstanding Citizen" by the House of Representatives in the State of Georgia in 1984, and received the "Outstanding Achievement and Service" award in 1986 by the Tabor College Alumni Association. In 1987, he received recognition by the Georgia Association for Marriage and Family Therapy for "Outstanding Contribution." He was named "Family Psychologist of the Year for 1994" by Division 43 (Family Psychology) of the American Psychological Association.

CONTRIBUTORS

Krisann M. Alvarez, BA, is a doctoral student in the Psychology Department of the University of Nevada at Las Vegas.

John Arias, BA, Individual Support Specialist, Bradley Cleveland Services, Cleveland, Tennessee.

Ellen Arledge, MSW, Clinical Supervisor, Community Connections, Washington, DC.

Joselyn Y. Barsfield, MA, Clinical Case Manager, Community Connections, Washington, DC.

Rubin Battino, PhD, is Professor Emeritus of Chemistry and an adjunct professor in the School of Psychology at Wright State University in Dayton, Ohio. He has an MS in mental health counseling, works part-time as a therapist, and has published two books: one on Eriksonian therapy and one on the use of metaphor in psychotherapy.

Giovanni Carrieri, MD, Psychiatrist/Researcher in the Department of Neurological and Psychiatric Sciences at the Medical School of the University of Bari, Italy.

Andrew Christensen, PhD, Professor of Psychology, University of California at Los Angeles.

Mario Cusinato, PhD, is Associate Professor in the Department of General Psychology at the University of Padua and Director of the Centro della Famiglia in Treviso, Italy.

Andrea De Giacomo, MD, Pediatric Neuropsychiatrist and Researcher in the Department of Neurological and Psychiatric Sciences at the Medical School of the University of Bari, Italy.

Piero De Giacomo, MD, Chair and Professor, Department of Neurological and Psychiatric Sciences, Medical School, University of Bari, Italy.

Donatella Fara, PhD, Chief Psychologist, Family Psychology Service, Associazione "La Nostra Famiglia," and Researcher, Scientific Institute "Eugenio Medea," Bosisio Parini (Lecco), Italy.

Krista S. Gattis, MA, is a doctoral candidate in the Psychology Department, University of California at Los Angeles.

Demián F. Goldstein, Licensed Biologist, Buenos Aires, Argentina.

Everett Gorman, PhD, is retired from public service in the province of Alberta, Canada.

Lorna L. Hecker, PhD, Associate Professor, Marriage and Family Therapy Program, Purdue University at Calumet, Hammond, Indiana.

David C. Hodgins, PhD, is Professor of Psychology, University of Calgary, Alberta, Canada.

Christopher A. Kearney, PhD, is Professor of Psychology, Department of Psychology, University of Nevada at Las Vegas.

Eleonora Maino, PhD, is a member of the Family Psychology Service, Associazione "La Nostra Famiglia," and Researcher, Scientific Institute "Eugenio Medea," Bosisio Parini (Lecco), Italy.

Terry Michael McClanahan, PsyD, is Director of Training, Post-Doctoral Residency in Psychology, Department of Psychiatry, Kaiser Permanente, Pleasanton, California, and Lecturer, College of Behavioral and Health Sciences, University of California, Berkeley Extension.

Oliver McMahan, DivD, PhD, Associate Dean, Church of God Theological Seminary, Cleveland, Tennessee.

Odilia Mele, MD, Psychiatrist/Researcher, Department of Neurological and Psychiatric Sciences at the Medical School of the University of Bari, Italy.

Katherine J. Miller, PhD, is a psychologist in private practice in Philadelphia.

Caroline L. Mitchell, MS, is Director of Day Services, Community Connections, Washington, DC.

Massimo Molteni, MD, Medical Director and Pediatric Neuropsychiatrist, Associazione "La Nostra Famiglia," and Researcher, Scientific Institute "Eugenio Medea," Bosisio Parini (Lecco), Italy.

Emily Moody, MSW, Clinical Supervisor, Community Connections, Washington, DC.

Massimiliano Morreale, MD, Psychiatrist/Researcher, Department of Neurological and Psychiatric Sciences at the Medical School of the University of Bari, Italy.

Silvia Pasinato, PhD, is a coordinator of psychological services at a center for handicapped children and a psychological consultant to the schools of a rural county in Como, Italy. She also has a part-time private practice.

James W. Pennebaker, PhD, Professor, Department of Psychology, University of Texas at Austin.

Carolina J. Quesada, MSW, Clinical Case Manager, Community Connections, Washington, DC.

Mia Sevier, MA, is a doctoral candidate in the Psychology Department of the University of California at Los Angeles.

Marco Storelli, MD, Psychiatrist/Researcher, Department of Neurological and Psychiatric Sciences at the Medical School of the University of Bari, Italy.

Umberto Talpone, MD, Pediatric Neuropsychiatrist, Family Psychology Service, Associazione "La Nostra Famiglia," and Researcher, Scientific Institute "Eugenio Medea," Bosisio Parini (Lecco), Italy.

Caterina Tarquinio, MD, Pyshiatrist/Researcher, Department of Neurological and Psychiatric Sciences at the Medical School of the University of Bari, Italy.

Francesco Vaira, MD, Psychiatrist and Consultant, Department of Mental Health of Termoli (Campobasso), Italy.

Foreword

The idea of using workbooks to help people deal with upsetting experiences is obvious. It is like giving schoolchildren homework, or giving graduate students take-home assignments. Everyone knows that the more time you spend thinking about a problem, the sooner you will be able to solve it. If written homework assignments are acknowledged by everyone to be of value, why has so little research been conducted on their best embodiment—workbooks?

The use of workbooks has been greatly overlooked. Although clinicians, counselors, and social workers have been encouraging the use of workbooks as homework for years, most researchers have been blind to their value because they have been looking in another direction, trying to find some new breakthrough in therapy. The irony is that the use of workbooks might represent one of the biggest breakthroughs in decades. That is why this book is so timely and important.

Using Workbooks in Mental Health is groundbreaking in bringing together the growing literature on workbooks. It is also the first to draw attention to this phenomenon across problem areas. That is, we are able to see for the first time the similarities and differences in workbooks across very different types of social, mental, and physical health problems. The practitioners represent a broad array of theoretical perspectives and training. More than anything, this book alerts us to the pervasiveness of workbooks and hints at their incredible potential.

As someone who has spent much of the past twenty years exploring the power of writing as a means of improving people's physical and mental health, the workbook world is particularly exciting for me. Although this book points to the possible value of workbooks, two broad questions need to be addressed in the coming years.

Do Workbooks Really Work?

Many of the chapters of this book point to some promising evidence that workbooks are indeed effective. However, the current findings are still very tentative. One of the central problems is in deciding the best way to experimentally test workbook effectiveness. The ideal study, for example, would involve a large number of people with a particular problem and randomly assign half of the participants to the workbook condition. What do you compare workbooks with? What do the other half of the participants get? Nothing? A workbook that is irrelevant for their problems? Perhaps the first studies should compare workbooks with nothing. However, future studies will need to be run like current-day drug-effectiveness trials. That is, we will need to compare proven workbooks with other workbooks to see which ones work best.

A related concern is to determine some of the limiting conditions of workbooks. Is their effectiveness dependent on the reading ability of the participant, type of problem, reading level of the book, nature of the assignments, degree of specificity, length of the workbook, compliance with the workbook, or other dimensions? Similarly, what are the best measures of effectiveness? Once people have finished their workbooks, do they go to the doctor less often, change their behaviors, or simply feel better?

It is likely that the majority of workbooks are bought at bookstores by people who are not in any form of therapy. One could safely predict that a high percentage of these books are never read beyond the first few pages. A compelling test would be to determine the degree to which bookstore-purchased workbooks are both read and ultimately bring about improvements in the purchasers.

Just as many workbooks are bought in bookstores, many are purchased in conjunction with traditional therapy. What roles do preventers, therapists, rehabilitators, and researchers play in getting workbooks to change people's lives? In other words, are workbooks primarily effective because they bolster the therapy sessions themselves, or are the workbooks adding something unique that goes beyond what respondents could ever gain from individual therapy sessions? The setting in which workbooks are used or encouraged may be as important as the workbooks themselves.

How Do Workbooks Work?

Let's assume that workbooks are truly effective in producing measurable benefits (and I suspect they are). What is the secret to their effectiveness? This is a far more complicated question than one might think. There are a number of candidates, including the following:

- *Translating experiences into words:* Once problems and solutions are written out, people have a better understanding of their situations.

- *The creation of a story:* As people gradually disclose their thoughts and feelings, they begin to put the pieces together. A workbook may encourage the creation of a narrative that helps to organize their experiences.
- *Altering thinking patterns:* By doing specific exercises, people learn to think differently. Writing in a workbook can be thought of as training in thinking.
- *Emotional relief:* Writing assignments can help people appreciate their emotional reactions to events. It is highly unlikely that the benefits of workbooks are due to some kind of emotional venting. Rather, the acknowledgment of emotions may be a critical feature of their effectiveness.
- *Providing a sense of control or perspective:* Once emotional upheavals are on paper, they can sometimes seem less daunting.
- *The freeing of working memory:* Writing in workbooks may help people to get past many of the problems with which they have been struggling. Recent research hints that this may allow for a greater capacity to think about other things, and to devote more concentrated attention on work, friends, and family.
- *Serving as a constant reminder to change:* By their very nature, workbooks remind people to stay on task. If people promise themselves to complete workbook assignments at set times, they must continue to remember to change their thoughts and their behaviors.

As is apparent, workbooks can exert their powers in multiple ways. Indeed, this possibility may explain why so many different types of workbooks, with such a broad range of approaches, are available. Most influence their readers along several dimensions at once. There will not be a single "magic bullet" that accounts for the effectiveness of any given workbook. However, with systematic study, we can begin to learn what features of workbooks are most powerful.

As this book demonstrates, workbooks are used for a large number of problems. In the coming years, we need to learn when workbooks work and when they don't. As many authors point out, workbooks are not meant to be a substitute for therapy; however, the reality is that they probably *can be and are* used in place of therapy at times. The remarkable cost-effectiveness of workbooks makes them ideal ways for bringing about change for large groups of people, people who are not able to see therapists, or those who simply refuse to see therapists.

Luciano L'Abate is visionary in bringing together such a broad and esteemed group of contributors for this volume. With the publication of *Using*

Workbooks in Mental Health, he is legitimizing a cottage industry and demanding that we begin to explore scientifically the effectiveness of workbooks in everyday life.

James W. Pennebaker
The University of Texas at Austin

Preface

Progress in many fields of human endeavor is based on a written record rather than on the spoken word. No business, political, or human enterprise can flourish and advance without a written record of its past and present transactions. Furthermore, the written medium has the advantage over the spoken medium of being explicit and specific, qualities that become confused in speaking, no matter how clearly one may talk (L'Abate, 1999; Lepore and Smyth, 2002). Psychotherapy is one of the few enterprises in which the process (and assumed progress) has been based mainly on the spoken word. Self-help workbooks, consisting of a series of homework assignments systematically written and administered either face to face or online, are "ganz Amerikanisch" technological inventions that can be used as cost-effective, mass-oriented, complementary, supplementary tools or as a sole form of intervention in addition to or as an alternative to verbal and nonverbal media. The latter includes medication, diet, and exercise, including body and awareness therapies. The combination of two or even all three media should provide synergistic outcomes that might increase the efficiency and efficacy of most psychological approaches, regardless of theoretical predilections.

Reliance on the written word may seem to limit the domain of possibilities that is wide open when there is reliance solely on talk. However, what respondents will say cannot be controlled or predicted any more than one can control and structure what professionals will say in response to what respondents say or do. Manuals and planners for therapists may decrease this variability. However, recording and coding of verbal therapist-respondent interactions is expensive and limited to few researchers rather than to most practitioners. Thus, manuals or planners do not increase the knowledge of process and outcome for psychological interventions. Indeed, one could argue that they are maintaining the status quo in this field because they still rely on talk.

To save time and energy as well as to avoid inevitable distortions from respondents, it is much more efficient to put instructions for homework assignments in writing. These instructions are to be followed step by step, matching approximately one hour of homework for each hour of prevention, therapy, or rehabilitation, in whatever ratio of sessions to homework is relevant to both practitioners and respondents. Often, when only talk was used for structuring directions, prescriptions, or directives, it was necessary to repeat instructions to the same respondent or from one respondent to another, when the same problem was presented. To avoid misunderstandings, selective forgetting, and blatant distortions, as well as to save professional time and energy, it became useful to write down, and indeed program, various instructions to be answered in writing. The systematic use of this approach—programmed writing—resulted in a large number of workbooks that cover a variety of clinical and nonclinical conditions, as the collaborators to this book amply demonstrate.

Writing is one method for increasing efficiency and effectiveness in psychological interventions. It can be used as an additional or alternative structuring skill to traditional talk-based psychological interventions. Writing is one way to increase the professional's or trainer's influence or generalization outside of the professional office. Its impact on treatment outcome has yet to be fully realized beyond the experience of a few clinician-researchers. Workbooks are not yet in the mainstream of current psychological interventions. They, of course, represent the most extreme structure in writing—*programmed writing,* by definition. Their importance in improving human conflicts and conditions is still in its infancy, and the contributions in this book constitute a step toward toddlerhood. It will take more than these contributions to bring workbooks up to adolescence.

Research contributions in the use of writing have highlighted its potential use in prevention, psychotherapy, and rehabilitation (Lepore and Smyth, 2002; Levy and Ransdell, 1996). Writing can be considered a secondary prevention because it can be applied alongside (before, during, or after) preventive (primary) and therapeutic (tertiary) interventions, that is, parapreventively as well as paratherapeutically. Overall, a robust and increasingly coherent body of literature points to the widespread use and benefits of writing as well as to its limitations. Writing is one tool in a growing repertoire of adjunct techniques to support psychological interventions and improve coping abilities and perceptions of control over stressful, debilitating, and traumatic events. Ultimately, classifications of writing and workbooks (Chapter 1) should facilitate the task of prescription, a task that thus far has taken place along subjective and difficult-to-replicate lines.

As long as talk remains the major modality of exchange between mental health professionals and respondents, the goal of linking evaluation with treatment will remain unrealistic and unreachable. In using written homework assignments, especially programmed ones, however, one can achieve a level of prescriptive specificity otherwise unreachable verbally. It may be possible to use prescriptive writing at the beginning of therapy followed by a more exploratory, relationship-oriented process later. The same approach could be recommended in working with character disorders, couples, and families. Such clients may have to finish written materials to demonstrate their willingness and motivation to change. If change is demonstrated in writing, they may benefit then from a personal, face-to-face relationship based on talk. Addicts, however, may have a hard time writing about painful events in their lives. With these clients, for instance, it may be helpful to start them writing about pleasant events, then increase the intensity to hurtful and even traumatic incidents. Many addicts fear writing because they equate it with past traumas to losing control, and even death. Hence, with critically or clinically severe cases, professionals need to be available in between written homework assignments to a much greater degree than would generally occur with less severe cases.

Workbooks do not in any way decrease or eliminate the need for professionals. Rather, they provide a way by which a professional's time and energy can be used more effectively, thereby possibly decreasing time and costs of psychological interventions. Workbooks are complementary and supplementary to the professional's personal contribution, when indeed there is one, to deal with subthreshold, subsyndromal, or comorbid disorders in individuals, couples, and families. This personal contribution may be effective with internalizers, but it is doubtful, if not questionable, whether this contribution is effective with externalizers, severe psychopathologies, as well as with couples and families. In the latter cases, workbooks can suggest alternatives that are still unavailable to professionals who are unable to treat most critical and criminal conditions.

Depending on their degree of structure and directives, workbooks can be administered by professionals regardless of their theoretical allegiance. For example, a central aim of cognitively oriented therapists may be to uncover current self-defeating thought patterns and self-directed statements. In contrast, therapists with psychodynamic or humanistic orientations could use workbooks to aid respondents to reflect on feelings associated with particular memories of past, traumatic events.

Three analogies have guided this editor's interest in using workbooks in practice and research. Workbooks are (1) the software for computer-assisted, offline or online interventions; (2) to psychological interventions what medications are to psychiatric interventions; and (3) the cost offset for psychotherapy as the latter was for medical treatments (Cummings, O'Donohue, and Ferguson, 2002). This volume is essentially an expansion of these three analogies.

In Section I, after an introductory Chapter 1 about the role of workbooks in the delivery of mental health services in prevention, psychotherapy, and rehabilitation, Chapter 2 summarizes background and research with self-administered workbooks in the editor's former laboratory. The rest of the following contributions have been organized on whether they apply to individuals, couples, or families. Each section starts with the least empirical and mostly impressionistic chapter progressing to chapters relying more and more on controlled observations.

In Section II on individuals, Gorman (Chapter 3) describes his gut-wrenching experience of finding out as a professional that many of his symptoms were due to dementia rather than depression. Nonetheless, depression was a natural concomitant of a severely deteriorating condition. In Chapter 4, Battino describes the background for developing workbooks for life-challenging conditions, such as cancer and Alzheimer's, that threaten not only individuals but, even more important, those who help them cope with the most stressful experiences of their entire lives: their caretakers. In Chapter 5, Goldstein describes his workbook based on cognitive schema derived in part from Erikson's developmental stages. Chapter 6 summarizes the experiences of working with a single workbook to help women recover from abusive relationships. In Chapter 7, Hodgins demonstrates how it is possible to deal with gambling problems using very brief interventions. Chapter 8 shows how a "circular" workbook called "The Wheel of Wisdom" can be used in conjunction with medications instead of face-to-face psychotherapy. Chapter 9 illustrates how using a workbook can help women with substance abuse issues. In Chapter 10, McMahan and Arias follow up a previous study using workbooks and psychotherapy with incarcerated felons.

In Section III, Chapter 11, Cusinato reports on his thirty years of experience in marriage preparation and maintenance with couples using, among others, David Olson's program, which includes written homework assignments. Cusinato's hierarchical structure of older couples supervising and helping younger couples helping couples-to-be is worthy of attention and replication by others interested in using a paraprofessional paradigm. In Chapter 12, Gattis, Sevier, and Christensen review the contribution that written homework assignments make in many self-help books for couples. In Chapter 13, Maino reports on her use of an intimacy workbook with couples.

In Section IV, Kearney and Alvarez (Chapter 14) report on their results with school refusals in adolescents. Miller (Chapter 15) reviews the literature about workbooks in the alimentary disorders of bulimia and anorexia nervosa. In Chapter 16, Maino and colleagues report on their interventions using an intimacy workbook with parents of handicapped children.

Finally, in Chapter 17, L'Abate and Hecker remark about the status and future of workbooks in the delivery of mental health services, including a research agenda about how workbooks can be related to physiological processes and used as in online interventions.

As Pennebaker noted in his Foreword, the crucial questions which have been attempted but not really answered by most contributions in this book, and which still need to be answered in the future, are:

> What percentage of the variance in the outcome of psychological interventions is due to face-to-face interactions?
> What percentage of the outcome variance is due to homework assignments in general?
> What percentage of the remaining variance is due to the contribution of written homework assignments?

Hopefully, future research will attempt to answer these and many other questions about the usefulness of workbooks in prevention, psychotherapy, and rehabilitation.

REFERENCES

Cummings, N. A., O'Donohue, W. T., and Ferguson, K. E. (Eds.) (2002). *The impact of medical cost offset in practice and research: Making it work for you.* Reno, NV: Context Press.

L'Abate, L. (1999). Taking the bull by the horns: Beyond talk in psychological interventions. *The Family Journal: Counseling and Psychotherapy for Couples and Families, 7,* 206-220.

Lepore, S. J. and Smyth, J. M. (Eds.) (2002). *The writing cure: How expressive writing promotes health and emotional well-being.* Washington, DC: American Psychological Association.

Levy, C. M. and Ransdell, S. (Eds.) (1996). *The science of writing: Theories, methods, individual differences, and applications.* Mahwah, NJ: Earlbaum.

SECTION I:
INTRODUCTION

Chapter 1

The Role of Workbooks
in the Delivery of Mental Health Services
in Prevention, Psychotherapy,
and Rehabilitation

Luciano L'Abate

[N]umerous issues [are] relevant to applying technology to the delivery of healthcare information and services. Many of the issues pertain
to questions about online therapy. The more appropriate questions are:
under what conditions, for what problems and with which interventions does the application of Internet technology facilitate the delivery
of healthcare services? (Newman, 2001, p. 56)

The often uncertain work of therapy would be simplified if special
techniques uniformly exerted powerful main effects for particular
complaints. Therapy could then be applied in this manner: "When
faced with problem _____ administer technique _____." (Asay and
Lambert, 1999, p. 41)

This chapter will argue that workbooks are one way to bridge the considerable gap that still exists between practitioners and researchers in the
mental health field, specifically psychological interventions in prevention,
psychotherapy, and rehabilitation. Workbooks consist of written homework
for out-of-session or between-sessions assignments. They contain systematically written instructions (exercises, prescriptions, questions, tasks) for a
specific topic in prepackaged forms, sheets, or handouts to be completed by
respondents either in writing or through talk and nonverbal communication.

I am indebted to Lorna L. Hecker for her thoughtful and detailed editing of a previous
draft of this chapter.

Chapters within this book should help demonstrate how the gap between researchers and practitioners can be filled through workbooks. Using workbooks implies using distance writing (DW) as an adjunct or alternative to face-to-face psychological interventions. This process implies having respondents write away from the eyes and presence of a mental health professional. DW can take place in between face-to-face sessions, either in the waiting room of the professional's office or at home, or it could take place at a distance, without ever meeting a professional helper face to face, via computers and the Internet. Although DW as an intervention tool is not new, systematic investigation of its efficacy has occurred only recently, as discussed also in the next chapter and elsewhere (Esterling et al., 1999; L'Abate, 1992; Smyth, 1998; Smyth and L'Abate, 2001; Snowdon, 2001).

The last decade has seen a dramatic increase in the number of such workbooks containing systematically written homework assignments (SWHAs) for respondents of all types (clients, consumers, patients, subjects, individuals, couples, and families) (L'Abate, 2002b). Workbooks represent the most structured extreme in a classification of writing that will be presented later in this chapter. In this regard they follow the much reviled medical model unabashedly, which, however, is as close to an empirical model as mental health services can follow, as indicated by Asay and Lambert's (1999) previous quote.

One or more workbooks are available for most distressing or troublesome conditions. An annotated bibliography and lists of workbooks available on the Internet contain more than 300 entries covering most known or frequent clinical and nonclinical conditions (L'Abate, 1996, 2002a,b). The increase in the number of workbooks available on the market parallels also the introduction of DW for preventive and paratherapeutic purposes (Lepore and Smyth, 2002). Furthermore, computers can help distressed people at a distance (Bloom, 1992; Williams, Boles, and Johnson, 1995). Adding such technology to workbook administration will produce another avenue or vehicle of service delivery unmatched by previously traditional mental health approaches that rely on face-to-face contacts and talk between professionals and respondents.

Workbooks are part of an increasing trend in the administration of homework assignments (Coon and Gallagher-Thompson, 2002; Freeman and Rosenfeld, 2002; Garland and Scott, 2002; Hudson and Kendall, 2002; Kazantzis et al., in press; Kazantzis and Lampropoulos, 2002; Tompkins, 2002). Therefore, chapters contained in this book try to answer qualitatively the question about how much of the total intervention outcome is due to workbooks and how much is due to factors other than workbooks. A related question, which is answered in part in the next chapter, is: "Can psychological interventions be based solely on workbooks?" As Kazantzis and Lampropoulos (2002), as well as most of the authors cited earlier, concluded: "There is now sufficient evidence to support the assertion that homework assignments enhance psychotherapy outcomes" (p. 577), provided, of course, that there is consistent compliance to complete homework customized to respondents' needs. Homework assignments, however, include more than workbooks (Dattilio, 2002). Therefore, the variance of treatment outcomes must include the type of homework assignments that have been delivered.

Consequently, workbooks fit within an overall model of psychological interventions that include

1. individual styles and personalities of professional helpers;
2. type of rapport, contract, or "therapeutic" alliance established between professionals and respondents;
3. field of intervention practiced (preventive, crisis intervention, rehabilitation);
4. type of intervention used (cognitive-behavioral, humanistic, psychodynamic, etc.);
5. type of clientele seen—individuals (children, adolescents, adults), couples, or families;
6. type of referral question treated as well as its severity;
7. context (private for fee versus public with minimal or no fees, office, clinic, hospital); and
8. homework assignments that can be administered or completed
   - verbally,
   - nonverbally (medication, exercise, diet, etc.), and
   - in various types of DW, as discussed later in this chapter.

Computers and the advent of Internet technology now allow mental health professionals to help distressed people at a distance (Maheu, Whitten, and Allen, 2001; Newman et al., 1997). Combined with SWHAs, this technology could well develop into an evolutionary, if not revolutionary, step in how mental health services will be delivered in this century and the future (Barak, 1999; Budman, 2000; Celio et al., 2000; Grohol, 1998; Heinlen et al., 2002; Jerome et al., 2000; Jones, 1995; Marks, Shaw, and Parkin, 1998; Nickelson, 1998; Smith and Senior, 2001; Stamm, 1998; Strom, Petterson, and Anderson, 2000). Despite this increasing trend, however, workbooks still are not part of mainstream psychological interventions. Nonetheless, they can and do fulfill important functions in prevention, psychotherapy, and rehabilitation, as chapters in this book will demonstrate.

In considering the mental health needs of the United States, the surgeon general's report on mental health (U.S. Department of Health and Human

Services, 1999) will be discussed from the viewpoint of pressing mental health needs that cannot and will not be solved through face-to-face talk-based psychological interventions alone. This report will serve as context for this as well as all other chapters in this book, especially in considering the limited contribution that traditional psychological interventions can make to satisfy those needs.

To bolster these arguments, it will be necessary to present

1. major differences between practitioners and researchers to understand how these two fields can reconcile with each other and come together through the use of workbooks, nested within a trend in psychological interventions that is leading toward their increased formalization and specificity;
2. a classification of distance writing;
3. another classification of workbooks, as well as their advantages, disadvantages, and dangers;
4. a classification of the evidence necessary to support the use of workbooks; and
5. the importance of a thorough evaluation and informed consent to support workbook administration and effectiveness along various sieves of stepped interventions in a continuum of care.

DW, and especially workbooks, should take place before moving on to more expensive, prolonged, and intense treatments, such as face-to-face talk-based interventions. What will it take to support their use in practice and in research?

One could conclude and even argue that workbooks are to psychological interventions what medications are to psychiatric interventions: (1) in most cases, more than one workbook is available to deal competitively with the same condition, (2) dosage can be administered and controlled by the number of assignments needed to complete one or more workbooks, and (3) if one workbook does not work (please forgive the pun!) perhaps another workbook might, or more aggressive and expensive treatment may be necessary (L'Abate, 2002a). The major difference between the two approaches lies in repetition. Although medication can be administered repeatedly, even for life, the same workbook usually cannot be administered repeatedly. Once a workbook is administered, it would be a waste of time to re-administer it to the same respondent, especially if the outcome has not been satisfactory.

Combining DW with computer and Internet technology could even represent a paradigmatic shift toward greater specificity in psychological interventions than cannot and will not be achieved through talk and face-to-face contacts alone (L'Abate, 1999a,e, 2001). Furthermore, in view of the surgeon general's report, it would be impossible for face-to-face talk-based interventions to take care of all those needs, especially when the usefulness of traditional methods of service delivery is questionable (Bickman, 1999). Traditional face-to-face talk-based psychological approaches are not going to reach all of the distressed and troubled people at risk, in need, and in crisis.

The multitude and diversity of psychological interventions make it difficult, if not impossible, to change extremely entrenched traditional professional practices as long as talk and face-to-face interaction remain the sole media of communication and possible healing. Mental health professionals seem so involved, invested, and even fixated in their ways to intervene that change is as difficult for them as it is for the very populations they claim to change (Bickman, 1999; L'Abate, 1997b, 1999a,e).

One way to upset and possibly change the status quo of current talk-based, face-to-face psychological interventions is to introduce the other two media of communication—nonverbal and writing—as additional or alternative avenues and vehicles of healing, since feedback loops should exist from one medium to another (L'Abate, 2002a; Szell, 1994). The issue here is to find which feedback loop is more effective from one medium to another, and from one respondent to another, as part of homework assignments that include all three media.

Before elaborating on the points considered in this chapter, it is important to review the status of mental health needs in general and of individual psychotherapy in particular. One cannot deal with more complex systems, such as couples and families, without ignoring individuals. Hence, if anything can be learned from research with individual psychotherapy, for instance, couple and family interventions might be better off.

THE STATUS OF MENTAL HEALTH NEEDS
IN THE UNITED STATES

This important report shows that only a fraction of people who need professional mental health help actually receive it. As Satcher (2000) commented on his report,

> The first ever Surgeon General Report on Mental Health is an historic document. For too long our nation has overlooked mental health as fundamental to overall health and has overlooked mental health promotion and prevention and has not considered treatment of mental illness as being essential to a quality health care system. With the

publication of this report, we hope to bring mental health and mental illnesses to the forefront of our nation's attention and to impact discussion on health and planning processes for our health care system. . . . It affirms that mental illnesses are real, that effective treatments are available, and that recovery is possible. (p. 9)

However, one important finding from this report shows that even though mental illness strikes one in five Americans each year, more than half of those who need treatment do not get it, either because they do not seek it or because they do not have access to it. This lack of access to mental health services has driven the most vulnerable individuals into the streets, hospitals, jails, prisons, or cemeteries.

Among the many reasons for this state of affairs, such as stigma, ethnic origin, socioeconomic level, is the fact that those who need help the most are also among those who refuse it the most (Albee, 2000; Torrey, 1997). However, another reason for this refusal may lie in the very nature of the most used medium of communication and supposed healing—talk. Some people may not want to talk about their problems to someone who represents authority and the unknown. A review of various studies, for example, demonstrated that psychiatric patients respond better to computers than to mental health professionals (Bloom, 1992). In addition to the nature of the medium, one needs to keep in mind that talk is cheap and expensive at the same time—anybody can talk, but talk may be inefficient and unreliable. It can be forgotten, distorted, or used for purposes of manipulation (L'Abate, 1999e). If, in addition to talk, one adds the requirement of personal face-to-face contact, the chances for people in distress presenting themselves under these conditions tend to decrease noticeably.

Furthermore, traditional psychological interventions may be effective for disorders of internalization, but they are relatively ineffective for disorders of externalization and serious psychopathology (Albee, 2000; L'Abate, 2002a). How are we going to deal with these problems? Psychotherapy manuals for professionals still require face-to-face verbal contact, and in so doing perpetuate the status quo in psychotherapy. Medication is another alternative or adjunct with possible side effects and forced lifelong consumption. However, issues of compliance are still present. Those who need medication the most tend to refuse it. Those who do accept it may need to use it for the rest of their lives, and usually fail to learn new, more effective ways of coping because medication renders them complacently unwilling or passively unable to learn those new ways.

The needs presented by the surgeon general (U.S. Department of Health and Human Services, 1999) are never going to be fulfilled and satisfied through traditional, face-to-face, personal verbal contacts, no matter how intensive or extensive these contacts may be (Albee, 2000; Kiesler, 2000). Cost-effective, mass-oriented psychological interventions will be necessary to deal with these needs satisfactorily. A combination of structured software, as in workbooks, with computers and the Internet will allow practitioners as well as researchers to reach much larger populations than has been possible through traditional, face-to-face, personal contact, talk-based paradigms—that is, one or more respondents with one or two professionals. It will be necessary to work at a distance from respondents using DW, either as an addition or as an alternative to talk and face-to-face contacts alone.

Here is where workbooks and structured computer-assisted interventions can make a contribution that cannot be replicated by more traditional methods of treatment, especially face-to-face talk-based interventions. They can be used at a distance from practitioners, provided responsible safeguards are set in place from the very outset. These safeguards have been discussed already (L'Abate, 2002a) and will be touched briefly at the end of this chapter.

THE STATUS OF INDIVIDUAL PSYCHOTHERAPY

In addition to recent criticisms about the effectiveness of psychotherapy (Albee, 2000) and a review of criticisms about it (L'Abate, 2002a), a veritable avalanche of works extremely critical of individual psychotherapy, its usefulness, and its efficacy have been published since the mid-1990s (Dineen, 1998; Sykes, 1992), including one which declares that psychotherapy is dead (Eisner, 2000). These attacks have been more frequent and perhaps more acerbic over the past few years. However, one is mindful that individual psychotherapy historically preceded couple and family therapy and its status is just as important to consider as the latter.

Dineen (1998) is somewhat more specific in her criticisms. Instead of a blanket indictment of psychotherapy as done by some critics, she focuses on obvious extremes—multiple personality misdiagnosis, past-life therapy, day care sex abuse hysteria, false recovered memories, and mythical satanic cults—as if these were the responsibility of the mental health professions. Her blanket, pall-mall use of the term "psychology industry" to lump together all the mental health disciplines, and the overuse of the "victim" metaphor taken from Sykes' (1992) diatribe, raises questions about her objectivity and, hence, her credibility.

Eisner (2000) contends that in spite of its apparent success and seeming progress, psychotherapy is no more than a placebo, lacking in essential evidence of effectiveness and in specificity. Inadequate specificity is an argument already presented by L'Abate (1999e). Eisner reached his conclusion about the "death of psychotherapy" by arguing that psychotherapy, including Haley's (1976) contribution to family therapy, was actually dealing with individuals and lacking in scientific evidence to justify its practice.

Inadequate specificity is especially stressed in another critical evaluation by Keen (2000). He argued that psychotherapy fails to distinguish between ultimacy (what is relevant) and triviality (what is irrelevant). L'Abate has argued (1999e) that both shortcomings in cost-effectiveness and specificity stem from the very medium solely used in psychotherapy—talk—let alone face-to-face contact and the personality of the psychotherapist, or the therapeutic alliance. Talk is usually nonspecific. Even if and when it is claimed to be specific, it is difficult to evaluate whether this seeming specificity is relevant or not to the eventual outcome.

As with many other critics of individual psychotherapy, Keen (2000) fails to give a realistic solution or, if not a solution, at least a practical and relevant suggestion for corrective approaches to differentiate superficial problems from serious problems. For example, if pre-posttreatment evaluations were adopted as standard operating procedures, as done routinely in some fields of commerce, medicine, and industry, the distinction between serious and superficial problems could be addressed more objectively.

Wampold (2001), in a more balanced review, covers issues relating to the relative efficacy of various types of treatments within the larger context of the illusory standard of "absolute" efficacy of therapy, or, for that matter, of any form of treatment. He also reviews presumed specific ingredients of various forms of therapy and their effects to these supposedly "common" factors. Psychotherapy outcome is related also to adherence and allegiance to therapy manuals, as well as to the effects and influence attributed to different personalities among psychotherapists.

Most of the criticisms listed earlier, however, are directed toward psychotherapies of individuals rather than psychotherapies of couples and families. On that matter, Roberts, Vernberg, and Jackson (2000) reported a "moderately high mean effect size of .71 for therapy with families of children younger that 12 years" (p. 502). They concluded their review of treatment outcome thusly: "[F]indings that support the efficacy of psychotherapy with children parallel those found within a meta-analysis of adult psychotherapy" (p. 503). In the same vein, a number of meta-analyses (Asay and Lambert, 2000; Forsyth and Corazzini, 2000) attest to the continued viability of psychotherapy. Karoly and Anderson (2000), however, concluded their review about the long-term effects of psychotherapy by siding with its critics: "[T]he extant literature on such effects remains inconclusive. Consequently, treatment gains for complex and chronic problems generally cannot be expected to persist" (p. 172). If long-term gains cannot be expected, then one could be led to conclude that psychotherapy may give temporary relief. However, whether such relief persists over time remains to be seen.

One characteristic of most if not all detractors and of critical results, as far as this writer can discern, is their common failure to suggest alternative courses of helpful, constructive action. The sources cited previously are long on criticisms and short on suggestions on how to change and improve the status quo in psychotherapy. Perhaps Dineen (1998) may be an exception to that conclusion, even though she lumps social workers, psychiatrists, and even psychologists together under the term "psychology." Her suggestions essentially deal with limiting their professional roles, including no insurance coverage, and greater accountability in and out of courts. If that were the case, with no alternative to and without psychotherapy, whether individual or family-oriented, the only traditional choices left to us would be either medication, incarceration, or hospitalization. Whether criticisms or results are valid does not make any difference to the thesis of this chapter.

The alternative or additional use of workbooks, therefore, is nowhere to be seen—even in critical reviews. Such criticisms sometimes offer a variety of solutions that range from strictly and ideally utopian (Albee, 2000) to either impractical, unrealistic, or no solutions at all (Snyder and Ingram, 2000). Limiting the role of mental health professionals, as Dineen (1998) would like to see, is another nonsolution. The mental health disciplines are institutionalized and here to stay, whether critics like it or not. The issue, then, lies in how to improve their practices. Will workbooks perform this function? This is not to say that workbooks are the solution to all our mental health needs and problems. However, they are one solution that merits consideration. One could also argue that workbooks represent the kind of "disruptive technology" that might upset traditional psychological interventions' apple cart.

Because of overreliance on talk, personal face-to-face contact, and the belief of mystique in the person or personality of the therapist and the therapeutic alliance, psychotherapists are still reluctant to use DW, and are even more reluctant to use systematically written homework assignments or workbooks (L'Abate, 1997b, 1999e). As discussed later, this reluctance explains, at least in part, the relative absence of homework assignments and workbooks in extant treatises on prevention, psychotherapy, and rehabilitation. This absence, fortunately, is being corrected by the forthcoming publication of Kazantzis et al. (in press) about homework assignments in cognitive-behavioral therapies and the references cited earlier relevant to this topic.

A conceptual and rather practical solution would distinguish among different levels of prevention, reflecting on the fact that most therapists are not interested or even knowledgeable about using structured primary and secondary prevention methods to deal with many of the issues that make up the majority of present-day private practice, leaving crisis intervention for really serious problems. The introduction of successive sieves (L'Abate, 1990, 2002a), which are now called "stepped treatments," as an exemplary solution could be one way of addressing the problem of a blanket approach for everybody without specificity, as concluded at the end of this chapter. This approach stresses the importance of differentiating among degrees and types of dysfunctionalities and among at least three preventive approaches: primary-universal, secondary-targeted, and tertiary-necessary.

On one hand, we have an increasing number of detractors regarding the usefulness of psychotherapy. On the other hand, we have a number of statistically significant meta-analyses that attest to the robustness of this approach. Even then, controversy exists about the meaning of these results. Barlow (2002) introduced a series of papers on this topic by stating,

> Among psychologists, seemingly diametrically opposed interpretations of the results of psychotherapy research have been proffered like ships passing in the night. . . . The first view is that we now have specific psychological interventions that necessarily differ from disorder to disorder. . . . The other view, based largely on meta-analytic studies, where the effects of psychotherapy are averaged across multiple studies without regard to the conditions being treated, is that the preponderance, if not the totality, of the effects of psychotherapy can be accounted for by common factors, and that specific psychological procedures are irrelevant beyond the extent to which they are credible and have meaning for the therapist and the patient. (p. 1)

Consequently, one can conclude that reports of psychotherapy's death are grossly exaggerated or premature. A more differentiated trend, however, is present in the field of psychological interventions.

TOWARD AN INCREASING FORMALIZATION OF PSYCHOLOGICAL INTERVENTIONS

The purpose of this section is to provide a historical and situational context for the use of workbooks and bring to light a trend that indicates an increasing formalization and specification in psychological interventions. The more the field of psychotherapy has grown, the more two processes of greater differentiation have taken place, as is the case in any growing system. One process is related to the emergence of psychotherapy textbooks becoming more and more focused on specific clinical conditions or symptoms (Norcross, 2002). For instance, a variety of texts are now focused strictly on treatments of anxiety or depression. This trend is partially documented by the increasing number of workbooks published since the 1990s. The reader can check on this trend by viewing advertisements, brochures, and flyers mailed to professionals by publishing houses.

A second trend, which parallels the first, is the formalization of psychological interventions. By formalization is meant greater reliance on clear, definite, prearranged, and predetermined steps in interventions, relying on nonverbal and writing media rather than just talk. Nonverbal techniques, working on facial, gestural, postural, and locomotor movements, have been reviewed elsewhere (L'Abate, 1997c). Unfortunately, the latter do not have a sufficiently solid and empirical base to be incorporated into the mainstream of psychotherapeutic practices. However, if nonverbal techniques also mean medication, exercise, and diet, then a plethora of evidence exists to support their use, and does not need to be reviewed here.

The trend in the formalization of psychological interventions includes prevention (Albee and Guillotta, 1997; Bloom, 1996; Mrazek and Haggerty, 1994), where many approaches were already formalized, as in psychoeducational and social skills training and rehabilitation (Corrigan, 1995; Frank, Gluck, and Buckelew, 1990). This trend is taking place in an increasingly, perhaps imperceptibly, visible fashion to many practitioners. The field of psychological interventions is becoming more and more "formalized."

In *Webster's New Collegiate Dictionary* (1959), the term "formal" is given four meanings:

1. not familiar and homelike,
2. conventional,
3. clear and definite, and
4. having to do with form rather than content.

The term "form" is given at least seven meanings that are relevant to the thesis of this section:

1. shape,
2. person or animal,
3. mold,
4. manner or method,
5. formality or ceremony,
6. kind, sort, and
7. arrangement.

Among the synonyms for formal, the last three meanings apply to the thesis of this section to show how recent psychological interventions are beginning to follow certain agreed upon "conventions." These agreed-upon conventions allow interventions to become more "clear and definite" in the manner of how symptoms and problems need to be addressed. The manner in which interventions are applied is just as important as their content, and is increasingly following a medical model requiring greater and greater specificity of interventions. For instance, given a variety of ways of addressing anxiety, it matters how each way approaches it.

Among synonyms for "form," two apply directly to an increasing trend toward following "methods" that involves repeatable "arrangements," i.e., a series of predesigned, predetermined steps in the administration of an intervention. One could say that although talk-based interventions are mostly indeterminate, one cannot predict how long the intervention will take, and that this trend, if valid, is determinate in the sense that the specificity of these interventions limits how long it will take to apply them successfully.

This formalization, as understood here, implies, therefore, an increase toward clear and definite conventions in how psychological interventions are to be delivered according to a series of prearranged steps, i.e., methods or arrangements. Formalized methods involve written procedures for interventions that differ from how psychological interventions have been administered traditionally. Instead of the verbal medium, i.e., talk, as the sole medium of communication and healing, certain psychological interventions are beginning to rely more and more on nonverbal, i.e., action, and on written media and less and less on amorphous, indefinite, nonspecific, and unclear talk.

Formalization is taking place through the production of standard protocols, steps, and procedures for treatment. Hence, here the term *formalization* has three meanings: (1) following a prearranged series of steps, (2) production of standard operating procedures as shown in written instructions (protocols, handouts, etc.) either for professionals or for respondents, and (3) making the process of intervention repeatable within each professional, and, therefore, repeatable and verifiable among different professionals in different settings. Formalization, of course, means more than just the use of "forms." The latter may be part of the process. However, this process implies going beyond just the simplistic use of forms. It implies also the use of systematic, step-by-step approaches. The process of intervention is carefully prepared and arranged before a specific intervention is applied.

This trend, therefore, implies an increasing tendency to codify, specify, and arrange interventions according to standard operating procedures, i.e., systematic methods and preset steps and operations for *specific* conditions, rather than all conditions. This formalization minimizes amorphous and unstructured talk and, instead, seems directed toward greater structure and clarification about the nature of specified interventions. Talk is included as well as the other two media: nonverbal and writing. At least nine interventions illustrate this trend well. They fall within the criteria of a preset, prearranged, systematic series of steps that is clearly repeatable among professionals:

1. manuals;
2. planners;
3. distance writing and workbooks;
4. systematically structured computer-assisted interventions (SCAI);
5. computer-assisted interventions (CAI) based on visual imagery, as in virtual reality therapy;
6. CAI based on physiological measures, as in neurobiofeedback;
7. autogenic training (AT);
8. psychoeducational social skills training programs; and
9. eye movement desensitization and reprogramming (EMDR).

Only manuals, planners, workbooks, and SCAI are considered here. The remaining approaches are left to sources supporting their usage in clinical practice, which are too lengthy to include here.

In these approaches, standard forms or formats with specific written questions, items, tasks, and homework assignments are used by respondents. Written instructions and homework assignments save time and involve respondents more actively in the process of sharing information as well as becoming more responsible for the outcome of the intervention. These interventions may vary in the extent to which they have been empirically supported. Some of them may still be controversial, as in the case of AT or EMDR. Almost all of them are not yet in the mainstream of current mental health practices, which are still based mainly on talk and face-to-face contact with a professional. Some approaches can be administered by paraprofessionals under the supervision of a doctorate level professional or at a distance from a professional, as in homework assignments.

These approaches fulfill most criteria to qualify as "methods," in the sense that most, if not all, show (1) sufficient empirical support in the scientific and professional literature, including journals of their own, and (2) a sufficiently large number of practitioners who apply each method routinely. The literature to support both criteria for each method is too vast to include here. Perhaps these interventions are not yet part of mainstream clinical practices because they are not yet taught in graduate training programs. Nonetheless, together they represent a trend that may make them worthy of incorporation in graduate training programs and in future preventive, clinical, and rehabilitative practices.

Put in historical perspective, this trend looks at talk therapies as

1. starting as a general approach without specificity;
2. moving on to more specific therapies for specific disorders;
3. changing from a relatively passive role to a more active and even intrusive role;
4. ultimately culminating in the use of homework assignments; and
5. eventually leading to the use of interactive self-help workbooks to be administered out of or between sessions, or online.

Evaluation

The search for a one-to-one correspondence between evaluation and treatment has been the Holy Grail of clinical psychology since the inception of the profession. This goal has been sought in many ways but not achieved fully because the medium of treatment has remained the spoken word. Once the medium of intervention is changed in part to workbooks, the goal of linking a specific diagnosis, i.e., understanding, with a specific treatment becomes much more reachable and real. The matching between problem and solution can be restricted and becomes possible once we know and limit the domain we want to change. For example, my co-workers and I coded more than 1,000 enrichment exercises according to nine nonoverlapping categories, following nonoverlapping criteria for the coding. We then constructed an evaluation instrument that was isomorphic with the nine categories which classified enrichment exercises. This instrument was found to be relatively reliable (test-retest) and to discriminate significantly between clinical and nonclinical couples. In addition, it correlated significantly with already well-established instruments, such as the Family Environment Scale and the Dyadic Adjustment Scale. On the basis of how a couple or family responds on this test, we can now administer enrichment exercises that fit in the area of deficit or conflict, as reported by the family. Hence, we can link evaluation with structured enrichment in primary prevention in a way that cannot be achieved as long as we rely on the spoken word (Kochalka and L'Abate, 1997; L'Abate, 1990).

Many preventers and therapists have avoided the use of standard objective measures of individual, couple, and family functioning, with a single overreliance on the interview. This avoidance seems based on the belief that testing could not capture the complexities found in human behavior, nor could it provide links with effective preventive or therapeutic strategies. Preventers, like therapists, have concluded that psychological assessment has very little to do with intervening and helping clients. However, prescriptive instruments can be constructed whenever the domain to be covered is definite and finite. In Structured Enrichment (SE), for example (L'Abate, 1985; L'Abate and Weinstein, 1987; L'Abate and Young, 1987), each exercise was coded for its specific relationship to nine nonoverlapping dimensions of family functioning, as illustrated earlier.

Although evaluation interviews are quite individualized and difficult to formalize, psychological tests, of course, are the major type of formalization to evaluate the process and outcome of psychological interventions. The fact that many intelligence and personality tests can now be scored and interpreted by computers is a major step toward formalization of evaluation. A notable example of formalization can be found in the *Forms Book* published by the American Association for Marriage and Family Therapy (1989). It contains forms for (1) intake (both long and short) assessment of families, treatment evaluation, and medical screening; (2) consent for therapy, release of information, including videotapes, and insurance; (3) evaluation, including a family therapist rating scale, supervisory evaluation, and termination summaries; and (4) record keeping of progress notes and financial information. Hecker, Deacon, and Associates (1998) published another book chock-full of forms for evaluation as well as interventions. L'Abate (1992) produced a structured interview to evaluate individual, developmental, and historical background forms with item weights to measure the extent of psychopathology from many of the items to be answered.

Another instance of formalization in evaluation can be found in the work of Cautela, Cautela, and Esonis (1998), who produced a veritable collection of forty-two reproducible assessment forms designed to aid professionals in making proper diagnoses and in developing treatment plans for children and adolescents. Hence, as far as evaluation is concerned, its formalization has been taking place for years, even though there may be strong resistances to its use on pre- and postintervention bases in psychotherapy.

Manuals

Manualized therapies, of course, are supported by those who limit themselves to empirically based interventions (Nathan and Gorman, 1998; Norcross, 2002). Manuals seem to detract from the creativity and self-determination of most psychotherapists, hence they are not as popular as one might expect. One can argue that manuals perpetuate the status quo in psychotherapy by their sole reliance on talk and face-to-face contact. They are not as radical a departure from traditional psychological interventions as workbooks.

Planners

Planners are a mixture of manuals of how to approach a particular condition, on one hand, and workbooks with specific homework assignments for respondents, on the other hand (L'Abate, 2002b). For instance, Perkinson and Jongsma's planner (1997) claims to contain

> pre-written treatment components for over 25 substance abuse programs. Featuring a sample treatment plan, it describes the behavioral manifestations of each problem, treatment objectives and goals, therapeutic interventions, and DSM-IV diagnoses to help create treatment plans that satisfy the requirements of. . . third-party payers. (from the publisher's advertisement)

Finley and Lenz (1998) produced a treatment documentation sourcebook for chemical dependency that contains more than eighty forms, handouts, and records that can be copied or customized using a CD-ROM included with the sourcebook. Wiger (1997) published a "clinical documentation sourcebook" that contains "25 ready-to-use blank forms for managing each phase of the mental health treatment process—including intake, assessment, evaluation, treatment planning, and termination" (from the publisher's advertisement). Schultheis, O'Hanlon, and O'Hanlon (1998) provided couples with over sixty prewritten homework assignments grouped by skill set. O'Leary, Heyman, and Jongsma (1998), on the other hand, provided a planner to help couples deal with anger management, conflict resolution, financial disagreements, infidelity, life transitions, and communication difficulties, among others.

The term *planner* therefore can be applied to a collection of forms, a collection of therapeutic guidelines to be administered directly to respondents, as well as written homework assignments. Planners are a mixture of treatment guidelines found in manuals and forms for written homework assignments (L'Abate, 2002b).

Internet Applications of SCAI

SCAI on the Internet are fast becoming an alternative source of service delivery in the mental health field (Childress, 2000; Gackenbach and Ellerman, 1998; Grohol, 1998; Heinlen et al., 2002; Johnson, 1998; King and Moreggi, 1998; Reid, 1998). With managed care pressuring for cost-effective and accountable therapies, SCAI can fulfill these requirements. It also fulfills a requirement of reaching populations and respondents who are either unwilling or unable to seek mental health facilities and interact in a face-to-face relationship with a mental health professional. Incarcerated offenders are another population that could profit from SCAI.

Of course, there is a growing controversy about whether rapport can be achieved on the Internet as well as can be achieved in face-to-face talk psychotherapy (Kraut et al., 1998; Parks and Roberts, 1998). Only empirical evidence will provide an answer to this controversy (Rabasca, 1998). Sufficient evidence exists that many relationships—romantic, sexual, exploitative, and collaborative—are formed every day via the Internet, with the participants never meeting face to face.

Thus far, SCAI using written communications has been found useful in the treatment of panic disorders, obesity, fear of relaxation, test anxiety, phobias, and depression (Newman et al., 1997). Before long, a variety of clinical conditions will be treated through SCAI to determine which clinical or subclinical conditions can be treated through this medium at a distance and which conditions need to be treated by a professional in a face-to-face relationship.

IMPLICATIONS OF AN INCREASING TREND IN FORMALIZATION

If this trend is indeed valid, then it represents an evolutionary step in the development of methods other than traditional, mainstream, artistic, and impressionistic talk-based approaches. It represents the greater differentiation that is peculiar in any growing system, leading to greater specialization of functions. This step indicates that psychological interventions are achieving a greater degree of specificity than talk-based ones and implies specific treatments for specific conditions, as is the case with workbooks. Specificity can be evaluated. Grandiose, unclear, nonspecific claims based on talk are very difficult and expensive to evaluate and compare with other nonspecific approaches.

Of course, specific approaches offer a much wider range of cost-effective options for professionals and their patients than would be possible with talk therapies. Since no single professional can master more than one or two methods of treatment, greater specificity of practice will lead to groups of professionals with different skills banding together to offer the same specialization that has been evident in the practice of law, industry, and medicine for many years.

The major implication of this trend lies in determining which method is more cost-effective than another competing method claiming to treat the same condition successfully. For example, VRT claims to treat many phobias successfully. By the same token, many of the other methods, such as AT and EMDR, claim the same results. Given two methods that treat the same condition successfully, the cheaper of the two wins.

Thus, showing that a particular method is successful with any condition is no longer a feasible or acceptable criterion. Each method has to demonstrate that one method is more cost-effective in comparison to another method that claims to treat the same condition, when effectiveness is the same for both methods. Psychological interventions based on method and on writing are much more amenable to comparative testing than verbally based psychotherapies because they specify various steps that need to be followed to hopefully achieve a positive outcome.

As Alpert (1985) indicated a generation ago, changing already-established professional practices is an arduous and questionable endeavor (L'Abate, 1997b, 1999a,e). Yet the evidence brought out here suggests that indeed an evolutionary step in clinical practices is taking place presently through increasing formalization of clinical interventions. Many of the interventions listed earlier are not yet in the mainstream of established, traditional interventions. Hence, the major issue facing mental health professions is whether to enlarge the repertoire of interventions and therefore reach more people than traditionally has been possible, or stay the same and embrace the comforts of the status quo (L'Abate, 1999e). The latter means that no change is desired and no expansion of clinical practices is necessary. This position would lead to stagnation and eventual irrelevance. There is no choice but to change.

The formalization trend discussed earlier has at least four implications:

1. This trend suggests an evolutionary step in the development of replicable methods other than idiosyncratic, nonreplicable verbal gimmicks or techniques that vary from one professional to another.
2. This trend leans toward greater specificity of interventions that are difficult or impossible to achieve through talk (L'Abate, 1990, 1992, 1997b, 1999a, 2001, 2002a). Specificity can be evaluated. It means one specific treatment for one specific condition rather than the same treatment for all conditions.
3. A wider range of options will be available for professionals and respondents relying on other media and modalities than just talk. Most options, except manualized therapies, tend to use either body or movement-oriented instructions or homework assignments to increase generalization from the office to the home. Of course, such a wide range of interventions would produce not only greater specificity of practice but, eventually, more cost-effective methods of treatment.
4. Professional practice will become more complex. Specialization in practice means that no single professional can be an expert in all as-

pects of human deviations. Specialization has led many mental health professionals to join group practices, where different specialties are represented. Such specialization is found in medicine, law, and industry. The alternative to specialization is to use workbooks that cover areas of expertise outside the knowledge of the professional. For example, if a therapist does not consider herself or himself knowledgeable enough to deal with phobias, using a workbook for phobias initially as a structured interview and later as homework assignments would allow the therapist to expand her or his practice beyond his or her training and expertise.

In conclusion, the methods briefly reviewed here attest to a trend toward a greater formalization in psychological interventions. Except for manualized and planned therapies, which are still based on talk, the others involve the two modalities of nonverbal and DW interventions in addition to talk. The latter promise a much greater degree of specificity than can be obtained through talk alone. Although they are not yet in the mainstream and are still controversial in their empirical support, they represent an increasing formalization of psychological interventions that offer a greater degree of potentially comparative evaluation among professionals and within clinical settings.

DIFFERENCES BETWEEN CLINICAL PRACTICE AND RESEARCH

The argument of this chapter is based on various considerations about differences existing between the two fields of endeavor in mental health: clinical practice and research (Table 1.1). We need to know what these differences are if we want to reconcile them. These considerations vary according to various dimensions.

1. *Contexts of discovery versus justification* (Kuhn, 1962; Rychlak, 1969): Clearly, most clinical professionals operate within a private, money-for-services context dedicated to finding whatever causes may be present in the referral question, leading respondents to find answers and ways to deal with that question more or less immediately. This context implies face-to-face personal contact between respondents and professionals that involves individual (couples and families as well) presence. Justification, on the other hand, does not involve personal contact, remuneration, or discovery in the individual sense. If the term *discovery* is to be used here, it would be to jus-

tify findings that support hypotheses derived from clinical practice. Whatever procedure is used in research, it must answer some definite hypothesis that is based on mass-produced data and not individual cases. The latter may be used to develop hypotheses, with no data except case studies and anecdotal evidence. Clinical practice is idiographic. Research is nomothetic.

2. *Value systems related to indeterminism in practitioners and determinism in researchers:* The former means an unpredictable and, therefore, uncontrollable behavior. The latter means a predictable and lawful reality (L'Abate, 2002a). If indeterminism is one's choice, it is difficult to reconcile this choice with a deterministic position. The former is based on emotionality, whereas the latter is based on rationality. If both positions are absolute rather than relative, it will be difficult, if not impossible, to reconcile them.

3. *Goals of immediacy in practice versus transcendence in research:* In private practice the immediate goal is to help someone in distress or in crisis. The medium to achieve such an immediacy is language (Pennebaker and King, 1999). Hence, *variability* is the norm, since help varies from one professional to another. In research, very little language is involved because most instructions are administered in standard ways and do not vary from one respondent to another. Hence, in research *uniformity* is the norm. Helping people in distress is secondary to finding evidence to support hypotheses.

4. *Operations of privacy versus visibility or public display:* Practitioners need to assure respondents of complete confidentiality and secrecy unless indications of abuse or destructive tendencies are present. Within this context, whatever happens between a professional and the respondents remains secret. Research, on the other hand, is completely public. Its operations are for anyone to follow and to replicate step by step.

5. *Relationships about denial of dependence in clinical practice versus acknowledgment and acceptance of dependency in research:* Even though this conclusion may seem paradoxical, private practitioners have long denied any dependence on anyone except their respondents. In research, one needs to depend not only on respondents but also on procedures and standards that will ensure the validity of conclusions reached. Researchers are as dependent on funding and temporal availability of respondents as clinicians are dependent on respondents. Nonetheless, at least in the past, private practitioners were proud to practice "independently." This claim, however, can no longer be made because practitioners need to depend on managed care companies as well as on their respondents to survive. Most re-

searchers with academic appointments do not need such income, even though many research-oriented universities increasingly require their faculty members to obtain and depend on grants to receive promotions, tenure, or salary increments.

6. *Nature of nonreplicability versus replicability:* Because of the very operations and characteristics just described, it is impossible to replicate what happens in the offices of private practitioners. In research, on the other hand, operations have to be publicly replicable. If they are not, they no longer can achieve the evidentiary status of being replicable.

7. *Methods—dialectic versus demonstrative* (Rychlak, 1969): Professional, face-to-face relationships based on talk rely mostly on dialectical processes, in which questions, counterquestions, suggestions, recommendations, or interpretations are based on a verbal give-and-take between professionals and respondents. In research, the process is to demonstrate that whatever results or conclusions one may have achieved or found, they are valid and reliable, with no individualization of process and complete reliance on replicable, step-by-step approaches.

8. *Evaluation—qualitative versus quantitative:* Most evaluations in clinical practice are conducted through an interview that at best is individualized and tailored to the needs of respondents. In its uniqueness to the specific needs of a specific respondent, the interview is eminently qualitative and nonreplicable. In research, to be replicable, interviews became structured to standardize and make them repeatable from one respondent to another. In practice, very few test instruments are used, and when they are, they are subjectively and qualitatively interpreted. In research, only test instruments are used, and group norms rather than individual scores are used for interpretation.

9. *Evidence—anecdotal/impressionistic/subjective versus factual/verifiable/intersubjective:* The nature of the evidence is different from practice to research. In the former, evidence is left mostly to the opinion of the professional. In the latter, evidence is made public so it may be evaluated by other researchers as well.

10. *Quality—community versus agency* (Bakan, 1968): Emphasis on the relationship between practitioners and clients/patients is different from the relationship between researchers and their "subjects." In the former, an attempt is made to reach community, a relationship that is both professional on one hand, yet also intimate based on sharing of feelings, liking and trust, and disclosure of painful events or experiences (plus money exchanged). In the latter, the relation-

ship is strictly agentic, based on what needs to be done to achieve whatever research goal is sought. Feelings, if they are involved, are secondary or irrelevant to the achievement of the research goal. If money is involved, it is exchanged the other way around—from researchers to subjects.

11. *Emphasis on emotionality versus rationality* (L'Abate, 1986): From the foregoing distinction, emphasis is different because in practice feelings of respondents are paramount, at least in some clinical schools. Rationality, instead, is paramount in research. Whatever feelings respondents may have about the research they can keep to themselves, unless, of course, the research deals specifically with feelings. By the same token, the most research-oriented therapy school, cognitive-behavioral, stresses impaired rationality and uses homework assignments as an integral approach to interventions.

12. *Possible hypothetical dominance in hemispheric functions:* Here is where any possible differences between practice and research may seem far-fetched. However, if all of the foregoing differences are valid, then one could conclude that practitioners are relatively more right-hemisphere dominant, whereas most researchers are relatively more left-hemisphere dominant. This difference is based on considering that most practitioners rely strictly on talk for immediate, personal contact and presence, i.e., community (Pennebaker and King, 1999). Subjective feelings and community, apparently, are right-hemisphere functions (Ornstein, 1997). On the other hand, stress on rationality, transcendence, agency, and objectivity may well be under the dominance of the left hemisphere. How else could one explain so many differences in value systems, personality characteristics, and methods between the two approaches? Of course, this is an extremely hypothetical long shot. However, this is one way to discriminate between the two enterprises. By the same token, this writer has argued (L'Abate, 2001; Reed, McMahan, and L'Abate, 2001) that face-to-face talk therapy might be mediated usually by right-hemisphere functions, whereas DW might be mediated relatively by left-hemisphere functions. Whether this simple-minded hypothesis is valid remains to be seen.

13. *Media of communication—mostly verbal versus mostly written:* The previous conclusion is further validated by reliance on different media of communication. While practitioners rely mostly on talk, researchers rely mostly on writing. Both processes depend on different hemispheric dominances as well (Ornstein, 1997).

14. *Functions—myth making versus myth breaking:* One could argue, as had Cassirer (1946), that language is the producer of myths, as in the

case of psychoanalysis and "the talking cures" (Wallerstein, 1995), whereas research has the function of breaking myths, since these cures have been built on language rather than reality. One can only look at the many psychotherapeutic schools to see how language can create so many diverse approaches, each claiming therapeutic superiority. Research, on the other hand, demonstrated that no single school of therapy, except perhaps cognitive-behavioral, can claim hegemony over the others (Chambless and Ollendick, 2001).

Table 1.1 was created before this writer became acquainted with Kinneavy's (1971) distinction between exploratory and scientific proof. However, similarities between Kinneavy's distinctions and those made in Table 1.1 are too overwhelming to ignore. For instance, according to Kinneavy (1971), exploration consists of opinions, whereas scientific proof consists of knowledge by dialectics, as originally proposed by Plato (Taylor 1966). Cicero, Albertus Magnus, Thomas Aquinas, and Hugh of St. Victor (Org, 1958) distinguished between invention and judgment.

Roger Bacon, Galileo, Sir Isaac Newton, and René Descartes (Carmichael, 1939) were among the first to show how actual demonstration was different from discovery. Kant (1952), of course, distinguished the dialectic of reason in exploration versus analytic understanding of science. Hegel

TABLE 1.1. Differences Between Clinical Practice and Research in Psychological Interventions

Realms of Endeavor	Clinical Practice	Research
Contexts	Discovery	Justification
Value systems	Indeterminism	Determinism
Goals	Immediacy	Transcendence
Operations	Private	Public
Dependency	Denial of	Acknowledgment of
Nature	Nonreplicable	Replicable
Methods	Dialectic	Demonstrative
Evaluation	Qualitative	Quantitative
Evidence	Anecdotal/impressionistic/subjective	Factual/verifiable/intersubjective
Quality	Community	Agency
Emphasis	Emotionality	Rationality
Hemispheric dominance	Right side?	Left side?
Media	Mostly verbal	Mostly written
Functions	Myth making	Myth breaking

(1959), on the other hand, proposed that analytic understanding belonged to exploration, whereas dialectic reason belonged to science. Pierce (1960) distinguished between proposing and testing, whereas Dewey (1938) distinguished between inquiry versus judgment. Day (1961), instead, distinguished between heuristic (hypothetical) versus probative/demonstrative. Kuhn (1962) distinguished between the context of discovery versus the context of justification. Hanson (1961) supported the distinction between discovery versus the hypothetic-deductive method. Rychlak (1969) stressed differences between dialectical versus demonstrative enterprises, a distinction expanded by L'Abate (1986, 1994, 1997c, 2002a).

Workbooks, therefore, represent the ultimate stress on a reproducible, replicable approach that is demonstrative rather than dialectical in the realm of justification rather than discovery, and empirical rather than impressionistic. Yet they are as clinically useful an any approach available at this time. Their usefulness will be discussed later.

How Can These Differences Be Reconciled?

If DW, and especially workbooks, were to become part of mainstream mental health practices, they could serve as a nexus between researchers and practitioners (L'Abate, 1997a,b). Clearly such a reconciliation could not be achieved ipso facto by fiat. It will take time and a desire from both parties to achieve such a conciliation. What would need to happen to achieve it? At least five distinct and not wholly independent steps will need to take place if a semblance of conciliation is to occur.

First, managed care companies, having seen the cost-effectiveness and mass orientation of most DW approaches, may require practitioners to start using DW and especially workbooks to support and document claims of usefulness and therapeutic success. Second, practitioners will need to start adding DW as another medium of intervention with synergistic results, together with talk and nonverbal interventions. Third, professional organizations may start questioning claims of success based strictly on subjective evaluations of practitioners without external evidence to substantiate such claims. Words, subjective interpretations of results based on anecdotal, impressionistic evidence, may not be sufficient to support and document claims of professional competence. Fourth, state boards creating standards of practice may start to require more than talk or paper credentials to license practitioners. Fifth, the burden will be on training programs to teach that words alone are not going to suffice in an increasingly competitive market, where objective evidence will be necessary to prove one's competence.

In addition to the foregoing, briefly stated, arguments, one needs to consider the trend in the formalization of psychological interventions that is germane to the use of DW and workbooks. It is within this very trend that workbooks represent the ultimate formalization of most psychological interventions, as discussed further in the next chapter.

WORKBOOKS IN CURRENT PSYCHOLOGICAL LITERATURE

When one reviews DW and workbooks for preventive, therapeutic, or rehabilitative purposes, one discovers that neither DW or workbooks, despite their distinguished history (L'Abate, 1992), has been used as a possible medium of therapeutic intervention (Freeman et al., 1986; Bergin and Garfield, 1994; Hubble, Duncan, and Miller, 1999; Livesley, 2001; Routh and DeRubeis, 1998). At best, DW or written homework assignments have been used for single-shot, ad hoc purposes, or to log behavior (Carroll, 1999; Kazantzis, 2000; Kazantzis, Deane, and Ronan, 2000). Both the surgeon general's report on mental health (U.S. Department of Health and Human Services, 1999) and selected, recent, treatises on psychotherapy (Hubble, Duncan, and Miller, 1999; Snyder and Ingram, 2000) and effective treatments for post-traumatic stress disorder (PTSD) (Foa, Keane, and Friedman, 2000), for instance, fail to mention either DW, computers, or workbooks, let alone assignments, homework, or working at a distance from respondents via computers and the Internet. If one were to interpret this void, one would assume that the major stance of most psychological interventions is still traditionally passive or, at best, reactive, receiving what respondents say without any active, proactive, or, heaven forbid, interactive component!

A recent series of articles about brief psychotherapy (Elliott, 2001; Gurman, 2001; McGinn and Sanderson, 2001; Messer, 2001a,b; Rohrbaugh and Shoham, 2001), for example, did not even mention homework assignments, let alone written homework assignments. What these articles do show, however, is the bewildering array of approaches, all claiming great therapeutic usefulness and little specificity, with the exception of one article about phobias (McCullough and Andrews, 2001). When one surveys the field of addiction treatments, one discovers only self-monitoring forms to identify high-risk situations (Carroll, 1999) and worksheets to serve as homework assignments to conduct functional analyses of substance use (Carroll, 1999).

When one reviews the treatment of incarcerated felons (Gaes et al., 1999), one finds that "adult correctional treatment is effective in reducing criminal behavior" (p. 361). "Behavioral/cognitive treatments, on the average, produce larger effects than other treatments" (Gaes et al., p. 361). Presumably, such treatments use some form of written homework assignments. On the other hand, a review of parole and prison reentry in the United States (Petersilia, 1999) concluded that "needed treatment programs are scarce, and parole officers focus on surveillance more than rehabilitation. About half of parolees fail to complete parole successfully, and their returns to prison represent about a third of incoming prisoners" (p. 479). If treatment programs for criminals are successful, as Gaes and colleagues (1999) want us to believe, why do one-third of parolees go back to jail?

In reviewing the field of rehabilitation of felons, Reed, McMahan, and L'Abate (2001) found very discouraging results and high rates of recidivism, suggesting that DW and workbooks may be a cost-effective alternative treatment of choice when words fail to make a dent in the number of incarcerated felons. Even if this treatment fails, it is not as expensive as face-to-face, verbal treatment based on professional contact. Furthermore, using workbooks administered through computers is a way of controlling what information criminals receive. In addition, one could argue that structured computer-assisted interventions, like workbooks, would allow criminals to use an asset area, that is, eye-hand coordination, supposedly under relative control of the right hemisphere, to access and reinforce their deficit area in cognitive functioning, supposedly under relative control of the left hemisphere (L'Abate, 2001; Reed, McMahan, and L'Abate, 2001).

Not only are workbooks not yet part of the mainstream of current psychological practices, they are not even part of empirically supported treatments (ESTs), despite being the most objective of all psychological interventions. ESTs are supposedly based on or developed from established practices, yet they insist on relying on face-to-face talk (Chambless and Ollendick, 2001; Dobson and Craig, 1998; Ingram, Hayes, and Scott, 2000; Nathan and Gorman, 1998; Norcross, 2002), even though the spoken medium is not as replicable. Workbooks do not appear anywhere in the established EST literature, as far as this writer has been able to assess. As argued earlier in this chapter and elsewhere (L'Abate, 1999a,e, 2001), manuals, the mainstay of all ESTs, function only to perpetuate the status quo in psychotherapy. Their practice still assumes and believes that talk remains the only medium of communication and healing. Manuals are presented as the sole salvation in the practice of psychotherapy, even though researchers and only a few practitioners use them. Furthermore, even if they were used more frequently by a larger number of practitioners, it is doubtful whether it can be demonstrated economically that a specific link exists between what the manual instructs a practitioner to do and say and what that particular practitioner says she or he did. As mentioned earlier, demonstration would be left to a few die-hard researchers with enough grant money to pursue this line of research.

Freeman and Fusco (2000) commented on the general use of homework in cognitive-behavioral therapy without further specification as to its nature:

> Therapy of necessity needs to take place beyond the confines of the consulting room. It is important for the patient to understand that the extension of the therapy work to the nontherapy hours allows for a greater therapeutic focus. The homework can be either cognitive or behavioral. It might involve having the patient complete an activity schedule . . . complete several dysfunctional thoughts records, or try new behaviors. . . .When therapy ends, everything will be homework for the patient. (p. 55)

In another short reference to homework, Dattilio and Kendall (2000) add that "homework is a very important aspect of cognitive-behavioral treatments of panic [disorders]" (p. 75). No other reference was made about writing, DW, or computer-assisted interventions. Nonetheless, in spite of this void, there are a few indications that DW, if not workbooks, is slowly creeping into the family therapy literature (Androutsopoulou, 2001; Penn, 2001; Penn and Frankfurt, 1994).

Therefore, to include DW in existing mental health practices, a conceptualization of the therapeutic process was necessary to find a responsible rationale for its use (L'Abate, 2002a). Instead of psychotherapy alone, we need to consider a continuum of preventive approaches, ranging from primary, universal prevention for almost everybody, to secondary prevention targeted to special populations, and tertiary prevention and crisis intervention necessary for critical or clinical populations (Heller, Wyman, and Allen, 2000; L'Abate, 1990, 2002a; Offord, 2000). DW and workbooks are located as secondary prevention tools that can be added to or substituted for primary and tertiary prevention approaches.

If the past is bleak as far as the role of workbooks in mental health, their future is, however, bright and well assured. In a review of interactive versus noninteractive interventions, for instance, Prochaska (1999) concluded,

> [The] results clearly support the hypothesis that interactive interventions will outperform the same number of noninteractive interventions. . . . The implications are clear. Providing interactive interventions via computers is likely to produce greater outcomes than relying on noninteractive communications, such as newsletters, media, or self-help manuals. (pp. 249-250)

In comparing proactive versus reactive interventions, Prochasha (1999) concluded,

I believe that the future of behavioral and mental health programs lies with stage-matched, proactive and interactive interventions. Much greater impacts can be generated by proactive programs because of much higher participation rates, even if efficacy rates are lower. I also believe that proactive programs can produce comparable outcomes to traditional reactive ("wait-till-they-come") programs. (p. 250)

In comparing results from counseling and computer-assisted interventions, Prochaska (1999) added this prophetic conclusion as far as the use of workbooks in the delivery of mental health services is concerned:

The results . . . were even more impressive. . . . If these results continue to be replicated, therapeutic programs will be able to produce significant impacts on entire populations . . . such impacts require scientific and professional shifts from (a) an action paradigm to a stage paradigm, (b) reactive to proactive recruitment [of respondents], (c) expecting participants to match the needs of therapeutic programs to having these programs match their needs, (d) clinic-based to population-based programs that still apply the field's most powerful individualized and interactive intervention strategies, and (e) specific strategies varying from therapy to therapy to common pathways and processes integrated from across competing theories that were once thought to be incomparable. (p. 250)

In conclusion, regardless of the foregoing arguments, it is abundantly clear that thus far workbooks are not part of the established psychotherapeutic or even preventive or rehabilitative armamentaria. Only a relatively small number of practitioners use homework assignments. An even smaller number use written homework assignments regularly. Of the latter, an even smaller percentage may use systematically written homework assignments or workbooks.

Then why bother to edit a whole book on workbooks? First, presenting the role of workbooks in prevention, psychotherapy, and rehabilitation is important on the basis of research showing the effectiveness of DW in general, and expressive, focused DW writing in particular (Esterling et al., 1999; Esterling and Pennebaker, 2001; Pennebaker, 2001). Second, this work is important on the basis of evidence summarized in previous work, including a meta-analysis of workbook effectiveness presented in Chapter 2. Third, publishing a book on workbooks is based on the possibility that when DW and workbooks are used in the context of a caring and compassionate therapeutic or paratherapeutic relationship, they can enhance, strengthen, and possibly shorten the process of helping, making them just as effective but less expensive than other approaches (L'Abate, 2002a). Workbooks have the potential to satisfy the private, pay-for-practice model as well as a larger public health model for the masses who cannot afford private practitioners, as well as researchers looking for inexpensive ways to intervene and collect results, while being helpful at the same time. If Prochaska's (1999) conclusions are correct, then this book and its contributors can be considered as harbingers of mental health service delivery in this century.

Clearly, advantages and even dangers of DW and workbooks have yet to be fully explored, along with their limitations. In spite of evidence already cited elsewhere (Smyth and L'Abate, 2001) and in Chapter 2, more empirical evidence needs to be gathered to support a wider applicability and specificity of workbook application. Because of their cost-cutting, time-saving potential and mass orientation, workbooks deserve more attention from preventive, psychotherapeutic, and rehabilitative communities than they have received heretofore. Hopefully, chapters contained herein will bring this message home to mental health students and practitioners.

OVERVIEW OF WORKBOOK ADMINISTRATION

The large number of workbooks available to deal with an extremely wide range of problems and symptoms makes it possible to match intervention with evaluation or diagnosis in a way that is difficult, if not impossible, using the spoken medium (L'Abate, 1996, 2002b).

Consequently, we will need to rely on a lattice or ladder of professional and paraprofessional personnel which will require some basic changes about how psychological interventions have been traditionally practiced. These changes include (1) working at a distance from respondents (2) through less trained and less experienced personnel with (3) greater reliance on nonverbal (medication, exercise, and diet) and written media. Any existing organization, to work efficiently, needs a hierarchy of personnel. We cannot build skyscrapers with our bare hands, for example—we need a hierarchy of architects, engineers, draftspersons, and bricklayers, working with a variety of tools and instruments. This process is what needs to occur in the mental health field, with the help of new technologies and with a hierarchy of personnel.

In the early twentieth century, we thought we could deal with immense human problems strictly through face-to-face, talk-based, individual psychotherapy (Wallerstein, 1995). In the middle of the century, we thought that adding couple, group, and family therapies to individual therapy would help improve on the single-professional, single-respondent paradigm. Later, in the second half of the century, preventive approaches came into being with little if any evidence of long-term effects. By the end of the twentieth century, these additions only indicated the need for more mass-oriented, cost-effective interventions that would go beyond the talk-based, face-to-face paradigm. Here is where workbooks can make a contribution.

When the mental health movement started after World War I, only professionals with a doctorate in medicine and further specialization in psychiatry were allowed to work (i.e., talk) face to face with patients who had critical or clinical conditions. Eventually, and not without a struggle, clinical psychologists and psychotherapists from various disciplines started to supplement and, later, partially supplant the psychiatric profession, at least in the talking role. A host of other professions, disciplines, and credentialed professionals have mushroomed in the past fifty years. Toward the end of the twentieth century, workbooks came into being, suggesting that it is possible to help people in distress at a distance from a professional, particularly through computers and the Internet (L'Abate, 2001, 2002a).

Matching Evaluation with Interventions

No matter which theory determines which treatment is used, as long as the treatment is based on talk, links between evaluation and treatment are going to be difficult if not impossible to apply and verify (L'Abate, 1992, 1999b,c,d, 2001, 2002a). This goal is possible to a few grant-receiving researchers but not to practitioners on the front line. When treatment is linked to evaluation through DW, and especially workbooks, it is possible to link the two processes together and achieve the match that mental health professionals have been looking for as the Holy Grail of clinical practice and research. This quest has been and will remain unfulfilled because no critical questions were raised on whether the spoken medium was appropriate or worth using for that purpose. Classifications according to three media of communication—nonverbal, verbal, and written—indicate that interventions need to take place using these three media. Combinations of these media may allow clinicians to intervene with more people in a more discriminating manner than has been the case heretofore (L'Abate, 2002a).

Working at a Distance from Respondents

Can we really and effectively change people's behavior without even seeing them? If words have that power, then any argument about their limitations will be seen as threats to professional power and, therefore, rejected out of hand (L'Abate, 1997b). When speaking into a microphone and writing about past traumas are compared experimentally in their effectiveness with control groups that write about emotionally neutral events, it cannot be denied that speaking into a microphone is slightly superior to DW (Esterling et al., 1994; Esterling et al., 1999; Smyth, 1998; Szell, 1994). However, this difference is not sufficiently significant statistically to justify its superiority over DW. Furthermore, as Weintraub (1981) argued then, and has been argued ever since (L'Abate, 1990, 1991, 1992, 1994, 1997c, 1999a,c), at least for research purposes, talk needs to be transcribed into writing, a process that is expensive, as indicated earlier. Consequently, talk is more expensive than writing, at least in that respect. If talk is inefficient, is it effective? If it is effective, then it is a very expensive way to help people change for the better. Can workbooks facilitate the process of helping people in distress? This and other questions will be answered later in this book.

Contributors to this work are the pioneers in their respective countries of origin in the use of workbooks. They all share a belief based on professional experience or empirical evidence about the usefulness and efficacy of workbooks.

TOWARD A CLASSIFICATION OF WRITING

Of course, classifications of writing abound but vary according to which criteria are used, aims, goals, special audience characteristics, etc. Even though the following sources refer to "language" and not directly to "writing," apparently they assume that a classification of writing derives directly from a classification of language (Britton, 1975; Bushman, 2000; Dean and Wilson, 1959; Heath, 1983; Howard, 1985). Of course, as Brandt (personal communication, November 27, 2000) asked: "What is the purpose of the classification?" To answer that relevant question, at least five major reasons exist for attempting such a task:

1. Develop a historical and situational context for the use of DW and workbooks
2. Serve as background for an even more specific classification of workbooks that would derive and follow from such a classification
3. Achieve a more systematic understanding of DW within the context of psychological interventions
4. Assuage fears of most practitioners about the use of DW by legitimizing it with a classification of DW first and a classification of workbooks second
5. Match workbooks with specific referral questions or problems

Without such a classification it would be impossible to achieve this kind of match and specificity.

Hughes (1985), for example, traced a classification of writing to its evolution from early ideographic, to pictographic, then syllabic, and finally alphabetic writing. Kinneavy (1971) distinguished language from metalanguage. Language per se deals with linguistics, which includes syntactics and semantics, discourse and pragmatics. Metalanguage, on the other hand, includes situational and cultural contexts. The first context deals with personal and social motivations for speaking, reading, and writing, concerned mostly with the immediate, personal, and social effects of discourse. This context includes proxemics, kinesics, haptics, and other topics. The second context deals with large social reasons, such as propaganda, science, philosophies, literature, and comparative ethnoscience, traditions, and period characteristics. Thus, Kinneavy (1971) comes close to a classification of DW as metalanguage that would be useful here. He also included a section on the structure of language consisting of the communication triangle composed of encoder, decoder, and reality. However, structure in his proposal does not mean or include the meaning of structure used within the present chapter.

There is no space to give full attention and credit to Kinneavy's (1971) otherwise encyclopedic and scholarly contribution. It would include his extremely relevant distinction between exploration, which in its characteristics (see p. 101) and in this context would include psychotherapy, versus scientific proof (see pp. 98-124), which in this context would include DW and workbooks. This distinction was elaborated earlier in this chapter to distinguish clinical practice from research.

In addition to its formal characteristics, i.e., expressive/instructive versus creative/spontaneous versus contrived, DW encompasses a wide range of possibilities on a continuum of structure (see Box 1.1), an area, that, as far as this writer knows, has been left untouched by previous classifications. Workbooks constitute the most stringent form of DW along a dimension of structure (Box 1.2), ranging from (1) an open-ended structure on one end, as in journals or diaries (Carney et al., 2000), to (2) expressive writing focused on a single topic, as in autobiography, or on past and recent traumas (Esterling et al., 1999; Esterling and Pennebaker, 2001; Lepore and Smyth, 2002; Pennebaker, 1997, 2001), (3) guided (de Vries, Birren, and Deutchman, 1990), consisting of questions based on previous writings, to (4) an extreme of structure or programmed writing, as in workbooks. In addition to structure, DW varies according to: (1) content (traumatic/trivial, varied), (2) specificity (high/low), (3) goals (cathartic/prescriptive), and (4) level of abstraction (high/low) (L'Abate, 1986, 1991, 1992, 1997a,b,c, 2001, 2002a,b; L'Abate and Kern, 2002).

BOX 1.1. A Classification of Writing

1. Expressive/instructive versus creative/spontaneous (contextual, constructive of stories) versus contrived (vocabulary, spelling, style, syntax, logic, sentence construction and combination)
2. Structure, ranging from unstructured to structured
   - Open-ended (journals, diaries)
   - Focused (one topic, as in autobiographies and Pennebaker's [1997] expressive format)
   - Guided (written questions about written compositions)
   - Programmed (as in workbooks)
3. Goals (prescriptive/cathartic)
4. Specificity (general/specific)
5. Content (traumatic/trivial; various categories)
6. Abstraction (high/low)

There is virtually no topic that cannot be dealt with in writing that is not already dealt with in speaking. In fact, people with certain character disorders, for example, tend to reveal more in writing than they can disclose verbally. Workbooks are available for just about any relevant topic one can think of for individuals, couples, and families: addictions, affective disorders (including anxiety and depression), fears, interpersonal conflict, intimacy, grief and loss, and many other clinical and semiclinical conditions (L'Abate, 2002b).

TOWARD A CLASSIFICATION OF WORKBOOKS

Workbooks for homework assignments are an instance of programmed distance writing (PDW) that represents a relatively new phenomenon supporting the thesis of greater formalization in the practice of psychological interventions. The large number of workbooks available to deal with a rather wide range of problems and symptoms makes it possible to match intervention with evaluation or diagnosis in a way that is difficult if not impossible to obtain using talk. Furthermore, workbooks written from different theoretical, therapeutic, or empirical perspectives may well become the next dynamic step (battleground?) in the comparative evaluation of cost-effectiveness for different approaches. For instance, the workbook about anxiety and panic developed by Barlow and Craske (1994) could be compared to an anxiety workbook developed by L'Abate et al. (1992) from the *Diagnostic and Statistical Manual of Mental Disorders,* Third Edition (APA, 1980). The depression workbook developed by Weissman (1995), based on interper-

---

BOX 1.2. A Classification of Workbooks

1. *Composition of respondents:* individuals, children, adolescents, adults, couples, and families
2. *Theoretical orientation:* as in theory-derived (behavioral, cognitive, humanistic, etc.) versus theory-related versus theory-independent (clinical practice, research, pop literature, etc.)
3. *Format:* fixed (nomothetic) versus flexible (idiographic)
4. *Derivation:* from referral question versus from single test score or from multidimensional test profile
5. *Style:* straightforward linear versus paradoxical, circular
6. Level and type of functionality versus dysfunctionality
   • Normalizing
   • Internalizing
   • Externalizing
   • Serious pathology
7. *Specific content:* addictions, affective disorders, couples, families, intimacy, loss and grief, etc.

---

sonal psychotherapy, could be compared with workbooks developed from Beck's Depression Inventory or Hamilton's Depression Scale (L'Abate, 1996, 2002a,b). A sexuality workbook developed by Wincze and Barlow (1997) could be compared to a sexuality workbook developed by L'Abate (1992). Hence, comparative testing of contrasting theoretical models could take place proactively and dynamically, above and beyond static, sterile, and unproductive laboratory testing on the statistical properties of test instruments based on self-report, paper-and-pencil tests.

On the basis of considerations made earlier, the following classification of workbooks is tentatively suggested in Box 1.2. Workbooks could be classified according to

1. composition of respondents (individual children, adolescents, adults, couples, and families);
2. referral reason as stated by respondents;
3. single test score or peaks and valleys of test profiles;
4. level of functionality derived from unstructured, initial contact, reason for referral, and results from a test battery:
   • normalizing, when no florid deviation is evident objectively and subjectively,
   • externalizations (anger, hostility, and aggression),
   • internalizations (anxiety, depression, and fear), and
   • severe psychopathology, combining contradictory extremes in both internalizations and externalizations; and

5. specific content of the workbook (addictions, affective disorders, anger, aggression, intimacy, etc.).

Furthermore, workbooks can be divided into a fixed, nomothetic versus a flexible, idiographic format. In this fashion, it seems possible to match a workbook with a referral question in a more specific way than would be possible with face-to-face talk.

Once PDW is used to match treatment with evaluation, it is possible to write workbooks that derived from either existing evaluation instruments or definite clinical symptoms. For example, a series of homework for individuals was written to match the fifteen content scales of the Minnesota Multiphasic Personality Inventory-2 (MMPI-2) (L'Abate, 1992). Another workbook on social training was written for impulsive individuals who score high on the psychopathic deviate scale of the MMPI-2. Various depression workbooks were written for individuals with high scores on either the depression scale of the MMPI-2 or on the Beck Depression Inventory (L'Abate, 2001; L'Abate et al., 1992). Other workbooks to match existing tests were written for the Neuroticism, Extraversion, and Openness (NEO) and the five-factor personality model, the Personality Assessment Inventory (PAI), and the Symptom Scale 77, among many others (L'Abate, 1996, 2002a,b). This will be discussed further in Chapter 2.

To match referral symptoms with treatment in couples, for instance, a program was written about arguing and fighting (L'Abate, 1992). In this program, partners are asked to describe individually the nature and content of arguing and fighting through ratings of frequency, rate, duration, content, and intensity of this behavior in the first assignment. They are to exchange their completed forms and discuss similarities and differences in their answers, a practice that applies to all couples and families who are administered this and other systematically written homework.

In the second assignment, partners are asked to rank ten "explanations" of arguing and fighting that are all positively reframed, including giving their own explanation if those given are not satisfactory to them. In the third assignment, partners are asked to have an argument or fight according to a series of instructions designed to mimic how couples argue/fight ("really dirty") in general, according to a prescription of the symptom technique (Weeks and L'Abate, 1982). Couples are instructed to tape-record this session and to bring the tape to their professional helper. Once the tape is brought in (some couples do not bring a tape because they have stopped arguing/fighting and have settled down to calm discussion/negotiation), they are given a rating sheet and asked to listen individually to the tape and score how often each partner has uttered abusive expressions already defined in the instructions of the previous assignments ("you" statements/blaming, reading the partner's mind, bringing up the past, finding excuses for self but not for partner, blackmail/bribery, threats and ultimatums, distracting). Once they bring back their scores on these categories, each partner is administered the assignment that matches the highest score achieved. If other high scores are found, each partner is administered the matching assignment in subsequent therapy sessions. Consequently, PDW is a nomothetic approach that can be administered idiographically to both individuals and couples.

As the foregoing workbook illustrates, the process of prescription between evaluation and written homework assignments can be achieved through links between a symptom, e.g., fighting, and a specific workbook. To make this process even more precise and accurate, it is possible to link specific test scores with a matching workbook, as in the case of the MMPI-2 for individuals. For couples, another workbook was written for problems in relationships. It consists of a questionnaire with assignments matching the same dyadic dimensions covered by the questionnaire (L'Abate, 1992). A series of twenty conflict areas cited frequently in the couple therapy literature (dominant/submissive, expressive/inexpressive, open/closed, etc.) provided the basis for 240 items rated on a five-point scale by each partner. Scores for each partner are meaningful only to the extent of how they compare with the scores of the other partner. Discrepancies among the twenty scales are added to obtain a total discrepancy score (McMahan and L'Abate, 2001).

The test profile (produced through a computer program) shows which dimensions for each couple have the widest discrepancy, producing a nomothetic instrument (for all couples) with idiographic features (for a specific couple). The profile of each couple is specific to that couple and to no other. Depending on the number of conflict areas, each couple is administered homework assignments that match the dimensions with the greatest discrepancy scores. A total discrepancy score correlated significantly and negatively with two subscales, dyadic satisfaction ($r = -.57, p < .01$) and dyadic cohesion ($r = -.53, p < .05$) of the dyadic adjustment scale ($r = -.51, p < .05$) in thirty-two married couples (McMahan and L'Abate, 2001). In addition to workbooks matching test scores for individual tests, other couple workbooks matching existing dyadic questionnaires have been written for marital satisfaction and marital conflict scales (L'Abate,1996, 2001, 2002a,b).

Workbooks for families have been written on the basis of the referral symptom, including abuse, lying, overeating, negativity, etc., either in the whole family or in the identified patient (L'Abate, 1990, 1992, 1996, 2002a,b), or on the basis of test profiles in the family evaluation scale.

ADVANTAGES OF WORKBOOKS

Advantages and disadvantages of workbooks have been considered elsewhere (L'Abate, 1992, 1996, 1999c,e, 2001, 2002a). The major advantage of workbooks, however, lies in their providing the software for structured Internet interventions, in addition to unstructured interventions, such as psychotherapy. They furnish a source documentation far above psychotherapy notes. Advantages of workbook administrations are summarized in Box 1.3, whereas disadvantages and even dangers are summarized in Box 1.4. It would take a great deal of time and space to elaborate on each advantage, disadvantage, and danger implicit in workbook administration.

However, as long as talk is the major medium of interaction between practitioners and respondents (consumers, participants, clients, patients, individuals, couples, families), research on the process and outcome of psychologically based interventions will be difficult and expensive to perform (L'Abate, 1999e, 2001). It will remain even more difficult, if not impossible, to link evaluation with a specific treatment as would be the case of DW, and especially programmed writing, as in workbooks. This conclusion is demonstrated by one study showing the possibility of performing research on the comparative use of different theoretical viewpoints in a relatively inexpensive fashion (L'Abate et al., 1992). Furthermore, specifically designed workbooks allow linking evaluation with treatment in a much more systematically explicit, efficient, and specific fashion that is going to be difficult to match when talk is used by itself.

Regardless of how many advantages, disadvantages, and even dangers this new technology may have, the major advantages that workbooks have over talk in current, talk-based, face-to-face contacts, as well as over manuals and self-help books, are

1. specificity,
2. explicitness,
3. interactivity,
4. versatility,
5. cost-effectiveness, and
6. verifiability.

Specificity, Explicitness, and Interactivity

Specificity relates to the notion that a workbook deals only with the particular condition it claims to confront and no other condition. For example, if a workbook claims to deal with anxiety, it cannot be used to treat depres-

BOX 1.3. Advantages of Workbook Administration

- Specificity: Close match between specific problem or referral questions and treatment.
- Explicitness: Questions, tasks, and assignments are made in writing, leaving little or no room for confusion.
- Interactivity: Written homework assignments force interaction according to three hypothetical metafunctions or—from written questions, tasks, or exercises to written answers; from written answers to comparisons or feedback from others (partners, family members, group members); from comparisons with others to professional helpers.
- Versatility: Workbooks can be used in prevention by themselves, or in psychotherapy as adjuncts, especially with comorbid conditions, and as alternatives before, during, or after talk-based, face-to-face prevention, psychotherapy, or rehabilitation.
- Workbooks can serve as written treatment plans since they are more specific than manuals.
- Workbooks can serve as structured interviews, especially to train students or even help professionals who are not familiar with how to treat a specific condition.
- Workbooks allow a 100 percent documentation of treatment plans since they are more specific, coming directly from respondents rather than psychotherapy notes written by professionals. Those notes are susceptible to self-serving interpretations and biases from the professional.
- Workbooks can be assigned after completion of psychotherapy, following up any unfinished business.
- Workbooks can function as software for computer-assisted psychological interventions, possibly decreasing respondents' dependency on professionals and increasing their sense of self-mastery and autonomy.
- The cost-effectiveness of workbooks seems plausible but still needs to be demonstrated.*
- Workbooks can be administered to masses of people through the mail, fax, TV, and the Internet.
- Workbooks are eminently verifiable—because of their written format they can be reproduced without limits.

*L'Abate, L'Abate, and Maino (2004) actually found that workbooks administered to individuals, couples, and families prolonged significantly the number of psychotherapy sessions.

**BOX 1.4. Disadvantages and Dangers
of Workbook Administration**

- Discovery or uncovering of avoided past traumas
- Mismatch between problem and workbook
- Confidentiality
- Cheating
- Poorly written workbooks (hortatory, verbose, etc.)
- Biases and resistance of mental health professionals

These and other potential dangers will not be discovered unless we take the risk of helping respondents at a distance without talk or face-to-face contacts.

---

sion, despite the overlap between these conditions. However, what is even more important is the link between evaluation and intervention.

The link between evaluation and intervention becomes even more specific when a respondent is found, for example, to be depressed through an interview and scores on depression or other clinical or personality scales. Whoever is depressed receives a depression workbook. Whoever is anxious receives an anxiety book and so on, as long as workbooks are available that: (1) match the specific referral question and (2) a single-dimension test score or (3) a profile from a multidimensional test. Under these conditions, treatment through a workbook should match: (1) the subjective referral question ("I need help with my depression"), (2) an interview, that does not need to be talk-based and face-to-face, and/or (3) objective results from a test and, preferably, from a test battery.

This specific link is difficult to achieve if the medium of communication and supposed healing is talk, because of its immediacy (Pennebaker and King, 1999). As long as the major vehicle of intervention is talk, it is going to be difficult and expensive to link and match evaluation with intervention. This link is available to a handful of researchers with grant money and to no one else. How are findings from that research to be disseminated and practiced by practitioners rather than just researchers? It is also very difficult and expensive to demonstrate that such a link exists. This process is clearly outside the realm of clinical practice to most psychotherapists (L'Abate, 1992, 1997b, 2001, 2002a,b).

Specificity, explicitness, and interactivity are difficult to achieve as long as talk remains the main medium of communication and healing (L'Abate, 1999e). Talk is liable to distortion, forgetting, and unwarranted generalizations that may make the process of therapy unduly lengthy and relatively more expensive than DW. The myth-making qualities of language (Cassirer, 1946) are reflected not only in the multitude of available psychotherapeutic approaches, but also in the possibility that there are as many therapeutic approaches as there are therapists. Each therapist has his or her individual style and approach, differing from one therapist to another. This variability has led to the existence of literally hundreds of psychotherapies, making it impossible to evaluate them. One has only to check on the myriad publications, let alone professionals, to become aware of such diversity and multiplicity. Is chaos the ultimate and inevitable outcome of such diversity and multiplicity?

Versatility

Versatility implies an ease of various applications. For instance, workbooks can be used as the following:

- Written treatment plans rather than talk-based treatment plans, which are difficult to link with the actual behavior of the therapist, as discussed previously.
- Structured interviews for beginning graduate students, or even professionals not familiar with a particular method of treatment (Jordan, 2001). In this fashion, they would function as being much more structured than the manuals advocated in some quarters as the answer to all evidence-based interventions (Chambless, 1997; Dobson and Craig, 1998; Nathan and Gorman, 1998; Wilson, 1997). By relying on talk as the only medium of communication and healing, manuals would perpetuate the status quo in psychotherapy. Treatment fidelity remains variable from one therapist to another, and recordings would be needed to evaluate such fidelity. As already noted, this process is expensive, limited to a few dedicated researchers with grant money, and out of reach of most professionals.
- A recent survey (Najavits et al., 2000) reporting positive views, extensive use, and few concerns about the use of manuals was limited to forty-seven cognitive-behavioral therapists. It failed to include a larger sample of therapists from different theoretical or practical persuasions. Nonetheless, these authors warned, "Be aware that reading a manual is not sufficient to attain mastery of a treatment" (Najavits et al., 2000, p. 407). This warning, of course, applies to the whole issue of treatment fidelity, a criterion that cannot and will not be met as long as treatment, including manuals, is talk-based. Hence, it is

doubtful whether practitioners will rely on manuals, unless forced by managed care companies. Even then, it would be impossible to evaluate their process and outcome because both are still based on talk.

- Straightforward written homework assignments administered in addition to or as alternatives before, during, or after talk-based, face-to-face prevention or psychotherapy serve as 100 percent documentation of treatment plans and the match between the referral questions and treatment. Before interventions, workbooks can serve as preparation as well as screening for actual face-to-face, talk-based interventions. What is learned from this administration would allow for a more precise intervention. For example, waiting-list controls could be used to evaluate the effects of talk-based therapy. Respondents on waiting lists could be helped immediately through workbooks even if no immediate, face-to-face, talk-based professional help is available. The use of workbooks may well reduce the number of distressed people in need of help who are waiting for it.

- After traditional interventions, workbooks could furnish a form of follow-up that would allow cleaning and clearing up of issues not completely dealt with during face-to-face interventions (Bird, 1992). Furthermore, certain workbooks are idiographic in nature. These assignments can be changed to accommodate to respondents' specific needs, as will be shown later. Other workbooks are nomothetic. They are the same for all respondents. Even idiographic ones, however, can be administered nomothetically, as discussed later.

- The major advantage of workbooks, however, lies in dealing with comorbid conditions. For instance, one could perform traditional fcae-to-face, talk-based psychotherapy or even medication, and at the same time administer referral-oriented, symptom-specific workbooks. One can help respondents in one's office but also help them with their symptoms through workbooks that match a symptom, provided there are as many workbooks as there are clinical conditions (L'Abate, 1996).

- It is virtually impossible to train any professional, even a seasoned one, to deal with so many existing clinical disorders and psychopathologies. How can one, trained to work with individuals, work with couples? By the same token, how can one trained to work with couples work with families, or groups, for that matter? Even within each field of prevention, psychotherapy, or rehabilitation, a plethora of problems require specialization and experience, well beyond what any single professional can master in a lifetime.

- Available workbooks represent a virtual encyclopedia of different treatment approaches to deal with many clinical issues foreign to the experience and training of many professionals. Workbooks could be concentrated, for instance, into one single CD-ROM that would be available for administration by professionals only. The basic clinical skills required would be history taking and interview techniques with statistical knowledge of psychometric instruments, psychopathology, and professional ethics. It would be necessary to arrive at a specific diagnosis that would match a specific workbook or a series of workbooks. If a workbook is not available for a specific condition, one could be written easily following detailed instructions (L'Abate, 1992, 2001, 2002a).

- If one conceives of workbooks as software for computer-assisted interventions, as this writer does, then one is aware that most commercial software programs undergo changes and improvements over years of application. This change applies to workbooks as well. They are not cast in stone. They can be improved if a feedback loop exists from respondents to providers and from providers to workbook authors. In the absence of objective pre- and postevaluations, one could at least use a questionnaire to evaluation participant satisfaction. as contained in the Appendix. Can the same change loop be applied to psychotherapists? Of course, this change loop would be faster if comparative research on workbook effectiveness took place more often (Smyth and L'Abate, 2001).

- Another possibility raised by writing and especially workbooks needs to be demonstrated: decreasing dependency on professionals and increasing the sense of self-mastery and autonomy in respondents.

Cost-Effectiveness

Workbooks available on the Internet (L'Abate, 1996, 2002a,b) cost a fraction of a traditional, face-to-face, talk-based therapy session. They can be reused ad infinitum, making them mass-oriented and cost-effective. Commercially available workbooks in print (L'Abate, 2002b) can be duplicated, increasing their cost from one xerox copy to another. Nonetheless, cost-effectiveness for the use of workbooks still remains to be demonstrated (Lombard et al., 1998). Even though most research, reviewed later, demonstrates their usefulness, no cost-effectiveness study has been undertaken, as far as this writer is aware.

These advantages are intrinsically interwoven with each other. It is believed that one cannot have cost-effectiveness without specificity, interactivity, and versatility. An increase in specificity should increase cost-effectiveness. These advantages, however, need more evidence to be substantiated fully.

Verifiability

Treatment fidelity (Moncher and Prinz, 1991) of workbooks by themselves, without any other intervening or interfering variable, should be 100 percent. They are completely replicable within each professional dealing with the same condition, e.g., depression, as well as from one professional to another and from one clinical setting to another. However, variance does exist in how workbooks and also manuals are administered, as shown by Weisman and colleagues (2002). They found that the therapist's fidelity to a manual was not related to treatment outcome. Each professional differs from another on how, when, and under what conditions each workbook is administered (Bryant, Simons, and Thase, 1999). The possibility of distortion is nil if the same protocols are used without any additional variables. As long as talk remains the only method of treatment, fidelity remains extremely variable from one professional to another. Hence, verifiability is decreased substantially when DW is the sole medium of intervention. Workbooks, on the other hand, when delivered via the Internet (L'Abate, 1996), are 100 percent replicable. No interpersonal or nonverbal cues or emotional overtones are present in workbooks. Therefore, under these conditions, variability remains in the characteristics of therapists and respondents rather than in the treatment. Furthermore, it is crucial to study the effectiveness of workbooks with a minimum influence from other uncontrolled and difficult to control factors, including the (1) influence of therapeutic modalities, such as the so-called therapeutic alliance, or (2) personality and style of the professional, as well as (3) degree and type of dysfunctionality present in respondents.

METAFUNCTIONS OF WORKBOOKS

Hypothetically, SWHAs put respondents in the position to think and respond about their behavior in an impersonal context. A piece of paper or a computer are relatively void of emotionally charged interpersonal relationships, either with a therapist, partner, or family members. This process requires reliance on a completely new medium, which is different from usual talk. It creates at least two, and perhaps three, change-related feedback loops in individuals, three or more feedback loops in partners, and multiple feedback loops in family members.

One feedback loop in individuals goes from questions and tasks to be answered on a piece of paper or computer screen to respondents. The second feedback loop goes from respondents to professionals, who will respond, either verbally or in writing, to completed SWHAs. In partners, assuming that they are required to meet to compare and discuss individual completions of each assignment (L'Abate, 1986), feedback loops go from partners answering questions singly (loop 1) to comparing individually completed assignments with each other (loop 2), then returning the completed assignments to the professional for feedback (loop 3). In families, again assuming that family conferences are taking place to compare and discuss individually completed assignments, the same process is multiplied by how many members are involved in the process: singly from paper to individuals (loop 1), from individuals to as many members are involved in the process (n), and eventually from the therapist (loops $n + 1$).

Nonetheless, one can still follow a generic, face-to-face, talk-based, personal-contact model dealing with respondents as individuals, while dealing also with the referral question and objective test scores, i.e., matching the referral question or the symptom with a workbook. Allegiance to a mechanistic model in no way excludes allegiance to other models dealing with respondents as persons. In dealing with human problems we need as many useful models as we can get. Indeterminism/dialectics in professional practice do not exclude determinism/demonstrability in practice as well as research. They are two sides of the same coin (L'Abate, 1986, 1999a, 2002a). We are not dealing with mutually exclusive models.

DISADVANTAGES AND DANGERS OF WORKBOOK ADMINISTRATION

Of course, dangers exist in working with respondents at a distance (L'Abate, 1999a). However, one cannot base this approach on fears alone (Box 1.4). One needs to use this approach to find with whom it will work well and at what price. Clearly, the mental health communities are still fearful of working at a distance with respondents using a medium other than talk.

A major issue in working at a distance from respondents is confidentiality. However, with so many advances in encryption technology available on the Internet, this fear is invalid.

What is valid is the fear that the respondents one is working with may not have been evaluated at the outset of treatment and may not have signed an informed consent form (ICF) to participate in the intervention. Even this fear can be controlled, if not eliminated, by passwords and measures that would guarantee the correct match between provider and consumer. Even more important, however, is obtaining the correct match between referral question or symptom and the workbook administered. This match can be achieved through a thorough initial interview (written as autobiography) and a battery of quick and short paper-and-pencil self-report tests. Pre- and postobjective evaluations should be mandatory if this practice is to be conducted responsibly and ethically.

Another danger lies in the inadequacy of the nature and structure of some workbooks themselves (when they are poorly written, poorly developed, etc.). This shortcoming will be obviated once comparative testing of workbooks competing for the same condition is undertaken (L'Abate et al., 1992).

Mismatch between referral question and administered workbook can occur if the information given about the referral question or symptom is faulty, incomplete, misleading, or misinterpreted. A more adequate match is possible when, in addition to the referral question, a battery of screening and self-report tests is administered on a pre- and posttreatment basis.

Another danger that looms in the background of any new attempt to change the status quo of current psychotherapy practices lies in the biases of professionals who resist this approach (L'Abate, 1997b, 1999a). This resistance might be based mainly on emotional grounds that may then parallel resistance from respondents themselves (Burns and Spangler, 2000). Both professionals and respondents may rely too much on the mystique of talk and of face-to-face, personal presence and contact, rather than on DW. Resistance to working at a distance from professionals may possibly result from (1) unmet dependency needs of respondents, who passively need professionals to be wholly responsible for the treatment process, (2) fear of the unknown, and (3) the discovery of painful experiences that have been strongly avoided, or that are still avoided in the professional's office.

Clearly, these and other potential dangers will not be discovered unless mental health professionals risk helping respondents at a distance without talk or face-to-face contacts.

TESTING THEORIES THROUGH WORKBOOKS

Workbooks can be used for theory testing through parapreventive applications with nonclinical populations and paratherapeutic applications with clinical ones. Workbooks are cost-effective, replicable, mass-produced methods to compare and contrast different theoretical viewpoints or models. Examples from testing a selfhood model illustrate how this process can take place once we have workbooks representing different viewpoints.

Most theory testing in prevention, counseling, and psychotherapy (hereafter referred to simply as interventions) has historically taken place in the laboratory through comparative evaluations of objective instruments, usually self-report paper-and-pencil tests, derived from competing theoretical viewpoints or perspectives (Maruish, 1999). As a result laboratory research had little if any impact on interventional practices. More recently, theory testing has taken place directly through intervention research. This is a very expensive enterprise that only a few highly qualified investigators can master and undertake (Beutler and Clarkin, 1990; Luborsky et al., 1988). This approach is certainly beyond the expertise of the average professional helpers, who can hardly afford to record sessions, let alone transcribe, rate, and classify them. As Gottman (1979) estimated, it takes twenty-nine hours of technical time to process one hour of psychotherapy. The outcome of this state of affairs is, of course, that few helpers can undertake any research because they see most objective tests irrelevant to the whole intervention enterprise.

Furthermore, helpers cannot even begin to record their sessions, except perhaps for their own personal consumption, if at all. Hence, we are at a standstill for comparative theory testing in interventions, as far as this writer can tell. Only a few investigators who qualify for harder-to-obtain grant monies can perform this research. The rest of the helping community does not even consume research because, like objective tests, it is seen as irrelevant to practicing helpers. Hence, the chasm between academic, clinical researchers and practicing helpers may be growing wider.

Can we find cost-effective, theory-derived methods of helping people and, at the same time, testing theories without relying solely on face-to-face verbal interventions? Can we intervene with high school and college populations that, although not in need of clinical interventions, could use a preventive "boost" that might make a difference in their lives? Can we help shut-ins, home-bounds, military, missionary, and Peace Corps volunteers, as well as criminals in jails and penitentiaries? How about sick people in hospitals or at home in bed? Yes, we can indeed help most of these people if they want our help and, at the same time, test comparatively different theoretical and therapeutic viewpoints, intervening preventively with nonclinical populations, helping clients in counseling and patients in psychotherapy through the application of workbooks.

Use of workbooks implies two changes in the way interventions are traditionally practiced: (1) use of DW with respondents away from the presence of professional helpers and (2) reliance on written homework assignments in addition to or as an alternative to face-to-face verbal interventions. The rationale and empirical basis for the use of DW are found in many reviews (Esterling et al., 1999; L'Abate, 1990, 1992, 1997b, 2001). The rationale for the use of homework assignments has become more prevalent in clinical practice once demands for cost-effective, empirically based, active interventions and cost containment coming from managed care companies are taken into account. Both approaches involve respondents in the process of intervention by requiring them to show that they are willing to work to produce changes in their lives for the better—above and beyond just talking about them.

ON THE NATURE OF EVIDENCE TO SUPPORT WORKBOOK AND STRUCTURED COMPUTER-ASSISTED INTERVENTIONS

Chorpita et al. (2002) furnished a stringent list of criteria necessary to evaluate treatments that are relevant also to the evaluation of workbook effectiveness. The use and practice of workbook administration can be validated at least seven different ways. They increase in rigor, progressing from simple anedoctal evidence to meta-analyses of workbook studies:

1. Anecdotal evidence, as in case studies (L'Abate, 1999a,b,c, 2001), is the simplest form of evidence, and is still used in many clinical treatises, including those by this writer. Unfortunately, most case studies may be subjected to bias (to make the presenter look good) or to questionable interpretations of subjective results, also given by the same presenter. Hence, case studies are questionable in their utility. As Howard Ruppell said, "Anecdotal evidence in an age of science is ridiculous" (Macy, 1996, p. 147). Nonetheless, case studies remain the first line of evidence to convince other professionals about the usefulness of a given approach. To make this type of evidence less biased and less unnecessarily self-serving, contributors planning to use case studies were asked to present one positive and one negative case study, since we learn more from our failures than we learn from our successes.
2. An example of a consumer satisfaction survey is available in the Appendix. These surveys are also questionable to the extent that they are based on the subjective opinion of respondents, as seen in the case of *Consumer Reports* survey on mental health (Seligman, 1998). Nonetheless, it is important to obtain such information because no treatment can be administered unless respondents are generally pleased with it.
3. Pre- and posttreatment evaluation of outcome through objective, self-report paper-and-pencil tests is the most common of standard evalua-

tions. Unfortunately, most studies evaluate short-term outcome at the end of treatment, and fail to follow up months or even years later to evaluate whether the treatment has produced long-lasting results.

4. A combination of steps 2 and 3 should be the ideal to the extent that with objective pre- and posttreatment data, one would be able to connect consumer satisfaction with change scores. Is subjective consumer satisfaction related to objective outcome? If so, how?

5. Comparative evaluation of different workbooks claiming to treat the same condition should show, as done originally by L'Abate and colleagues (1992), that this comparison will be crucial to the development of workbook technology. They evaluated three workbooks based on three different models of depression—one based on Beck's cognitive theory of depression, one based on L'Abate's (1986) relational model of depression, and one based on an empirical description of depression derived from the MMPI-2 Content Scale (L'Abate, 1992). All three workbooks, as is often the case with different schools of psychotherapy, showed similar results. No single workbook produced better results.

6. The relative effectiveness of workbooks requires experimental manipulation of different variables (workbook versus workbook, workbook versus face-to-face psychotherapy, workbooks administered at a distance versus workbooks administered at a distance from professionals). For example, would a workbook claiming to treat depression work less well than an anxiety workbook to treat anxiety? Even better, how about comparing talk-based, face-to-face psychotherapy with workbook administration without face-to-face personal contact? L'Abate (see Chapter 2) has provided evidence to support the latter position. How about comparing medication versus workbooks?

7. Ultimately, meta-analyses of studies performed in 3, 4, 5, and 6, as shown by the meta-analyses by Rosenthal and DiMatteo (2001), have become the gold standard for the evaluation of treatment effectiveness. In evaluating eighteen studies, Smyth and L'Abate (2001) found a moderate effect-size estimate (d) of .44, a figure that compares well with the effect-size estimates of other therapeutic approaches.

IMPORTANCE OF EVALUATION AND INFORMED CONSENT FOR WORKBOOK ADMINISTRATION

In an exhaustive review of the evidence and issues surrounding psychological testing and assessment, consisting of 125 meta-analyses and 800 samples, Meyer and colleagues (2001) concluded that in addition to the "strong and compelling" validity of psychological testing that is "comparable to medical test validity, distinct assessment methods provide unique sources of information" (p. 128) about respondents. However, because "clinicians who rely exclusively on interviews are prone to incomplete understanding," Meyer and colleagues (2001) recommended the use of a multimodal, structured battery "to maximize the validity of individualized assessment" (p. 128). These conclusions support's this writer's arguments (L'Abate, 1994, 2002a; L'Abate and Bagarozzi, 1993) that interviews are insufficient to develop a responsible treatment plan, and that workbooks provide a more accurate match between objective evaluation and workbook selection.

Especially when working at a distance from respondents, not only should an objective evaluation be conducted with a multidimensional battery of reliable self-report paper-and-pencil tests, but an informed consent form (L'Abate, 2002b) should be also required of respondents. These are the two sine qua non conditions for workbook administration and working with respondents at a distance, in addition to a complete, historical, developmental, and situational understanding of the problem at hand.

SUCCESSIVE SIEVES AND STEPPED TREATMENT IN THE DELIVERY OF MENTAL HEALTH SERVICES

Because of their alleged cost-effectiveness, mass orientation, versatility, and verifiability, workbooks could become the first line of attack/defense on prevention in and by themselves or in combination with traditional preventive approaches (Kaplan, 2000). The presence of significant subthreshold, subsyndromal depressive experiences indicates the importance of cost-effective, mass-oriented approaches to deal with those as well as many other subthreshold conditions, in addition to depression (Lewinsohn et al., 2000). If one conceived of a continuum of care ranging on at least three dimensions: from least to most expensive, or from most general to most specific, or from nomothetic to idiographic, consisting on one hand by DW in its four structures (open-ended, focused, guided, and structured), versus psychotherapy, medication, and hospitalization/incarceration on the other, one would obtain at least ten steps or sieves of intervention (Davison, 2000; Haaga, 2000; Newman, 2000; Otto, Pollack, and Maki, 2000; Sobell and Sobell, 2000; Wilson, Vitousek, and Loeb, 2000). Stepped care along a continuum of care would range from DW alone, to primary prevention alone, to DW with primary prevention approaches, to secondary prevention alone, to DW combined with secondary prevention, to tertiary prevention such as psychotherapy and crisis intervention alone, the latter plus primary prevention and DW, etc. It is believed that a combination of approaches, including medication, would produce synergistic effects on the outcome. A more specific proposal is summarized in Box 1.5.

CONCLUSION

Workbooks are not yet part of the mainstream of psychological interventions. A great many changes will need to occur before reaching the goal of including them in the mainstream. Cost-effectiveness and increasing evidence of comparative effectiveness over face-to-face talk will eventually allow their entry in everyday, preventive, psychotherapeutic, and rehabilitative armamentaria of mental health professionals. Their potential for the betterment of much larger numbers of troubled people needing help is too great to bypass. Eventually, no other alternatives will be left to most mental health professionals, except to rely on workbooks and learn to help and heal distressed people at a distance.

BOX 1.5. Successive Sieves and Stepped Interventions in a Continuum of Care

I. Sieve 1. Primary prevention: Proactive, pre- and posttherapeutic, and universal group interventions:

1. Use the following screen respondents to determine whether they are appropriate for this sieve or whether they should be placed in Sieves 2 or 3:
   a. Distance writing in its four structures (open-ended, focused, guided, and structured)
   b. Workbooks for normalizing experiences
   c. Workbooks for screening experiences
2. Combine the previous step with a traditional preventive program (psychoeducational, social skills training, or equivalent) that is appropriate for the respondents (individuals [children, adolescents, or adults], couples, families, or groups).
3. Administer the program through the appropriate medium of intervention (radio, TV, Internet, etc.).
4. If this sieve fails, proceed to Sieve 2.

II. Sieve 2. Secondary prevention: Para-active, para-, pre-, or posttherapeutic interventions targeted and selective:

1. Reevaluate respondents to determine whether they are appropriate for this sieve or the next one.

(continued)

(continued)

    a. Use targeted workbooks for specific internalizing and external-
    izing conditions that produced failure in Sieve 1, either through re-
    ferral questions, preclinical conditions, or group membership (e.g.,
    children of alcoholics).
    b. Have paraprofessional personnel administer structured programs
    to screened individuals, couples, or families face-to-face.
  2. Combine substeps a and b as necessary.
  3. If this sieve fails, proceed to Sieve 3.

III. Sieve 3. Tertiary prevention: Reactively therapeutic, necessary and indicated:

  1. Reevaluate reasons for the failure of previous sieves or for referral.
  2. Apply crisis intervention.
  3. Administer workbooks that are directed toward specific symptoms,
    conditions, and psychopathologies.
  4. Use medication as necessary.
  5. Combine steps 2, 3, or 4 as required.

IV. Sieve 4. Hospitalization or incarceration: Implementation of approaches used in previous sieves, workbooks, psychotherapy, and medication.

REFERENCES

Albee, G. W. (2000). Critique of psychotherapy in American society. In C. R. Snyder and R. E. Ingram (Eds.), *Handbook of psychological change: Psychotherapy processes and practices for the 21st century* (pp. 689-706). New York: Wiley.

Albee, G. W. and Guillotta, T. P. (1997). *Primary prevention works.* Thousand Oaks, CA: Sage.

Alpert, J. L. (1985). Change within a profession: Change, future, prevention, and school psychology. *American Psychologist, 40,* 1112-1121.

American Association for Marriage and Family Therapy (1989). *Forms book.* Washington, DC: AAMFT.

American Psychiatric Association (APA) (1980). *Diagnostic and statistical manual of mental disorders,* Third edition. Washington, DC: APA.

Androutsopoulou, A. (2001). Self-characterization as a narrative tool: Applications in therapy with individuals and families. *Family Process, 40,* 79-94.

Asay, T. P. and Lambert, M. J. (1999). The empirical case for the common factors in therapy: Quantitative findings. In M. A. Hubble, B. L. Duncan, and S. D. Miller

(Eds.), *The heart and soul of change: What works in therapy* (pp. 23-55). Washington, DC: American Psychological Association.

Bakan, D. (1968). *Disease, pain, and sacrifice: Toward a psychology of suffering.* Boston, MA: Beacon Press.

Barak, A. (1999). Psychological applications on the Internet: A discipline on the threshold of the new millennium. *Applied and Preventive Psychology, 8,* 231-245.

Barlow, D. H. (2002). Editor's introduction. *Clinical Psychology: Science and Practice, 9,* 1.

Barlow, D. H. and Craske, M. G. (1994). *Client workbook: Mastery of your anxiety and panic II.* San Antonio, TX: Psychological Corporation.

Bergin, A. E. and Garfield, S. L. (1994). *Handbook of psychotherapy and behavior change.* New York: Wiley.

Beutler, L. E. and Clarkin, J. F. (1990). *Systematic treatment selection: Toward targeted therapeutic interventions.* New York: Brunner/Mazel.

Bickman, L. (1999). Practice makes perfect and other myths about mental health services. *American Psychologist, 54,* 965-978.

Bird, G. (1992). Programmed writing as a method for increasing self-esteem, self-disclosure, and coping skills. Doctoral dissertation, Department of Counseling and Psychological Services, Georgia State University, Atlanta, Georgia.

Bloom, B. L. (1992). Computer-assisted psychological intervention: A review and commentary. *Clinical Psychology Review, 12,* 169-197.

Bloom, M. (1996). *Primary prevention practices.* Thousand Oaks, CA: Sage.

Britton, J. (1975). *The development of writing abilities.* New York: Macmillan Education.

Bryant, M. J., Simons, A. D., and Thase, M. E. (1999). Therapist skill and patient variables in homework compliance: Controlling an uncontrollable variable in cognitive therapy outcome research. *Cognitive Therapy and Research, 23,* 381-399.

Budman, S. H. (2000). Behavioral healthcare dot-com and beyond: Computer-mediated communications in mental health and substance abuse treatment. *American Psychologist, 55,* 1290-1300.

Burns, D. D. and Spangler, D. L. (2000). Does psychotherapy homework lead to improvements in depression in cognitive-behavioral therapy or does improvement lead to increased homework compliance? *Journal of Consulting and Clinical Psychology, 68,* 46-56.

Bushman, J. H. (2000). *Teaching the English language.* Springfield, IL: Thomas.

Carmichael, R. D. (1939). *The logic of discovery.* Chicago, IL: Open Court Publishing Company.

Carney, M. A., Armeli, S., Tennen, H., Affleck, G., and O'Neil, T. P. (2000). Positive and negative daily events, perceived stress, and alcohol use: A diary study. *Journal of Consulting and Clinical Psychology, 68,* 788-798.

Carroll, K. M. (1999). Behavioral and cognitive-behavioral treatments. In B. S. McCrady and E. E. Epstein (Eds.), *Addictions: A comprehensive guidebook* (pp. 250-267). New York: Oxford University Press.

Cassirer, E. (1946). *Language and myth*. New York: Dover.

Cautela, J. R., Cautela, J., and Esonis, S. (1998). *Forms for behavioral analysis with children*. Champaign, IL: Research Press.

Celio, A. A., Winzelberg, A. J., Wilfley, D. E., Epstein-Herald, D., Springer, E. A., Dev, P., and Taylor, C. B. (2000). Reducing risk factors for eating disorders: Comparison of an Internet and a classroom-delivered psychoeducational program. *Journal of Consulting and Clinical Psychology, 68*, 650-657.

Chambless, D. L. (1997). In defense of dissemination of empirically supported psychological interventions. *Clinical Psychology: Science and Practice, 4*, 230-235.

Chambless, D. L. and Ollendick, T. H. (2001). Empirically supported psychological interventions: Controversies and evidence. *Annual Review of Psychology, 52*, 685-716.

Childress, C. A. (2000). Ethical issues in providing online psychotherapeutic interventions. *Journal of Medical Internet Research, 2*, 5-15.

Chorpita, B. F., Yim, L. M., Donkervoet, J. C., Arendorf, A., Amundsen, M. J., McGee, C., Serrano, A., Yates, A., Burns, J. A., and Morelli, P. (2002). Toward large-scale implementation of empirically supported treatments for children: A review and observations by the Hawaii empirical basis to services task force. *Clinical Psychology: Science and Practice, 9*, 165-190.

Coon, D. W. and Gallagher-Thompson, D. (2002). Encouraging homework completion among older adults in therapy. *Journal of Clinical Psychology, 58*, 549-563.

Corrigan, P. W. (1995). Wanted: Champions of psychiatric rehabilitation. *American Psychologist, 50*, 514-521.

Dattilio, F. M. (2002). Homework assignments in couple and family therapy. *Journal of Clinical Psychology, 58*, 535-547.

Dattilio, F. M. and Kendall, P. C. (2000). Panic disorder. In F. M. Dattilio and A. Freeman (Eds.), *Cognitive-behavioral strategies in crisis intervention* (pp. 59-83). New York: Guilford.

Davison, G. C. (2000). Stepped care: Doing more with less? *Journal of Consulting and Clinical Psychology, 68*, 580-585.

Day, J. P. (1961). *Inductive probability*. New York: Humanities Press.

de Vries, B., Birren, J. E., and Deutchman, D. E. (1990). Adult development through guided autobiography: The family context. *Family Relations, 39*, 3-7.

Dean, L. F. and Wilson, K. G. (Eds.) (1959). *Essay on language usage*. New York: Oxford University Press.

Dewey, J. (1938). *Logic: The theory of inquiry*. New York: Holt and Co.

Dineen, T. (1998). *Manufacturing victims: What the psychotherapy industry is doing to people*. Montreal: Robert Davies Multimedia.

Dobson, K. S. and Craig, K. D. (Eds.) (1998). *Empirically supported therapies: Best practice in professional psychology*. Thousand Oaks, CA: Sage.

Eisner, D. A. (2000). *The death of psychotherapy: From Freud to alien abductions*. Westport, CT: Praeger.

Elliott, R. (2001). Contemporary brief experiential psychotherapy. *Clinical Psychology: Science and Practice, 8*, 38-50.

Esterling, B. A., Antoni, M. H., Fletcher, M. A., Margulies, S., and Schneiderman, N. (1994). Emotional disclosure through writing or speaking modulated latent Epstein-Barr virus reactivation. *Journal of Consulting and Clinical Psychology, 62,* 130-140.

Esterling, B. A., L'Abate, L., Murray, E., and Pennebaker, J. M. (1999). Empirical foundations for writing in prevention and psychotherapy: Mental and physical outcomes. *Clinical Psychology Review, 19,* 79-96.

Esterling, B. E. and Pennebaker, J. M. (2001). Focused expressive writing, immune functions, and physical illness. In L. L'Abate (Ed.), *Distance writing and computer-assisted interventions in psychiatry and mental heath* (pp. 47-60). Westport, CT: Ablex.

Finley, J. R. and Lenz, B. S. (1998). *The chemical dependence treatment documentation sourcebook.* New York: Wiley.

Foa, E. B., Keane, T. M., and Friedman, M. J. (Eds.) (2000). *Effective treatments for PTSD.* New York: Guilford.

Forsyth, D. R. and Corazzini, J. G. (2000). Groups as change agents. In C. R. Snyder and R. E. Ingram (Eds.), *Handbook of psychological change: Psychotherapy processes and practices in the 21st century* (pp. 309-336). New York: Wiley.

Frank, R. G., Gluck, J. P., and Buckelew, S. P. (1990). Rehabilitation: Psychology's greatest opportunity? *American Psychologist, 45,* 757-761.

Freeman, A. and Fusco, G. (2000). Treating high-arousal patients: Differentiating between patients in crisis and crisis-prone patients. In F. M. Dattilio and A. Freeman (Eds.), *Cognitive-behavioral strategies in crisis intervention* (pp. 27-58). New York: Guilford.

Freeman, A. and Rosenfeld, B. (2002). Modifying homework in patients with personality disorders. *Journal of Clinical Psychology, 58,* 513-524.

Freeman, A., Simon, K. M., Beutler, L. E., and Arkowitz, H. (Eds.) (1986). *Comprehensive handbook of cognitive therapy.* New York: Plenum.

Gackenbach, J. and Ellerman, E. (1998). Introduction to psychological aspects of Internet use. In J. Gackenbach (Ed.), *Psychology and the Internet: Intrapersonal, interpersonal, and transpersonal implications* (pp. 1-26). San Diego, CA: Academic Press.

Gaes, G. G., Flanagan, T. J., Motiuk, L. L., and Stewart, L. (1999). Adult correctional treatment. In M. Tonry and J. Petersilia (Eds.), *Prisons: Crime and justice, a review of research* (pp. 361-426). Chicago, IL: University of Chicago Press.

Garland, A. and Scott, J. (2002). Using homework in therapy for depression. *Journal of Clinical Psychology, 58,* 489-498.

Gottman, J. M. (1979). *Marital interaction: Experimental investigations.* New York: Academic Press.

Grohol, J. M. (1998). Future clinical directions: Professional development, pathology, and psychotherapy online. In J. Gackenbach (Ed.), *Psychology and the Internet: Intrapersonal, interpersonal, and transpersonal implications* (pp. 111-140). San Diego, CA: Academic Press.

Gurman, A. S. (2001). Brief therapy and family/couple therapy: An essential redundancy. *Clinical Psychology: Science and Practice, 8,* 51-65.

Haaga, D. A. (2000). Introduction to the special section on stepped models of psychotherapy. *Journal of Consulting and Clinical Psychology, 68,* 547-548.

Haley, J. (1976). *Problem-solving therapy.* San Francisco, CA: Jossey-Bass.

Hanson, N. R. (1961). *Patterns of discovery.* Cambridge, UK: University Press.

Heath, S. B. (1983). *Ways with words: Language, life, and work in communities and classrooms.* New York: Cambridge University Press.

Hecker, L. L., Deacon, S. A., and Associates (1998). *The therapist's notebook: Homework, handouts, and activities for use in psychotherapy.* Binghamton, NY: The Haworth Press.

Hegel, G. (1959). *Encyclopedia of philosophy.* New York: Philosophical Library.

Heinlen, K. L., Welfel, E. R., Richmond, E. N., and O'Donnell, M. S. (2002). Internet psychologists: Scope, ethics, and advertising of Web-based services. Paper read at the Annual Meeting of the American Psychological Association, Chicago, IL, August 16.

Heller, K., Wyman, M. E., and Allen, S. M. (2000). Future directions for prevention science: From research to adoption. In C. R. Snyder and R. E. Ingram (Eds.), *Handbook of psychological change: Psychotherapy processes and practices for the 21st century* (pp. 660-680). New York: Wiley.

Howard, P. (1985). *The state of the language: English observed.* New York: Oxford University Press.

Hubble, M. A., Duncan, B. L., and Miller, S. D. (1999). *The heart and soul of change: What works in therapy.* Washington, DC: American Psychological Association.

Hudson, J. and Kendall, P. C. (2002). Showing you can fit: Homework in therapy for children and adolescents with anxiety disorders. *Journal of Clinical Psychology, 58,* 525-534.

Hughes, J. P. (1985). Languages and writing. In V. P. Clark, P. A. Eschholz, and A. E. Sosa (Eds.), *Language: Introductory readings* (pp. 698-717). New York: St. Martin's Press.

Ingram, R. E., Hayes, A., and Scott, W. (2000). Empirically supported treatments: A critical analysis. In C. R. Snyder and R. E. Ingram. (Eds.), *Handbook of psychological change: Psychotherapy processes and practices for the 21st century* (pp. 40-60). New York: Wiley.

Jerome, L. W., DeLeon, P. H., James, L. C., Folen, R., Earles, J., and Geney, J. J. (2000). The coming of age of telecommunications in psychological research and practice. *American Psychologist, 55,* 407-420.

Johnson, A. (1998). Causes and implications of disinhibited behavior on the Internet. In J. Gackenbach (Ed.), *Psychology and the Internet: Intrapersonal, interpersonal, and transpersonal implications* (pp. 43-60). San Diego, CA: Academic Press.

Jones, S. G. (Ed.) (1995). *Cybersociety: Computer-mediated communication and community.* Thousand Oaks, CA: Sage.

Jordan, K. B. (2001). Teaching psychotherapy through workbooks. In L. L'Abate (Ed.), *Distance writing and computer-assisted interventions in psychiatry and mental heath* (pp. 171-190). Westport, CT: Ablex.

Kant, I. (1952). *The critique of pure reason.* Chicago, IL: Encyclopedia Brittanica.

Kaplan, R. M. (2000). Two pathways to prevention. *American Psychologist, 55,* 382-396.

Karoly, P. and Anderson, C. W. (2000). The long and short of psychological change: Toward a goal-centered understanding of treatment durability and adaptive success. In C. R. Snyder and R. E. Ingram (Eds.), *Handbook of psychological change: Psychotherapy processes and practices in the 21st century* (pp. 154-176). New York: Wiley.

Kazantzis, N. (2000). Power to detect homework effects in psychotherapy outcome research. *Journal of Consulting and Clinical Psychology, 68,* 166-170.

Kazantzis, N., Deane, F. P., and Ronan, K. R. (2000). Homework assignments in cognitive and behavioral theory: A meta-analysis. *Clinical Psychology: Science and Practice, 7,* 189-202.

Kazantzis, N., Deane, F. P., Ronan, K. R., and L'Abate, L. (Eds.) (in press). *Homework assignments in cognitive-behavioral therapy.* Mahwah, NJ: Earlbaum.

Kazantzis, N. and Lampropoulos, G. K. (2002). Reflecting on homework in psychotherapy: What can we conclude from research and experience? *Journal of Clinical Psychology, 58,* 577-585.

Keen, E. (2000). *Ultimacy and triviality in psychotherapy.* Westport, CT: Greenwood.

Kiesler, C. A. (2000). National mental health issues. In C. R. Snyder and R. E. Ingram. (Eds.), *Handbook of psychological change: Psychotherapy processes and practices for the 21st century* (pp. 681-688). New York: Wiley.

King, S. A. and Moreggi, D. (1998). Internet therapy and self-help groups—The pros and cons. In J. Gackenbach (Ed.), *Psychology and the Internet: Intrapersonal, interpersonal, and transpersonal implications* (pp. 77-109). San Diego, CA: Academic Press.

Kinneavy, J. L. (1971). *A theory of discourse: The aims of discourse.* New York: Norton.

Kochalka, J. and L'Abate, L. (1997). Linking evaluation with structured enrichment: The family profile form. *American Journal of Family Therapy, 25,* 361-374.

Kraut, R., Patterson, M., Lundmark, V., Kiesler, S., Mukopadhyay, T., and Scherlis, W. (1998). Internet paradox: A social technology that reduces social involvement and psychological well-being? *American Psychologist, 53,* 1017-1031.

Kuhn, T. S. (1962). *The structure of scientific revolutions.* Chicago, IL: University of Chicago Press.

L'Abate, L. (1985). Structured enrichment (SE) with couples and families. *Family Relations, 34,* 169-175.

L'Abate, L. (1986). *Systematic family therapy.* New York: Brunner/Mazel.

L'Abate, L. (1990). *Building family competence: Primary and secondary prevention strategies.* Newbury Park, CA: Sage.

L'Abate, L. (1991). The use of writing in psychotherapy. *American Journal of Psychotherapy, 45,* 87-98.

L'Abate, L. (1992). *Programmed writing: A self-administered approach for interventions with individuals, couples, and families.* Pacific Grove, CA: Brooks/Cole.

L'Abate, L. (1994). *A theory of personality development.* New York: Wiley.

L'Abate, L. (1996). Workbooks for better living. Available at <www.mentalhealthhelp.com>.

L'Abate, L. (1997a). Distance writing and computer-assisted training. In S. R. Sauber (Ed.), *Managed mental health care: Major diagnostic and treatment approaches* (pp. 133-163). Bristol, PA: Brunner/Mazel.

L'Abate, L. (1997b). The paradox of change: Better them than us! In S. R. Sauber (Ed.), *Managed mental health care: Major diagnostic and treatment approaches* (pp. 40-66). Bristol, PA: Brunner/Mazel.

L'Abate, L. (1997c). *The self in the family: A classification of personality, criminality, and psychopathology.* New York: Wiley.

L'Abate, L. (1999a). Decisions we (mental health professionals) need to make (whether we like them or not): A reply to Cummings and Hoyt. *The Family Journal: Therapy and Counseling for Couples and Families, 7,* 227-230.

L'Abate, L. (1999b). Increasing intimacy in couples through distance writing and face-to-face approaches. In J. Carlson and L. Sperry (Eds.), *The intimate couple* (pp. 328-344). Philadelphia, PA: Taylor and Francis.

L'Abate, L. (1999c). Programmed distance writing in therapy with acting-out adolescents. In C. Schaefer (Ed.), *Innovative psychotherapy techniques in child and adolescent therapy* (pp. 108-157). New York: Wiley.

L'Abate, L. (1999d). Structured enrichment and distance writing for couples. In R. Berger and T. Hannah (Eds.), *Preventative approaches in couples therapy* (pp. 106-124). Philadelphia, PA: Taylor and Francis.

L'Abate, L. (1999e). Taking the bull by the horns: Beyond talk in psychological interventions. *The Family Journal: Therapy and Counseling for Couples and Families, 7,* 206-220.

L'Abate, L. (2001). Distance writing (DW) and computer-assisted interventions (CAI) in psychiatry and mental health. In L. L'Abate (Ed.), *Distance writing and computer-assisted interventions in psychiatry and mental heath* (pp. 3-31). Westport, CT: Ablex.

L'Abate, L. (2002a). *Beyond psychotherapy: Programmed writing and structured computer-assisted interventions.* Westport, CT: Ablex.

L'Abate, L. (2002b). *A guide to self-help workbooks.* Atlanta, GA: Workbooks for Better Living.

L'Abate, L. (in press). *Personality in intimate relationships: Socialization and psychopathology.* New York: Kluwer Academic.

L'Abate, L. and Bagarozzi, D. A. (1983). *Sourcebook of marriage and family evaluation.* New York: Brunner/Mazel.

L'Abate, L., Boyce, J., Fraizer, L., and Russ, D. A. (1992). Programmed writing: Research in progress. *Comprehensive Mental Health Care, 2,* 45-62.

L'Abate, L. and Kern, R. (2002). Workbooks: Tools for the expressive writing paradigm. In S. J. Lepore and J. M. Smyth (Eds.), *The writing cure: How expressive writing promotes health and emotional well-being* (pp. 239-255). Washington, DC: American Psychological Association.

L'Abate, L., L'Abate, B. L., and Maino, E. (2004). Reviewing 25 years of clinical practice: Workbooks and length of therapy sessions. Manuscript submitted for publication.

L'Abate, L. and Weinstein, S. E. (1987). *Structured enrichment programs for couples and families.* New York: Brunner/Mazel.

L'Abate, L. and Young, L. (1987). *Casebook of structured enrichment programs for couples and families.* New York: Brunner/Mazel.

Lepore, S. J. and Smyth, J. (Eds.) (2002). *The writing cure: How expressive writing influences health and well-being.* Washington, DC: American Psychological Association.

Lewinsohn, P. M., Solomon, A., Seeley, J. R., and Zeiss, A. (2000). Clinical implications of "subthreshold" depressive symptoms. *Journal of Abnormal Psychology, 109,* 345-351.

Livesley, W. J. (2001). *Handbook of personality disorders: Theory, research, and treatment.* New York: Guilford.

Lombard, D., Haddock, C. K., Talcott, G. W., and Reynes, R. (1998). Cost-effectiveness analysis: A primer for psychologists. *Applied and Preventive Psychology, 7,* 101-108.

Luborsky, L., Crits-Christoph, P., Mintz, J., and Auerbach, A. (1988). *Who will benefit from psychotherapy? Predicting therapeutic outcomes.* New York: Basic Books.

Macy, M. (1996). *Working sex: An odyssey into our cultural underworld.* New York: Carroll and Graf.

Maheu, M., Whitten, P., and Allen, A. (2001). *E-health, and telemedicine: A guide to startup and success.* San Francisco, CA: Jossey-Bass.

Marks, I., Shaw, S., and Parkin, R. (1998). Computer-aided treatments of mental health problems. *Clinical Psychology: Science and Practice, 5,* 151-170.

Maruish, M. E. (Ed.) (1999). *The use of psychological testing for treatment planning and outcome assessment.* Hillsdale, NJ: Earlbaum.

McCullough, L. and Andrews, S. (2001). Assimilative integration: Short-term dynamic psychotherapy for treating affect phobias. *Clinical Psychology: Science and Practice, 8,* 82-97.

McGinn, L. K. and Sanderson, W. C. (2001). What allows cognitive behavioral therapy to be brief: Overview, efficacy, and crucial factors facilitating brief treatment. *Clinical Psychology: Science and Practice, 8,* 23-37.

McMahan, O. and L'Abate, L. (2001). Programmed distance writing with seminarian couples. In L. L'Abate (Ed.), *Distance writing and computer-assisted interventions in psychiatry and mental heath* (pp. 135-156). Westport, CT: Ablex.

Messer, S. B. (2001a). What allows therapy to be brief? Introduction to the series. *Clinical Psychology: Science and Practice, 8,* 1-4.

Messer, S. B. (2001b). What makes brief psychodynamic therapy time efficient. *Clinical Psychology: Science and Practice, 8,* 5-22.

Meyer, G. J., Finn, S. E., Eyde, L. D., Kay, G. G., Moreland, K. L., Dies, R. R., Eisman, E. J., Kubiszyn, T. W., and Reed, G. M. (2001). Psychological testing and psychological assessment: A review of evidence and issues. *American Psychologist, 56,* 128-165.

Moncher, F. J. and Prinz, R. J. (1991). Treatment fidelity in outcome studies. *Clinical Psychology Review, 11,* 247-266.

Mrazek, P. J. and Haggerty, R. J. (Eds.) (1994). *Reducing risks for mental disorders: Frontiers for preventive intervention research.* Washington, DC: National Academy Press.

Najavits, L. M., Weiss, R. D., Shaw, S. R., and Dierberger, A. E. (2000). Psychotherapists' views of treatment manuals. *Professional Psychology: Research and Practice, 31,* 404-408.

Nathan, P. E. and Gorman, J. M. (Eds.) (1998). *A guide to treatments that work.* New York: Oxford University Press.

Newman, M. G. (2000). Recommendations for a cost-offset model of psychotherapy allocation using generalized anxiety disorder as an example. *Journal of Consulting and Clinical Psychology, 68,* 549-555.

Newman, M. G., Kenardy, J., Herman, S., and Barr-Taylor, C. (1997). Comparison of palmtop-computer-assisted brief cognitive-behavioral treatment to cognitive-behavioral treatment for panic disorder. *Journal of Consulting and Clinical Psychology, 65,* 178-183.

Newman, R. (2001). Not a question of "for" or "against." *Monitor on Psychology, 32,* 56.

Nickelson, D. W. (1998). Telehealth and the evolving health care system: Strategic opportunities for professional psychology. *Professional Psychology: Research and Practice, 29,* 527-535.

Norcross, J. C. (2002). *Psychotherapy relationships that work: Therapist contribution and responsiveness to patient needs.* New York: Oxford University Press.

Offord, D. R. (2000). Selection of levels of prevention. *Addictive Behaviors, 25,* 833-842.

O'Leary, K. D., Heyman, R., and Jongsma, A. E. Jr. (1998). *The couple psychotherapy treatment planner.* New York: Wiley.

Org, W. J. (1958). *Ramus: Method and the decay of dialogue.* Cambridge, MA: Harvard University Press.

Ornstein, R. (1997). *The right mind: Making sense of the hemispheres.* New York: Harcourt Brace.

Otto, M. W., Pollack, M. H., and Maki, K. M. (2000). Empirically supported treatment for panic disorder: Costs, benefits, and stepped care. *Journal of Consulting and Clinical Psychology, 68,* 556-563.

Parks, M. R. and Roberts, L. D. (1998). "Making Moosic": The development of personal relationships online and a comparison to their offline counterparts. *Journal of Social and Personal Relationships, 15,* 517-537.

Penn, P. and Frankfurt, M. (1994). Creating a participant text: Writing, multiple voices, narrative multiplicity. *Family Process, 33,* 217-231.

Pennebaker, J. M. (1997). *Opening up: The healing power of expressing emotions.* New York: Guilford.

Pennebaker, J. M. (2001). Explorations into the health benefits of disclosure: Inhibitory, cognitive, and social processes. In L. L'Abate (Ed.), *Distance writing and computer-assisted interventions in psychiatry and mental health* (pp. 34-44). Westport, CT: Ablex.

Pennebaker, J. W. and King, L. K. (1999). Linguistic styles: Language use as an individual difference. *Journal of Personality and Social Psychology, 77,* 1296-1312.

Perkinson, R. R. and Jongsma, A. E. Jr. (1997). *The chemical dependence treatment planner.* New York: Wiley.

Petersilia, J. (1999). Parole and prisoner reentry in the United States. In M. Tonry and J. Petersilia (Eds.), *Prisons: Crime and justice, a review of research* (pp. 479-529). Chicago, IL: University of Chicago Press.

Pierce, C. S. (1960). *Collected papers.* Cambridge, MA: Harvard University Press.

Prochaska, J. O. (1999). How do people change, and how can we change to help many more people? In M. A. Hubble, B. L. Duncan, and S. D. Miller (Eds.), *The heart and soul of change: What works in therapy* (pp. 227-255). Washington, DC: American Psychological Association.

Rabasca, L. (1998). Study probes how patients are affected by telehealth. *Psychological Monitor* (August), 31.

Reed, R., McMahan, O., and L'Abate, L. (2001). Workbooks and psychotherapy with incarcerated felons: Research in progress. In L. L'Abate (Ed.), *Distance writing and computer-assisted interventions in psychiatry and mental health* (pp. 157-167). Westport, CT: Ablex.

Reid, E. (1998). The self and the Internet: Variations on the illusion of one self. In J. Gackenbach (Ed.), *Psychology and the Internet: Intrapersonal, interpersonal, and transpersonal implications* (pp. 29-42). San Diego, CA: Academic Press.

Roberts, M. C., Vernberg, E. M., and Jackson, Y. (2000). Psychotherapy with children and families. In C. R. Snyder and R. E. Ingram (Eds.), *Handbook of psychological change: Psychotherapy processes and practices in the 21st century* (pp. 500-519). New York: Wiley.

Rohbraugh, M. J. and Shoham, V. (2001). Brief therapy based on interrupting ironic processes: The Palo Alto model. *Clinical Psychology: Science and Practice, 8,* 66-81.

Rosenthal, R. and DiMatteo, M. R. (2001). Meta-analysis: Recent developments in quantitative methods for literature reviews. *Annual Review of Psychology, 52,* 59-82.

Routh, D. K. and DeRubeis, R. J. (Eds.) (1998). *The science of clinical psychology: Accomplishments and future directions.* Washington, DC: American Psychological Association.

Rychlak, J. F. (1969). *A philosophy of science for personality theory.* New York: Houghton Mifflin.

Satcher, D. (2000). *Report of the surgeon general on mental health.* Washington, DC: Office of Public Health and Science.

Schultheis, G., O'Hanlon, B., and O'Hanlon, S. (1998). *Brief couples therapy homework planner.* New York: Wiley.

Seligman, M. E. P. (1998). Why therapy works. *Psychological Monitor* (December), 2.

Simon, L. (1998). Do offender treatments work? *Applied and Preventive Psychology, 7,* 137-159.

Smith, M. A. and Senior, C. (2001). The Internet and clinical psychology: General review of the implications. *Clinical Psychology Review, 21,* 129-136.

Smyth, J. M. (1998). Written emotional expression: Effect size, outcome types, and moderating variables. *Journal of Consulting and Clinical Psychology, 66,* 174-184.

Smyth, J. M. and L'Abate, L. (2001). A meta-analytic evaluation of workbook effectiveness in physical and mental health. In L. L'Abate (Ed.), *Distance writing and computer-assisted interventions in psychiatry and mental health* (pp. 77-90). Westport, CT: Ablex.

Snowdon, D. (2001). *Aging with grace: What the nun study teaches us about leading longer, healthier, and more meaningful lives.* New York: Bantam.

Snyder, C. R. and Ingram, R. E. (2000). Psychotherapy questions for an evolving field. In C. R. Snyder and R. E. Ingram (Eds.), *Handbook of psychological change: Psychotherapy processes and practices for the 21st century* (pp. 707-726). New York: Wiley.

Sobell, M. B. and Sobell, L. C. (2000). Stepped help as a heuristic approach to the treatment of alcohol problems. *Journal of Consulting and Clinical Psychology, 68,* 573-589.

Stamm, B. H. (1998). Clinical applications of telehealth in mental health care. *Professional Psychology: Research and Practice, 29,* 536-542.

Strom, L., Petterson, R., and Anderson, G. (2000). A controlled trial of self-help treatment of recurrent headache conducted via the Internet. *Journal of Consulting and Clinical Psychology, 68,* 722-727.

Sykes, C. J. (1992). *A nation of victims: The decay of the American character.* New York: St. Martin's Press.

Szell, E. (1994). *Comparison of therapeutic interactions between face-to-face and telemediated communication conditions.* Doctoral dissertation, University of Miami, Florida.

Taylor, A. E. (1966). *The mind of Plato.* Ann Arbor, MI: University of Michigan Press.

Tompkins, M. A. (2002). Guidelines for enhancing homework compliance. *Journal of Clinical Psychology, 58,* 565-576.

Torrey, E. F. (1997). *Out of the shadows: Confronting America's mental illness.* New York: Wiley.

U.S. Department of Health and Human Services (1999). *Mental health: A report of the surgeon general.* Rockville, MD: Center for Mental Health Services, National Institute of Mental Health.

Wallerstein, R. S. (1995). *The talking cures.* New Haven, CT: Yale University Press.

Wampold, B. R. (2001). *The great psychotherapy debate.* Mahwah, NJ: LEA.

Weeks, G. R. and L'Abate, L. (1982). *Paradoxical psychotherapy: Theory and practice with individuals, couples, and families.* New York: Brunner/Mazel.

Weintraub, M. D. (1981). *Verbal behavior: Adaptations in psychopathology.* New York: Springer.

Weisman, A., Tompson, M. C., Okazaki, S., Goldstein, G. J., Rea, M., and Miklowitz, D. J. (2002). Clinician's fidelity to a manual-based family treatment as predictor of the one-year course of bipolar disorder. *Family Process, 41,* 123-131.
Weissman, M. M. (1995). *Mastering depression: A patient's guide to interpersonal
  psychotherapy.* San Antonio, TX: Psychological Corporation.
Wiger, D. E. (1997). *The clinical documentation sourcebook.* New York: Wiley.
Williams, R. B., Boles, M., and Johnson, R. E. (1995). Patient use of a computer for
  prevention in primary care practice. *Patient Education and Counseling, 25,* 283-
  292.
Wilson, G. T. (1997). Empirically validated treatments: Reality and resistance.
  Clinical Psychology: Science and Practice, 4, 241-244.
Wilson, G. T., Vitousek, K. M., and Loeb, K. L. (2000). Stepped care treatment for
  eating disorders. *Journal of Consulting and Clinical Psychology, 68,* 564-572.
Wincze, J. P. and Barlow, D. H. (1997). *Client workbook—Enhancing sexuality: A
  problem-solving approach.* San Antonio, TX: Psychological Corporation.

Chapter 2

Systematically Written Homework Assignments: The Case for Homework-Based Treatment

Luciano L'Abate

In writing, it is possible to move beyond the surface, to intimate as well as to inform, to touch as well as make a point. (Bennett, 2000, p. 35)

The purpose of this chapter is to give a professional background and a rationale to expand on how workbooks, combined with computer-assisted interventions (CAI) on the Internet, could well constitute a substantive advance in the delivery of mental health services as we know them. Distance writing (DW), in its four structures reviewed in the previous chapter (open-ended, focused, guided, and programmed) and additional characteristics of specificity, content, goals, and level of abstraction, is not yet part of accepted, mainstream mental health practices. However, concerns about its clinical and research background and usefulness need to be addressed before greater acceptance of DW and its introduction, addition, and acceptance into future psychological interventions, be they preventive, psychotherapeutic, or rehabilitative, occurs.

This background is limited to the experience of this writer. It is not designed to detract and take credit from those who have developed other workbooks.

PROFESSIONAL ANTECEDENTS OF SYSTEMATICALLY WRITTEN HOMEWORK ASSIGNMENTS

At least eight antecedent sources led to the development of systematically written homework assignments (SWHAs) in this writer's professional experience. These sources do not imply that the same process took place for authors of other workbooks.

The first source consisted of the advent of programmed instruction (PI) and teaching machines in the 1960s (Brown and L'Abate, 1969). Both contributions helped to break down instructions into manageable, sequential parts. Instructions could be administered through teaching machines and mechanical devices rather than face-to-face verbal interaction with another human being. Both PI and teaching machines predated computers and helped dispel the notion that human interaction was necessary to teach, learn, and perhaps even help distressed people to change for the better. Both PI and teaching machines are the most direct antecedents of workbooks and computer-assisted interventions.

A second source consisted of believing that the laboratory method, based on replicable clinical procedures, would help combine evaluation with treatment, theory with practice, research with treatment, and prevention with psychotherapy/rehabilitation. Direct services would be provided by paraprofessional intermediaries (with BA- or MA-level education) between respondents, and supervising/supporting doctorate-level professionals, according to a hierarchy of personnel. The former would deliver services through standard operating procedures in evaluation and interventions, i.e., methods. This point applies most directly to working with minorities who may not trust a professional from a different ethnic or cultural background. The doctorate-level professional would facilitate service delivery, deal with most difficult and critical cases, and perform research (L'Abate, 1973).

The third source, long ignored by the mental health community, was the possibility that help for distressed people could be given through DW rather than through talk and face-to-face contacts. This switch from the spoken to the written medium in clinical practice, with a history of its own (L'Abate, 1987, 1991, 1992), was initially advocated by the late Boston neurologist Weintraub (1981). Not only did Weintraub compare both media, but he also advocated how DW, rather than automatically learned speech, can be used for therapeutic purposes. Years later, as discussed in Chapter 1, L'Abate (1994, 1997) expanded on this comparison by adding the nonverbal medium as a third avenue of intervention.

A fourth source in this development was the increasing influence of the cognitive-behavioral approach in assigning homework (Shelton and Levy, 1981; Levy and Shelton, 1990). Initially, this approach was verbally based and mostly ad hoc. Assignments were administered in a helter-skelter fashion according to the specific needs of respondents with little, if any, systematic thought given to their administration. They were given as convenient, one-shot additions to psychotherapy to make it more efficient than just passive nods and reflections of feelings from a therapist. Nonetheless, this early approach mushroomed into a veritable movement in which homework assignments were found to contribute significantly to the therapeutic process

(Detweiler and Whisman, 1999; Primakoff, Epstein, and Covi, 1986), as already discussed in Chapter 1.

A fifth source of influence in the importance of DW as an additional or alternative medium of intervention came from the work of the Milano group. They used written paradoxical messages in family therapy (Selvini-Palazzoli et al., 1978) that were believed to be powerful enough to destabilize rigidly defended or chaotic families. This work became very influential in the United States and produced a flurry of copycats. However, as with many fashions in the mental health field not supported by empirical evidence, it eventually lost its seductive appeal. However, it did help to establish the alleged effectiveness of writing as a means of producing changes. Nonetheless, it was a one-way street in the sense that families answered behaviorally rather than in writing. It was not as interactive as workbooks. More on this point later.

A sixth source of influence in the creation of workbooks was the production of fifty structured enrichment programs with more than 1,500 questions, tasks, and exercises for couples and families (L'Abate, 1985; L'Abate and Weinstein, 1987; L'Abate and Young, 1987). Trainers were instructed to follow programs verbatim. These programs represented the early influence of PI and the laboratory method in the development of systematic, sequential instructions to be delivered as standard operating procedures by semi, quasiprofessional personnel (i.e., beginning graduate students). The administration of these programs introduced the possibility that people in distress could be helped at a distance from a professional through the use of less trained and less experienced intermediaries using structured interventions. Intermediaries could administer evaluation instruments and repeatable instructions, away from a supervising and supporting professional. These intermediaries now have been supplanted by workbooks, computers, TV, and the Internet.

What is more relevant to the development of workbooks is their direct derivation from single-score or multiple-score tests was the development of a self-report, paper-and-pencil rating sheet based on matching enrichment exercises. This instrument links an area of reported disturbance in a couple or family with matching enrichment exercises (Kochalka and L'Abate, 1997). Once all enrichment exercises were classified into nine categories (L'Abate and Weinstein, 1987), it was possible to create items to describe each category. Hence, depending on what scores a couple or family would receive on this instrument, they could be administered matching exercises in their reported area of disturbance. This instrument showed statistically significant correlations with the dyadic adjustment and family environment scales. The instrument's high concurrent validity ($p < .001$) showed that it was possible to match evaluation directly with intervention provided that the domain of intervention was defined precisely in writing.

This expansion added another dimension to test instruments. Instead of being strictly evaluative, diagnostic, and predictive, workbooks developed from test instruments added a prescriptive function that enlarged in a more interactive fashion the many functions of test instruments in psychological interventions, as already discussed in the previous chapter (L'Abate, 1990, 1997, 2001a,b, 2002, 2003; L'Abate and De Giacomo, 2003).

A seventh and much more recent source of influence and reinforcement for the use of DW in psychological interventions came from the research of Pennebaker (2001) and Esterling et al. (1999), as already reviewed in Chapter 1, with the support of a meta-analysis by Smyth (1998). Their findings, plus additional research from many other sources that cannot all be cited here, including the development of a science of writing (Levy and Ransdell, 1996), led to the possibility that DW could become the wave of the future in mental health services. This possibility has been reinforced by the recent edited work by Lepore and Smyth (2002).

An overall consideration—one that loomed large in the laboratory method and the production of workbooks—lies in what constitutes a method of intervention. For a method of treatment to be useful it needs to be replicable to the point of 100 percent fidelity. To obtain such a result, the method, e.g., workbooks, needs to be administered without the interfering and intervening influence of extraneous factors, such as face-to-face talk-based alliances, nonverbal cues, as already noted. Only through such fidelity can we measure the impact that this method has or can have on the outcome it claims to produce.

As long as the method of intervention is verbal, requiring face-to-face contact between professionals and respondents, it will be extremely difficult to determine which factors are responsible for which result. Even manuals, so strongly advocated by professionals who need evidence-based methods of treatment, require talk and personal, face-to-face contact. These factors make it difficult and expensive to discern which variable produced which change. In this regard, manuals perpetuate the status quo in psychotherapy because they still rely on talk and face-to-face contact. Unless mandated by managed care companies, manuals are difficult if not impossible to use in private practice, regardless of what a recent survey of psychotherapists concluded (Najavits et al., 2000).

Hence, the issue is: What part of the outcome variance in psychological interventions is due to the influence of workbooks and what part of that variance is due to other factors?

WORKBOOKS AS EXTENSIONS
OF EXISTING KNOWLEDGE

Workbooks are applied embodiments and practical encapsulations of existing, clinical, professional, and scientific knowledge, lore, and information. This bold statement, of course, needs explanation, expansion, and support. To wit, workbooks have been developed from the following sources of information:

1. At the outset of workbook development, *clinical experience* was the only basis relied upon, since no written guidelines were available. For example, early workbooks derived from this writer's experience as a child and family clinical psychologist dealt with sibling rivalry, temper tantrums, and time-out procedures with children, as well as arguing and fighting in couples (L'Abate, 1992). As this writer's practice changed to family therapy, the importance of depression in couples, negotiation skills, and intimacy became paramount, producing workbooks that matched theoretical models (L'Abate, 1986),

2. Related mostly to development of workbooks for acting-out, impulsive, and aggressive individuals was *semantic reconditioning* (L'Abate, 1992). This approach consists of having respondents answer assignments about the meaning of words that control behavior, such as "mistake," "law," "goal," "love," "parent," with corrective feedback about errors in thinking familiar to cognitive-behavioral therapists. Prime examples of this approach are found in at least two workbooks on social training, in the case studies of an incarcerated felon (L'Abate, 1992, 1996) and an acting-out teenager (L'Abate, 1999), and in preliminary research, still in progress, with incarcerated felons found in Chapter 10.

3. The *Diagnostic Statistical Manual of Mental Disorders,* Fourth Edition (DSM-IV, APA, 1994), which provides a list of signs or symptoms describing clinical conditions. The primary example of a workbook derived from the DSM is one on anxiety developed by this author and David Rupp (L'Abate et al., 1992). The DSM-IV is a major, untapped, source in the development of future workbooks, particularly if one were to use a list of symptoms or behaviors as a foundation. This process is described later.

4. Another source in the development of workbooks was *paper-and-pencil self-report tests or rating sheets.* Some workbooks were developed from unidimensional single-score tests, such as the Beck Anxiety and Depression Inventories (Alloy et al., 1999; Dozois, Dobson, and Ahnberg,

1998; Wilson et al., 1999), Hamilton's Anxiety and Depression Inventories (Kobak and Reynolds, 1999; Moras, Di Nardo, and Barlow, 1992), the Brief Psychiatric Rating Scale (Faustman and Overall, 1999; Mueser, Curran, and McHugo, 1997), and Hare's Psychopathic Behavior scale (Kosson et al., 1997), among many others. Several workbooks were also developed from multidimensional tests, including the Minnesota Multiphasic Personality Inventory-2 (MMPI-2) (Greene and Clopton, 1999), the Personality Assessment Inventory (Morley, 1999), and the Big Five Factors model (Goldberg, 1999), as well as a host of others.

5. A fifth source consisted of *theoretical models or books.* For example, after developing theoretical models of depression, negotiation, and intimacy, isomorphic workbooks to match these models were written (L'Abate, 1986). This process has been repeated with other models. When workbooks are developed from tests that represent theoretical and empirical models, it follows that workbooks thus developed become active, interactive, and dynamic ways to evaluate those very models. From the laboratory, one can go directly into the clinic and apply preventively and therapeutically what has been learned empirically. For instance, a workbook was developed from works published recently on the development of emotional competence (L'Abate and Kern, 2002).

6. A sixth source of information in the development of workbooks was *empirical knowledge.* For instance, several workbooks were developed from factor analyses for character disorders (Clark, 1990), personality dissociation (Goldberg, 1999), and personality disorders (Davis and Millon, 1999).

7. A seventh source that is everywhere consists of *omnipresent, easily available self-help popular literature* (Norcross et al., 2000). Most self-help books can be transformed easily into an interactive workbook format. An early example, however, discouraged their development into workbooks because of the exorbitant fee requested by the publisher of the original book. Nonetheless, this writer has in his files many workbooks developed by students based on existing and popular self-help materials. By basing a workbook on many sources, rather than one specific source, it might be possible to transform the relatively passive process of using a workbook into dynamic, interactive interventions.

The creation of workbooks from clinical or personality tests, especially single-score evaluations and published factor-analyses, raises relevant and important professional issues. Can one use information that is printed in copyrighted journals? Sources relevant to each workbook are always cited and copies of workbooks sent to the respective authors or publishers of either tests or factor analyses as a standard operating procedure. However, in most cases no response was ever received, or at best a letter of acknowledgment of receipt with best wishes was sent to the requestor. Only in one case was permission to use test materials obtained directly from the publisher of the test, who requested a citation of the publisher's permission with the workbook.

In one case, still pending, the author of the test expressed "serious questions" about the use of his test items to develop a workbook. This author submitted the workbook to the publisher of the test for an opinion. The publisher's relatively negative response prompted a look at the current code of conduct from the American Psychological Association (which had nothing to say on this issue), consultation with at least two colleagues with acknowledged expertise of ethical and professional standards, and, eventually, review of a book on copyright laws (Fishman, 1997). To avoid the possibility of future legal actions, formal permissions were obtained from most publishers of books and journals from which some workbooks were developed, and especially the American Psychological Association, whose journals became a major source of workbooks based on research studies. Development of at least two workbooks based on tests—one based on the Myers-Briggs Inventory and one based on a well-documented family evaluation test—was stopped in its tracks because of the absolute unwillingness of their publishers to allow this development.

Although workbooks thus developed could be considered "derivative works" that are covered under fair use copyright laws, if they are derived from copyrighted materials, a host of professional issues follow that remain as yet unresolved. They fall into a limbo of seemingly contradictory laws, including the never-never land of fair use laws. One argument that can be used in the creation of workbooks from single-item tests or factor analyses lies in the fact that "Individual words are always in the public domain, even if they are invented by a particular person" (Fishman, 1997, p. 6/8). One could also argue that workbooks as transformative works, fit the "goal of copyright to promote human knowledge" (Fishman, 1997, p. 11/4).

Counterarguments may be made against both points, since a pattern of words related to a single topic or test becomes copyrighted material requiring permission. Furthermore, the goal of derivative tranformations brings about another relevant issue. If this writer's expressed goal (L'Abate, 1996) is to produce "low-cost mental health workbooks," would a test producer or publisher agree to that goal? Hence, the creation of workbooks from copyrighted materials is fraught with new professional issues that deserve consideration from various viewpoints. Which viewpoint is correct remains to be seen.

BRIDGING THE SEMANTIC GAP

An overall source of influence in the production of workbooks is the semantic gap between the mystique of professional mental health jargon and the knowledge base of most respondents (L'Abate, 1992). This gap cannot be filled through talk, as argued by this author ad nauseam, because talk is a rather ineffective medium of communication and teaching, especially with distressed and troubled people. Talk can be distorted and forgotten. It may be effective in functional relationships, but it is clearly ineffective in dealing with serious psychopathology because of semantic distortions present in severe pathologies (Kerns and Berenbaum, 2000; Sheppard and Teasdale, 2000). It may even be counter-therapeutic with criminal and related conditions (Reed, McMahan, and L'Abate, 2001). A survey conducted by the National Depressive and Manic-Depressive Association (2001) found that more than 75 percent of patients receiving treatment for major depression felt that their illness was not under control, and more than 50 percent stopped taking antidepressants because of side effects caused by the medication. More to the point of a semantic gap, this survey found that the root of the problem was "a significant communication gap" (p. 26) between patients and their primary care physicians. One reason for primary care physicians' reluctance to refer their depressed patients to mental health professionals was the "complex terminology in the mental health field" (p. 26). This terminology loomed as a significant barrier to effective communications between primary care physicians and therapists. Thus, a semantic gap exists not only between patients and therapists but also among professionals.

It takes more than talk to help human beings change. Talk is not a medium through which we can impart effectively and efficiently new information and knowledge to be learned, practiced, rehearsed, and retained interactively. For instance, when professionals arrive at the conclusion that a respondent is depressed, they use cues—verbal, nonverbal, and written (as in a test)—given by respondents. From that label they supposedly derive an alleged treatment plan (Beutler, 1989; Beutler and Clarkin, 1990; Hurt, Reznikoff, and Clarkin, 1991). Under managed care guidelines, they are to write these plans. Has anyone evaluated the relationship between written treatment plans and what therapists claim they have done through repeated, face-to-face, verbal contacts? How it is possible to conduct such an evaluation? What would it take to follow up and evaluate what therapists claim they have said and done that conforms to, let alone matches with, their original treatment plans? An unpublished study by this author found very little connection between what professionals said they wrote and what they said they did (L'Abate, 1995).

A diagnostic conclusion, then, is couched professionally into a label that may have an important impact—positive or negative—on the lives of respondents. After informing respondents of such a conclusion, professionals may give an explanation about the meaning and prognostic and therapeutic implications of that label. Supposedly, this explanation will be followed by a specific method of treatment that will relieve respondents of such a painful condition. However, how are respondents to know whether the method of treatment to treat depression, for instance, is different from a method of treatment for anxiety? Are these methods different enough to make a specific difference? As Seligman (1998) reported, the most significant similarity among most, if not all, talk psychotherapies is their "lack of specificity." He did not expand on the possibility that this inadequacy lies in the very characteristic of talk as a medium of communication and possible healing.

However, the gap between professionals' understanding of most clinical conditions or diagnoses and respondents' understanding of those conditions is still present. Respondents still remain passive recipients of a label and often very little more than a pill or a verbal, usually vague and general, treatment plan, for example, "We shall meet once a week to talk about your depression and let's see what happens between us." Respondents still remain passive recipients of a therapist's knowledge and experience, which is sometimes imparted to them piecemeal during the process of psychotherapy, with a two-thirds chance of obtaining positive results. How can we make the process less passive and more dynamic, involving respondents interactively by making them more responsive and responsible for whatever changes they may want in their lives? Workbooks can and do impart this knowledge and help bridge this semantic gap by increasing shared meanings between professionals and respondents in a more efficient manner than can be achieved verbally. Examples of how this gap is filled semantically follow.

Workbooks can help bridge the semantic gap between professionals and respondents in a more efficient and, one hopes, cost-effective way than talk. This process implies learning the meaning of behaviors by defining any clinical and nonclinical condition or symptom according to its component parts, i.e., behaviors. This gap was originally filled by asking respondents to answer assignments composed of single terms, as in the social training workbook derived from clinical practice with acting-out, impulsive teenagers and adults (L'Abate, 1992). Respondents define and answer questions or tasks directed to terms, as mentioned earlier. The order of presentation here was fixed and nomothetic—the same for all respondents.

From a fixed, nomothetic sequence it was later possible to move to a more fluid, flexibly idiographic sequence by requiring respondents to define and give two examples for all of the terms comprising a single-score test, such as the Beck Depression Inventory and many others, or a list of terms resulting from factor analyses or other research (Clark, 1990; Livesley, Jackson, and Schroeder, 1989; Sajatovic and Ramirez, 2001). A dictionary, friends, or relatives could be used to define each term. The point is that respondents have to search actively for the meaning and definition of each term, including two examples to demonstrate actual understanding. After definitions and examples are provided, respondents are asked to rank the same list of terms according to personal preferences, that is, from what term applies to them the most to what term does not apply to them at all, or from most troublesome and relevant to what is least troublesome or irrelevant.

This ranking then becomes the order of administration for all subsequent assignments, following a standard assignment format (L'Abate, 1996, 2002). For instance, if X behavior was ranked first in the first assignment, the second assignment would receive the title of that X behavior. Standard questions would be asked about the meaning, developmental background, intensity, duration, frequency, and rate of occurrence for that behavior, sometimes with its paradoxical prescriptions according to an ordered sequence. The third assignment would be titled according to the Y term ranked second in preference, and so on, until all terms ranked as relevant to each respondent's awareness and experience have been administered. In most cases, a follow-up debriefing assignment ends the workbook. In some cases, a conflict may arise when the sequence of assignments derived from test results is compared to the sequence of assignments derived from respondents' rank-orders. This discrepancy can be used to highlight differences in viewpoints derived from objective tests versus subjective viewpoints derived from personally felt experiences in respondents, increasing the chances of bridging the semantic gap.

In this fashion, the order of presentation for assignments becomes specific and idiographic to the individual needs and preferences of respondents. Even for research purposes, one could administer a fixed, constant number of assignments that would vary in content from one respondent to another. Rankings would be idiographic, combining them with a constant nomothetic approach. Thus, workbooks constructed from rating scales, single-score tests, or lists of behavior symptoms can become a much more active and interactive way to help respondents fill a semantic gap and become more aware of their symptomatic behaviors. Whether this awareness and practice of symptomatic behavior leads to change for the better remains to be seen.

RESEARCH WITH SWHAs

The use of SWHAs is based on a program of research performed over the years in the Family Study Center of Georgia State University, with the help of my collaborators. They are listed chronologically to indicate how each study was one stepping stone after another toward helping people at a distance through workbooks rather than through face-to-face contacts and talk. These studies were originally conducted without effect-size estimates. Consequently, these estimates were calculated from the original data available and reported here in their entirety. Results of studies not published previously, are also included here.

Wildman

The first study by Wildman (1977) explored whether structured interventions, such as enrichment programs, would be as helpful as unstructured marital interventions, such as psychotherapy. Enrichment was usually performed with undergraduate couples who denied any problems (i.e., "nonclinical"), whereas psychotherapy was performed with couples who came to the University Family Clinic for help with their relationships ("clinical"), indicating two different groups with different characteristics. In this study, however, "clinical" couples who referred themselves for "therapy," were administered structured enrichment programs instead, providing a cell that was necessary to compare which approach produced better outcomes.

Couples were assigned randomly to four groups: Group 1 consisted of eight "clinical" couples who referred themselves for help and received structured enrichment for five sessions instead; Group 2, consisted of eleven "clinical" couples who referred themselves for therapy and received it; Group 3 consisted of twenty-five "nonclinical" couples who received structured enrichment programs; and control Group 4 consisted of fourteen "nonclinical" couples who did not receive any treatment, either enrichment or therapy, but completed the test-battery on a pre and post basis.

The number of either enrichment or therapy sessions was constant (five) for all couples. If, after posttesting, couples required or needed further help, it was made available and administered to them. Both therapy and enrichment were administered by graduate students, usually with the more advanced students administering therapy and the less advanced administering enrichment. In addition to the initial identifying information, couples were administered the following paper-and-pencil self-report tests on a before and after intervention basis: (1) Marital Happiness Scale (MHS), (2) Revised Marital Happiness Scale (RMHS), and (3) Marital Progress Sheet

(MPS). These instruments correlated highly with each other ($p < .001$). On posttest, only the MPS and total battery mean scores showed any significant improvements ($p < .01$). The control condition failed to show any improvement. Enrichment applied to nonclinical couples produced statistically significant improvements in mean scores. Marital therapy applied to clinical couples produced highly significant improvement in mean change scores, whereas enrichment administered to clinical couples instead of therapy also produced highly significant improvement in mean change scores. As the size estimates shown in Table 2.1 suggest, enrichment did not produce any greater results than therapy. In fact, these estimates are in line with effect-size estimates resulting from psychotherapy extant in that literature. Because of the small *n,* one can only claim a size estimate of .50 for all of the large values of this study.

These results suggested that structured intervention, as a replicable intervention method, may be as helpful as unstructured intervention. Given a replicable, structured method, such as enrichment administered by facilitators with minimal if any clinical experience, results were comparable to those obtained by unstructured therapy by more experienced therapists. The results of this study were the basis for the next one.

Wagner and L'Abate

Wagner and L'Abate (1977) evaluated the effects of enrichment and of written homework assignments with couples. Thirty-two married or cohabiting couples participated in this study as volunteers for experimental class credit. They were defined as nonclinical to the extent that they denied any problems and scored in the nonclinical ranges of evaluation instru-

TABLE 2.1. Effect-Size Estimates for Therapy versus Enrichment

Groups Treatments	n	d
Enrichment	8	.72
Therapy	11	.73
Enrichment	25	.54
Nonclinical control	14	.02
Clinical versus nonclinical		.19
Treatments versus control		.49
Enrichment versus therapy		.18

Source: Wildman, 1977.

ments. They were randomly assigned to four groups with eight couples each: Group 1 received enrichment as well as written homework assignments specifically designed to improve communication. Group 2 received the same written homework assignments as Group 1 but did not receive enrichment, meeting with the experimenter being present for a few minutes only at the beginning and at the end of the study; Group 2 received and returned completed written homework assignments in sealed envelopes. Group 3 received enrichment but no written homework assignments. Group 4 received no intervention and served as control for the other groups. Groups 1 and 3 received six sessions each. Couples in Group 2 received and returned six homework assignments.

All couples were evaluated before and after intervention with five paper-and-pencil self-report rating scales: (1) Marital Adjustment Test (MAT); (2) Primary Communication Inventory (PCI); (3) Marital Happiness Scale; (4) Communication Behaviors Rating Scale (CBRS); and (5) Family Information Rating Scale (FIRS). Change scores for these rating scales were defined as the sum of the difference for each item (110 items total) on each rating scale obtained from subtracting preintervention scores from postintervention scores for each individual. Results were presented in terms of percentage improvement for each group. Group 1, enrichment plus assignments, produced a 75 percent improvement. Assignments alone produced a 62 percent improvement. Enrichment produced a 37 percent improvement, whereas the control group produced a 25 percent improvement in change scores. An effect-size estimate produced a high $d = +1.16$ score for treatment over the control group.

This study suggested that synergistic effects can be obtained by combining two different treatments, making it possible to help respondents at a distance using written homework assignments with a minimum of personal face-to-face verbal contact. To verify this hypothesis, an additional study was performed.

Clark and L'Abate

Clark and L'Abate (1977) studied the effects of enrichment programs and tape recordings with couples to see whether respondents could be helped at a distance, with a minimum of verbal interaction between semiprofessionals (beginning graduate students) and respondents. In addition, the question asked here was whether written instructions directed toward increased self-revelation and self-disclosure would bring about positive change in nonclinical couples. Again, couples who volunteered for experimental class credit were randomly assigned to three groups. Group 1 consisted of

eight couples who served as controls by receiving credit for completing the
test battery on a before-and-after basis; Group 2 consisted of eight couples
who received enrichment, and Group 3 consisted of ten couples who were
instructed though a written contract (to be signed in order to participate) to
speak about themselves as individuals into a tape recorder. After speaking in
the tape recorder, they were asked to listen to each other's tapes and to make
an appointment to discuss their respective reactions with each other. The
couples were guaranteed anonymity with the assurance that all the tapes
they returned would be kept under lock and key at all times. Instructions on
what to say in each recording were given in writing. They consisted of detailed questions about six topics: future, fears, sex, fantasy, feelings, and reactions about finishing up. The first five instructions were administered randomly to avoid serial effects. The same battery of tests administered in the
previous study was administered.

Instead of results for each separate test, given the high intercorrelations
among them, all individual pre- and postintervention scores were combined
to produce mean change scores obtained by subtracting individual pretest
scores from posttest scores. Percentage estimates indicated that the control
group improved 25 percent, the enrichment group improved 50 percent,
whereas the tape-recording group improved 70 percent.

Recently performed effect-size estimates (Table 2.2) produced equivalent effect sizes for both enrichment and tape recordings, suggesting that it
is possible to produce change in nonclinical couples at a distance, with minimal interaction with "professionals." Given two treatment methods that
produce approximately similar results, e.g., enrichment, requiring face-to-
face verbal contact with a "professional," versus tape recordings, requiring
minimal face-to-face personal contact and therefore less expensive, one
chooses the least expensive method. These results, in spite of the small sample size and the possibility of compensatory rivalry for the control group,
therefore, encouraged the use of written messages to see whether even one
single letter would produce positive results.

TABLE 2.2. Effect-Size Estimates for Tape Recordings with Couples

Groups treatments	n	d
Control	8	1.31
Enrichment	8	1.13
Tape recordings	10	1.15
Treatments versus control		.58

Source: Clark and L'Abate, 1977.

Wagner et al.

Wagner et al. (1977) studied the effects of linear versus circular methods of intervention with couples. However, this was strictly an anecdotal, exploratory, explicatory, and qualitative study that did not involve empirical data. Nonetheless, it was the basis for the next, more empirical study.

Wagner, Weeks, and L'Abate

Wagner, Weeks, and L'Abate (1980) explored the effects of structured enrichment programs and written messages with couples. Following the example of the Milano school of family therapy (Selvini-Palazzoli et al., 1978), it seemed crucial at that time to determine whether paradoxical, i.e., circularly worded letters (Weeks and L'Abate, 1982) would be more effective than straightforward, linearly worded letters.

To evaluate which approach was more effective, fifty-six nonclinical, undergraduate couples were randomly assigned to four groups: Group 1 ($n = 14$) were assigned to a waiting list, do-nothing control; Group 2 ($n = 14$) consisted of couples who were administered enrichment programs only; Group 3 ($n = 14$) consisted of couples who received enrichment plus linear letters; Group 4 ($n = 14$) consisted of couples who received enrichment plus circular letters. All experimental couples were administered enrichment for six weeks. Letters were given at the conclusion of the fourth enrichment session. There was no discussion of the letters until the posttest was completed, if a couple asked for it.

Couples were administered the Revised Marital Happiness Scale, Marital Progress Sheet, and a Communication Reaction Form (CRF) before and after completion of the six sessions. Analysis of variance (ANOVA) for all three tests found near significance in change scores for both the RMHS and CRF but not for the MPS. A 2×2 chi-square analysis of most improved versus least improved by treatment versus no treatment produced a chi-square value of 3.84 ($p < .05$). The largest mean change score for couples in Group 3 on the RMHS and on the total battery change scores suggested that written communication in the form of linear letters may be a useful adjunct to enrichment and, perhaps, to other forms of interventions.

A more recent effect size estimate analysis of results (Table 2.3) showed the greater overall moderate effect size for enrichment with linear letters (average effect size .43), with paradoxical letters producing a rather small effect size (.16). Of course, in view of other negative results in studies to be cited, one cannot conclude that paradoxical letters did not produce any results. One must keep in mind that only short-term (immediately after termi-

TABLE 2.3. Effect-Size Estimates *(d)* of Pre and Post Mean Scores for Enrichment, Linear, and Paradoxical Letters

Groups	Letters		Treatments		versus control	
	Control	Enrich	Linear	Paradox		
n	14	14	14	14	Pre	Post
Tests						
RMHS	−.03	.28	.57	.26	−.53	−.19
MPS	−.06	.08	.35	.13	−.49	−.17
CRF	−.20	.61	.38	.08	−.48	−.06
Avg. *d* =	−.09	.32	.43	.16	−.50	−.15

Source: Wagner, Weeks, and L'Abate, 1980.

nation) results were evaluated. One cannot arrive at a negative conclusion unless long-term results are evaluated.

Nonetheless, these results suggested (more than twenty years ago!) that it may be possible to change behavior at a distance through written communications. What would happen if instead of respondents being relatively passive recipients of these communications, they would become involved and interactive participants of written homework assignments? This question was tentatively answered in the next study.

Ganahl

As a follow-up to previous studies, Ganahl (1981) evaluated the results of various treatment modalities with 126 married couples and one cohabiting couple. Approximately half of these couples were used in previous studies of Wildman (1977) and Wagner and L'Abate (1977). Eighty-four nonclinical couples did not seek help for their relationships and volunteered either to improve their relationships or to earn class credit for participation. Eighteen clinical couples requested assistance for their relationship difficulties. Ethnic, economic, religious, educational, and occupational levels were quite various and rather heterogeneous. One-way ANOVA and chi-square analyses failed to find significant between-group differences. In addition to an identifying information sheet, most, not all, couples were evaluated on a pre- and posttreatment basis with a battery of self-report questionnaires, including the Marital Happiness Scale, the Revised Marital Happiness Scale, Communication Reaction Form, Marital Progress Sheet, Locke-Wallace

Short Marital Adjustment Test, and Primary Communication Inventory. The test-rested reliability of all these measures varied from .54 to .89, significant at either the .01 or 001 levels. Most measures correlated highly ($p < .001$) with one another, to the point that change scores were added to produce a total battery score.

Couples were assigned to treatments on a semirandomized basis. Clinical couples were assigned to either structured enrichment (clinical enrichment, $n = 15$) or therapy (T, $n = 15$). Nonclinical couples were assigned to either structured enrichment (nonclinical enrichment, $n = 48$), homework assignments only (H, $n = 8$), or combination of both structured enrichment and homework (CEH, $n = 8$). All couples received six sessions of either structured enrichment, therapy, homework, or both enrichment and homework before being retested after termination.

ANOVAs of change scores produced a variety of results. Of relevance to this area of research was the conclusion that structured enrichment in its three forms, alone, homework only, and enrichment plus homework, was effective in producing positive changes in nonclinical couples' marital adjustment and satisfaction. Significant ($p < .02$) positive improvement was found for clinical couples relative to control couples using analysis of covariance (ANCOVA) for both structured enrichment and marital therapy, with the latter showing superiority over the former with clinical couples.

Size estimates for both husbands and wives (Table 2.4) produced inconsistent results for either gender. In husbands, for instance, on the total battery gain scores, homework alone showed an extremely high (.82) effect size, with clinical enrichment and therapy showing some effect sizes (.38 and .34, respectively), whereas, surprisingly, nonclinical enrichment plus homework showed absolutely no effect (.08), which was even lower than the control group (.04). On the PCI, the control group showed the highest effect size (.70), followed by homework alone (.59), and trailed by nonclinical enrichment and nonclinical enrichment plus homework. On the MAT, nonclinical enrichment showed a medium effect size (.50), followed by a low effect size (.35) for homework alone, followed by nonclinical enrichment (.18) and no effect for the control group (.09). On the MHS, homework alone and clinical therapy showed the relatively highest effect size (.65 and .67 respectively) followed by clinical enrichment (.37) and lower nonclinical enrichment (.13). Control and nonclinical enrichment plus homework failed to show any effect size (.03 and .09 respectively).

In wives, the same pattern of inconsistent results persisted. On total battery scores, wives had the highest effect size on homework alone (.88), followed by nonclinical enrichment plus homework (.58), clinical enrichment (.35) and clinical therapy (.30), with the control group showing the lowest effect size (.09). On the PCI, wives in the control group matched their hus-

TABLE 2.4. Effect-Size Estimates (d) of Various Interventions for Husbands and Wives

Meaures and Groups	n	Husbands	n	Wives
Total Battery Scores				
Nonclinical enrichment	50	.01	49	.04
Clinical enrichment	15	.38	16	.35
Clinical therapy	16	.34	16	.30
Control	23	.04	21	.09
Homework only	8	.82	7	.88
Nonclinical enrichment and homework	8	.08	8	.58
Primary Communication Inventory				
Nonclinical enrichment	15	.26	17	.27
Control	8	.70	7	.67
Homework only	8	.59	7	.47
Nonclinical enrichment and homework	7	.21	4	.06
Locke-Wallace Short Marital Adjustment Test				
Nonclinical enrichment	13	.50	16	.45
Control	9	.09	8	.17
Homework only	8	.35	7	.31
Nonclinical enrichment and homework	8	.18	4	.57
Marital Happiness Scale				
Nonclinical enrichment	23	.13	25	.25
Clinical enrichment	12	.37	12	.40
Clinical therapy	7	.67	6	.82
Control	16	.03	16	.15
Homework only	5	.65	5	.65
Nonclinical enrichment and homework	6	.09	4	1.68

Source: Ganahl, 1981.

bands in showing the highest effect sizes (.67), followed by homework alone (.47), with nonclinical enrichment and nonclinical enrichment plus homework showing the lowest effect sizes (.27 and .06, respectively). On the MAT, nonclinical enrichment and nonclinical enrichment plus homework showed relatively medium effect sizes (.45 and .57, respectively), with homework alone trailing behind (.31), and the control group showing no effect size (.17). On the MHS, clinical enrichment plus homework showed the highest effect size of all the measures (1.68), followed by clinical therapy (.82), homework alone (.65), and nonclinical enrichment (.25), with the control group showing the lowest effect size (.15).

Due to these inconsistent and variable results, all effect sizes for both husbands and wives for the three tests (PCI, MAT, and MHS) were averaged to see whether a more consistent pattern could be found for the control and the three major interventions. Nonclinical enrichment showed an average effect size of .31, control showed an average effect size of .30, homework alone .50, and nonclinical enrichment plus homework .45. These averages are more in line with what would be expected. However, they do show that written homework alone is slightly and relatively more effective than the other two types of intervention: enrichment and enrichment plus homework. Again, given the same results from different treatments, one chooses the least expensive treatment. From this study it became apparent that we could initiate studying the effectiveness of specific workbooks, as showed in the next study.

L'Abate

This study evaluated results from the administration of a negotiation and intimacy workbook with couples (see pp. 58-63 of L'Abate, 1992) under two experimental conditions (completion of workbook assignments in the presence of a "therapist," [trainer-conducted] lasting forty-five minutes, and completion of the same assignments with minimal [five minutes] "therapist" presence [trainer-assisted]). In this group, instead of being invited into the "therapist's" office couples were met at the door of the office to return completed assignments and receive the next assignment.

Thirty-seven couples (seventy-four partners) in committed relationships (at least six months or longer), engaged or married, participated in this study after signing an informed consent form. They were selected from the student body of an urban university via personal solicitation and introductory psychology classes. For the negotiation workbook, the control group was composed of ten couples. For the intimacy workbook, six couples were assigned to the control group.

Couples were administered a battery of tests on a pre- and posttest design to assess the extent of workbook intervention consisting of the Dyadic Adjustment Scale (DAS), Primary Communication Inventory, Marital Issues Questionnaire (MIQ), and the Sharing of Hurts Scale (SOH). Couples received six weekly assignments for both workbooks. The first three tests showed improvement with increased scores, whereas the SOH showed improvement with decreasing scores.

ANOVA yielded positive and significant ($p < .01$) results on all assessment instruments. Estimates of effect sizes (Table 2.5) show that trainer-assisted (TA) groups produced consistently greater effect-size estimates

TABLE 2.5. Effect-Size Estimates of Two Workbooks for Couples

Workbook	Groups	Tests				
		DAS (d)	MIQ (d)	PCI (d)	SOH (d)	Overall (d)
Negotiation						
TA	$n = 16$	+1.07*	−.52	−1.19*	−1.20*	−.43*
TC	$n = 16$	+.53	+.22	−1.09*	−.44	−.17
Intimacy						
TA	$n = 12$	−1.31*	+.36	−1.32*	−.16	−.53*
TC	$n = 14$	−.71	+.51	−.67	−.20	−.25

Source: L'Abate, 1992.
*$p < .01$; TA = trainer assisted; TC = trainer conducted

than trainer-conducted (TC) groups ($d = -.43$ and $-.53$ versus $-.17$ and $-.25$ respectively), all in the negative direction. However, major differences exist among the effect-size estimates of the two workbooks. For instance, the negotiation workbook produced a rather large, positive effect size ($d = 1.07$), whereas the intimacy workbook produced a somewhat larger but negative effect size ($d = -1.31$). The latter result might support the view that intimacy, defined as sharing of hurts and fears of being hurt, is not an easy condition to achieve even on a normative basis (L'Abate, 1997), as found also with seminarian couples (McMahan and L'Abate, 2001).

Therefore, one would conclude that, all other variables being equal, the less expensive (of therapist's time) condition (TA) was less effective in producing change than the more expensive condition (TC). Therefore, if face-to-face, verbal psychotherapy is deemed necessary, it could be enhanced synergistically by additional homework assignments, especially if these assignments produced effects independent from verbal, face-to-face contacts.

L'Abate et al.

Three studies about the administration of workbooks at a distance from respondents were reported by L'Abate et al. (1992). The first study was performed with college students who scored high on self-report instruments designed to assess depression, the Beck Depression Inventory (BDI) and the Center for Epidemiological Studies-Depression scale (CES-D). The second study was also performed with undergraduates using workbooks developed from the MMPI-2. The third study assessed the outcome of an anxiety workbook developed from the *Diagnostic and Statistical Manual of Mental Disorders,* Fourth Edition. In all three studies, workbook interventions were the experimental condition. Control conditions included either focused writing about trivial topics or no intervention.

The results from the first study appeared promising. High and medium depression scores for the BDI and the CES-D showed significant decreases to a normal, lower level. On the BDI, the level of depression was significantly affected by the three workbooks interventions, $F(3, 60) = 5.91, p < .001$. The effects were similar for high- and low-depression groups, suggesting that workbooks may be effective in lowering depression scores, regardless of the initial level of depression, except, of course, for scores at the normal level, usually below ten points. The same results were found for CES-D scores, which decreased significantly for the three experimental groups over the control group, $F(3, 60) = 7.18, p < .001$. A follow-up study to assess the lasting effects of workbook interventions was conducted (L'Abate et al., 1992).

Of the sixty-four students who participated in this study, four could not be located. Of the remaining sixty, a total of twenty-eight respondents completed the BDI and the CES-D, which was mailed to them six months after completion of the posttest in the original study. In the analysis of results for the original study, respondents had been divided into two groups of high and medium depression. Because of the meager number of responses at followup, these two groups were combined into one group. Pre- and posttreatment scores of those who returned the follow-up tests were compared with the scores of those who did not return the follow-up tests. Scores of completers and noncompleters did not differ except for the posttreatment scores.

All groups improved regardless of experimental or control condition. Consequently, a Tukey-HSD procedure was used to determine which groups were significantly different from one another on posttest. One workbook seemed to produce slightly more gain scores than the other two experimental workbooks. A more recent effect-size estimate of this study (Smyth and L'Abate, 2001) produced a moderate score ($d = +.44$) that is similar to the average effect-size score obtained from a meta-analysis of mental health workbooks reported later.

In a second, unpublished study, specification of personality characteristics, regardless of theory, can be accomplished with individuals using an objective test, such as the MMPI-2. To determine the effectiveness of workbooks in lowering the peak scores on the MMPI-2 content scales, fifty-four undergraduate students were administered this test on a before-and-after basis. They were randomly assigned to one of three groups: (1) a control group that did not receive homework assignments; (2) an experimental group that received workbooks designed to match each of the MMPI-2's fifteen content scales (L'Abate, 1992); and (3) another experimental group that, in addition to workbook assignments, received written feedback about and after each completed assignment was turned in. As in all the previous studies, personal contact between respondents and experimenters was either nonexistent or minimized.

One-way MANOVA was used to examine mean differences in peak scores subtracted from average profile elevation of the remaining fourteen scores on the content scales on a pre-posttreatment basis. Although between-groups effects yielded no significant difference ($F = 2.03$; df. 2, 5, $p>.14$) among the three groups, the within-groups effect yielded a significant difference among these same groups ($F = 24.12$; df. 2, 51, $p < .001$. Although mean peak scores decreased significantly, in this study the control group's mean peak scores decreased as well as those of the two experimental groups, weakening the validity of the initial hypothesis that the experimental group would improve more than the control group. Some additional findings concerned the validity of the content scales, as related by the students' behavior during the study. For instance, students scoring highest on the Type A personality scale were the most prompt in returning assignments, whereas those scoring highest on the antisocial practices scale handed in incomplete assignments, made the most excuses, were often late, and dropped out the most from the study.

A third, unpublished study focused on the impact of workbook intervention on anxiety. Two different forms of programmed writing were used with the two experimental groups. In one group, a workbook consisted of detailed questions set in a sequential order. In another group, respondents were asked to write about their anxiety. This approach was similar to an open-ended format developed by Esterling et al. (1999). As in the depression study, students were obtained by announcing the purpose of the study to undergraduates who would volunteer and were willing to admit to being anxious according to the definition of anxiety in the recruitment announcement. After signing a consent form, all volunteers were asked to complete the anxiety content scale of the MMPI-2, which was also readministered at completion of the study. If the respondents' t scores were at or above sixty-five, they were asked to continue in the experiment, whereas those who scored lower than sixty-five were not considered. The seventy-two respondents who remained in the study, thirty-five males and thirty-seven females, were administered the State-Trait Anxiety Inventory (STAI) on a pre- and post-intervention basis.

Respondents were randomly assigned to either the two experimental groups or to the no-intervention control group ($n = 23$). The first experimental group ($n = 26$) received an anxiety workbook derived from the DSM-III-R's definition of generalized anxiety disorder (L'Abate, 1996). It consisted of six assignments. The second experimental group ($n = 23$) was asked to write at least thirty minutes once a week for six weeks about their anxieties at pre-arranged times.

A factorial ANCOVA showed significant ($p < .05$) treatment effects for the MMPI-2 anxiety content scale and the state anxiety of the STAI with no significant interaction effects. Tukey's HSD post hoc comparisons found significant differences ($p < .01$) between scores of experimental and control groups on both the MMPI-2 anxiety content scale and the state scale of the STAI. Consequently, this workbook was effective in reducing state anxiety scores but not trait anxiety. Very likely, a different workbook could be designed to deal more specifically with trait anxiety.

A six-month follow-up found that, of the seventy-two undergraduates who participated in the original study, only fifty-two respondents could be located after six months. Of the remaining fifty-two, twenty-one completed the STAI mailed to them. The size of the follow-up sample was too small to arrive at relevant conclusions. Nonetheless, the experimental group maintained greater change scores than the control group. Note that all previous studies were performed with undergraduates. The next study was performed with psychotherapy outpatients.

Bird

This study was designed to evaluate the effectiveness of psychotherapy and a workbook created to increase self-esteem, self-disclosure, and coping skills (Bird, 1992). Respondents were patients currently in therapy or former patients of three therapists who collaborated in contacting former patients for the purposes of participating in this study. All respondents signed an informed consent form that described the study and gave them the freedom not to participate. A total of thirty-two women and twenty men participated in this study, with eight women and five men in each group. Group 1 was made up of patients who were currently in psychotherapy and who simultaneously completed PDW assignments. Group 2 consisted of patients who participated in psychotherapy without writing assignments. Group 3 included patients who were formerly in psychotherapy (within the last two years) and who completed PDW assignments. Group 4 was a control group of former patients who did not complete PDW assignments. All respondents completed evaluation instruments administered on a pre- and postintervention design format. Evaluation instruments were the Tennessee Self-Concept Scale (TSCS), the Self-Other Profile Chart (SOPC) (L'Abate, 1992, 1994, 1997, 2002; L'Abate and De Giacomo, 2003), and the Coping Resources Inventory for Stress (CRIS).

The workbook included four assignments. Respondents were required to complete one assignment per week for four weeks. Patients in psychotherapy brought in their weekly assignments at each session and discussed them with their therapist, whereas former patients received their weekly assignments through the mail. Each assignment contained a stamped and addressed envelope for returning completed assignments. Writing assignments dealt with the topic of moral and ethical values, the meaning of life, coping with stress, emotional experiences, friendships, family relationships, close relationships, body, health, appearance, attitudes toward sex, identity, past influences, decisions and accomplishments, future life, goals, and decisions. These topics were divided into four writing assignments, each containing three topics, administered in a constant order in what could be called a semistructured rather than programmed writing format. Unlike patients in psychotherapy, former patients were not given any feedback about their writing during the course of the study. However, on request, they were given feedback after they completed the study.

A 2×2 ANCOVA analyzed the significance of results. On the TSCS, only psychotherapy produced a main effect, $F(1, 43) = 5.29$, $p < .05$. For patients currently in psychotherapy, the writing group did not differ significantly from the nonwriting group. On the CRIS, writing produced a significant main effect, $F(1, 47) = 3.94$, $p < .01$. However, among former patients, the writing group did not differ significantly from the nonwriting control group on all three measures. Thus, respondents to the workbook did not differ significantly from the two nonwriting groups on two of the three dependent measures (SOPC and TSCS).

This workbook failed to produced significant results in the two psychotherapy groups, in which the workbook group differed from the nonwriting control group on only one dependent measure. Hence, the mixed results found in this study with current and past psychotherapy patients offer only tentative support for the use of workbooks with clinical populations.

In summary, results from the foregoing studies suggest that workbooks could be used with other psychological interventions, but not as a replacement for psychotherapy, especially in clinical populations. Perhaps they could be used preventively with functional populations that do not need psychotherapy but that could use some alternative approach to psychotherapy, as argued in Chapter 1 and elsewhere (L'Abate, 1990, 2002).

Blatt et al.

An individual differences approach suggests a distinction of the kind suggested by Blatt and his co-workers (Blatt et al., 1982). According to them, depression is related either to overdependency or to self-criticism. To test the validity of a two-factor model of depression and compare it with a self-hood model of personality propensities derived from L'Abate's (1994, 1997) personality theory, Lambert and L'Abate (1996) predicted different levels of depression and differential results as an outcome of two depression workbooks tailored after Blatt et al.'s (1982) model. This study was designed to identify personality differences between improvers and nonimprovers in homework writing assignments matched for personality characteristics.

A call sheet for the study specified that respondents had to admit being depressed, as well as describing symptoms associated with this condition. The study was explained in detail through an informed consent form that described the nature of the study, anonymity, and dropout conditions. Respondents were mailed the test instruments, with instruction on how to return them. No scheduled face-to-face contact with respondents and experimenters took place except by happenstance or, when necessary, by telephone. Experimenters, as was the case in all of these studies, had no knowledge of theories or models under investigation.

Two hundred undergraduates participated in this study in exchange for course credits. Three respondents were dropped because of invalid test scores, leaving a total of 197 respondents. They were administered four self-report instruments on a before-and-after basis. The instruments administered were the Beck Depression Inventory; the Center for Epidemiological Studies-Depression Scale (CES-D), the Depression Experiences Questionnaire (DEQ) developed by Blatt and his co-workers (1982), and the Self-Other Profile Chart, based on L'Abate's (1997, 2002) selfhood model.

The interventions for this study consisted of two written workbooks derived isomorphically from Blatt et al.'s (1982) model. One workbook focused on the nature of depression related self, as seen through hyper-criticalness, whereas the other focused on the interpersonal nature of depression, as seen through overdependency. Both workbooks were distributed randomly via mail to respondents. All test instruments were scored after the workbook intervention was completed. Both depression workbooks consisted of four assignments administered once a week for four weeks. All respondents were randomly assigned to one of three groups: overdependency workbook ($n = 41$), self-criticalness workbook ($n = 31$), and a no-treatment control group ($n = 25$). All respondents, with the exception of one group that also received the DEQ, completed the BDI, CES-D, and the SOPC.

For the BDI completers and noncompleters, pretest scores showed a significant interaction ($p < .01$) between self and other factors. There was a significant main effect for the self factor, indicating that low-self individuals are higher on depression than high-self individuals ($p < .04$), as predicted from

L'Abate's (1997, 2002, 2003, in press) selfhood model. To understand further the nature of this significant interaction, Tukey's HSD procedure was used. The no-self group showed significantly ($p < .05$) higher depression scores than the other three groups. On the CES-D, no significant interaction was observed between self and other factors, but significant main effect ($p < .001$) existed for self.

Sizes and statistical significance of correlations among the tests support the prediction that depression scores are highly related to personality propensities as measured by the SOPC. Furthermore, this matrix showed significant ($p < .01$) correlations among the SOPC self-other measures before and after intervention. The magnitude of these correlations supports the reliability of this rating scale, whereas its negative correlations with both BDI and CES-D support its concurrent validity, even though an intervention occurred between the two time periods.

As far as the two workbooks are concerned, on pretest the three groups did not differ from one another on either the BDI or the CES-D, demonstrating pretreatment equivalence in depression scores. There was a group × time significant interaction on the BDI ($p < .02$) and on the CES-D ($p < .03$). Tukey's procedure was used to understand further the nature of this interaction. The two experimental groups showed significant declines on depression scores on both the BDI ($p < .05$) and CES-D ($p < .05$), whereas the control group scores remained the same. When an ANCOVA was applied to the data set, significant differences were observed on adjusted posttest means for both BDI ($p < .03$) and the CES-D ($p < .001$). On post hoc comparisons, the control group was significantly higher on depression scores than both treatment groups on both tests ($p < .05$). Hedges's Unbiased Effect Sizes were calculated to illustrate the magnitude of the treatment effects. Both workbooks produced high effect sizes: BDI = 1.11, CES-D = .84 for the other (overdependency) workbook, and BDI = .70, CES-D = .66 for the self (criticalness) workbook. The theoretical selfhood model was supported to the extent that low-self individuals showed higher depression scores than high-self individuals.

As suggested by this study, workbooks can be made isomorphic with specific theoretical models, a feature that is absent in less structured forms of DW, such as expressive writing (Pennebaker, 2001; Esterling et al., 1999), and certainly in talk-based psychotherapy.

McMahan and L'Abate

McMahan and L'Abate (2001) studied the effects of two workbooks on personal and marital adjustment of thirty-two seminarian couples, obtaining no effect size ($d = -.012$), suggesting that, at least with this sample, workbooks may have had temporary disruptive effects, as in the case of couples working with the intimacy workbook discussed earlier (L'Abate, 1992). A long-term follow-up would have been necessary to test this hypothesis.

Reed, McMahan, and L'Abate

Reed, McMahan, and L'Abate (2001) are still studying the effects of combining psychotherapy with the social training workbook on incarcerated felons. Even though partial results are promising, they are only one step up from anecdotal evidence since no control group has been used to date and no long-terms results were reported.

Summary of Research Studies

In conclusion, the research efforts summarized earlier include at least three major shortcomings: (1) they were conducted by the author of the workbooks and his collaborators, introducing an evident experimenter bias that raises questions about the validity of these results, (2) they were not published in primary, main-line, refereed journals—they were published instead in secondary works published by the author (L'Abate, 1977, 1983, 1987) or appeared in low-impact journals with little if any refereed feedback, and (3) at least three studies were unpublishable because they produced paradoxically negative results, i.e., control groups did better than experimental groups. These negative results at best suggest, as Pennebaker (2001) found, that expressive, focused DW about one's traumas does, indeed, have disruptive effects on respondents. Another hypothesis for the relative success of control groups is compensatory rivalry. Whether these effects are only immediate and initial rather than long term remains to be seen. Whether these effects are stronger with some individuals than with others also remains to be seen.

Unexpected and paradoxical results obtained from MMPI-2 workbooks, the questionable results obtained by Bird (1992) with outpatients, as well as those with couples reported earlier (L'Abate, 1992), and from McMahan and L'Abate's study (2001) with seminarian couples, suggest that workbooks may not be as beneficial as one would like them to be. The possibility exists that, depending on their content, specific workbooks may elicit pent-up anxieties and issues that were either denied, repressed, or suppressed, as found by Pennebaker (2001) in his studies.

The undeniable fact that in a few studies control groups obtained higher gain scores than experimental groups suggests that this is an important area to investigate in the future. What is the nature of these lowered workbook scores? Are they temporary or long-lasting? Are lowered gain scores indications of an antitherapeutic workbook effect? Consequently, future research would need to evaluate comparatively workbooks developed from different empirical and theoretical sources, to answer the same question asked of psychotherapy: "Which workbook is effective with what problems and populations?" The issue of cost-effectiveness, relevant to psychotherapy, may no longer apply here.

A META-ANALYSIS OF WORKBOOK EFFECTIVENESS

Smyth and L'Abate (2001) performed a meta-analysis of eighteen workbook studies in mental and physical health. The goal of this meta-analysis was to examine this assumption within the limited domain of workbooks. It attempted to determine to what degree workbooks led to improvements in mental and/or physical health. Meta-analytical methods for the cumulation and examination of research studies can thus provide an alternative, and in many ways preferable, approach to evaluate a research literature. However, some unique difficulties were posed by the literature on workbooks. Vast differences existed among studies in overall design and quality of methods and statistics used. A relatively small number of studies contrasted workbooks to a control condition (often a delayed treatment condition).

All studies had to include the use of a workbook in conjunction with, or solely as, therapy (with the explicit aim of producing positive change on some outcome measure). Studies were also required to contain some outcome measure of health, although, for the purposes of this chapter, the authors defined health in the broadest possible terms. Such health outcomes could be in the domain of either mental or physical health, or more general measures of performance (e.g., student grades, cognitive performance). Studies also had to contain statistical information necessary to calculate an effect size.

Following these criteria, eighteen studies were included in this analysis. Magnitude and significance of the overall mean weighted effect size was computed for all outcomes and all studies. One effect size was computed for each study by generating effect sizes for each outcome in the study, and then averaging across all outcomes. These effect sizes were then cumulated across all studies (corrected for bias) for an overall effect size of workbooks.

The overall effect size across all outcomes and all studies was $d = .30$. Considerable variability was observed in effect sizes between studies, ranging from $-.22$ to $+1.16$. Effect size for workbooks alone was $d = .36$, whereas the effect size for workbooks used in conjunction with other treatment was $d = .26$. The difference between these two effect sizes was not significant. The overall effect size for mental health outcomes was $d = .44$. The overall effect size of workbooks on physical health outcomes was $d = .25$. Unlike mental health outcomes, the test for homogeneity of effect sizes was significant.

Results of this analysis, as well as the studies summarized earlier, suggest that workbooks may produce a medium effect size in mental health and a somewhat lower effect size for physical health (although great variability was present for such outcomes). This effect size is quite similar to the one obtained from a recent meta-analysis of psychological treatment in ninety studies conducted across a broad range of clinical settings (mean $d = .41$) (Shadish et al., 2000). This analysis supports the use of workbooks as additions or as alternatives in preventive, psychotherapeutic, and rehabilitative practices, making them ancillary as well as independent methods of intervention. It behooves practitioners using them to include informed consent and pre- and postintervention evaluation as standard operating procedures because of still unresolved professional issues facing this practice.

PROFESSIONAL IMPLICATIONS

Professional implications in the use of DW, workbooks, and Internet interventions, that is, working at a distance from respondents, must focus on at least six relevant areas, including:

1. evaluation;
2. presence;
3. structure, content, and process;
4. ethical and professional issues;
5. the relationship between theory and practice; and
6. the possibly gendered nature of the workbook approach.

First, evaluation can take place at a distance, as available from a variety of sources and with an increasing variety of test instruments (Stamm and Perednia, 2000; Snyder, Lacher, and Wills, 1988). Hence, one can no longer argue about the impossibility of evaluation at a distance from respondents. What one can argue relates to the second implication of working at a distance.

Second, one of the major criticisms leveled against DW relates to the absence of nonverbal cues (voice, gazes, hand and body motions, etc.) in the process of both evaluation and intervention. This criticism has been taken very seriously and counterargued by those who have demonstrated that it is possible to evaluate this variable in more precise ways on the Internet than it is possible in face-to-face situations (Darken et al., 1999; Parks and Roberts, 1998).

Third, most psychological interventions are composed of two sets of skills (L'Abate, 1986, 2002). The first set is the ability to establish and maintain a professional relationship in terms of the old triad of warmth, unconditional regard or acceptance, and empathy, qualities which stem from the personality of the therapist and which constitute style. These qualities may determine, in some still unknown ways, the process of how the intervention will take place. They are content-free and reach above and beyond how interventions should take place. This set of skills falls within the confine of presence, being emotionally available to another human being. A great many publications in the psychotherapy literature, too many to cite, deal with the style of the therapist rather than the substance or content of the interventions. Bohart and Tallman (1999), among many others, would be representative examples of this set of skills.

L'Abate (2002) has questioned the importance of relationship skills (i.e., presence) especially with acting-out and externalizing character disorders, couples, and families. In some cases, especially in externalizations, and perhaps in multirelational systems, these relationship qualities may be even countertherapeutic (Simon, 1998). L'Abate (1986, 1992, 2002) does not question that these skills are relevant in dealing with internalizations, where presence may be more important than method. He has argued that in general both sets of skills are necessary but not necessarily sufficient when talk is used by itself. Furthermore, these skills do not need face-to-face personal contact to be expressed and shared between professionals and respondents. They can be expressed and shared at a distance, through DW and CAIs rather than through talk, as discussed in the previous chapter.

The second set of skills consists of the ability to structure interventions through a method or repeatable sequence of well-defined steps or components, that is, the *substance* or content of interventions. This chapter and the use of workbooks represent and epitomize the second set of skills, constituting a method of intervention. In some cases, yet to be specified, both sets of skills may be necessary for a successful outcome.

The reason for stressing the second set of skills here is not to deny or eliminate the first set. The latter is so exquisitely individual and personal that it cannot be replicated, even though, undoubtedly, there are common factors to it that could be replicated with proper research grants but not by a typical therapist. A method, by definition, is replicable. Workbooks are economical and eminently replicable ad infinitum from one therapist to another and from one setting to another. Of course, if therapy is conceived solely as art or religion, stressing what therapists say or do on faith, without any questions or evaluation, there will not be room for any method. Apparently, the presence and words of the therapist and the alleged establishment of a therapeutic alliance will suffice to guarantee a satisfactory if not successful outcome.

As argued in Chapter 1 and elsewhere, a method may restrict the style of the therapist, but it also allows to conceive of psychological interventions as science rather than as art or religion. In spite of these differences, this writer has argued that both sets of skills—style and process, combined with method and content—may be necessary under certain conditions (L'Abate, 2001a). For instance, with internalizing conditions, practically any positively responsible approach will do well, where perhaps style and process may be more important than method and content. With externalizing conditions, the latter may be more relevant than the former. With serious psychopathology, either set of interventions may need pairing with medication.

Would using a method imply that practically anybody can use it, limiting and even excluding professionals? On the contrary, even and especially at a distance, sensitive and responsible professionals who are attuned to the needs of their respondents are necessary to:

1. determine the nature, background, and situational factors for the referral question, why help is needed at this time, and what kind of help is necessary;
2. establish a therapeutic contract and, after proper evaluation, a signed informed consent form, especially if workbooks, DW, and SCAI are going to be used in the treatment plan;
3. carry out the administration and follow through of weekly, biweekly, SWHAs with proper support and continuous feedback to respondents;
4. read between the lines of what has been written, interpreting not what has been said but what is implied or suggested indirectly;
5. determine objective evaluation of results, and, on the basis of these results;
6. decide what course of action would be most helpful for the respondent and for the referral question.

Using DW/SCAI as methods of intervention does not mean or imply using shortcuts. On the contrary, it means complicating therapeutic issues by adding alternative or additional media of intervention.

Fourth, working at a distance from respondents is replete with possible, likely, and potential ethical and professional issues. These issues have been considered in the extant literature already cited in the previous chapter and elsewhere (L'Abate, 2001a, 2002). An excellent summary of these issues in the practice of telehealth can be found and recommended by Reed, McLaughlin, and Milholland (2000). A responsible and responsive therapist should abide by the ten commandments summarized by these authors, as well as by similar points raised by Maheu, Whitten, and Allen (2001).

Fifth, if workbooks are derived from a particular theory or model, as in the case of depression, negotiation, and intimacy models (L'Abate, 1986, 2001), then theories and models can be evaluated much more directly and more quickly than can be achieved verbally, as in the research summarized earlier concerning Blatt and colleagues (1982) two-factor model of depression. Instead of relatively sterile (from an interventional viewpoint) laboratory research (Jensen, 1999), with no additional characteristics except for the search of the statistical properties of self-report tests, workbooks could become the next interactive step of theory testing through direct interventions. Test instruments, to be sure, are necessary to evaluate outcomes. Workbooks are necessary to produce that outcome and test the theories and models from which they were derived (L'Abate and De Giacomo, 2003).

Sixth, Michele Harway (personal communication, October 18, 2000) argued that "effective expression may be more constrained by workbook therapy in contrast to talk therapy." Harway's prediction that men may feel more comfortable with a structured, workbook approach is in part supported by the findings of L'Abate, L'Abate, and Maino (2004). Women, instead, may prefer talk with a therapist because they value a relationship that may not be available with men. Undoubtedly, this is an interesting and relevant hypothesis that merits serious empirical evaluation, especially in the light of sex differences found in Ganahl's (1981) study (Table 2.4).

CONCLUSION

Combinations of workbooks, computers, and Internet technologies may represent a paradigmatic shift from how traditional mental health practices have been delivered in the past century. These new technologies have the immense potential of reaching more people at risk, in need, or in crisis per unit of professional and paraprofessional time and energy than can been achieved through individual, face-to-face, talk-based interactions between professionals and respondents. There are inherent dangers in working at a distance from respondents. However, these dangers will not be discovered unless various combinations of distance technologies and psychological interventions are applied.

REFERENCES

Alloy, L. B., Abramson, L. Y., Whitehouse, W. G., Hogan, M. E., Tashman, N. A., Steinberg, D. L., and Donovan, P. (1999). Depressogenic cognitive styles: Predictive validity, information processing and personality characteristics, and developmental origins. *Behavior Research and Therapy, 37,* 503-531.

American Psychiatric Association (APA) (1994). *Diagnostic and statistical manual of mental disorders,* Fourth edition. Washington, DC: APA.

Bennett, J. B. (2000). *Time and intimacy: A new science of personal relationships.* Mahwah, NJ: Erlbaum.

Beutler, L. E. (1989). Differential treatment selection: The role of diagnosis in psychotherapy. *Psychotherapy, 26,* 271-281.

Beutler, L. E. and Clarkin, J. F. (1990). *Systematic treatment selection: Toward targeted therapeutic interventions.* New York: Brunner/Mazel.

Bird, G. (1992). Programmed writing as a method for increasing self-esteem, self-disclosure, and coping skills. Doctoral dissertation, Department of Counseling and Psychological Services, Georgia State University, Atlanta, Georgia.

Blatt, S. J., Quinlan, D. M., Chevron, E. S., McDonald, C., and Zuroff, D. (1982). Dependency and criticism: Psychological dimensions of depression. *Journal of Consulting and Clinical Psychology, 50,* 113-124.

Bohart, A. C. and Tallman, K. (1999). *How clients make therapy work: The process of active self-healing.* Washington, DC: American Psychological Association.

Brown, E. C. and L'Abate, L. (1969). An appraisal of teaching machines and programmed instruction. In C. M. Franks (Ed.), *Behavior therapy: Appraisal and status* (pp. 396-414). New York: McGraw-Hill.

Clark, L. A. (1990). Toward a consensual set of symptom clusters for assessment of personality disorders. In J. H. Butcher and C. D. Spielberger (Eds.), *Advances in personality assessment* (pp. 243-266). Hillsdale, NJ: Erlbaum.

Clark, D. and L'Abate, L. (1977). Enrichment and tape recordings with couples. In L. L'Abate (Ed.), *Enrichment: Structured interventions with couples, families, and groups* (pp. 203-213). Washington, DC: University Press of America.

Darken, R. P., Bernatovich, D., Lawson, J. P., and Person, B. (1999). Quantitative measures of presence in virtual environments: The roles of attention and spatial comprehension. *CyberPsychology and Behavior, 2,* 337-347.

Davis, R. D. and Millon, T. (1999). Models of personality and its disorders. In T. Millon, T. H. Blaney, and R. D. Davis (Eds.), *Oxford textbook of psychopathology* (pp. 485-522). New York: Oxford University Press.

Detweiler, J. B. and Whisman, M. A. (1999). The role of homework assignments in cognitive therapy for depression: Potential methods for enhancing adherence. *Clinical Psychology: Science and Practice, 6,* 267-282.

Dozois, D. J. A., Dobson, K. S., and Ahnberg, J. L. (1998). A psychometric evaluation of the Beck Depression Inventory-II. *Psychological Assessment, 10,* 83-89.

Esterling, B. A., L'Abate, L., Murray, E., and Pennebaker, J. M. (1999). Empirical foundations for writing in prevention and psychotherapy: Mental and physical outcomes. *Clinical Psychology Review, 19,* 79-96.

Faustman, W. O. and Overall, J. E. (1999). Brief psychiatric rating scale. In M. E. Maruish (Ed.), *The use of psychological testing for treatment planning and outcomes assessment* (pp. 791-830). Mahwah, NJ: Erlbaum.

Fishman, S. (1997). *The copyright handbook: How to protect and use written works.* Berkeley, CA: Nolo Press.

Ganahl, G. F. (1981). Effects of client, treatment, and therapist variables on the outcome of structured marital enrichment. Doctoral dissertation, Georgia State University, Atlanta.

Goldberg, L. R. (1999). The Curious Experiences Survey: A revised version of the Dissociative Experiences Scale: Factor structure, reliability, and relations to demographic and personality variables. *Psychological Assessment, 11,* 134-145.

Greene, R. L. and Clopton, J. R. (1999). Minnesota Multiphasic Personality Inventory (MMPI-2). In M. E. Maruish (Ed.), *The use of psychological testing for treatment planning and outcomes assessment* (pp. 1023-1050). Mahwah, NJ: Erlbaum.

Hurt, S. W., Reznikoff, M., and Clarkin, J. F. (1991). *Psychological assessment, psychiatric diagnosis, treatment planning.* New York: Brunner/Mazel.

Jensen, P. S. (1999). Links among theory, research, and practice: Cornerstone of clinical scientific progress. *Journal of Clinical Child Psychology, 28,* 553-557.

Kerns, J. G. and Berenbaum, H. (2000). Aberrant semantic and affective processing in people at risk for psychosis. *Journal of Abnormal Psychology, 109,* 728-732.

Kobak, K. A. and Reynolds, W. M. (1999). Hamilton Depression Inventory. In M. E. Maruish (Ed.), *The use of psychological testing for treatment planning and outcomes assessment* (pp. 935-970). Mahwah, NJ: Erlbaum.

Kochalka, J. and L'Abate, L. (1997). Linking evaluation with structured enrichment: The Family Profile Form. *American Journal of Family Therapy, 25,* 361-374.

Kosson, D. S., Steuerwald, B. L., Forth, A. E., and Kirkhart, K. J. (1997). A new method for assessing the interpersonal behavior of psychopathic individuals: Preliminary validation studies. *Psychological Assessment, 9,* 89-101.

L'Abate, L. (1973). The laboratory method in clinical child psychology: Three applications. *Journal of Clinical Child Psychology, 2,* 8-10.

L'Abate, L. (1977). *Enrichment: Structured interventions with couples, families, and groups.* Washington, DC: University Press of America.

L'Abate, L. (1983). *Family psychology: Theory, therapy, and training.* Washington, DC: University Press of America.

L'Abate, L. (1985). Structured enrichment (SE) with couples and families. *Family Relations, 34,* 169-175.

L'Abate, L. (1986). *Systematic family therapy.* New York: Brunner/Mazel.

L'Abate, L. (1987). *Family psychology II: Theory, therapy, enrichments, and training.* Lanham, MD: University Press of America.

L'Abate, L. (1990). *Building family competence: Primary and secondary prevention strategies.* Newbury Park, CA: Sage.

L'Abate, L. (1991). The use of writing in psychotherapy. *American Journal of Psychotherapy, 45,* 87-98.

L'Abate, L. (1992). *Programmed writing: A self-administered approach for interventions with individuals, couples, and families.* Pacific Grove, CA: Brooks/Cole.

L'Abate, L. (1994). *A theory of personality development.* New York: Wiley.

L'Abate, L. (1995). The use of notes in psychotherapy: A survey. Unpublished papers, Department of Psychology, Georgia State University, Atlanta.

L'Abate, L. (1996). Workbooks for better living. Available at <www.mentalhealthhelp.com>.

L'Abate, L. (1997). *The self in the family: A classification of personality, criminality, and psychopathology.* New York: Wiley.

L'Abate, L. (1999). Programmed distance writing in therapy with acting-out adolescents. In C. Schaefer (Ed.), *Innovative psychotherapy techniques in child and adolescent therapy* (pp. 108-157). New York: Wiley.

L'Abate, L. (2001a). Distance writing (DW) and computer-assisted interventions (CAI) in psychiatry and mental health. In L. L'Abate (Ed.), *Distance writing and computer-assisted interventions in psychiatry and mental heath* (pp. 3-31). Westport, CT: Ablex.

L'Abate, L. (2001b). Psychoeducational strategies. In J. Carlson and L. Sperry (Eds.), *Brief therapy strategies with individuals and couples* (pp. 346-396). Phoenix, AZ: Zeig/Tucker.

L'Abate, L. (2002). *Beyond psychotherapy: Programmed writing and structured computer-assisted interventions.* Westport, CT: Ablex.

L'Abate, L. (2003). *Family psychology III: Theory building, theory testing, and psychological interventions.* Lanham, MD: University Press of America.

L'Abate, L., Boyce, J., Fraizer, L., and Russ, D. A. (1992). Programmed writing: Research in progress. *Comprehensive Mental Health Care, 2,* 45-62.

L'Abate, L. and De Giacomo, P. (2003). *Intimate relationships and how to improve them: Integration of theoretical models with prevention and psychotherapy.* Westport, CT: Ablex.

L'Abate, L. and Kern, R. (2002). Workbooks: Tools for the expressive writing paradigm. In S. J. Lepore and J. M. Smyth (Eds.), *The writing cure: How expressive writing promotes health and emotional well-being* (pp. 239-255). Washington, DC: American Psychological Association.

L'Abate, L. and Weinstein, S. E. (1987). *Structured enrichment programs for couples and families.* New York: Brunner/Mazel.

L'Abate, L. and Young, L. (1987). *Casebook of structured enrichment programs for couples and families.* New York: Brunner/Mazel.

Lambert, R. G. and L'Abate, L. (1996). Changing depression test scores through programmed writing: A test of a selfhood model of personality propensities. Paper read at the Annual Meeting of the American Psychological Association, August 9, Toronto, Canada.

Lepore, S. J. and Smyth, J. (Eds.) (2002). *The writing cure: How expressive writing influences health and well-being.* Washington, DC: American Psychological Association.

Levy, C. M. and Ransdell, S. (Eds.) (1996). *The science of writing: Theories, methods, individual differences, and applications.* Mahwah, NJ: LEA.

Levy, R. L. and Shelton, J. L. (1990). Tasks in brief therapy. In R. A. Wells and V. J. Giannetti (Eds.), *Handbook of the brief psychotherapies* (pp. 145-163). New York: Wiley.

Livesley, W. J., Jackson, D. N., and Schroeder, M. L. (1989). A study of the factorial structure of personality pathology. *Journal of Personality Disorders, 3,* 292-306.

Maheu, M., Whitten, P., and Allen, A. (2001). *Health, telehealth, and telemedicine: A practical guide to startup and success.* San Francisco, CA: Jossey-Bass.

McMahan, O. and L'Abate, L. (2001). Programmed distance writing with seminarian couples. In L. L'Abate (Ed.), *Distance writing and computer-assisted interventions in psychiatry and mental heath* (pp. 135-156). Westport, CT: Ablex.

Moras, K., Di Nardo, P. A., and Barlow, D. H. (1992). Distinguishing anxiety and depression: Reexamination of the reconstructed Hamilton scales. *Psychological Assessment, 4,* 224-227.

Morley, L. C. (1999). Personality Assessment Inventory. In M. E. Maruish (Ed.), *The use of psychological testing for treatment planning and outcomes assessment* (pp. 1083-1122). Mahwah, NJ: Erlbaum.

Mueser, K. T., Curran, P. J., and McHugo, G. J. (1997). Factor structure of the Brief Psychiatric Rating Scale in Schizophrenia. *Psychological Assessment, 9,* 196-204.

Najavits, L. M., Weiss, R. D., Shaw, S. R., and Dierberger, A. E. (2000). Psychotherapists' views of treatment manuals. *Professional Psychology: Research and Practice, 31,* 404-408.

National Depressive and Manic-Depressive Association (2001). *Family Therapy News,* February-March.

Norcross, J. C., Santrock, J. W., Campbell, L. F., Smith, T. P., Sommer, R., and Zuckerman, E. L. (2000). *Authoritative guide to self-help resources in mental health.* New York: Guilford.

Parks, M. R. and Roberts, L. D. (1998). "Making moosic": The development of personal relationships online and a comparison to their offline counterparts. *Journal of Social and Personal Relationships, 15,* 517-537.

Pennebaker, J. M. (2001). Explorations into the health benefits of disclosure: Inhibitory, cognitive, and social processes. In L. L'Abate (Ed.), *Distance writing and computer-assisted interventions in psychiatry and mental health* (pp. 34-44). Westport, CT: Ablex.

Primakoff, L., Epstein, N., and Covi, L. (1986). Homework compliance: An uncontrolled variable in cognitive therapy outcomes research. *Behavioral Therapy, 17,* 443-446.

Reed, G. M., McLaughlin, C. J., and Milholland, K. (2000). Ten interdisciplinary principles for professional practice in telehealth: Implications for psychology. *Professional Psychology: Research and Practice, 31,* 170-178.

Reed, R., McMahan, O., and L'Abate, L. (2001). Workbooks and psychotherapy with incarcerated felons: Research in progress. In L. L'Abate (Ed.), *Distance writing and computer-assisted interventions in psychiatry and mental heath* (pp. 157-167). Westport, CT: Ablex.

Sajatovic, M. and Ramirez, L. F. (2001). *Rating scales in mental health*. Hudson, OH: Lexi-Comp.

Seligman, M. E. P. (1998). Why therapy works. *Psychological Monitor*, December 2.

Selvini-Palazzoli, M., Boscolo, L., Cecchin, G. E., and Prata, G. (1978). *Paradox and counterparadox*. New York: Brunner/Mazel.

Shadish, W. R., Matt, G. E., Navarro, A. M., and Phillips, G. (2000). The effects of psychological therapies under clinically representative conditions: A meta-analysis. *Psychological Bulletin, 126*, 512-529.

Shelton, J. L. and Levy, R. L. (1981). *Behavioral assignments and treatment compliance: A handbook of clinical strategies*. Champaign, IL: Research Press.

Sheppard, L. C. and Teasdale, J. D. (2000). Dysfunctional thinking in major depressive disorder: A deficit in metacognitive monitoring? *Journal of Abnormal Psychology, 109*, 768-776.

Simon, L. (1998). Do offender treatments work? *Applied and Preventive Psychology, 7*, 137-159.

Smyth, J. M. (1998). Written emotional expression: Effect size, outcome types, and moderating variables. *Journal of Consulting and Clinical Psychology, 66*, 174-184.

Smyth, J. M. and L'Abate, L. (2001). A meta-analytic evaluation of workbook effectiveness in physical and mental health. In L. L'Abate (Ed.), *Distance writing and computer-assisted interventions in psychiatry and mental health* (pp. 77-90). Westport, CT: Ablex.

Snyder, D. K., Lacher, D., and Wills, R. M. (1988). Computer-based interpretation of the Marital Satisfaction Inventory: Use in treatment planning. *Journal of Marital and Family Therapy, 14*, 397-409.

Stamm, B. H. and Perednia, D. A. (2000). Evaluating psychosocial aspects of telemedicine and telehealth systems. *Professional Psychology: Research and Practice, 31*, 184-189.

Wagner, V. and L'Abate, L. (1977). Enrichment and written homework assignments with couples. In L. L'Abate (Ed.), *Enrichment: Structured interventions with couples, families, and groups* (pp. 184-202). Washington, DC: University Press of America.

Wagner, V., Lockridge, J., Hardin, S., Gallope, R. H., Sloan, S., and L'Abate, L. (1977). Linear and circular models: Combination of enrichment and written interpretations with couples. In L. L'Abate (Ed.), *Enrichment: Structured interventions with couples, families, and groups* (pp. 214-237). Washington, DC: University Press of America.

Wagner, V., Weeks, G., and L'Abate, L. (1980). Enrichment and written messages with couples. *American Journal of Family Therapy, 8*, 36-44.

Weeks, G. R. and L'Abate, L. (1982). *Paradoxical psychotherapy: Theory and practice with individuals, couples, and families*. New York: Brunner/Mazel.

Weintraub, M. D. (1981). *Verbal behavior: Adaptations in psychopathology*. New York: Springer.

Wildman, R. W. II (1977). Structured versus unstructured marital interventions. In L. L'Abate (Ed.), *Enrichment: Structured interventions with couples, families, and groups* (pp. 154-183). Washington, DC: University Press of America.

Wilson, K. A., de Beurs, E., Palmer, C. A., and Chambless, D. L. (1999). Beck Anxiety Inventory. In M. E. Maruish (Ed.), *The use of psychological testing for treatment planning and outcomes assessment* (pp. 971-992). Mahwah, NJ: Erlbaum.

SECTION II:
INDIVIDUALS

Chapter 3

Dementia, Depression, and Workbooks: A Personal Odyssey

Everett Gorman

The purpose of this chapter is to describe the results of two workbook applications taken from L'Abate (1992). The contexts for these two applications were from individual therapeutic practice in treating depression that I experienced and the results of a program aimed at developing impulse control behavior within a group of adult offenders.

The impulse control application followed the programmed writing approach described by L'Abate (1992). From 1992 to 1995 I was working as a psychologist in a federal prison in Alberta, Canada. A fellow psychologist referred me to a text by McCown, Johnson, and Shure (1994). In this text I came upon L'Abate's (1992) reference to his programmed writing approach. It was also during this time that I purchased and used this approach in my work with federal offenders to address the problem of impulsive behavior. I employed the sixteen assignments of the social training workbook taken from the case of JEF described in the Appendix (L'Abate, 1992).

Two methods were used in my study, including writing assignments and face-to-face contact and feedback with each offender. The procedures included administration of the Basic Personality Inventory (BPI), which was developed and validated using norms for Canadian offenders. The BPI was administered on a pre- and posttest basis to ten offenders who volunteered to participate in what was called and described as an impulse control preventive program.

Pre- and posttest scores for each individual were gathered and analyzed using a group t-test. A significant difference was found between pre- and posttest scores. Based on these results it was recommended that the impulse control program be continued and evaluation of the results be published (Reed, McMahan, and L'Abate, 2001) even though no control group was established. Unfortunately, I was unable to carry on due to medical reasons, which led to early retirement from the prison system. This in turn led to the second application of programmed writing, which is described here.

THE PROBLEM OF DEPRESSION

The second application employed assignments found in L'Abate (1992). At the time, I was dealing with a personal bout of depression resulting from burnout that had resulted in my early retirement. The workbook assignments were used as a guided self-directed learning project based on my own experiences with depression. Each assignment focused on and documented the feelings I experienced over a period of four weeks.

Background to the Problem of Depression:
A Personal Odyssey

The following is a brief chronology of the problem I experienced. The seeds of my depression began when I was working as a college instructor and began noticing signs that my memory was slipping. I would miss appointments and meetings, getting dates mixed up. I also noticed that I would get angry and frustrated because I could not understand why I was having difficulty remembering such small details. It was the winter of 1991, and I was completing the last steps toward my doctorate. My ability to get this far with a full-time workload, family responsibilities, and all the other pressures I experienced was due primarily to the support and assistance of my wonderful wife and helpmate Mariette. Although I knew that I had taken on an impossible load, I was determined to finish, and with her helping hand and support, I knew I had a chance.

The fall trimester passed quickly and I was able to complete a rough draft of my dissertation in time for Christmas. All was not well at the college because my administrative and teaching skills began to slip and lapses in attention to details resulted in performance issues being reported to my boss, the chair of the Criminal Justice Program. Although my teaching skills suffered, my research skills and writing skills seemed to be becoming sharper and stronger. Understandably, my performance at the college was being judged primarily on the output of the former not the latter. Based on feedback from my colleagues who were becoming frustrated with my attitude toward them and the program, I was viewed by others, including administrators at the college, as the proverbial "pain in the butt."

Completing the doctorate became my obsession and coping with stress became my nemesis. I was like Sisyphus, the legendary king in Greek mythology who has often been depicted in the classical literature as the absurd hero. Like this man, I was (metaphorically) sentenced to repeatedly push a rock to the top of a mountain and then watch its descent.

The winter of discontent was cold and cruel, but I pushed on toward completion of the dissertation one chapter at a time. I began to see the end or summit of this self-imposed mountain-climbing obsession. My wife Mariette went on a long-overdue holiday to Hawaii with her mother, and my daughter Christine went away on a student exchange program to the province of Quebec. My son Andrew kept me busy, but he was now twenty-one and becoming more independent, living in an apartment of his own. This helped relieve the pressures on the home front and gave me time for the last big push. With my final chapter completed by the end of March 1991, I waited for final approval from my dissertation committee at Nova Southeastern University in Fort Lauderdale, Florida.

On the front line at work the situation went from bad to worse. I was under increased fire from my colleagues who by this time had reached the end of their patience with me because of my lack of attention to work details. Knowing that the end was nigh, my rationalization was that I would take my lumps and recoup my losses during the spring trimester when the teaching and administrative load at the college was minimal. This would give me time to graduate with the doctorate, rest a bit during the summer, and start afresh in the fall. In April 1991, I received official word that all requirements for the doctorate were met.

There was only one more hurdle to overcome: getting the college to recognize the doctorate for salary purposes. Up to this point, the only way for instructors to further their postgraduate education was to take the traditional PhD or a doctorate based solely upon approval of the University of Alberta. I requested that the university evaluate my EdD from Nova Southeastern University. A closed meeting was arranged with the college, the university, and Nova Southeastern University. The following week a meeting was held between the three parties with a lawyer from Nova Southeastern University's legal department. I was not invited to attend, nor was I told what had transpired. But after the meeting was over, the president of the faculty association knocked on my door to report that the university had approved my degree and it could be used for academic and salary purposes.

The following day, I was taken by ambulance to the Grey Nuns Hospital for observation because I thought I was having a heart attack. The diagnosis at that time was that I had suffered a major physical and emotional breakdown and depression. My family doctor gave me a doctor's excuse and ordered an MRI because she wanted to get as much evidence as she could to support the diagnosis. The MRI showed some structural abnormalities in my brain. After a complete medical evaluation, the doctor concluded that I was suffering from major acute depression and immediately prescribed antidepressant medication. I was placed on long-term disability, on which I remained for one year.

By the end of the one-year recuperation, I told my doctor that I felt I could return to work, despite my feelings of extreme vulnerability. I felt like an animal left alone to die in the desert of starvation and thirst. Soon, the vultures began to circle overhead, realizing that my tenured position, the only one left, would soon be vacant and ripe for the picking, and my twenty-year life as a college instructor was probably over. I decided not to stay in the same spot and get away from my vulnerable position. I made a few phone calls to my psychology colleagues in the prison system, and the Alberta Solicitor General Psychology Department rescued me just in time. They offered me a position as a full-time psychologist at Grande Cache, Alberta, which is located in the heart of the Canadian Rockies. In the beginning, this new location became my sanctuary and deliverance. I applied for a leave of absence from the college, which was immediately granted. My absence was based on a one-year leave without pay. Everyone was happy, and the result was a win-win situation. There followed three rewarding years as a prison psychologist. I was free to innovate and had control over my own destiny once again.

This experience of Selfulness, as described by L'Abate (1997, 2002, 2003, in press) in his Selfhood model, came to an abrupt end in the summer of 1995 when the Alberta provincial solicitor general decided to sell the Grande Cache Institution to the Federal Department of Corrections of Canada. My position and all my resources were transferred, and I became the sole property of the Federal Canadian Corrections System. This transfer became a disaster for any hope of ending my career with them on a positive note. I knew the Federal System of Corrections well since I had worked for them from 1970 to 1978. Suffice it to say that the summer of 1995 was a turning point in my life.

That summer my life as a psychologist began to unravel at an alarming rate. First, the new deputy warden decided that health care and psychology did not belong together, which resulted in the breakup of our team of psychiatric nurses. Second, this resulted in the loss of secretarial support. The federal corrections solution was to provide each psychologist with a computer, which replaced secretarial help. Health care and psychology became separate units. I was lost without training on how to use the new federal computer system. My production of reports began to fall short of the quota. New procedures were introduced to my responsibilities of overseeing our segregation unit without any discussion of the changes. I soon began to make mistakes and was assigned new duties. I was told that a person with a doctorate should be able to manage without any training. It soon became clear to me that the writing was on the wall and my days at Grande Cache were numbered. I began to feel the symptoms of depression beginning to develop again. I had already experienced enough stress and the old negative feelings of fear and anger began to surface again. My wife helped me cope, but the stress became too intense and unbearable. I finally went to my doctor who immediately referred me to the hospital for evaluation. The final psychiatric assessment was dementia of the Alzheimer type combined with depression. It was at this time that I began my prescribed treatment and was placed on a permanent medical pension.

COMPLETING PERSONAL ASSIGNMENTS FOR DEPRESSION

At this time I began my writing program for depression developed by L'Abate (1992). The primary method was self-study. The following questions were answered over a period of four weeks and helped me cope with my major depression. For purposes of illustrating how I used the workbook, I will describe my answers to the following questions.

1. *Depression means different things to different people. What does depression mean to you? Please describe it as you see it.* Depression for me can be explained by using the following analogy: When I go into a state of depression it is analogous to driving a vehicle and suddenly I feel my tires going flat one by one. Soon, I realize that I can no longer control the vehicle because of the following problems: steering is difficult, my reaction time and braking ability become slow, I become aware that I am no longer capable of driving. Fear, panic, and anger begin to flood my mind and it becomes necessary to pull over to the side of the road until my outlook becomes positive. The best way to deal with these feelings of depression is to take my medication and sleep. This downtime lasts between three to four weeks, after which my mind and body begin to synchronize and I begin to feel better and more in control of my life. My feelings and attitude gradually become more positive and I feel capable of navigating the highway of daily living.

2. *Following is a list of feelings related to depression. Which of these feelings apply specifically to you?* The feelings that apply specifically to me are:
   - *Feeling blue:* I begin to feel down in the dumps. My energy level drops and I find it difficult to get out of bed. I do not seem to have a "why" to live for. I therefore sleep in and miss the better part of the day.
   - *Uncertainty about the future:* Without a "why" to live for I begin to lose motivation and my future seems to become clouded with the

feeling of uncertainty. This often results in a lack of confidence in my ability to cope with tasks of daily living.

- *Lack of interest in living:* The lack of confidence in my ability to cope with the tasks of daily living further erodes my motivation to get out and do everyday tasks.
- *Feeling hopeless and empty:* When I go into this depressed state I sometimes feel that my life is hopeless. My career is over and I have been a failure and I have no future.
- *Broodiness:* When I am in my depressed state I sometimes brood over my predicament. I begin to feel sorry for myself and become angry with myself and sometimes blame others. I think, "If only they understood that my depression is related to my dementia and that I would not be this way if I was not inflicted with this horrible disease or mental illness." This sometimes leads to me becoming angry and blaming others, and this is when I begin to act like a pain in the butt. This drives my wife sometimes to her wits' end, and places stress on our marital relationship.
- *Unhappiness:* When I begin to feel down, my feelings sometimes turn to despair and I feel very unhappy with my life and situation. However, when I look at the positive aspects of my life, which are many, I find it easier to accept my predicament and this feeling of unhappiness diminishes.
- *Crying often:* I must say that I seldom cry about my situation. The time I remember crying was the day I received my diagnosis that I had dementia. I remember feeling angry and sorry for myself. I remember saying to myself, "Why me?" I was sitting in my beautiful two-bedroom condominium, well heated and furnished, warm and comfortable. Then I stood up and walked to the window. I looked first at the thermometer, which indicated the outside temperature to be –30° Celsius, then my eye caught sight of this old man very shabbily dressed who was retrieving empty beer cans and bottles from a large garbage bin in the side alley below. I remember after I saw this scene, saying to myself, "Why *not* me? I am no more special than anyone else. Look at that poor old man out there freezing in the cold." Then I realized I was sitting in a comfortable home, with a great wife who has stuck with me through all this, a beautiful daughter who has given me a sweet little granddaughter, and a son who loves and cares about me. How lucky a man I really was. What was I whining about? I have too many blessings to enjoy. My tears at that point dried up and disappeared.
- *Thinking of killing oneself:* Although this idea has crossed my mind when I was deep in a depressed state, I have never tried or at-

tempted suicide in my life. I guess I have too much to live for and therefore suicide is not an alternative I would choose.

- *Wishing to be dead:* I must admit that when I came home from seeing my neurologist the day I was told that I had dementia of the Alzheimer type I did feel as if I had been sentenced to death. However, after experiencing the episode described earlier under "crying often," my death wish turned to a resolve of making the best out of my life.
- *Lacking supports:* My family and friends have always been supportive. However, there were times at work that I felt not supported. For example, the college cut off financial support when I was pursuing my doctorate and did not support it for salary purposes until Nova University threatened the University of Alberta and the college with a legal action.

3. *Now rank the feelings just listed, giving a 1 to the feeling that is the strongest for you, a 2 to the second strongest feeling, and so on.*
   1. Feeling blue
   2. Uncertainty about the future
   3. Feeling hopeless and empty
   4. Broodiness
   5. Unhappiness
   6. Lacking supports
   7. Thinking of killing myself
   8. Lack of interest in living
   9. Crying often
   10. Wishing to be dead

Assignment for Week One

Focus on the feeling you rated number 1. FEELING BLUE. This blue feeling will usually occur when I feel my self-esteem beginning to deflate. It seems to happen gradually and becomes progressively worse when I dwell on negative thoughts and ideas such as, I cannot cope with the stresses today, I have so many things to do but do not have the energy to cope with the load of daily living. I begin to forget where I leave things, e.g., keys, letters, briefcase. I cannot get up out of bed in the morning and decide to sleep in. I think to myself that when I awake the blue feelings will be gone. I awake and feel even worse. I fear that I am getting behind and will not be able to catch up to my tasks of daily living. I do not go for my daily walks, and I stop visiting or talking with friends and people in general. I become a recluse and spend my waking hours worrying about my health, whether I will ever get over this blue feeling hanging over me like a dark cloud. I see darkness and feel hopeless. I keep wondering when will I see the light again. I take my medication, which helps me sleep. This seems to be the only thing that will help me cope with the blue feelings.

Assignment for Week Two

Focus on the feeling you rated number 2. UNCERTAINTY ABOUT THE FUTURE. This depressive feeling lasted for about another week. It seems to develop from my worry over my diagnosis dementia of the Alzheimer type. In my mind it is like a death sentence. The uncertainty about my future, how long I have to live, and how my wife will cope with my disease are my main concerns. The more I read about Alzheimer's the more bleak becomes my picture of my future and the greater the uncertainty of how my wife will be able to cope with the burden of caregiving. I have been told that in the later stages of the disease the stress on the caregiver increases. Finally, it becomes necessary to place the Alzheimer's patient in an institution. The feelings of uncertainty about how my family will cope becomes my main concern and worry at this point. This feeling does not seem to want to go away. Nothing seems to help to make this feeling go away.

Assignment for Week Three

Focus on the feeling you rated number 3. FEELING HOPELESS AND EMPTY. These feelings seem to stem from a loss of independence. When I was told that I could not drive a vehicle I was very upset because driving a car symbolized for me freedom and independence. I began to feel a great sense of loss. Now I was to become dependent and my freedom to go places was limited. In my own mind I felt capable of driving, but how could I prove this to others? I decided to be assessed by an organization called Driveable, which was set up to determine whether persons with dementia had the cognitive skills to operate a motor vehicle. I took the cognitive skills test, which involved making judgments and decisions based on problems and situations simulated by a computer program. The cognitive skills test was then followed up with a standard road test. The day of the road test it snowed heavily, but I attempted to drive under these unfavorable road conditions. Despite the adverse weather, I was able to navigate through the city, on the freeway, and through the downtown district and return safely to the Driveable office without any major mishaps. A report on my test results was sent to my doctor. When I called him for the results, he said, "Congratulations, you passed the tests with flying colors." My feelings of hopelessness and emptiness went away. I felt more empowered and capable now that I was able to drive again.

Assignment for Week Four

Focus on the feeling you rated number 4. BROODINESS. I decided that I would be up front with people about my diagnosis of early stage Alzheimer's disease. This, however, resulted in being rejected by some members of my family, friends, and colleagues. This rejection caused me to begin to develop a feeling of broodiness. Some of them said, "You don't have Alzheimer's disease—there is nothing wrong with your memory, you are articulate and just can't convince us that you have it." My mother and father told me they were convinced I was faking it. This reaction by them made me brood even more, and I interpreted this denial of my condition as a deeper feeling of broodiness and rejection. I just stated to others what the neurologist had concluded from the MRI results from 1999. I related these feelings of anger and resentment to my neurologist who decided to have me take another MRI in February 2002. The new results confirmed that the size of the atrophy found in the prefrontal lobe of my brain had not changed. This finding brought into question the early-stage Alzheimer's diagnosis. The doctors concluded, therefore, that it was dementia of another type, and said that it was impossible to accurately diagnose what type at that time. This change in diagnosis helped lower some of the feelings of broodiness that I felt from the rejection of me based on the original diagnosis. However, a burning question still remained: What exactly was the cause of my illness?

CONCLUSION

The process of writing this chapter has had some very significant effects on my self-awareness. Looking back on the events and actions that I have taken helped me realize that in many ways I have moved from a position of immaturity to a more mature Selful position in my life. This movement or development was central to the model of personality development described by L'Abate (1997). In the beginning of my odyssey, I was an immature, selfish, and young professional psychologist with many noble causes to fight for. In the end, writing about my battle with dementia and depression marked for me the call to become a more humble, Selful, and mature person. I have learned to accept my limitations and live more peacefully for my noble causes.

Writing about this experience provided me with material to search for answers to my problem and helped me to face life's struggles, which have given deeper meaning to my life. A major breakthrough came when I began volunteering for the Alzheimer Society of Edmonton (ASE). I was asked to tell my story of hope to patients in the Edmonton area who have been diagnosed with early-stage Alzheimer's disease. Talking to them about the role that writing has played in helping me better understand myself and strengthening the mind gives them some hope that they too may use writing to slow down the process of this debilitating disease. Although no cure exists, exercising the mind helps stimulate the neuropathways in the brain. The executive director and program director of the ASE have approached me to develop a program that would use programmed writing as a means of follow-up to allow professionals to keep in touch with their patients via the Internet.

Writing this chapter has helped me to identify specific feelings related to my periods of depression, which covered a time period of approximately four weeks. The assignments helped me focus on the four most prominent feelings experienced during my episodes of depression. They also helped me focus my attention on the dynamics of my behavior, allowed me to increase my awareness of what depression means to me, and increased my understanding of how the feelings developed, what triggered these feelings, and what strategies and activities helped to make these feelings go away. I have learned to cope more effectively with my depression. In the beginning, the period of depression lasted for almost four weeks. Completing the homework assignments helped me manage the depression more efficiently and decrease the length of the depressive episodes to one to two weeks. The results support the efficacy of program writing in the treatment of depression and dementia.

REFERENCES

L'Abate, L. (1992). *Programmed writing: A self-administered approach for interventions with individuals, couples, and families.* Pacific Grove, CA: Brooks/Cole.

L'Abate, L. (1997). *The self in the family: A classification of personality, criminality, and psychopathology.* New York: Wiley.

McCown, W., Johnson, J. L., and Shure, M. B. (Eds.) (1994). *The impulsive client: Theory, research, and treatment.* Washington, DC: American Psychological Association.

Reed, R., McMahan, O., and L'Abate, L. (2001). Workbooks and psychotherapy with incarcerated fellows. In L. L'Abate (Ed.), *Distance writing and computer-assisted interventions in psychiatry and mental health* (pp. 156-167). Westport, CT: Ablex.

Chapter 4

Life-Challenging Conditions and Helpers

Rubin Battino

About fourteen years ago I read Siegel's (1986) *Love, Medicine, and Miracles*. After reading the book, perhaps as a midlife crisis of conscience, I asked myself, "Rubin, you have all of these skills as a therapist, why aren't you using them to help people with serious diseases?" This led me to track down the Charlie Brown Exceptional Patient Support Group in Dayton, Ohio. They follow Siegel's precepts in their group and kindly allowed me to attend their semimonthly meetings. Eventually, I led my own support group for people with life-challenging diseases and their caregivers, and when that group folded I joined the Charlie Brown group as one of the facilitators.

I am frequently asked how I can do this work as a volunteer. "Doesn't it get you down?" Actually, the opposite is true—I always leave the meetings feeling uplifted by the incredible power of the human spirit and the bravery of my friends, who continually instruct me about hope and love and living in the moment. Paradoxical as it may seem, just about every one of my friends with a serious disease has said at some time, "You know, this has been a blessing." This strange statement comes out of the awareness that the cancer, for example, has forced them to be actively cognizant of their lives, love and loving, the environment, relationships, and what is really important, and given them a perspective that makes each moment and each day a special experience to be lived with heightened awareness. Our support group is a sharing and caring one in which people can say whatever they wish and know that they are being heard by others who have lived and are living through the same challenges. Viktor Frankl has written (1984) about the incredible power of the human spirit to find meaning when unexpected and uncontrollable bad things happen.

About three years ago, on a visit to Atlanta, my old friend and colleague Luciano L'Abate told me about the work he was doing in structured (or distance) writing. I read what he gave me with great excitement, for I immediately recognized the potential for expanding the work of the support group and the private volunteer work I do to a much larger population. A major difference between L'Abate et al.'s (1986, 1992) workbooks and those developed for my intended population is that these workbooks are intended for private personal use and are only shared (in part or otherwise) with others at the writer's discretion. So, these workbooks are more in the nature of a structured diary or journal than an extension of a psychotherapy session. In the loneliness and isolation of having a life-challenging disease, being a caregiver, or grieving, these workbooks are designed to organize the writer's thinking and emotions and responses.

Earlier versions of the three workbooks appear in Battino (2000, 2001). In this chapter they will be described separately. The results of a brief survey are then reported. (Unfortunately, there was neither time nor resources to carry out a proper evaluation.) A case history is presented of a woman with whom I worked intensively. Finally, some concluding comments and recommendations are made.

DESCRIPTION OF WORKBOOKS

The "style" of these workbooks has been influenced by my training in Ericksonian hypnosis and psychotherapy, a background in solution-focused brief therapy, the use of guided imagery for healing, the uses of metaphor for psychotherapy and healing, my experiences as a facilitator of a support group, the volunteer private work I do with people who have life-challenging diseases and their caregivers, and the importance of confidentiality in the support group. The workbooks are designed to be a structured writing exercise that is intended to be *private*—the writer can always share, of course, but they are encouraged to keep this private, as in a personal diary.

One of the relevant exercises follows:

> Take some time to write about your hopes and dreams, and what it is you would like to do with the remainder of your life. What are the things that you always wanted to do? Which of them can you do now? As your health improves, what are the things that you would like to do?

Although this exercise is aimed primarily at a person with a serious disease, its variants are also significant for caregivers and grievers. LeShan (1989) has stressed the importance of hopes and dreams in helping people with serious ailments find direction and meaning in their lives. In fact, in his extensive experience, he finds the elucidation of, and work toward fulfillment of, hopes and dreams to be the single most important factor for survival.

The three workbooks with their instructions follow.* A grid for interpersonal relationships is a feature of each workbook.

WORKBOOK FOR PEOPLE WHO HAVE A LIFE-CHALLENGING DISEASE

The questions in this workbook have been designed to help you cope with a diagnosis of a life-challenging disease and its treatment. Please find a quiet time and place to do this writing over a period of successive days. What you write is personal and should be kept private. It is your decision about sharing any part of this, or all of it, with someone you trust. If you need more than the allotted space, please continue your responses on the back of the paper, on separate sheets, or in a journal. There are no "correct" responses—whatever you write is the right thing for you. Take whatever time you need to respond. You should know that a number of research studies have shown that the very act of writing responses to the kinds of questions in this workbook have been beneficial for both physical and mental health. This process is most helpful when you "write from the heart."

1. Respond to the following three related questions. You may not be able to answer them with any certainty—in that case, a guess or a theory about how to answer the questions is fine.
   Why is this happening to me (versus someone else)?
   Why is this happening to me at this particular time of my life?
   Why do I have this particular kind of disease?
2. Do you know, have a theory, or can you guess why you are doing better, worse, or staying the same at this particular time?
3. What ways of taking care of yourself are you waiting to explore? (These can be second or third opinions, more research on available medical treatments, alternative or complementary treatments, support groups, support networks, or personal methods such as counseling/psychotherapy.)
4. What is stopping you from exploring such options now? What resources do you need to be able to do whatever is necessary to help yourself?
5. Take some time to write about your fears for yourself, your family, and your future.
6. Take some time to write about your hopes and dreams and what it is you would like to do with the remainder of your life. What are the things that you always wanted to do? Which of them can you do now? As your health improves, what are the things that you would be sure to do?

---

*The author appreciates feedback on these workbooks.

7. Write about your feelings about surgery, radiation, chemotherapy, or other treatments.

8. Some surgeries (such as mastectomies and prostatectomies) involve the loss of body parts, particularly those that are related to body- and self-image. Please write about your feelings concerning these surgeries, if you have undergone one.

9. Write about your feelings about being in a hospital.

10. This question has to do with being able to communicate openly about your condition and your feelings about this condition with the people in your life who care. Think carefully about who you can talk to about the following items, listing *specific* people in each row (for example, you may write the name of a particular cousin in the row for relatives). For your guidance a number of general categories of people are listed in the first column (see Table 4.1). In each box put a "+" if you would feel comfortable talking with them about that item, a "−" if this would be a mistake and they would be unresponsive, and a "?" if you are unsure of their responsiveness. Feel free to write additional comments in each box. Where more than one person can be listed in a category, such as friends, please list them separately.

11. Write about your feelings about interacting with medical personnel—doctors, nurses, technicians, others—including follow-up visits.

12. Write about what frustrates you about having this disease.

13. It is not unusual for people who have been diagnosed with a serious or life-challenging disease to have the seemingly paradoxical reaction of considering the disease to be a "blessing" in some way. What things have you learned about yourself and about the people around you that are beneficial to you?

14. How has having this disease changed your spiritual life?

15. Knowing what you know now about your life, if you could, how would you have lived differently? That is, what would you change about your past?

16. Knowing what you know now about your life, what things will you do differently starting right now?

17. Sometimes opportunities for saying things to people just pass us by. Are there significant people in your past or in the present that you never had a chance to tell what was really on your mind? Write what you would have told them if you had the chance. (These people may be living or dead.)

18. This is related to the previous question. Write out the things for your spouse and children (or specific others) that you want to have them know; leave them (personal items or thoughts); and say to them. You may wish to share these writings with them now, later, leave for them, or continue to keep private.

19. Although this is a trying time, it is always wise to take care of certain "mechanical" things, such as wills, living wills, powers of attorney, durable powers of attorney for health, financial matters, and funeral ar-

rangements as soon as possible. Most people make these arrangements when they are well and not faced with difficult times. Once taken care of, you no longer need to be concerned about them. If you have not already done so, make appointments to take care of these items. This would also be a good place to write about your feelings about these items. (*Note:* This item may be difficult to handle at this time, and you may wish to put it off for awhile and/or discuss it with someone you trust. The author of this workbook and his wife attended to these items many years ago, just so no surprises or difficulties would be left for their children. They also regularly review these items. However, please respond to this item only when you feel comfortable doing so.)

20. Write about anything else that concerns you at this time. This is *your private* journal and you can write whatever you wish.

TABLE 4.1. Life-Challenging Illness Support Table

People	Physical feelings	Emotional feelings	Fears	Treatments	Information	Fun and relaxation
Spouse						
Children						
Parents						
Relatives						
Friends						
Doctors						
Counselor						
God						

TABLE 4.1 *(continued)*

Minister						
People at work						
Support group						
Strangers						
Others						

WORKBOOK FOR CAREGIVERS

The questions in this workbook have been designed to help you cope with the stresses of being a caregiver. Please find a quiet time and place to do this writing over a period of successive days. What you write is personal and should be kept private. It is your decision about sharing any part of this, or all of it, with someone you trust. If you need more than the allotted space, please continue your responses on the back of the paper, on separate sheets, or in a journal. There are no "correct" responses—whatever you write is the right thing for you. Take whatever time you need to respond. You should know that a number of research studies have shown that the very act of writing responses to the kinds of questions in this workbook have been beneficial for both physical and mental health. This process is most helpful when you "write from the heart."

1. The following three questions are related. You may not be able to answer them with certainty—in that case, you may have a guess or a theory about how to answer these questions.
   Why is this happening to the person I love (versus someone else)?
   Why is this happening to him or her at this particular time?
   Why does he or she have this particular disease (versus a different one)?
2. Do you know, have a theory, or can you guess why he or she is doing better, worse, or staying the same at this time?
3. Write in detail about the good times you had with the person for whom you are caring.
4. Write about special memories or experiences the two of you have shared.

5. Write about losses that you shared and experienced together.
6. What special personal characteristics will see you through this time?
7. What are your special strengths?
8. What additional ways of taking care of *yourself* are you willing to explore at this time? How will you overcome things that are in the way of taking care of yourself?
9. What are ways you can share the work of caring? Who can help? Can you set up a network of helpers or have someone do this for you?
10. It is not unusual to feel anger and frustration, sometimes about the person for whom you are caring. There can even be occasional thoughts about wishing it were all over already. If you are experiencing any of these things, here is a private place to write.
11. Write about fears for yourself, for your family, for your loved one, for your future.
12. Write about how these circumstances have changed your life. How do you plan to adapt to or overcome these changes and go on with your life?
13. How have these circumstances affected your spiritual life?
14. How has your involvement with caregiving affected your relationship with the person you are caring for? Relationships with your family? Friends? Acquaintances? Social life? Work life?
15. Are there things you would like to tell the person you are caring for at this time? When will you take an opportunity to do that? On the other hand, some private things you may prefer to write rather than speak. Do that here.
16. Sometimes opportunities to say things to people pass us by. Are there other significant people in your past that you never had a chance to tell what was really on your mind? Write what you would have told them if you had the chance. The people you write to in this workbook may be deceased or still alive.
17. Who can you communicate with openly about being a caregiver and/or about your feelings? Think carefully about who you can talk to about the items in Table 4.2, listing *specific* people in each row (for example, in the row marked relatives you might list a particular cousin). (You can add more rows if needed or write your responses elsewhere.) Mark boxes with a "+" if you feel comfortable talking with them about that item, a "−" if this is a mistake and they would be unresponsive or unhelpful, and a "?" if you are unsure about their responsiveness. You may write additional comments in each box.
18. Although this is a trying time, it is always wise to take care of certain "mechanical" things, such as wills, living wills, powers of attorney, durable powers of attorney for health, financial matters, and funeral arrangements as soon as possible. Most people make these arrangements when they are well and not faced with difficult times. Once taken care of, you no longer need to be concerned about them.

If you have not already done so, make appointments to take care of these items. This is also a good place to write about your feelings about these items. (*Note:* This item may be difficult to handle at this time, and you may wish to put it off for awhile and/or discuss it with someone you trust. The author of this workbook and his wife attended to these items many years ago, just so no surprises or difficulties would be left for their children. They also review these items regularly. However, please respond to this item only when you feel comfortable doing so.)

19. You may think that it is premature to write about your hopes and dreams and what it is you would like to do with the rest of *your* life. This may be an appropriate time. If it is, what are the things that you always wanted to do? When will you do them?

20. Write about anything else that concerns you at this time. This is *your private* journal and you can write whatever you wish.

TABLE 4.2. Caregivers Support Table

People	Physical feelings	Emotional feelings	Fears	Memories	Loneliness	Hopes and dreams
Spouse						
Children						
Parents						
Relatives						
Friends						
Doctors						
Counselor						

God						
Minister						
People at work						
Support group						
Strangers						
Others						

WORKBOOK FOR GRIEVING

The questions in this workbook have been designed to help you cope with a traumatic loss. Please find a quiet time and place to do this writing over a period of successive days. What you write is personal and should be kept private. It is your decision about sharing any part of this, or all of it, with someone you trust. If you need more than the allotted space, please continue your responses on the back of the paper or on separate sheets or in a journal. There are no "correct" responses—whatever you write is the right thing for you. Take whatever time you need to respond. You should know that a number of research studies have shown that the very act of writing responses to the kinds of questions in this workbook have been beneficial for both physical and mental health.

1. Write in detail about the good times you had with the person whose loss you are grieving.
2. Write about losses that you shared and experienced together.
3. What special personal characteristics will see you through this time?
4. What are your special strengths?
5. What ways of taking care of yourself are you willing to explore at this time? How will you overcome obstacles that are in the way of taking care of yourself?
6. What is different about the times when you are able to function normally? How can you extend those times?
7. Write about fears for yourself, for your family, for your future.

8. Write about your hopes and dreams and what it is you would like to do with the rest of *your* life. What are the things that you always wanted to do? When will you do them?

9. Write about how this loss has changed your life. How do you plan to adapt to or overcome these changes and go on with your life?

10. How has this loss affected your spiritual life?

11. How has this loss affected your social life? Relationships with your family? Friends? Acquaintances? Fellow workers?

12. Who can you communicate with openly about your loss and your feelings? Think carefully about who you can talk to about the items in Table 4.3, listing *specific* people in each row (for example, in the row marked relatives you might list a particular cousin). (You can add more rows if needed.) Mark boxes with a "+" if you feel comfortable talking with them about that item, a "−" if this is a mistake and they would be unresponsive or unhelpful, and a "?" if you are unsure about their responsiveness. You may write additional comments in each box.

13. Sometimes opportunities to say things to people pass us by. Are there significant people in your past or in the present that you never had a chance to tell what was really on your mind? Write what you would have told them if you had the chance. The people you write to in this workbook may be deceased or still alive. Think especially about things you still have to say to your lost loved one.

14. People grieve deeply for different lengths of time. How long in months have you grieved deeply? If you are still grieving deeply, can you estimate in months how long you expect this to continue? Write down what things you are doing that may shorten the deep grieving time.

15. Write about anything else that concerns you at this time. This is *your private* journal and you can write whatever you wish.

RESULTS FROM A BRIEF SURVEY

Since so few responses were received (four for life-challenging disease, five for caregivers, two for grieving—about a 40 percent response rate), neither the questionnaire used for feedback nor the responses in each category will be given. Instead, some general comments will be made for each workbook.

1. *Life-challenging disease:* More satisfaction was observed with this workbook than the others. Comments from four thoughtful respondents follow:

- "This workbook has been useful in getting my thoughts and feelings down so family may one day be able to look inside my head at this point in my life."
- "This workbook has been most helpful because I feel a sense of comfort going over my professional writings in the book."
- "Quite a thorough all-encompassing document. Good to stimulate and trigger unexpected reactions, especially the grid. Very thought-provoking."
- "Good for the newly diagnosed."

2. *Caregivers:* One respondent liked the support table, which he found to be "very revealing." By and large, caregivers seem to prefer support groups with personal sharing and interactions than writing.

3. *Grieving:* Several people responded directly that they were not ready or willing to encounter themselves via the structured writing in this workbook. Grief work is so individual in its timing that it is difficult to know when to administer a workbook such as this. The one person who did all of the exercises reported a 70 percent contribution of the workbook to her well-being and welfare. She wrote, "Writing in this workbook helped me to see my journey more clearly."

TABLE 4.3. Grievers Support Table

People	Physical feelings	Emotional feelings	Fears	Memories	Loneliness	Hopes and dreams
Spouse						
Children						
Parents						
Relatives						
Friends						
Doctors						

TABLE 4.3 *(continued)*

Counselor						
God						
Minister						
People at work						
Support group						
Strangers						
Others						

SUSAN AND BILL: A CASE STUDY

I am writing briefly about Susan and Bill, not as an example of the use of workbooks in their lives but rather as a prime example of people who would have benefited from these workbooks if they had been available. Susan worked in a local school system doing a variety of administrative jobs. Bill is an engineer. They were both deeply religious and believed in a personal savior. I first met them in a hospice at a time when Susan was given seven to ten days to live. She walked out seventy-seven days after her admission using a walker, progressed to a cane, went back to work part-time, and then full-time. She died about two years later when the cancer returned and overwhelmed her defenses in a very short time.

During this time I saw her regularly and did guided imagery work with her—she had a personal healing angel named Gwen, and a bone-rebuilding specialist angel named Rosie—along with the other support things I do. I worked primarily with Susan. Bill was the ever-present, ever-supportive caregiver. He would have benefited in his quiet and private way with systematically working his way through the caregiver's workbook. Caregivers, who are the unsung heroes and heroines of these sagas, need the recognition and the support that a workbook can supply with its structured format. Susan, too, would have benefited in her own introspective way from the workbook for people with a serious disease. Even though Susan and Bill were with each other almost twenty-four hours each day for several years, they were also isolated and alone with their own thoughts and feelings much of the time. For them, the workbooks would have literally been a god send.

IMPLICATIONS AND CONCLUSIONS

Although the responses were limited, sufficient positive feedback was given about the utility of these workbooks—both verbally and via the questionnaire—to recommended their use for people who have life-challenging diseases (especially in the early stages in which much confusion and turmoil exists), for caregivers, and for grievers. For example, several people told me that they would have welcomed the workbook when they were first diagnosed, but that by now they had worked through the major hurdles that the initial diagnosis and treatments engendered.

Caregivers are a population that is often overlooked in my experience. These people frequently suffer more emotional and physical strain than those for whom they care. One respondent commented that the very act of being singled out for testing a workbook designed specifically for caregivers reassured him that he was not alone and that he was valued. This recognition of the importance of caregiving is underappreciated.

Grievers are a variable population in the sense that the course of grief is both so individual and so culture controlled. Several personal contacts were made about why the griever did not use the workbook—the common denominator had to do with timing, i.e., they had completed their major grieving and did not wish to revisit those feelings, or they were not ready at this point to confront the issues raised in the grieving workbook. Timing is crucial with grievers, and once they are made aware of the workbook's availability, the timing for its use (or nonuse) must be left to them.

My experience with these three workbooks and with my volunteer work led me to recommend that the workbooks be a private activity for these populations.

REFERENCES

Battino, R. (2000). *Guided imagery and other approaches to healing.* Carmarthen, UK: Crown House.

Battino, R. (2001). *Coping: A practical guide for people with life-challenging diseases and their caregivers.* Carmarthen, UK: Crown House.

Frankl, V.E. (1984). *Man's search for meaning.* New York: Simon and Schuster.

L'Abate, L. (1986). *Systematic family therapy.* New York: Brunner/Mazel.

L'Abate, L. (1992). *Programmed writing: A self-administered approach for interventions with individuals, couples, and families.* Pacific Grove, CA: Brooks/Cole.

LeShan, L. (1989). *Cancer as a turning point.* New York: Penguin Books.

Siegel, B. (1986). *Love, medicine, and miracles.* New York: Harper and Row.

Chapter 5

Schema-Focused Cognitive Therapy: A Stage-Specific Workbook Approach

Demián F. Goldstein

The purpose of this chapter is to present a workbook to help clients achieve more adaptive ways of understanding themselves and the world, and to guide their behaviors. By challenging maladaptive beliefs through programmed writing, the therapist can confront the clients with their own thought foundations, the behaviors derived from them, and the resulting affective states that appear as characteristic and dysfunctional. These affective states cause impairment in various areas of the clients' lives. A wide range of participants could benefit from the use of this workbook as a para-therapeutic tool. These include those diagnosed with personality, mood, and anxiety disorders. It is also intended for those who are simply seeking to add new resources to better cope with particular situations in life.

RATIONALE AND BACKGROUND FOR THE CREATION AND DEVELOPMENT OF THE WORKBOOK

The development of this stage-specific schema workbook (3SWB) (Goldstein, 2001b) was based on a thesis set forth by Arthur Freeman (1993) in which he looks at a developmental theory of personality from a cognitive therapy perspective. The developmental model for the under-standing of schematic development devised by Freeman borrows from Erikson's (1950) psychosocial crisis model. All of the stages described by Erikson present the individual with a conflict (see Table 5.1). The resolution of that conflict is the condition for going on to the next stage. Resolutions can be successful or not so successful, the latter leading to the formation of attitudes and beliefs that are maladaptive.

Erikson's stages are not taken into consideration using a psychoanal-ytical basis of psychosexual development. Instead, they are viewed under the light of schematic rooting and formation, through an environmental-

TABLE 5.1. Developmental Stages and Matching Conflict Areas in Erikson's (1950) Framework

Stage	Approximate Age Span	Conflict
I	Infancy	Trust versus mistrust
II	Toddlerhood	Autonomy versus dependence
III	Preschool	Initiative versus guilt
IV	Middle childhood	Productivity versus inferiority
V	Adolescence	Identity versus identity confusion
VI	Young adulthood	Intimacy versus isolation
VII	Middle age	Generativity versus self-absorption
VIII	Maturity	Integrity versus despair

biological course of action. This course encompasses all of the basic cognitive variables centered on attention, perception, and information processing, among others, leading to the conceptualization of a particular mode (see Beck, 1996). According to Freeman (1993), "By dealing with beliefs in a direct manner, better resolution of life crises can be effected, with a concomitant impact on present functioning" (p. 85). Freeman also states a list of therapeutic steps that have been taken into consideration for the development of this workbook:

1. Explication of the beliefs based on the patient's verbalizations (in the case of the 3SWB, based on the writings of the respondent)
2. Exploration of the beliefs to ascertain the value and power they have for the individual
3. Assessment of the thoughts and ideas that maintain particular beliefs;
4. Identification of and focusing on the attendant feelings and behaviors that derive from the beliefs
5. Structuring specific interventions based on the patient's idiosyncratic personal, familiar, and cultural beliefs
6. Structuring relapse prevention strategies to assist the patient in generalizing the therapeutic gain to other situations and occurrences

These therapeutic steps work together with the sequential model of intervention for workbooks as proposed by L'Abate (1992):

1. *Crisis intervention:* At this beginning stage, an assignment or a series of assignments devoted to the topic of crises and how one copes before, during, and after a crisis may be relevant.

2. *Treatment proper:* This step details the steps one must undertake to change oneself.
3. *Relapse prevention:* Because relapse could be a major part of any biological regulated process one must plan for it rather than waiting for it to happen.
4. *Maintenance or support:* This final part pertains to the long-range outcome, that is, how one is going to take care of oneself.

DESCRIPTION OF THE WORKBOOK

An initial definition of the beliefs by the respondent gives way to facing the core of the problem itself. It also helps respondents to familiarize with the beliefs they may possess but were unaware of. To produce change at the cognitive level, each assignment contains specific subassignments of certain relevant behaviors. The respondent needs to monitor or practice them for at least a week. By matching the beliefs to overt behaviors as recognized by the respondent, a reduced field of action is delineated. Therefore the belief, in relationship to its associated behaviors, will be under siege. To create a more effective paratherapeutic tool, strategies and exercises specific to each proposed belief were developed. Many of these interventions are based on paradoxes, whereas others come from the cognitive therapy (Beck, 1976), and behavior therapy realms (Lazarus, 1981; Persons, 1989).

An evaluation form accompanies each assignment, both for accountability and research purposes. A strategy to prevent relapse could be implemented by adding extra assignments from other workbooks, such as the negative treatment indicators workbook, or from L'Abate's (1992) social training workbook the assignment on goals and wants, and the one on control. If therapists need to occasionally depart from the workbook modality for any given reason, they can accommodate alternative ways of engaging the client in the therapeutic process. They can later evaluate whether returning to the workbook modality is appropriate, or continue with the most useful option that benefits the client.

ADMINISTERING THE WORKBOOK

A sequence was followed in planning each assignment, stating its purpose, and separating diagnostic from problem-solving questions. Respondents are asked to define terms, describe the possible benefits of proposed changes, and elaborate on ways each topic is relevant to their specific condition. Participants who can read and write can be given this workbook one assignment at a time, possibly with discussion after each assignment has been completed (Perris, 1989; L'Abate, 1992).

Participants can move on to the next assignment when they have completed the homework assignment satisfactorily. Supplementary assignments from other workbooks can be administered on an as-needed basis. The choice of an additional program or workbook after this one has been completed should be based on how the respondent did on the workbook, pre- and postworkbook test results, and goals the respondent wants to achieve.

The stage-specific schema inventory (3SI) makes way to a focused treatment modality in which using the 3SWB therapeutic assignments aims to maximize outcome gains. The focus of the treatment is indeed cognitive modification at the schematic level. Thus the 3SI provides a target area based on the client's schematic anchorage, whereas the 3SWB provides the means to implement the modification. The behavioral component is also a focus of treatment since the schemas are reflected in the everyday actions and choices of the individuals.

Assignments proposed within the workbook are mostly solution-focused therapeutic interventions. These interventions operate directly upon the client's dominating schemas, minimizing other variables in the periphery of treatment that might make the conceptualization of the case rather misleading. The most transparent example in the 3SWB is the use of problem-solving therapy techniques to define a problem, generate alternative ways to cope with it, and make decisions to finally implement a strategic plan.

Clients are active participants in the development of the treatment plan. The first assignment of the workbook deals with the conflictive stages from the clients' point of view, regarding how much negative resolutions have an impact in their lives. Involvement of family and other support systems is also encouraged both actively and in reminiscing. At times, clients are asked to interact with others in order to have an experiential grasp of their operational schemas. In other assignments, they are prompted to think about their past and present experiences, singling out who or what is involved in the perpetuation of their dysfunctional schemas.

A sample assignment that deals with the crisis initiative versus guilt is included in the appendix to this chapter. This assignment would be administered to an individual who obtained a high score in this particular area of conflict.

THE STAGE-SPECIFIC SCHEMA INVENTORY

Listed in this section are fifteen of the forty-eight statements that make up the 3SI. These are statements a person might use to describe his or her way of thinking about and interpreting things. The individual is asked to choose from a rating scale ranging from "I never think that way" to "I think that way most of the time."

1. People cannot be trusted.
2. I am not prepared to make decisions.
3. I feel guilty when things go wrong.
4. I feel inferior to others.
5. I am afraid of acting the way I feel.
6. Nobody loves me.
7. My life is worthless.
8. I could have done things better.
9. I do not have a special interest in things.
10. I will always be alone.
11. My abilities are extremely limited.
12. To give is to lose.
13. There is no purpose in life.
14. My present situation is a consequence of mistakes I have made in the past.
15. I need the opinion of others in order to consider my actions as valid.

The therapist may then score each statement and come up with a potential area of conflict. Based on these scores, the therapist may decide which assignment is appropriate for administration. At times, more than one area will qualify for high-level priority conflict status. However, the therapist must decide which area is more relevant to the client's present conflict and situation. Once a match is established, administration of the workbook's assignment follows.

IMPLICATIONS FOR THE ROLE OF WORKBOOKS IN COGNITIVE-BEHAVIORAL THERAPY

The use of this and other workbooks has a relevant role in cognitive-behavioral therapy practice. The administration process includes a strong role for assessment, in this case represented by major instruments such as the current versions of the MMPI, MCMI, and the BDI. In addition to these instruments, a new proposed measure was specifically designed to use with this workbook: the 3SI (Goldstein, 2001a). The 3SI remains to be tested and validated, and currently represents an approximation to clients' underlying schematic structures. Workbooks facilitate well-organized and documented clinical records that are easily accessible and storable, increasing therapists' accountability. In addition, they may serve as instrumental aids for clinical research or client follow-ups. The added bonus is having the client's un-altered thoughts in writing.

IMPLICATIONS OF THE PRESENT AND FUTURE USE OF WORKBOOKS IN MENTAL HEALTH INTERVENTIONS

Workbooks are especially competent in a number of ways that would support their inclusion in standardized managed mental health care. They could be consistent and systematically used in private practice psychother-apy, complying with at least the basic features required of an acceptable modality for mental health interventions (Sauber, 1997). A better access to psychotherapeutic services is guaranteed—geographic convenience being one of the hit features of this approach. The workbook can be administered through face-to-face appointments, the mail, or the Internet. This makes it available "here, there, and everywhere." The 3SWB is currently available in English and Spanish, and may eventually be translated into other languages.

Therapists could also be considered as being more available (close to a hypothetical twenty-four-hour basis) through a phone or e-mail consulta-tion, even though they may not respond instantly to the demand. In the case of the 3SWB and other similar workbooks, therapists who intend to use these types of distance media have to be aware of the importance of timely responses and appointments, especially when treating clients with personal-ity disorders.

Accessibility of records to external review is facilitated through a thor-oughly annotated progress of each particular case done by the therapist. This would make billing easier and more contained. In the case of the 3SWB, the way it is structured allows for a specific count of sessions, an evaluation of the outcome of each segment of the workbook, and a compari-son between initial and final specific assessment. This could be the case of using the 3SI at pre- and posttreatment, indicating at least an internal mea-sure of the treatment modality.

Outcome of treatment is measured by symptom relief, improvement in general, and improvement in the person's specific level of functioning. Symptom relief is a main goal with the 3SWB; however, when symptoms are severe, a more direct intervention may prove more appropriate. Such is the case of delusional thought, extreme anxiety, suicidal thoughts, or severe depression. Workbooks designed specifically for these extreme conditions still need to yield data to be considered the first choice of treatment.

Improvement in general level of functioning can be tracked through the clients' writings. When combined with face-to-face traditional psychotherapy, comparing what the client writes and what she or he says in person could be useful. Pre- and postworkbook administration testing also serves as a measure of improvement in general level of functioning.

Billing for specific interventions (such as face-to-face sessions) or distance writing (the cost of the workbook plus a fixed number of consultations) could eventually demonstrate that services are indeed cost-effective when compared to other expensive medical or social interventions. Such is the case of the man who could not afford to commute to my office and arranged his visits according to his work schedule and the time he spent completing written homework assignments.

Clients' satisfaction can be measured using the Clients Satisfaction Survey (L'Abate et al., 2001), a questionnaire developed for use with any workbook. In the case of the 3SWB, a shorter version of this questionnaire is provided at the end of each homework.

Programmed distance writing appears to be the most accessible system in which the amount paid for the results produced considerably reduces expenditure. However, more data are needed to consider this modality as effective or even superior to face-to-face psychotherapy. Therefore, further solid empirical research in the area is needed to support these hypotheses, as well as test the limitations of this modality. This will perhaps help develop and install a now-novel then-mainstream method in the field of mental health.

APPENDIX: A SAMPLE ASSIGNMENT FROM THE 3S WORKBOOK— CRISIS THREE, INITIATIVE VERSUS GUILT

Assignment 1. Becoming Aware of the Belief

The purpose of this assignment is to help you become more aware of your underlying belief and, perhaps, learn how to express it in a more helpful and constructive fashion than may have taken place in the past. You need to come up with an explanation of the belief based on your own understanding of it, as well as your personal experience. You will then focus on the thoughts and behaviors that keep the belief active, and finally you will utilize some techniques to try to readapt in a positive way this so-called maladaptive attitude. Now go on to the first assignment!

1. Define "initiative" in your own words, and give examples that come from your personal experience. Do you take on new things? Explain in detail how.

Appendix has been shortened to conserve space.

2. Define "guilt" in your own words, and give examples that come from your personal experience.
   Do you find it difficult to find a purpose for your actions? Explain in detail why.
3. Please answer the following questions regarding your perception of willingness, sense of purpose, and feelings of guilt. Explain in detail and give examples related to your personal experience.
   a. During your childhood (at home, in school):
      i. Did you feel willing to seek new activities? Explain in detail why you did or you did not. Please circle the percentage of how willing to seek new activities you believe you were:
         0   10   20   30   40   50   60   70   80   90   100
      ii. Did you have a purpose or goal? Explain in detail why you did or you did not.
      iii. Did you feel guilty? Explain in detail why and of what: Items i, ii, and iii are also asked for adolescence and adulthood.

Assignment 2. Reinterpreting Beliefs

1. Here you will find some maladaptive thoughts that reflect a negative resolution of the crisis initiative versus guilt, and are also characteristic of this belief of guilt. Please define them according to how much they relate to you and your behavior. Make sure to include examples.
   a. Life has no purpose.
   b. I cannot get started; I am paralyzed.
   c. I blame myself when things go wrong.
2. Now that you have already defined them according to the implications they have in your life, rank them by giving the number 1 to the thought that is the strongest in you, number 2 the next strongest, and so on.

Maladaptive thought	Rank
a. Life has no purpose.	_____
b. I cannot get started; I am paralyzed.	_____
c. I blame myself when things go wrong.	_____

Assignment 3. Modifying Beliefs

Thus far, you know you are ready to initiate some things, and become paralyzed and uninventive in others. A fair goal for you would be to gain a stronger sense of initiative in certain situations in order to have more resources readily available to you, and to feel more at ease while perceiving yourself as being more efficient.

Following is a grid containing five areas that are involved in this belief of guilt. Three characteristic features of each area are included, as well as a matching activity for each. Choose the characteristic you feel is the strongest in you and its matching activity. Circle them. Do one area per day, starting on Monday with behavior, Tuesday with mood, and so on, until you have finished all five. State the way you will be implementing this area during that day, and finally indicate your affinity to the characteristic you chose. Make sure you fill it in based on your real assumptions:

Area	Proposed Activities	How You Will Implement It
Behavior		
1. Delaying	1. Do not do what you planned on doing. Postpone it.	
2. Doubt	2. Think over and over before making any decisions.	
3. Lethargy	3. Do not do *anything at all!*	
		Percent of affinity between me and this behavior:
Mood		
1. Frustrated	Try to feel that way about everything during this day.	
2. Uninterested		
3. Bored		
		Percent of affinity between me and this way of feeling:
Thought		
1. Self-defeating	1. "I cannot be creative."	
2. Self-debasing	2. "I cannot do anything right."	
3. Wishy-washy	3. "I am not sure of what I want."	
		Percent of affinity between me and this way of thinking:

Area	Proposed Activities	How You Will Implement It
Sensation		
1. Numbness	1. Avoid any sensation whatsover. Do not feel!	
2. Anxiety	2. Develop anxiety before any situation you face.	
3. Tension	3. Be alert. Do not relax!	
		Percent of affinity between me and this type of sensation:
Relationships		
1. Submissive	1. Do whatever the other person wants. Obey!	
2. Gullible	2. Believe anything others say.	
3. Make excuses	3. Make excuses for your behavior: "I did this because ..."	
		Percent of affinity between me and this way to relate to others:

REFERENCES

Beck, A.T. (1976). *Cognitive therapy and the emotional disorders.* New York: Meridian.

Beck, A.T. (1996). Beyond belief: A theory of modes, personality, and psychopathology. In Salkovskis, P.M. (Ed.), *Frontiers of cognitive therapy* (pp. 1-23). New York: Guilford.

Erikson, E. (1950). *Childhood and society.* New York: W.W. Norton.

Freeman, A. (1993). A psychosocial approach for conceptualizing schematic development for cognitive therapy. In Kuehlwein, K.T. and Rosen, H. (Eds.), *Cognitive therapies in action* (pp. 54-87). San Francisco: Jossey-Bass.

Goldstein, D.F. (2001a). *3SI: Stage-specific schema inventory.* Available from the author upon request.

Goldstein, D.F. (2001b). *Stage-specific schema focused therapy workbook (3SWB).* Available from the author upon request.

Goldstein, D.F., Cairo, Y.S., and Molina, F.A. (2004). Reducion de conflictos en mujeres con crisis decompensatoria de su transfomo de personalidad (Reduction of conflicts in decompensating women in crisis through transformation of their personalities). Paper submitted for publication.

L'Abate, L. (1992). *Programmed writing: A self-administered approach for interventions with individuals, couples, and families.* Pacific Grove, CA: Brooks/Cole.

Lazarus, A.A. (1981). *The practice of multimodal therapy.* New York: McGraw-Hill.

Perris, C. (1989). The adult depressed patient. In Freeman, A., Simon, K.M., Beutler, L.E., and Arkowitz, H. (Eds.), *Comprehensive handbook of cognitive therapy* (pp. 309-313). New York: Plenum Press.

Persons, J.B. (1989). *Cognitive therapies in practice: A case formulation approach.* New York: Norton.

Sauber, S.R. (1997). *Managed mental health care: Major diagnostic and treatment approaches.* Bristol, PA: Brunner/Mazel.

Chapter 6

Healing the Trauma of Abuse:
A Women's Workbook

Ellen Arledge
Joselyn Y. Barsfield
Caroline L. Mitchell
Emily Moody
Carolina J. Quesada

In this chapter, the development and use of a self-help book designed especially for women survivors of childhood and/or adult trauma is presented. *Healing the Trauma of Abuse: A Women's Workbook* (Copeland and Harris, 2000) was written to address the profound impact physical, sexual, and emotional abuse or neglect have on a woman's view of herself and her world. Without treatment, the wounds from these traumas do not simply heal in time. A large percentage of women who have substance abuse disorders and/or mental illnesses report histories of trauma. Further, women who have been abused are often unsure of appropriate boundaries in relationships, unaware of their basic body functioning, feel anxious and fearful, and may struggle with anger that can feel out of control. Although no formal research has been conducted on this recently published manual, anecdotal information regarding women's use of this manual is presented. Further, use of the book as a prophylactic tool in primary, secondary, and tertiary prevention as well as its use in crisis intervention, psychotherapy, and rehabilitation will be examined. Predictions are made regarding future use of this book in various settings.

DESCRIPTION OF WORKBOOK

Development, Core Assumptions, and Format

Healing the Trauma of Abuse: A Women's Workbook (Copeland and Harris, 2000) provides a practical, step-by-step approach to healing for women

141

who have experienced physical, sexual, and/or emotional abuse in their lives. The workbook provides the structure for undertaking trauma work on one's own as opposed to work in a group or with a therapist. This book was developed as a supplement to the Trauma Recovery and Empowerment (TREM) group intervention, a model of practice developed by clinicians and survivors of abuse at Community Connections (an outpatient mental health and substance abuse agency) in Washington, DC. The TREM intervention is a thirty-three-week group that provides a safe forum in which female survivors of abuse begin to understand the connections between abuse experiences in their lives and other problems they may experience, such as substance abuse, emotional problems, and relationship difficulties.

The TREM group has a psychoeducational format. The model helps a woman to understand trauma as a core event that continues to affect multiple dimensions of her life. The sessions are topic specific, so that the healing process for a survivor of abuse occurs in a safe, contained manner. The emphasis is not on reexperiencing abuse but on building skills and improving a woman's current level of functioning.

A core assumption of the trauma recovery approach on which the workbook is based is that "women who experienced repeated trauma in childhood were deprived of the opportunity to develop certain skills necessary for adult coping" (Harris and the Community Connections Trauma Work Group, 1998, p. xiii). Using a step-by-step format, the workbook elucidates the connection between past abuse and current feelings and behaviors. It introduces the user to successful problem-solving techniques to replace destructive patterns, and facilitates "the development of skills in assertiveness, self-advocacy, self-management, and successful relationship building" (Copeland and Harris, 2000, p. 2).

This workbook is designed for women who have experienced physical, sexual, and/or emotional abuse at any point in their lives and who wish to gain greater understanding of the impact of trauma experiences on their current functioning. The workbook provides women the option to engage in trauma recovery work in a private forum. Some women are unable to participate in TREM groups for practical reasons, such as work schedules or family demands. The workbook is an alternative for others who may not choose to participate in groups because of concerns about sharing sensitive material in the presence of others.

Structure and Content of Sessions

Although the workbook is structured to match the Trauma Recovery and Empowerment intervention session by session, it is intended to be a standalone book. The workbook is grouped into four primary sections: empower-ment (eleven sessions), trauma recovery (ten sessions), creating life changes (nine sessions), and closing rituals (three sessions). The workbook opens with a section on preparing to do trauma work, with the understanding that the challenge of addressing one's abuse history is great. The authors stress the importance of timing the work well, and they offer general guidelines to assist the reader in assessing her readiness to work with her trauma issues. The introduction also provides some general ground rules that emphasize strategies for keeping oneself safe and healthy while working through each session. These strategies include the option to pass on certain activities that feel too stressful, the importance of setting aside dedicated time to complete each session, having a support network available to talk about difficult is-sues as they arise, and the need to care for one's physical and emotional health while doing trauma work. Session One, Taking Stock and Getting Started, is dedicated exclusively to helping a woman prepare for what fol-lows. Activities include identifying goals, setting aside time and space, identifying healthy activities to keep oneself well, and listing a support net-work that a woman can turn to when she needs help from another.

Each session follows a similar format, opening with an introductory ra-tionale that outlines the importance of the particular topic at hand as it re-lates to the effects of trauma. For example, in the session Intimacy and Trust, the introduction highlights how experiences of abuse are violations of trust that affect one's ability to establish and sustain trust in subsequent in-terpersonal relationships. Activities then follow each introduction, begin-ning often with general definitions of the topic issue (e.g., "What is an inti-mate and trusting relationship?"). Each session offers concrete examples from the lives of other trauma survivors and spaces for a woman to write about her own life experiences. For example, in the session on intimacy, the authors ask women to identify their own list of "red flags," or signs that warn them that a relationship may not be a healthy and trusting one. Follow-ing the activities in each session are lists of optional activities that women can complete if they wish to do additional work on a particular topic. These activities may include a reading list, art therapy activities, journaling topics, or additional skill-building exercises. Each session concludes with a list of Things to Remember: affirmations that validate the work in which women are engaging and that allow them to end each session on a positive note.

Workbook Goals

The sessions of the Empowerment section (Part One) set the tone for trauma recovery within a feminist framework, allowing women the opportunity to explore their roles within family and society. The emphasis is on providing information and building skills, particularly in the areas of a woman's life that are most likely to have been affected by traumatic experiences. Sessions in the Empowerment section include What It Means to Be a Woman, What Do You Know and How Do You Feel About Your Body?, Physical Boundaries, Emotional Boundaries, Self-Esteem, Self-Soothing, Intimacy and Trust, Female Sexuality, Sex with a Partner, and a transition session to the next section of the workbook.

The goals of the sessions in the first part of the women's workbook focus on providing education and information, as well as assisting trauma survivors in reframing their life experiences within the context of abuse. For example, many survivors of trauma either lack basic information or sustain inaccurate knowledge about their own bodies. The abuse experience has resulted in a disconnection from their physical self. Simple body awareness may trigger disturbing flashbacks of how they feel their body has betrayed them. Consequently, the women want to avoid thinking about their bodies at all. This section encourages survivors to increase their awareness of their bodies, physical space, and their basic interactions with others. The goal is not to relive experiences of abuse but rather to identify the skill deficits that abuse may cause and to develop coping strategies in their place. These new skills may include increased self-awareness, or the ability to cope with stressful or negative feelings and situations in a positive and healthy way. Women examine their current coping skills and plan to emphasize the healthy practices rather than the negative practices that may have costly consequences. This section lays the groundwork for the rest of the book, in which women are encouraged to create their own path to healing so they can regain a sense of control over their lives.

Section Two, Trauma Recovery, moves with more depth into specific discussion of abuse experiences. The primary goal for this section of the workbook is to assist women in gaining an understanding of what experiences constitute abuse. Many survivors of abuse may not regard certain encounters as abusive, and may inaccurately label their experiences as a result (e.g., the belief that "if it happens between a husband and a wife, it isn't rape"). The sessions in this section of the workbook include, but are not limited to, Understanding Trauma; The Body Remembers What the Mind Forgets; three separate sessions on physical, emotional, and sexual abuse; Physical Safety; Psychological and Emotional Symptoms; and Abuse and Relationships.

Again, the goal is not to relive experiences of abuse but rather to focus on current concerns and building skills that specifically address the issue. These sessions also serve to educate survivors of abuse that the recovery process occurs not only in the mind but in the body as well, since the body may store its own memories of abuse experiences as physical pain or other somatic problems. Many of the exercises in this section of the book focus on helping women begin to tell their stories of abuse and share the experience with safe others in their network. As women learn to share the stories of their abuse, they begin to cut through the isolation that is a hallmark of abuse.

This section also introduces a central concept of the intervention, that emotional and psychological symptoms may have originated as legitimate attempts to cope with trauma. Consider the woman who currently experiences symptoms of extreme anxiety and hypervigilance. This woman may have experienced physical and sexual abuse from a family member, occurring with no predictable pattern. Consequently, she had to be hypervigilant to protect herself. In Session 19, Psychological or Emotional Symptoms, the exercises facilitate this woman's understanding that maintaining a high degree of alertness and readiness at one point in her life may have protected her from additional abuses. It is only now that these symptoms have become maladaptive. In the process of reframing these symptoms, women come to a new and more empowering self-concept that embraces their own strengths and abilities to cope, rather than merely labeling symptoms as problematic.

Section Three, Creating Life Changes, builds on the information acquired in the first two sections of the workbook by assisting women in utilizing their newly acquired skills in broader domains so that they can make lasting life changes, not only within themselves but in how they relate to others. Sessions that are included in this section were added at the request of trauma survivors, who felt that the trauma recovery work begun in the previous sections needed to be expanded and addressed in more depth. Sessions in this section include Current Family Life; Decision Making: Trusting Your Judgment; Communication: Making Yourself Understood; Blame, Acceptance, and Forgiveness; Relationships; and Goal Assessment. Once again, the focus in this section is on daily life, coping with current relationships, and issues that arise in those relationships as a result of trauma. Issues of family life are explored in depth, which is particularly critical given that many survivors may continue to sustain relationships with family members who may have perpetrated abuse in the past. In this section, women are also provided an opportunity to evaluate their progress.

The final three sessions are dedicated exclusively to closing rituals, given that many abuse survivors experience problems regarding abandonment and unhealthy endings. These final three sessions facilitate a woman's creation of positive closure not only in her trauma work but in other areas of her life as well. In these sessions, truths and myths about abuse are explored, providing the opportunity to see clearly one's own shift in labeling and self-concept. The session titled What It Means to Be a Woman is revisited here to demonstrate progress from the initial sessions of the workbook. Women take stock of their progress and set goals for future trauma recovery work if they so choose.

RESULTS OF WORKBOOK ADMINISTRATION

Existing Research

As women at Community Connections use the workbook, we have found that completed research in the field of self-help reflects our experience. Mental health providers have begun to evaluate the notion that self-help books are, in many cases, a useful alternative to therapy. Self-help is considered to be an intentional coping mechanism (Tucker-Ladd, 1996a). That is, the person seeking help is consciously choosing and willing to take an active part in this method of support and recovery. Over the past decade, innumerable self-help workbooks have been introduced to the field of mental health. The intent has been to create a "support system" through self-help workbooks that protects people from psychological stress by providing the structure through which they might change their lives. At Community Connections, we have certainly seen that *Healing the Trauma of Abuse* (Copeland and Harris, 2000) fills a gap for women who have a very thin and/or dangerous·network. There is no trustworthy, supportive person with whom they can talk about their trauma issues. The book provides a safe, consistent arena in which to do that work.

Many studies have shown the usefulness of self-help workbooks as an alternative to face-to-face therapy. Scogin et al. (1990) conducted a meta-analysis review of forty well-designed outcome studies of self-help books and treatments. The focus was on written or audiotaped material used by persons with various mental health problems, including depression, phobias, and compulsive behaviors, who did not participate in traditional one-on-one therapy. In many cases, it was determined that this sort of intervention was as helpful as if one were in traditional face-to-face therapy sessions and certainly more effective than seeking no treatment at all. Self-help workbooks often use a specific therapeutic technique as the agent of change: confrontation, a behavioral focus, or the use of rehearsal or journaling. Bergin and Lambert (1978) contend that treatment-specific methods have been shown to work dependably with no more than ten or so disorders such as generalized anxiety disorder, eating disorders, and sleep disorders. The results tend to be more positive when people take control of their treatment and work toward self-improvement (Smyrnius and Kirby, 1993). *Healing the Trauma of Abuse* explicitly encourages this type of control over one's treatment and further enables the user to develop trust in one's own perception of reality and to be able to articulate the validity of those perceptions.

Tucker-Ladd (1996b) conducted a study with more than 300 students who had a wide range of problems. He employed the use of self-help books with the participants. The results of his study concluded that 10 to 20 percent of subjects who devoted six to eight hours a week to working in the book made notable progress, reporting impressive self-improvement. In his follow-up study, which was conducted over an eight-year period, 69 percent of participants reported having remembered making progress and 8 percent reported that the problems worked on had actually gone away. Of those respondents, 75 percent reported that they were still "working on it" and 40 percent expected it to always be a problem (Tucker-Ladd, 1996b). With respect to trauma issues, some aftereffects may always be present since trauma forever alters one's life. Consequently, the goal is management of the problems rather than the elimination of them. This is an important idea to pass on to the users of the book, since survivors often experience themselves as failures because they have not completely healed or been "cured."

CLIENTS' COMMENTS CONCERNING WORKBOOK UTILIZATION

Through the workbook's application at Community Connections, clinicians are gaining a sense of the patterns of use of the book and how it supports recovery. When women at Community Connections choose to participate in trauma recovery groups, they receive a copy of the workbook in the first session of the group. Group leaders instruct the women to use the workbook as they would like, but do suggest that the workbook be used each week along with the group intervention. To assess the effectiveness of the workbook, women have been informally approached to discuss how they were using the book, how it supports their trauma recovery work, and what general impressions they had of the workbook. Several positive themes emerged in discussing the self-help workbook with the consumers.

First, women spoke of the ease of using the workbook. Mary liked the workbook because it was "written in plain and understandable language," and if something was not clearly written, the "book provided the definition." She related that typically she has to look up many words in the dictionary just to understand what she is reading. She reported that in the past she had attempted to use several other self-help workbooks, but they were too difficult to understand. Toya echoed this sentiment when she reported that the workbook was "easy to skim, easy to read and understand." She went on to state that she was never "a very good reader" and recently had more difficulty reading due to brain damage resulting from her alcoholism. She felt proud of her accomplishment of being able to complete the workbook. Others shared their impressions of the comprehensiveness of the topic material. Mary said that this was her first time using a workbook "this deep and this comprehensive," adding, "it doesn't beat around the issues of abuse." Many survivors, such as Mary, learn to keep experiences of trauma a secret, and therefore benefit from the directness of the material in the book. Sarita thought the workbook was very effective because it "touches upon everything," stating that she likes it because it "breaks [my recovery process] down into steps." For women whose lives often feel chaotic as a result of the emotional impact of abuse, having the recovery process feel manageable is an important component in their treatment.

Women also spoke of the sense of control they felt while completing the workbook. Many survivors live with chaos and unpredictability and feel overwhelmed by even minor decisions. To be able to direct the material and the treatment process is empowering for trauma survivors. Toya liked the workbook because it gave her the opportunity to read over the material before every trauma group and "think about the questions before the group starts." For Toya, this element of predictability was significant because she had endured an abusive marriage for many years, living with tremendous anxiety over not knowing what feelings or events would trigger an abusive episode. Similarly, Sarita would read the corresponding chapter before each trauma group "to help get my thought processes going and emotionally prepare me for the group." Sarita's previous efforts in treatment had failed, because she felt too flooded by painful memories to continue her work effectively.

Other women spoke of how difficult it was to look at some of the material in the workbook, stating that at times they had to skip over difficult topics. Sonya said that just seeing the front cover of the workbook with the word "trauma" on it was a trigger of painful memories for her, so her strategy was to hide the workbook from herself until she felt strong enough to work on the material. Shakira stated that sometimes the work becomes "too intense" and that she has to "put the book away and wait to bring it up in group" where she would have the support of others. Jane, whose controlling partner had prevented her from making even small decisions, such as what clothes to wear, put it very succinctly when she stated that the workbook "gives me control over when and what to address. I can control what to say and how I feel." After a lifetime of severe abuse, Jane feels that she can manage the choices she is making now. Other women shared how reviewing their workbook responses was very helpful. Mary stated that she liked the workbook because she could "refer back and see how much I have progressed."

Women also report using the workbook as a resource when they experience distress in their daily lives. Several women shared that they utilize the workbook when they are coping with major stressors, such as experiencing flashbacks or intrusive thoughts, or when coping with more minor issues, such as saying "no" to a friend. Cindy uses the workbook "anytime a problem comes up" by going back to a topic that helped her in the past. She experiences considerable difficulty communicating with others and finds herself using the workbook in times of "crisis" to help her through those difficult periods. Kim states that the workbook "helped me through some difficulties that I have been experiencing personally and at home." She also states that using the workbook sometimes triggers her flashbacks, but that her strategy to cope with this is to utilize a technique she had learned in the self-soothing chapter to help her calm herself. Mary's strategy to deal with difficulties or stress is to reread her previous responses "as a reminder of what I want and how much I have changed."

Use of the workbook is also reported to help women increase their self-awareness and their understanding of their relationships to others. Sarita is beginning to notice favorable effects as a result of using the workbook, stating, "I am beginning to perceive others differently." She went on to share a recent experience of riding on a bus next to a man she did not know. She reports that during the bus ride he placed his arm across the back of the seat. Sarita felt that through using the workbook she had developed an improved ability to understand her own physical boundaries, and she felt more comfortable moving to another seat. Others spoke of how much change they see within themselves. Several women shared that they feel they are better able to communicate their thoughts and feelings to others. Sonya experienced severe physical abuse by her stepfather, and recalls that whenever she said "no" as a child, she received a severe beating. Sonya notices now that her communication with her husband is different, and that they are now "talking more and doing other activities." She also said she feels the power to say "no to sex" if she is not in the mood without feeling guilty. Overall, several women say use of the workbook has increased their positive view of themselves, stating they have more "confidence, patience, and self-respect" or feel "more outgoing, independent, and sassy."

In addition, women talked about their heightened sense of connection to others as a result of using the workbook. Jane liked "the stories from other women" because the stories help her know that she is "not the only one" who has experienced abuse. For trauma survivors, this is a critical component because often they experience deep feelings of isolation and loneliness. Still others mention the positive self-statements that conclude each topic (Things to Remember Every Day). Terri says the statements help to put her "mind at ease" and provide some "relief before I go on to the next chapter."

Many trauma survivors lack anything positive to say to themselves after years of emotional abuse, and struggle to find something positive and encouraging about themselves. The book provides the words for them. Shakira says that the positive statements give her "something to hold onto." Other women mention that they like the optional activities the most because, as Shakira commented, "it suggests things I can do and gives me ideas . . . and helps to encourage me to make steps that I haven't been able to before." Sarita mentioned that so many ideas were suggested she could "keep what works [for her] and discard what doesn't."

Finally, women shared how the workbook helped them understand what a major role trauma played in their life experience. Many trauma survivors, such as Cindy, experience multiple treatment episodes in hospitals or drug rehab centers where their abuse is never mentioned, let alone treated. Cindy reports that she had been hospitalized many times in the past, but no one ever mentioned the word *trauma*. The workbook helps her to "understand myself more." She goes on to share that she had children at a very young age and "I never really knew much about myself," adding that what she likes most about the workbook is that she can "relate to the material." Toya experienced a lot of emotional abuse growing up and believes that the workbook is helping her to improve her understanding of how the emotional abuse destroyed her self-esteem and prevented her from graduating from high school and keeping a job. She states that initially she thought the workbook was "a bunch of bunk" but that she has come to appreciate its power to change her life.

Summary of Clients' Comments

The women's comments on their use of the workbook lead to several conclusions. Primarily, the workbook may be used as a way to prepare women for initiating trauma recovery work. By reading over specific topics and questions, women can make an informed decision regarding their readiness to engage in treatment, either through the self-help workbook itself, or through other interventions, such as individual or group therapy. The use of the workbook may also increase the cost-effectiveness of treatment interventions that are used concurrently, because women's level of investment in treatment increases as they become more self-directive and empowered to guide themselves through the process, rather than depending exclusively on the direction of a care provider.

Use of the workbook helps consumers gain a sense of control over their treatment and thus have more control over the outcome of the intervention. For survivors, who experience a total loss of control during traumatic experiences, the need to feel that they can direct the intensity and content of their treatment is imperative. Women can gain an improved sense of control when they utilize the workbook on their own time and work at their own pace. The workbook also becomes a reference to mark their progress or keep them on task with the new skills they are attempting to develop.

THE ROLE OF WORKBOOKS IN PREVENTION

In addition to understanding patterns of use, one can look further at specific ways in which the women's workbook can be used for primary, secondary, and tertiary prevention, as well as in crisis intervention, psychotherapy, and rehabilitation. The following poem by Portia Nelson (1993) illustrates the process of recovery and is used describe how workbooks can be used at the various levels of prevention.

Autobiography in Five Chapters

1) I walk down the street.
There is a deep hole in the sidewalk
I fall in.
I am lost . . . I am hopeless.
It isn't my fault.
It takes forever to find a way out.

2) I walk down the same street.
There is a deep hole in the sidewalk.
I pretend I don't see it.
I fall in again.
I can't believe I'm in the same place.
But it isn't my fault.
It still takes a long time to get out.

3) I walk down the same street.
There is a deep hole in the sidewalk
I see it is there.
I still fall in . . . it's a habit
My eyes are open
I know where I am
It is my fault.
I get out immediately.

4) I walk down the same street.
There is a deep hole in the sidewalk
I walk around it.

5) I walk down another street.

Portia Nelson

This well-known poem illustrates the process of recovery. Although it is often used in twelve-step substance abuse programs, it also speaks to the process by which many female trauma survivors recover from trauma's negative effects. However, these survivors have an important preface to this autobiography:

Preface

I walk down the street.
It is a pleasant day.
A stranger lunges at me and assaults me.
I jump into a deep hole in the sidewalk to get away
from my attacker.
I'm scared . . . I'm hurt,
It isn't my fault.
It takes a long time to get out.

Portia Nelson

This poem is an apt analogy of the impact that trauma has on women's behaviors, thoughts, and perceptions. Behaviors that began as adaptive responses to trauma evolve into dysfunctional behaviors. For example, many women who were sexually or physically abused as children learned to protect themselves by dissociating from the experience and allowing their mind to "wander" to another place and time while their body was being abused. However, for many of these women in adulthood, this adaptive response to childhood abuse has evolved into extreme dissociation that has resulted in their being unaware of the passage of entire blocks of time, such as a class in school or a shift at work. In these situations, even though the survivor was physically present she cannot tell you what happened in the class or during the shift. As a consequence, because this severe dissociation has interrupted their ability to concentrate and learn, they have had difficulty being successful in school and on the job. As a result of limited education or vocational skills, one might then be unable to finish school or maintain a job, resulting in lack of income, inability to support oneself, and even homelessness. One can understand, then, the profound consequences of dissociation. The preface to Portia Nelson's (1993) poem illustrates that this woman had walked down that street earlier in her life. During that walk it was a pleasant day and she intentionally jumped into the hole in the sidewalk to avoid further abuse by the perpetrator—the jump was adaptive because it protected her. However, during the next three chapters of the autobiography, this adaptive reaction evolves into a dysfunctional behavior, in which the woman falls rather than jumps into the deep hole. She knows that the behavior is maladaptive yet is powerless at first to stop it, but then slowly finds a way out of it.

Goals of Prevention

Mental health providers have attempted to address trauma with a variety of primary, secondary, and tertiary prevention approaches. For the purposes of this chapter, primary prevention is defined as an intervention that focuses on all persons who are currently functioning well and "aims at improving existing strengths to minimize future risk of breakdown" (L'Abate, 1999, p. 207). With respect to a trauma intervention, an example might be a curriculum in elementary schools that teaches all students the difference between "good touch" and "bad touch." The goal of secondary prevention "is to help specific populations in need [such as trauma survivors] to avoid future breakdown" (L'Abate, 1999, p. 207). In contrast, the goal of tertiary prevention is "to restore adequate functioning to clinical and diagnosed populations who are already in crisis or whose crisis level is chronic" (L'Abate, 1999, p. 207). Although the workbook provides useful information about the devastating impact that trauma has on women's lives and supports the necessity of primary prevention, the workbook's target audience is those women who have already experienced abuse in childhood and/or adulthood. Therefore, as an intervention, it can be considered both a secondary and tertiary prevention approach. The workbook provides secondary prevention to women who have experienced abuse, are at risk of future breakdown, but who have teetered on an unsteady beam of adequate functioning (L'Abate, 1999). These women may have avoided frequent hospitalizations, arrest, drug abuse, and homelessness, but remain vulnerable. However, the workbook's key role is to restore adequate functioning to those female trauma survivors who are frequently in crisis and have been marginalized as a result of the dysfunction born of the trauma.

Tertiary Prevention

Through validation, consciousness raising, and skill building, the women's workbook focuses on tertiary prevention for female survivors of trauma. Some estimates of the prevalence of trauma against women are that one in three women have experienced some form of abuse during their lifetimes. Clearly, tertiary prevention is essential. The workbook is an important alternative intervention for women who otherwise would avoid services due to distrust and anxiety about the process of therapy and its prohibitive cost.

At Community Connections, the workbook plays multiple roles in tertiary prevention. These include a means through which survivors can prepare themselves prior to trauma group, a guide used by a group of female survivors to form their own self-help group, and a vehicle for discussion of trauma issues between a survivor and her partner. Some women have chosen to work through the book chapter by chapter, whereas others have chosen specific chapters they feel to be most relevant to their current struggles. Because those who have experienced abuse at the hands of family members or partners have learned that they cannot trust even primary caregivers or family, they may find it difficult to trust a therapist enough to discuss the abuse. Each session is structured and predictable in contrast to traditional talk therapy, in which the next topic or the next question the therapist might ask is an unknown. For women with trauma histories, the workbook takes control out of the hands of the therapist and allows the female survivor to progress though the book at her own pace, noting upcoming questions, and closing the book if she wants to. Many survivors have stated that having the option to choose and direct their recovery process has been an important aspect of their own empowerment and healing.

An additional role in tertiary prevention is the use of the book with a mental health provider. Although the women's workbook is not useful on its own for survivors with low or limited literacy skills, many of these survivors have used it with a therapist who can verbally guide them through the information and exercises in the book. The workbook has also served as a basis for clinical work between clinicians and individual female survivors whose literacy level allows them to use the book on their own, but who benefit from discussion and review with the therapist in conjunction with more traditional talk therapy. In some situations, the survivor completes a chapter on her own and then suggests a few questions to discuss further with her therapist.

Jill is a survivor who had suicidal thoughts during most of her adult life. She suffered with depression and often found it difficult to get out of bed. She would isolate herself and not schedule any activities during the day for fear that she would later cancel due to her disabling depression. Jill used the workbook independently and, at the suggestion of her clinician, discussed an exercise (the Wellness Recovery Action Plan) she had completed in the workbook. The Wellness Recovery Action Plan is discussed in Topic 18, Institutional Abuse, and is a way to plan in advance for difficult times. This plan enables the woman to exert greater choice and control during an "out of control" time, because she has already specifically outlined what is helpful and what she would like to happen when she is not doing well and having difficulty making decisions and communicating her wishes. Jill had been hospitalized on several occasions and was often in a state of crisis. She had earlier disclosed that one hospitalization had retraumatized her because she was brought to a hospital she never would have chosen and was given medications to which she previously had bad reactions.

In creating her Wellness Recovery Action Plan, Jill listed activities she could do on a daily basis to keep herself feeling safe and as psychiatrically stable as possible (e.g., taking medications as prescribed). She also listed red flags, or early warning signs, she and the clinician may see that indicate a stressor has occurred and some action may need to be taken. Jill also shared her Personal Crisis Plan with the clinician. The plan indicated her supporters, who she did and did not want contacted in the event of a crisis, and what specific task she would like each of the supporters to perform. The plan included medications and health care treatments she wanted and those she wanted to avoid. It also allowed her to specify her preference of treatment facilities. This plan was completed when Jill was well, and it allowed her to have some control over her care and prepare for a time when she might feel out of control. Completing this plan also helped her combat her fear of scheduling an activity and enrolling in music lessons once a week.

Restoration of Functioning

In addition to tertiary prevention through the creation of concrete self-management plans, the workbook assists female trauma survivors to restore adequate functioning by drawing the connection between past abuse and current feelings and behaviors. As with traditional talk therapy, this process of writing "may alter the way an event is represented and organized in memory. . . . Writing, like talking, forces a structure on an otherwise overwhelming and often times chaotic experience" (Esterling et al., 1999, p. 85). Through programmed writing about an experience, the woman is able to interpret past abuse through a new lens of understanding. For example, a woman may have called a physically abusive partner "overprotective." However, after reviewing the list of warning signs of physical abuse in the workbook and a statement that men often explain abusive behavior as being "overprotective" or "caring," the woman begins to accurately label her partner's treatment as "abusive" rather than "overprotective."

IMPLICATIONS FOR USING THE WORKBOOK IN PRACTICE

After discovering patterns of use of the workbook by both survivor and clinician, one is able to expand the use of the book with other populations and in various settings, either with or without a clinician, singly or in groups. Beyond the success of this book with women at an inner-city mental health agency, we believe that the workbook fills a niche for other populations that may not have the time or resources to devote to face-to-face therapy. In 1998, staff at Community Connections conducted trauma groups at a women's prison. We quickly confronted the limitations of doing trauma work in a group format in that setting. At that time, the self-help book was not available. In retrospect, we believe that the workbook would be an excellent alternative to that kind of group. The female inmates would be able to do the work on their own and not run the very real risk of sharing their story with a group of women with whom they also had to live. By default, many levels of relationships existed among group members. Many of the women had intense relationships with other members of the group, varying from romantic to parental to platonic. These current or past relationship dynamics complicated their trauma work when they had reason not to trust or feel safe with certain individuals. The prison environment was a difficult place at best to try to be vulnerable and explore one's feelings and experiences with respect to abuse.

Another limitation of psychotherapy is the expense. Even with insurance, many consumers cannot afford the ongoing expense of weekly therapy. Further, most insurances cover only a minimal number of sessions—ultimately, the consumer assumes the full burden of the cost of therapy. With a one-time expenditure of the price of the book, a woman gains access to a thirty-three-session journey in which she can participate as she is able.

CONCLUSION

This workbook was developed to address the needs of female trauma survivors who might not otherwise have the opportunity to heal from their experiences. It is an accessible, affordable way for women to begin to address the impact of abuse on their lives. The book provides a great deal of instructional material that in itself helps women gain a better understanding of their experience. After women make some connections and gain a new understanding of their abuse, the workbook helps survivors develop those skills necessary for adult coping, such as self-awareness, recognizing and labeling abuse, and establishing boundaries. An explicit message throughout all of the exercises is that the abuse the women experienced was serious and it is understandable that they are experiencing serious aftereffects. The ultimate goal of this progress through empowerment, recovery, and healing is that the individual will have a better understanding of the causes of her behaviors that are currently problematic and will have the basic skills to change these behaviors.

REFERENCES

Bergin, A. E. and Lambert, M. J. (1978). The evolution of therapeutic outcomes. In S. L. Garfield and A. E. Bergin (Eds.), *Handbook of psychotherapy and behavior change: An empirical analysis* (pp. 139-189). New York: Wiley.

Copeland, M. E. and Harris, M. (2000). *Healing the trauma of abuse: A women's workbook*. Oakland, CA: New Harbinger Publications, Inc.

Esterling, A., L'Abate, L., Murray, E., and Pennebaker, J. (1999). Empirical foundation for writing in prevention and psychotherapy: Mental and physical health outcomes. *Clinical Psychology Review, 19*(1), 79-96.

Harris, M. and The Community Connections Trauma Work Group (1998). *Trauma recovery and empowerment: A clinician's guide to working with women in groups*. New York: Free Press.

L'Abate, L. (1999). Taking the bull by the horns: Beyond talk in psychological interventions. *The Family Journal: Counseling and Therapy for Couples and Families, 7,* 206-220.

Nelson, P. (1993). *There's a hole in my sidewalk*. Hillsboro, OR: Beyond Words Publishing, Inc.

Scogin, F., Bynum, J., Stevens, G., and Calhoon, S. (1990). Efficacy of self-administered treatment programs: Meta-analytic review. *Professional Psychology: Research and Practice, 21,* 42-47.

Smyrnius, K. X. and Kirby, R. J. (1993). Long-term comparison of brief versus unlimited psychodynamic treatments with children and their parents. *Journal of Counseling and Clinical Psychology, 61,* 1020-1027.

Tucker-Ladd, C. E. (1996a). *Psychological self-help*. Dwight, IL: Self-Help Foundation.

Tucker-Ladd, C. E. (1996b). Teaching personally useful psychology. Unpublished manuscript.

Chapter 7

Workbooks for Individuals with Gambling Problems: Promoting the Natural Recovery Process Through Brief Intervention

David C. Hodgins

Problem gambling, defined as persistent and recurrent maladaptive gambling behavior, affects approximately 1 to 2 percent of the adult population in North America (American Psychiatric Association [APA], 1994). With increased recognition of the negative consequences of problem gambling has come increased interest in developing and evaluating effective treatment interventions. Unfortunately, outcome research for problem gambling treatment is limited (Kassinove, 1996; Walker, 1993). In a comprehensive review, nineteen published treatment studies were identified (Kassinove, 1996). These studies focused on a variety of treatment approaches including psychoanalysis, supportive therapy, Gamblers Anonymous (GA), marital therapy, multimodal inpatient care, drug treatments, and various cognitive-behavioral techniques. Of the nineteen studies, nine were case studies with one to three gamblers. Nine others were uncontrolled studies with small to moderate samples, leaving one controlled study. Most recently, *The Cochrane Review* published the results of a systematic review of randomized clinical trials (Oakley-Brown, Adams, and Mobberley, 2000). Only four studies were identified, and all were noted to have small sample sizes and methodological weaknesses. The review concluded that the experimental interventions, behavioral or cognitive-behavioral therapies, were more efficacious than the control interventions in the short-term. However, the review also concluded that more research is urgently required. In this chapter we describe the rationale and steps that we have taken to develop an empirically supported brief workbook intervention for problem gamblers.

RECOVERY FROM PROBLEM GAMBLING

We initially studied the recovery process of a group of media-recruited recovered gamblers versus a comparison group of active problem gamblers in a descriptive study (Hodgins, 2001; Hodgins and el-Guebaly, 2000). In-depth interviews were conducted with the group of forty-three recovered gamblers, about half of whom had received some treatment or Gamblers Anonymous exposure and about half who were "naturally recovered." We asked the recovered gamblers about the factors that precipitated their resolution (the "why?") and about the short-term and long-term strategies that they used to be successful (the "how?"). The group comprised eighteen women and nineteen men with a mean age of forty-four years (SD = 11) and an age range of twenty-one to seventy years. The largest group was employed full-time (46 percent) and 30 percent were unemployed. High school education or greater was reported by 73 percent. About half (47 percent) were married or living in common-law relationships, and 23 percent were single and never married. The mean South Oaks Gambling Screen (SOGS) (Lesieur and Blume, 1987) was twelve (SD = 4), which indicated a substantial degree of gambling difficulties, and all but one met the *Diagnostic and Statistical Manual of Mental Disorders*, Fourth Edition (DSM-IV) criteria for pathological gambling (APA, 1994). About half reported that their primary problem was video lottery terminals (VLTs), and 45 percent had problems with mixed casino games, often including VLTs. The remainder reported problems with horses (4 percent) and bingo (2 percent). The mean age of onset of problems was thirty-four (SD = 11), and mean length of problem resolution was forty-one months.

A substantial proportion of participants reported mood, alcohol, and other drug use disorders. Almost half reported a lifetime mood disorder, with 18 percent meeting DSM-IV criteria for a current mood disorder. Similarly, about half reported lifetime alcohol abuse or dependence with 5 percent reporting a current problem. Other lifetime drug use disorders were found in 27 percent of participants, with 4 percent reporting current problems. These results are consistent with findings from clinical samples of pathological gamblers (Crockford and el-Guebaly, 1998).

Recovered gamblers reported a variety of reasons for their resolutions, most of which were related to the emotional and financial consequences of their gambling. For example, depression, stress, panic, and guilt were frequently reported emotional consequences. Financial concerns such as "always losing money," "money getting tight," and "missing having a lot of money" were reported. About one-third indicated that their decision was related to a specific event, and one-third reported that it evolved over time.

Participants routinely provided a number of reasons for recovery (M = 3) versus only one trigger, suggesting that the process has multiple influences.

The recovered gamblers did not experience a greater number of negative life events in the year before recovery compared with the active problem gamblers. Instead, they reported more positive events and fewer negative events in the year after recovery. These results are similar to studies of the recovery process from alcohol problems (Sobell, Ellingstad, and Sobell, 2000) and run counter to the notion that "hitting bottom" is a necessary precursor to recovery. Recovery is clearly precipitated by a complex array of factors, although emotional reactions to consequences and financial aspects are pivotal.

Eighty-four percent reported that they stopped "cold turkey" versus tapering their involvement over time. When asked to describe their change strategies, recovered gamblers reported two major tactics. The first tactic was stimulus control—recovered gamblers reported that they curtailed their exposure to gambling opportunities and cues. For example, VLT players reported that they stayed away from bars and lounges where the machines are located. Horse-racing gamblers stopped reading the race results. The second common tactic was the development of activities incompatible with gambling. In recognition of the amount of time that gambling can take, the gamblers made a specific plan for how to fill the time. Examples included starting an exercise program, taking on a new work project, and spending more time reading or with family. A third tactic often reported was using a cognitive strategy such as reminding oneself of the negative consequences or the benefits of quitting, self-talk, or stopping oneself from thinking about gambling.

NATURAL VERSUS TREATMENT-ASSISTED RECOVERY

We found no differences in the types of recovery strategies used by treated and nontreated gamblers in the sample. However, treated gamblers had more severe gambling problems than did those who changed without treatment. As had been found in other areas of addiction (e.g., Humphreys, Moos, and Cohen, 1997; Klingemann et al., 2001; Sobell et al., 1996), individuals with less severe problems were more likely to report engaging in a self-recovery process. Significant gambling treatment involvement (broadly defined as either self-help group membership or talking with a professional about gambling issues on five or more occasions) was reported by 23 percent, minimal treatment by 18 percent (less than five exposures), and 59 percent reported no previous treatment. Of a wide range of demographic variables, only severity of gambling problem (number of DSM-IV criteria met, SOGS score) was related to treatment seeking. Those with less severe problems more likely reported "self-change," those with moderate problems reported "minimal treatment," and those with more severe problems reported significant treatment involvement.

These naturally recovered individuals and the active gamblers who had not been exposed to treatment in the comparison group were asked to complete a checklist of reasons for not seeking treatment. The responses are displayed in Table 7.1. As shown, the large majority of both groups reported that they "wanted to handle the problem on their own." This finding is consistent with the notion of a stepped care matching approach to problem gambling intervention. Such an approach has been advocated in treatment for other addictions, such as smoking (Abrams et al., 1996) and alcohol (Breslin et al., 1997; Sobell and Sobell, 2000) as well as other areas of medicine (Haaga, 2000).

APPLYING THE STEPPED CARE MODEL
TO PROBLEM GAMBLING

Application of the stepped care model to problem gambling is presented in Figure 7.1. As can be seen, problem and pathological gamblers are grouped into individuals ready to change and those not ready to change. Interventions for this latter group include public health efforts and efforts of family members to enhance the gamblers' readiness to tackle their problem. For example, we recently developed a self-help program for concerned significant others to help them engage the problem gambler into treatment (Makarchuk, Hodgins, and Peden, 2002).

TABLE 7.1. Reasons for Not Seeking Treatment for Gambling Problems

Reason	Recovered (n = 23) (%)	Active (n = 39) (%)
Wanted to handle problem on own	78.3	79.5
No problem/no help needed	60.9	35.9
Embarrassment/pride	34.8	59.0
Stigma	39.1	51.3
Ignorance of treatment or availability	34.8	51.3
Unable to share problems	21.7	33.3
Negative attitude toward treatments	8.7	25.6
Cost of treatment	0	23.1

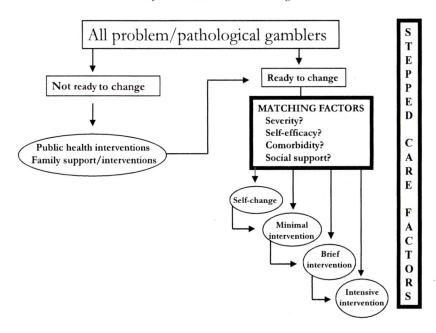

FIGURE 7.1. Stepped Care Process for Problem Gambling Resolution

Those individuals who are ready to tackle their problem are matched to or select the appropriate level of intervention, ranging from self-change (natural recovery) to intensive interventions such as residential programs. The initial intervention recommended is the one that is least expensive and least intrusive on the gambler's lifestyle, but one that is reasonably likely to be effective. Failure in a less intensive intervention is followed by interventions of increasing intensity.

The stepped care model is a heuristic to support our efforts to develop and evaluate an effective intervention system. Support for the stepped care model comes from the fact that it is difficult to attract problem gamblers to intensive treatment programs, particularly women (Lesieur and Rosenthal, 1991). Less than 3 percent of problem gamblers in the United States seek out the available treatments (National Gambling Impact Study Commission, 1999). To some of these remaining individuals, self-help materials or brief interventions may be an attractive and nonthreatening effective alternative. Self-help materials have a number of other potential advantages as well. They can be readily provided to problem gamblers in remote areas without gambling treatment resources. Individuals in remote areas have increased access to gambling opportunities because of advances in technology (e.g., Internet gambling, satellite bingo). Also, self-help materials are relatively inexpensive and time efficient. Finally, self-help materials are easily transferable.

SELF-HELP WORKBOOKS IN ADDICTIONS

Self-help workbooks have been successfully used in a number of areas of behavior change, most notably problem drinking. Meta-analyses of comparisons between self-help interventions and no treatment controls or therapist-directed interventions have indicated that self-help approaches are more effective than controls and are comparable to the same programs administered by therapists (Gould and Clum, 1993). One uncontrolled study with problem gamblers conducted in Australia compared self-help materials with and without an additional personal interview (Dickerson, Hinchy, and Legg England, 1990). General improvement was found after six months with no difference between the groups.

Minimal interventions, including self-help workbooks, have been described as "dissuasions," reflecting their motivational qualities (Babor, 1994). The majority of the individual's behavior change takes place during the first few sessions before much skill development is possible. Consistent with this notion, the effectiveness of self-help workbooks for problem drinkers was enhanced by specific motivational telephone contact with a therapist in advance of receiving the workbook (Sanchez-Craig, Davila, and Cooper, 1996).

DEVELOPING A SELF-HELP WORKBOOK
FOR PROBLEM GAMBLERS

To capitalize on the desire of some problem gamblers to recover without formal help, the techniques that were identified as significant in the recovery process in our study were compiled into a self-help workbook. The self-help workbook (*Becoming a Winner: Defeating Problem Gambling,* Hodgins and Makarchuk, 1997) is based on a cognitive-behavioral model of problem gambling (Sharpe and Tarrier, 1993; Blaszczynski and Silove, 1995), relapse prevention techniques (Marlatt and Gordon, 1980), as well as the results of our study of the recovery process of problem gamblers (Hodgins and el-Guebaly, 2000). The workbook underwent pilot testing with a small group of problem gamblers, and was reviewed by experienced gambling counselors. It is written in simple language with an estimated grade level of 5.8 (Flesch-Kincaid formula calculated by Microsoft-Word).

The workbook includes the following sections:

1. *Self-assessment:* This section focuses on increasing individuals' awareness of the consequences of their gambling and the situations that commonly precipitate gambling. The consequences are identified in a number of ways. The SOGS is included, which allows individuals to compare their overall score to cutoffs for problem and pathological gamblers. A checklist of negative consequences and a calendar used to reconstruct the financial costs of gambling for the past month serve to highlight specific negative consequences for the individual. The situations associated with gambling are identified in two additional exercises. The first exercise involves reconstructing the last three gambling situations in terms of situations, affect, and cognition. The second exercise involves completing a checklist of reasons for gambling.

2. *Goal setting:* The goal-setting section begins with a decisional balance exercise (Janis and Mann, 1977) designed to facilitate a cognitive appraisal of the perceived costs and benefits of gambling. This technique is commonly used to make apparent the benefits of change and to identify potential obstacles to change. It has been used successfully with behavior change in a number of areas, including smoking (Velicer et al., 1985) and drinking (Sobell et al., 1996). This section also includes a discussion of abstinence or controlled gambling as a goal. The individual is asked to specify a goal, and if it involves some gambling to specify the types, frequency, and amount of money allowed.

3. *Strategies:* Various cognitive-behavioral strategies are reviewed in this section: cognitive restructuring, dealing with urges using cognitive or behavioral coping, stimulus control (staying away from gambling and limiting access to money), and eliciting social support (telling others of the plan).

4. *Maintenance:* The goal of this section is to help prepare the individual for preventing and coping with relapses. Individuals are asked to review the previous sections to ensure that they have a plan for dealing with high-risk situations. They are also asked to identify other major life problems that need attention in order to stop problematic gambling.

5. *Other resources:* The final section contains information on accessing other resources if additional help is needed.

CLINICAL TRIAL

In our first clinical trial, two alternative self-help protocols were compared to a waiting-list control (see Hodgins, Currie, and el-Guebaly, 2001, for details). The first approach involved simply providing a self-help workbook via the mail (Group 1); the second involved a telephonic motivational interview prior to the receipt of the workbook (Group 2). After the waiting period, which was one month in length, wait-list participants were reassigned to either Group 1 or Group 2. The workbook was distributed as a bound booklet with the instruction that the participant work through the exercises at his or her own pace. The participant was asked to give his or her impressions of the workbook but completions of the exercises was not monitored.

There were two primary hypotheses. It was hypothesized that participants in Groups 1 and 2 would show greater reduction in gambling at one month than those assigned to the control group. It was further hypothesized that participants receiving the motivational interview would show greater improvement than those receiving only the self-help workbook.

Recruitment of Problem Gamblers

Media announcements (press releases, paid advertisements, and flyers) were used to recruit individuals:

> Are you concerned about your gambling? We are seeking individuals who are interested in overcoming their problem with gambling and who would like to quit or cut back on their own. This free program is being offered by telephone and through the mail as part of a research project at the University of Calgary. You must be willing to participate in four or five brief telephone interviews. For more information call 1-800- . . . . Confidentiality ensured.

The goal was to target both urban and rural settings within the province of Alberta. However, because of substantial media interest, 20 percent of the sample was recruited from other areas of Canada. Interested individuals telephoned a toll-free number and were provided with information about the study by the research assistant. Inclusion criteria were minimum age of eighteen, perception of a gambling problem, not presently involved in treatment, willing to read a short book as treatment (to ensure reading ability), willing to provide follow-up data on gambling, willing to provide the name of a collateral to help locate them for follow-up interviews and the name of the same or a different collateral for data validation.

Calls were received from 196 individuals, but about half the callers were inappropriate. Most calls came from individuals hoping to get the self-help workbook for a family member or friend with a gambling problem. These individuals were asked to encourage the gambler to call back personally and were also given information about other resources. This group inspires our ongoing development of self-help materials for concerned significant others (Makarchuk, Hodgins, and Peden, 2002). A large number of calls were also received from therapists hoping to get the workbook for use with their clients. Inclusion criteria were met by 102 individuals. Thirty-five were assigned to Group 1, thirty-two to Group 2, and thirty-five to Group 3.

The mean age of the 102 participants was forty-six years (SD = 9), and 52 percent were women. Cultural group was identified as Canadian by 91 percent, native 2 percent, and other 7 percent. In terms of marital status, 59 percent were married or in a common-law relationship, 23 percent separated or divorced, 14 percent never married, and 4 percent widowed. The mean education level was 11.3 years (SD = 1.2), and 64 percent were employed full-time. Eighty-six percent reported that VLTs were a major problem, 19 percent casinos, 10 percent bingo, 4 percent horse racing, 4 percent lotteries, 3 percent slot machines, 3 percent card games, 1 percent speculative investments, and 1 percent games of skill. The mean SOGS score was twelve (SD = 3.7) with a range of three to nineteen. Previous treatment was reported by 56 percent, mostly Gamblers Anonymous attendance (42 percent). In the month before entry into the study, the median amount of money lost was $1,000, and participants reported gambling a mean of ten days (SD = 8). Quitting was the goal of 84 percent, with 16 percent wishing to cut back on gambling.

Of the 102 participants, ninety-three were interviewed at one month, eighty-four at three months, eighty-two at six months, and eighty-five at twelve months. Because participants could provide some data for earlier missed assessments, follow-up data are available for 96 percent of participants at one month, 94 percent at three months, 90 percent at six months, and 83 percent at twelve months.

Motivational Interview Equals Motivational Nudge

The basic assessment information described earlier was obtained during the motivational interview (e.g., Sanchez-Craig et al., 1996). In contrast to the friendly but task-oriented information-gathering approach of the research assistant, the motivational interview attempts to build a commitment to change by using the principles of motivational enhancement therapy (Miller and Rollnick, 1991). This interview took between twenty and forty-five minutes to conduct, and the brief assessment that was conducted with other participants was built into the interview. The general style of the interview was to be supportive, empathetic, and interested. The interview had four goals in addition to collecting the assessment information. The interviewer attempted to elicit the gambler's concerns, including the difficulties experienced (e.g., "What worries have you had about your gambling?" and "What makes you think you need to change your gambling?"). The interviewer queried effects on financial and legal status, relationships, and emotional functioning, and elicited advantages of quitting. The second and third goals were to explore the gambler's ambivalence about change and promote self-efficacy: "What might make it difficult to accomplish this? How successful do you think you will be? Looking back, what makes you think you can accomplish it?" Finally, the interview suggested specific strategies for the individual based on past successful change attempts. These strategies were tied to a section of the workbook. For example, "It sounds like starting exercising was helpful when you quit smoking. There is a section in the workbook that recommends taking on new activities. That might be helpful."

The interview concluded by recording some contact information for the participant. The interviewer prepared a brief personalized note to the gambler that was sent along with the workbook.

Summary of the Results

Detailed results from the study are available elsewhere (Hodgins, Currie, and el-Guebaly, 2001; Hodgins et al., in press). A number of the findings are of particular interest. First, it was very easy to recruit participants to the study. Participants who showed clear evidence of significant gambling problems, with SOGS scores similar to other clinical samples, were very interested in this self-help approach to treatment. This finding supports the need for a range of intervention options for problem gamblers, consistent with the stepped care model. We were particularly struck by the fact that more than half of the participants were women. It is not clear what aspect of the approach appeals to women—the privacy, the ability to integrate it into a busy life, and the focus on self-management are possibilities.

The second important finding from this trial was that participants on the waiting list showed improvement over the one-month period. We recruited motivated individuals who wanted to change "on their own." It is not surprising that they initiated the change process while on the waiting list. This may have been, in part, in response to the enrollment and brief assessment procedure. However, despite improvement in waiting-list participants, participants in the active treatments were more than twice as likely to show improvement in the first month. This finding supports the notion that the materials promote a natural recovery process.

The initial gains made by participants early in the follow-up period were maintained at twelve and twenty-four months. At twelve months, about 84 percent showed a reduction of at least 50 percent in the amount of money lost per month and 25 percent were entirely gambling free. At the twenty-four-month follow-up, 77 percent were improved with 37 percent reporting six months of abstinence. According to the SOGS for the past year, 55 percent scored below the cutoff for pathological gambling (i.e., five), compared with 30 percent at twelve months. Women and men did equally well. Almost half (47 percent) of the participants rated their needs as mostly or completely met. Seventy-eight percent indicated that they would recommend the program to a friend.

An additional important finding for this trial was that an early advantage existed for the group receiving the motivational intervention. Figure 7.2 displays the outcome of participants at three-, six-, twelve-, and twenty-four-month follow-up assessments. A statistical difference exists between the two groups at three, six, and twenty-four months with a nonsignificant trend for

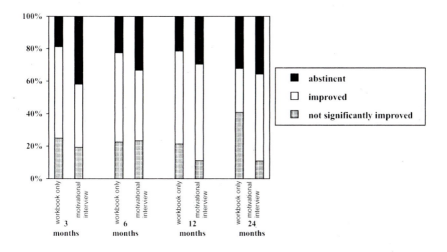

FIGURE 7.2. Clinical Classification of Outcome of Participants at Each Follow-Up Period

twelve months. The brief telephone intervention appears to be a wise investment of resources to enhance the likelihood of individual success.

We attempted to identify individual characteristics that would suggest better outcome with the workbook only or motivational intervention plus the workbook. As would be predicted by the stepped care model in Figure 7.1, we hypothesized that greater severity (as measured by the SOGS) would be associated with better outcome from the relatively more intensive intervention (i.e., workbook plus motivational intervention). We found the opposite—both interventions were equally effective with higher severity, and the motivational enhancement group had improved outcomes at twelve months with lower severity. This finding is intriguing, and may suggest that more intensive or more sustained motivational work is necessary for more severe problems. However, the SOGS is not designed as a severity measure, and replication with other indicators of severity is important.

CONCLUSION

The interest in developing an effective treatment for problem gambling is growing rapidly. Because few formal treatments are offered in many jurisdictions, we are well positioned to impact the thinking about treatment systems as they develop. The promotion of self-change or natural recovery as a treatment intervention is one way to broaden the system to maximize valuable resources, maximize the number of problem gamblers seeking intervention, and, ultimately, minimize gambling-related harms (Hodgins, Wynne, and Makarchuk, 1999).

REFERENCES

Abrams, D. B., Orlean, C. T., Niaura, R. S., Goldstein, M. D., Prochaska, J. O., and Velicer, W. (1996). Integrating individual and public health perspectives for treatment of tobacco dependence under managed health care: A combined stepped-care and matching model. *Annals of Behavioral Medicine, 18*, 290-304.

American Psychiatric Association (1994). *Diagnostic and statistical manual of mental disorders,* Fourth edition. Washington, DC: APA.

Babor, T. F. (1994). Avoiding the horrid and beastly sin of drunkenness: Does dissuasion make a difference? *Journal of Consulting and Clinical Psychology, 62,* 1127-1140.

Blaszczynski, A. P. and Silove, D. (1995). Cognitive and behavioral therapies for pathological gambling. *Journal of Gambling Studies, 11,* 195-220.

Breslin, F. C., Sobell, N. B., Sobell, L. C., Buchan, G., and Cunningham, J. A. (1997). Toward a stepped care approach to treating problem drinkers: The predictive validity of within-treatment variables and therapist prognostic ratings. *Addiction, 92,* 1479-1489.

Crockford, D. and el-Guebaly, N. (1998). Psychiatric comorbidity in pathological gambling. *Canadian Journal of Psychiatry, 43,* 43-50.

Dickerson, M., Hinchy, J., and Legg England, S. (1990). Minimal treatments and problem gamblers: A preliminary investigation. *Journal of Gambling Studies, 6,* 87-102.

Gould, R. and Clum, G. (1993). A meta-analysis of self-help treatment approaches. *Clinical Psychology Review, 13,* 169-178.

Haaga, D. A. (2000). Introduction to the special section on stepped care models in psychotherapy. *Journal of Consulting and Clinical Psychology, 68,* 547-548.

Hodgins, D. C. (2001). Processes of changing gambling behavior. *Addictive Behaviors, 26,* 121-128.

Hodgins, D. C., Currie, S. R., and el-Guebaly, N. (2001). Motivational enhancement and self-help treatments for problem gambling. *Journal of Consulting and Clinical Psychology, 69,* 50-57.

Hodgins, D. C., Currie, S. R., el-Guebaly, N., and Peden, N. (in press). Brief motivational treatment for problem gambling: 24-month follow-up.

Hodgins, D. C. and el-Guebaly, N. (2000). Natural and treatment-assisted recovery from gambling problems: Comparison of resolved and active gamblers. *Addiction, 95,* 777-789.

Hodgins, D. C., and Makarchuk, K. (1997). *Becoming a winner: Defeating problem gambling.* Calgary: Alberta Alcohol and Drug Abuse Commision.

Hodgins, D. C., Wynne, H., and Makarchuk, K. (1999). Pathways to recovery from gambling problems: Follow-up from a general population survey. *Journal of Gambling Studies, 15,* 93-104.

Humphreys, K., Moos, R. H., and Cohen, C. (1997). Social and community resources and long-term recovery from treated and untreated alcoholism. *Journal of Studies on Alcohol, 58,* 231-238.

Janis, I. L. and Mann, L. (1977). *Decision-making: A psychological analysis of conflict, choice, and commitment.* New York: Free Press.

Kassinove, J. I. (1996). Pathological gambling: The neglected epidemic. *The Behavior Therapist, 19,* 102-104.

Klingemann, H., Sobell, L., Blomquist, J., Cloud, W., Finfgeld, D., Granfield, R., Hodgins, D. C., Hunt, G., Junker, F., Moggi, F., et al. (2001). *Promoting self-change from problem substance use. Practical implications for policy, prevention, and treatment.* New York: Kluwer Academic.

Lesieur, H. and Blume, S. (1987). The South Oaks Gambling Screen (SOGS): A new instrument for the identification of pathological gamblers. *American Journal of Psychiatry, 144,* 1184-1188.

Lesieur, H. R. and Rosenthal, R. J. (1991). Pathological gambling: A review of the literature (prepared for the American Psychiatric Association Task Force on DSM-IV Committee on Disorders of Impulse Control Not Elsewhere Clarified). *Journal of Gambling Studies, 7,* 5-39.

Makarchuk, K., Hodgins, D. C., and Peden, N. (2002). Development of a brief intervention for concerned significant others of problem gamblers. *Addictive Disorders and Their Treatment, 1*, 126-134.

Marlatt, G. A. and Gordon, J. J. (1980). Determinants of relapse: Implications for the maintenance of behavior change. In P. O. Davidson and S. M. Davidson (Eds.), *Behavioral medicine: Changing health lifestyles* (pp. 410-452). New York: Brunner/Mazel.

Miller, W. R. and Rollnick, S. (1991). *Motivational interviewing. Preparing people to change addictive behavior.* New York: Guilford.

National Gambling Impact Study Commission (1999). *Final report.* Washington, DC: Government Printing Office.

Oakley-Brown, M. A., Adams, P., and Mobberley, P. M. (2000). Interventions for pathological gambling (Cochrane Review). *The Cochrane Library, 3.* Available online at <www.cochrane.org>.

Sanchez-Craig, M., Davila, R., and Cooper, G. (1996). A self-help approach for high-risk drinking: Effect of an initial assessment. *Journal of Consulting and Clinical Psychology, 64*, 694-700.

Sharpe, L. and Tarrier, N. (1993). Toward a cognitive-behavioural theory of problem gambling. *British Journal of Psychiatry, 162*, 407-412.

Sobell, L. C., Cunningham, J. A., Sobell, M. B., Agrawal, S., Gavin, D. R., Leo, G. I., and Singh, K. N. (1996). Fostering self-change among problem drinkers: A proactive community intervention. *Addictive Behaviors, 21*, 817-834.

Sobell, L. C., Ellingstad, T. P., and Sobell, M. B. (2000). Natural recovery from alcohol and drug problems: Methodological review of the research with suggestions for future directions. *Addiction, 95*, 749-764.

Sobell, M. B. and Sobell, L. C. (2000). Stepped care as a heuristic approach to the treatment of alcohol problems. *Journal of Consulting and Clinical Psychology, 68*, 573-579.

Velicer, W. F., Di Clemente, C. C., Prochaska, J. O., and Brandenberg, N. (1985). Decisional balance measures for assessing and predicting smoking status. *Journal of Personality and Social Psychology, 48*, 1279-1289.

Walker, M. B. (1993). Treatment strategies for problem gambling: A review of effectiveness. In Eadington, W. R. and Cornelius, J. A. (Eds.), *Gambling behavior and problem gambling* (pp. 533-566). Reno, NV: Institute for the Study of Gambling and Commercial Gaming.

Chapter 8

The Wheel of Wisdom
with Depressed Inpatients

Piero De Giacomo
Marco Storelli
Andrea De Giacomo
Caterina Tarquinio
Giovanni Carrieri
Odilia Mele
Massimiliano Morreale
Francesco Vaira

Every year nearly 100 million people in the world become affected by depression, which is the second most common psychological disturbance worldwide if subclinical forms are included in the count (American Psychiatric Association [APA], 2000). The associated individual, social, and economic costs of this disorder are immense, and for this reason diagnosis, therapy, and prevention of depression and its recurrences are among the most urgent challenges that researchers and clinicians have to face at the present time, in both hospital and outpatients settings.

Moreover, the widespread dissatisfaction at the length of time required with traditional methods, now that larger numbers of patients need to be helped in shorter times, confirms the importance of integrated treatments combining psycholeptic drugs and brief, strategic, patient-centered therapeutic techniques.

The Wheel of Wisdom (De Giacomo and De Giacomo, 1997) was created as a diagnostic-psychotherapeutic tool with the goal of helping patients acquire greater knowledge of themselves by using it to jot down thoughts that can be fitted into a precise way of thinking (or constructions—containers in which the patients classify their processes of thought). These can then be reread and commented upon.

In the psychiatric clinic at Bari University Hospital in Bari, Italy, clinical experimentation with this tool has confirmed its efficacy and utility in treating depression.

OBJECTIVES AND RESEARCH HYPOTHESIS

1. To integrate psychotrophic drugs in the treatment of major depression syndromes with moderate symptoms
2. To use the wheel for depression syndromes secondary to a general medical condition and dysthymias

The Wheel of Wisdom has been used together with the pantheoretical method of scriptotherapy (Riordan, 1996) to assess their combined efficacy.

SCRIPTOTHERAPY

Psychotherapy generally relies on language, whereas nonverbal communication and the written word tend to be ignored and are often not used in therapy. In practice, blending the use of the various language forms provides better results, because events one can see naturally leave a stronger impression on visual memory, and because putting images down in writing is a way to objectify the patient's problem. Clinical and experimental studies have frequently pointed out how writing is a good way to clear one's thoughts. Writing helps one to acquire and retain new mental schemes and fosters problem solving. The issue of the use of workbooks in psychotherapy has been dealt with in the literature (L'Abate, 2001).

In our experimentation, we explored the possibility of exploiting the combined effect of two models (the wheel and scriptotherapy). One such experience had already been reported using "The Tape of the Mind Workbook" (Jordan and L'Abate, 1999). Our original goal, therefore, was to help depressed patients to analyze the flow of their cognitive processes and capture the beginning of an improvement at the moment when, for instance, their thinking was previously stuck on the "Great Tragedies," moving on to less pessimistic thinking. To do this, patients were asked to write their thoughts three times a day, at set times previously agreed upon with them, and to classify these thoughts using as reference a sheet that listed the ten possible ways of thinking and feeling and their relative explanations. Patients were assisted with this task by trained health personnel. They learned how to correlate changes in their thoughts with changes in their emotions, as well as changes in mood. The working hypothesis was that this could provide patients with a handy, useful tool that could act synergistically with prescribed drugs.

THE TECHNIQUE

Thinking implies running along a series of thoughts that follow one after another as a result of external events or of continual internal fluctuations. During this free flow of thoughts, we feel emotions that tinge the content of these thoughts with tragic, neutral, or sometimes comic colors. Our thinking can be compared to a wheel that turns and alternates different kinds of thoughts, reflecting our emotions and feelings.

Our thinking processes are a stable representation of the reality we experience, as determined by a given event, be it external or internal. They encompass thoughts, emotions, mental images, and external behavior. By diligently filling out the Wheel of Wisdom, it is possible to learn to know the dominant colors of our thoughts and also the mechanisms for bringing about changes.

According to this model, we think in ten different ways or "constructions." The ten ways of thinking are outlined here, with a brief explanation of their meanings:

1. *Great tragedies:* This means that we keep on thinking about tragic, sad, anguishing, and desperate events, dwelling on them with great intensity. It seems to us there is no way out: great loss, great disappointments, great pangs of conscience and remorse, huge mistakes we have made, terrible events and experiences, etc.
2. *Moderate tragedies:* We think with a lower intensity of pessimism—the darkness is not total, there is a slight ray of light, and things are just about tolerable. The points at issue are the same: loss, mistakes, very bad experiences, humiliations, but to a lesser degree.
3. *Small tragedies:* Consist of unpleasant experiences, but with a very low degree of intensity, that are all quite tolerable: loss, mistakes, humiliations, etc.
4. *Very amusing comedies:* Thoughts that are very amusing and that make us laugh and put us in a good mood.
5. *Moderately amusing comedies:* Thinking about very pleasant and enjoyable events that put us in a good mood, but certainly do not make us laugh as hard.
6. *Not particularly amusing comedies:* Unlike the very amusing and moderately amusing comedies, thinking about pleasant, gratifying episodes that bring a faint, pleased smile to our lips.
7. *Instrumental tasks:* Moments when we are intent on carrying out a given task, such as, "Now I must do this, now I must do that." For ex-

ample, "Now I am writing at the computer," "I am getting ready to go out and buy bread."

8. *Triumphs:* Times when we feel very clever, very proud of ourselves.
9. *Neutral past memories:* When we remember something neutral that is neither tragic nor comic but is just simply a memory.
10. *Dreams for the future:* These are daydreams, fantasies, ambitions, and hopes for the future—about what things we would like to happen in our lives to make us feel happy.

METHOD AND EXPERIMENTAL PROCEDURE

Subjects with a diagnosis of major depressive disorder or those in the depression phase of bipolar disorder who were admitted to our psychiatric clinic at Bari University Hospital (Italy) were enrolled in this study after having been examined by the ward medical staff. Subjects were randomly assigned to the control or experimental group by tossing a coin. The control group was administered pharmacological treatment only, whereas the experimental group was administered pharmacological treatment and the Wheel of Wisdom. Both groups completed psychodiagnostic tests for depression (Beck, 1969; Zung, 1965), usually three days after admission to the ward, so as not to interfere with normal ward activities (taking medical history, psychological testing, treatment decision making). The personnel who administered the Wheel of Wisdom were unaware of the type of psychotrophic drugs administered to the subjects in the two groups. Only the ward doctors knew what type and dosage of drugs had been administered.

Neither of the two groups received any kind of psychological support (apart from the Wheel of Wisdom in the experimental group).

The two groups were allowed to receive visits from family and friends. The ward doctors held clinical interviews with the subjects in each group once every two days to monitor their clinical conditions.

Subjects assigned to the experimental group underwent a preliminary session during which the experiment was carefully explained. The following is a faithful transcript of what was said to them when they were given the Wheel of Wisdom:

We are doing this to help you feel better. This will be possible if you can understand better how you think. If you try and read what you have in your mind at the moment you will get a series of confused impressions, feelings of not very clearly defined malaise, thoughts that make you suffer, fantasies, emotions, and behavior that seem to you unbearable. You should know that you think as a running tape, a revolving wheel. This tape contains your processes of thought, that are linked with your ideas, emotions, and affections.

If, for instance, you have suffered a deep sorrow for the loss of a person you love, you will have very tragic thoughts. If, instead, you think about a friend you met the other day who made you laugh, you will give your thoughts an amusing shade and it is you yourself who will establish whether it is very amusing, moderately so, or not very amusing. Alternatively, if you are thinking about a piece of work you want to do, you will think of instrumental tasks.

We believe that if you can succeed in identifying how you think and consequently the working of your processes of thought, you will be able to see the things that happen to you in the right light, and this will help you to overcome your problems.

At this stage the patient was given a sheet of paper defining the ten possible ways of thinking, and the researcher commented on them and gave some examples.

Regarding the administration technique, it should be borne in mind that the first author of this work has patented an object shaped like a mandala called the Wheel of Wisdom (see Figure 8.1) (De Giacomo, 2001). In this Wheel, the ten ways of thinking or "constructions" are listed in the fixed wheel with a time sheet under the rotating disk and blank spaces for various times of the day. The same author also developed a computer program called The Tape of the Mind, which is available in English (De Giacomo, 1999). The computer program, the procedure described earlier for the wheel and its use in our experimentation with sheets of paper on which to mark our processes of thought that run through the mind at various times, classifying them into the ten possible ways of thinking, are different methods of practical application of this psychotherapeutic technique.

ANALYSIS AND DESCRIPTION OF THE SAMPLE

The experimental sample was composed largely of women, which is in line with the epidemiological data showing that depression is 1.5 to two times more prevalent in women than in men (APA, 2000). Patients were of different ages, but the greatest number of patients, 73.6 percent, belonged to the age range from thirty to sixty years. As for education, 55.2 percent of the subjects had attended middle school, 31 percent high school, and 13.8 percent university.

The study had a 14.3 percent dropout rate, consisting of six subjects who dropped out within the first four days of the experimentation: three said they

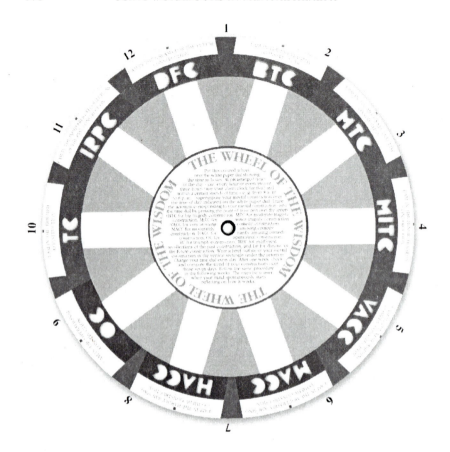

FIGURE 8.1. The Wheel of Wisdom

were too depressed to fill out the wheel, two patients said they had no faith in such things, and one patient offered no explanation.

The description of the sample and the results of the experimentation are reported in Table 8.1 and Tables 8.2 to 8.11 respectively.

ANALYSIS OF RESULTS

One-way analysis of variance (ANOVA) (Fisher, 1956; Scheffè, 1959; Stapleton, 1995) is used separately in experimental and control groups to

TABLE 8.1. Distribution and Educational Level of Subjects

Attribute	Number
Sex	
Men	32
Women	55
Age	
< 20	1
21-30	12
31-40	29
41-50	18
51-60	17
61-70	7
> 70	3
Education	
Middle school	48
High school	27
University	12

Note: Based on a random selection method.

test mean score reductions of the self-administered Beck and Zung tests, each week for three weeks. In addition to determining that differences exist among the means, one-way ANOVA provides the information on which means differ. The post hoc Tukey-Kramer (T-K) multiple comparisons test allows researchers to compare means. One-way ANOVA assumes that the data are sampled from populations that follow Gaussian distributions with identical variances. These assumptions are tested using the Kolmogorov-Smirnov and the Bartlett method respectively.

Two-way ANOVA is used to analyze the different treatments (Factor 1) during the three weeks (Factor 2). The Beck and Zung tests can be grouped by defining the within-subjects factor having three levels (first, second, and third week). The treatment can be specified as a between-subjects factor to study the differences between experimental and control groups. Two-way ANOVA allows researchers to determine the effect of the treatments.

The descriptive statistics for the Beck and Zung tests in the control and experimental group are contained in Tables 8.2, 8.3, 8.4, and 8.5.

In the control group, one-way ANOVA produced significantly time decreasing of the Beck and Zung test results ($p < 0.0001$ and $p < 0.004$ respec-

TABLE 8.2. Descriptive Statistics for the Beck Test in the Control Group

Week	n	Mean	Standard Deviation	Standard Error	95 Percent Confidence Interval for Mean		Minimum	Maximum
					Lower Bound	Upper Bound		
1	39	35.5128	9.2619	1.4831	32.5105	38.515	15.00	54.00
2	39	26.1282	10.6232	1.7011	22.6846	29.571	3.00	48.00
3	23	23.2609	7.0789	1.4761	20.1997	26.322	6.00	31.00
Total	101	29.0990	10.6691	1.0616	26.9928	31.205	3.00	54.00

TABLE 8.3. Descriptive Statistics for the Zung Test in the Control Group

| Week | n | Mean | Standard Deviation | Standard Error | 95 Percent Confidence Interval for Mean | | Minimum | Maximum |
					Lower Bound	Upper Bound		
1	39	52.8462	9.7563	1.5623	49.6835	56.008	26.00	74.00
2	39	45.3846	10.5572	1.6905	41.9624	48.806	20.00	65.00
3	18	46.5000	9.4324	2.2232	41.8094	51.190	30.00	64.00
Total	96	48.6250	10.5384	1.0756	46.4897	50.760	20.00	74.00

TABLE 8.4. Descriptive Statistics for the Beck Test in the Experimental Group

| Week | n | Mean | Standard Deviation | Standard Error | 95 Percent Confidence Interval for Mean | | Minimum | Maximum |
					Lower Bound	Upper Bound		
1	42	36.3333	12.2846	1.8955	32.5052	40.1615	9.00	63.00
2	42	21.6429	11.7532	1.8136	17.9803	25.3054	4.00	55.00
3	24	16.0833	6.9715	1.4230	13.1395	19.0271	2.00	34.00
Total	108	26.1204	13.8785	1.3355	23.4730	28.7678	2.00	63.00

TABLE 8.5. Descriptive Statistics for the Zung Test in the Experimental Group

Week	n	Mean	Standard Deviation	Standard Error	95 Percent Confidence Interval for Mean		Minimum	Maximum
					Lower Bound	Upper Bound		
1	42	55.0952	9.6545	1.4897	52.0867	58.1038	40.00	72.00
2	42	40.2619	9.8031	1.5126	37.2070	43.3168	19.00	60.00
3	21	33.6667	7.8888	1.7215	30.0757	37.2576	18.00	50.00
Total	105	44.8762	12.7571	1.2450	42.4074	47.3450	18.00	72.00

tively). For the Beck test, the multiple comparison by the post hoc test of the T-K produced a very significant difference between the first and second week ($p < 0.0001$) and between the first and third week ($p < 0.0001$). The difference between the second and third week was not significant. For the Zung depression test, the post hoc test is significant only for the first and the second week ($p < 0.004$).

One-way ANOVA produced extremely significant results ($p < 0.0001$) for the both of the depression tests in the experimental group. For the Beck test, the multiple comparisons produced the same results as the control group. For the Zung test, the post hoc test is significant for the first and second week ($p < 0.0001$), between the first and third week ($p < 0.0001$), and between the second and third week ($p < 0.0027$).

The results of the two-way ANOVA, in which the Beck test was measured each week for three weeks, are shown in Table 8.6.

The test of within-subjects effect (time factor) is very significant ($p < 0.0001$), showing a significant contrast for the first and second week ($p < 0.0001$) and the third and the second week ($p < 0.0001$). The test of between-subjects effect (control and experimental group) is significant ($p < 0.05$). Tables 8.7 and 8.8 show the estimated marginal means for both factors.

The results of a two-way ANOVA for the Zung test measured each week for three weeks are shown in Table 8.9.

The test of within-subjects effect (time factor) is very significant ($p < 0.0001$), showing a significant contrast for the first and second week

TABLE 8.6. Two-Way Table for the Beck Test

Type	Mean	Standard Deviation	n
Week 1			
Control group	40.1579	6.1848	19
Experimental group	38.5000	11.6320	24
Total	39.2326	9.5490	43
Week 2			
Control group	28.9474	9.7381	19
Experimental group	22.5000	10.7137	24
Total	25.3488	10.6788	43
Week 3			
Control group	23.4211	8.9896	19
Experimental group	16.0833	6.9715	24
Total	19.3256	8.6512	43

TABLE 8.7. Estimated Marginal Means for the Beck Test in the Different Treatments

Type	Mean	Standard Error	95 Percent Confidence Interval	
			Lower Bound	Upper Bound
Control group	30.842	1.904	26.996	34.688
Experimental group	25.694	1.695	22.272	29.117

TABLE 8.8. Estimated Marginal Means for the Beck Test in the Different Weeks

Week	Mean	Standard Error	95 Percent Confidence Interval	
			Lower Bound	Upper Bound
1	39.329	1.478	36.344	42.314
2	25.724	1.581	22.531	28.917
3	19.752	1.216	17.296	22.208

TABLE 8.9. Two-Way Table for the Zung Test

Type	Mean	Standard Deviation	n
Z0			
Control group	55.2778	9.3608	18
Experimental group	56.5238	9.6779	21
Total	55.9487	9.4283	39
Z1			
Control group	48.8333	8.9064	18
Experimental group	41.5714	8.0906	21
Total	44.9231	9.1317	39
Z2			
Control group	46.5000	9.4324	18
Experimental group	33.6667	7.8888	21
Total	39.5897	10.7035	39

TABLE 8.10. Estimated Marginal Means for the Zung Test in the Different Treatments

| | | | 95 Percent Confidence Interval | |
| | | Standard | Lower | Upper |
Type	Mean	Error	Bound	Bound
Control group	50.204	1.922	46.309	54.099
Experimental group	43.921	1.780	40.314	47.527

TABLE 8.11. Estimated Marginal Means for the Zung Test in the Different Weeks

| | | | 95 Percent Confidence Interval | |
| | | Standard | | |
Week	Mean	Error	Lower Bound	Upper Bound
1	55.901	1.531	52.798	59.003
2	45.202	1.361	42.444	47.960
3	40.083	1.386	37.274	42.892

($p < 0.0001$) and for the third and second week ($p < 0.0001$). The test of between-subjects effect (control and experimental group) is also significant ($p < 0.022$). Tables 8.10 and 8.11 show the estimated marginal means for both of the factors.

DISCUSSION AND CONCLUSIONS

The results obtained lead us to conclude that the Wheel of Wisdom acts in synergy with pharmacological treatment in cases of moderate and severe depression in the acute phase. The score reductions in the cases treated with the combined therapy were practically twice those obtained with pharmacological therapy alone, as shown by the Beck test, which mainly explores the cognitive aspect of depression, and the Zung test, which gives greater weight to the somatic symptoms of the disease (APA, 2000). In the latter test, the reduction was 2.5 times higher in the experimental group compared to the control group.

In conclusion, we can confirm the utility and importance of the Wheel of Wisdom. When used together with traditional therapy, it not only encourages the expression of inner feelings but also helps the patient face past and present events. This psychotherapeutic support makes it possible to give a new meaning and interpretation to events that occurred in the past, exploring unexpressed memories, and reelaborating painful experiences and insults to the ego, that were then turned into negative perceptions (Bara, 1996).

The Wheel of Wisdom helps the patient to work through painful and traumatic events and experiences, providing cognitive reframing to build on systematically. For example, it could be useful in bipolar subjects during the manic phase, since they have a hypertrophic ego and very often think of themselves as almighty persons (according to the "triumphs" way of thinking).

In fact, carefully filling out the wheel could help them to realize when an imminent crisis is coming and induce them to contact the specialist and have the dosage of their pharmacological treatment adjusted.

Other subjects could discover through filling out the wheel that they are living their lives in a tragic way of feeling—for instance, depressed subjects who often use the "great tragedies" way of thinking will notice after the first few days that an "instrumental tasks" or a "dreams for the future" way of feeling starts to appear. They can see a ray of light in the darkness, a sign that their minds are changing.

The tool also allowed us to make other interesting discoveries. We found that some subjects entirely lack particular processes of thought. For instance, people who always think in an "instrumental tasks" way started to wonder why they never have alternative courses of thought. In short, this self-observation task takes the subject on a mental journey, along a path that helps the subject to change.

The processes that seem to be activated with written homework assignments follow:

1. an increased sense of involvement and responsibility in the process of change—instead of leaving all responsibility in the doctor's hands patients who are involved only as passive containers of malaise become active self-observers;
2. intensification of the therapeutic effects of treatment thanks to the assignment of systematic, programmed tasks to be completed outside the therapeutic session;
3. use of these as stimuli for discussion in the next therapeutic session;
4. reduction of the costs and duration of treatment, because the patient works on the tasks between sessions;

5. help in working through forgotten events, memories, and traumatic experiences; and
6. the therapist is given a more complete idea of the patient's problem (Jordan and L'Abate, 1999; Jordan, 2001).

Subjects who worked on the Wheel of Wisdom entered into a new way of looking at reality, themselves, their world, and their disease, experiencing the possibility of being able to actively influence their own thinking. This process, inserted in the wider context of cognitive-behavioral therapy, provides respondents with tools to help them change their cognitive schemes and gain a new mental equilibrium, an essential requirement for them to be able to understand their own history and discover values they were previously unaware of or dismissed as unimportant.

The results of the experimentation need to be confirmed in further work, but they may act as a spur to all those operating in the psychological aid sector to adopt this new intervention model. We hope this support may also be beneficial to subjects suffering from organic diseases and convalescing from surgical procedures. These patients are affected by a drop, and sometimes a very sharp one, in the tone of their mood, brought on by their disease or operation. The professional administering the Wheel of Widsom does not need to possess complex psychotherapeutic skills. The instrument will do the work for the professional.

We would also like to stress that a low cultural level is not a contraindication for the administration of the Wheel of Wisdom, since it was found to be efficacious, as we have seen, in subjects with relatively little schooling.

Scriptotherapy seems to be the ideal therapeutic follow-up to the Wheel of Wisdom. The observation that some subjects passed straight on from the task of filling out the Wheel to doing scriptotherapy can be seen as a passage from theory to practice: some subjects can restore their equilibrium using only the wheel, whereas others need to keep themselves under control and move onto writing.

We do not, of course, wish to present the Wheel of Wisdom as a replacement for psychotherapy, still less for pharmacological treatment. However, we hope it may also be beneficial to patients outside the psychiatric field, who are affected by diseases such as cancer, and help them to face their problems with greater serenity. It may also help the doctors promote health care that aims to cure the patient in both body and soul.

REFERENCES

American Psychiatric Association (2000). *Diagnostic and statistical manual of mental disorders,* Fourth edition, Text revision. Washington, DC: American Psychiatric Association.

Bara B. G. (1996). *Manuale di psicoterapia cognitiva* (Manual of cognitive psychology). Torino: Bollati Boringhieri.

Beck A. T. (1969). Measuring depression: The depression inventory. In M. M. Katz and J. A. Shields (Eds.), *Recent advances in the psychology of depressive illness.* Washington, DC: U.S. Government Printing Office.

De Giacomo P. (1999). *Mente e creatività* (Mind and creativity). Milano: Franco Angeli.

De Giacomo P. (2001). Dispositivo a disco per autoriflessione (A rotating disk procedure for self-reflection). Patent no. 00242584. Ministero delle Attività Produttive: Italy.

De Giacomo P. and De Giacomo A. (1997). *Psicoterapia: Un metodo basato su un modello relazionale della mente* (Psychotherapy: A method based on a relational model of the mind), First edition. Fasano: Schena Editore.

Fisher R. A. (1956). *Statistical methods for research workers.* New York: Wiley.

Jordan K. B. (2001). Teaching psychotherapy through workbooks. In L. L'Abate (Ed.), *Distance writing and computer-assisted interventions in psychiatry and mental health* (pp. 171-190). Westport, CT: Ablex.

Jordan K. B. and L'Abate, L. (1999). The tape of the mind workbook: A single case study. *Journal of Family Psychotherapy, 10,* 13-25.

L'Abate L. (2001). Distance writing (DW) and computer-assisted interventions (CAI) in psychiatry and mental health. In L'Abate, L. (Ed.), *Distance writing and computer-assisted interventions in psychiatry and mental health* (pp. 3-31). Westport, CT: Ablex.

Riordan R. J. (1996). Scriptotherapy: Therapeutic writing as a counseling adjunct. *Journal of Counseling and Development, 74,* 263-269.

Scheffè H. (1959). *Analysis of variance.* New York: Wiley.

Stapleton J. H. (1995). *Linear statistical models.* New York: Wiley.

Zung, W. W. K. (1965). A self-rating depression scale. *Archives of General Psychiatry, 12,* 63.

Chapter 9

Substance Abuse in Women: An Empirical Evaluation of a Manualized Cognitive-Behavioral Protocol

Terry Michael McClanahan

Female substance abuse in America has reached epidemic levels (Substance Abuse and Mental Health Services Administration [SAMHSA], 1997a). The problem has become so prolific that morbidity data indicate an estimated 200,000 females will die annually of substance-related illness (Blumenthal, 1998). This morbidity is more than four times the number of females who will succumb to breast cancer.

Growing evidence indicates differences in both the etiology as well as epidemiology of substance abuse between males and females. For example, neurochemical research indicates that females are more sensitive than males to the rewarding effects of substances (Leshner, 1998). This results in more rapid addiction in females who abuse substances than in males. Emergency room data indicate that female mentions exceed those of males for many substances (e.g., methamphetamine and other stimulants, tranquilizers, and sedatives) (SAMHSA, 1998). These data also indicate that medical complications for females are more severe than are those of their male substance-abusing counterparts (SAMHSA, 1997b).

Although the aforementioned data indicate an obvious need, treatment for substance abuse has focused on male etiology and patterns of use (Hatsukami et al., 1997). Another complicating factor in the treatment of female substance abuse is the fact that a psychodynamic paradigm (and derivations thereof), continues to dominate treatment. Psychodynamic treatment paradigms focus on the intrapsychic underpinnings and are nondirective. The treatment approach espoused in this chapter is an adaptation of Carroll's (1998) model which is based on Beck's (1979), Ellis's (1962, 1986), and Meichenbaum's (1977) cognitive-behavioral treatments. Carroll's model, however, was developed for male veterans who were addicted to cocaine. The Carroll model was adapted for female substance abusers in order to introduce more client-centered aspects into their treatment. The Carroll (1998) model was also shortened due to treatment constraints of the original study (McClanahan, 2002).

A plethora of anecdotal pontifications postulates that treatment for females must be process oriented, thus eliminating manualized treatment, behavioral interventions, and workbooks entirely. As the following data indicate, these postulations are not borne out. In fact, behavioral interventions, of which the use of workbooks is paramount, indicate that an insight-oriented approach is contraindicated in the treatment of substance abusing females.

DESCRIPTION OF THE MANUALIZED COGNITIVE-BEHAVIORAL PROTOCOL

The CBT model utilized in this chapter is a manualized, short-term, highly structured, goal-oriented approach. The treatment is based on the use of a patient workbook wherein each session is divided into three sections (Carroll, 1998). The first portion of each session includes the therapist conducting an assessment of the status of each patient, which should be conducted transparently to the patient. This would include assessing relapse indicators, conducting a mental status examination, updating the functional analysis, and reviewing the homework assignment for that particular session. Although clinically necessary, these preliminary items also serve to further develop the therapeutic relationship while gleaning clinically relevant data. The middle portion of each session is dedicated to presenting a high level of content-specific information from the workbook (i.e., what is CBT?, why use workbooks?, the ABCs of substance use, coping with urges to use, the cognitive triad, problem solving high-risk situations, developing a coping plan, and maintaining treatment gains). The last portion of each session is dedicated to developing group cohesion through patient disclosure and discussing the homework assignment from the workbook. Each session ends with problem-solving strategies for remaining clean and sober until the next treatment session. The sessions are organized as follows:

1. Initiating treatment
   - *Goals:* Although the first session is often crucial in treatment compliance, this session is parament with female substance abusers. The first session focuses on introducing a CBT treatment approach, obtaining historical information, and forming a therapeutic relationship with each patient.

- *Assignment:* Begin to complete the functional analysis of addiction (Box 9.1).
2. The cycle of addiction
   - *Goals:* This session focuses on the cycle of addiction (ABCs). The patients are presented with the premise that everyday life is filled with biopsychosocial stressors, and although some may handle these situations effectively, others turn to substances as a method of coping. Thus the beginning stages of addiction and dysfunctional coping mechanisms are confronted from the outset.
   - *Assignment:* Complete the functional analysis of addiction (Box 9.1).
3. Coping with cravings
   - *Goals:* This session focuses on healthy ways of coping with the craving or urge to use substances to alleviate pain and suffering in an attempt to cope with environmental stressors.
   - *Assignment:* Continue to track thoughts, feelings, and behaviors through the functional analysis form (Box 9.1) and complete the Coping with Urges to Use form (Box 9.2).
4. Thoughts, feelings, and behaviors
   - *Goals:* This session focuses on the cognitive triad—thoughts, feelings, and behaviors—and how these are interrelated. For many substance abusers, this relationship leads to feelings of incompetence, shame, guilt, etc., and should be addressed in the session.
   - *Assignment:* Continue to track thoughts, feelings, and behaviors through the functional analysis form (Box 9.1) and complete the Coping with Urges to Use form (Box 9.2).
5. High-risk situations
   - *Goals:* This session focuses on developing strategies for handling high-risk situations. For instance, problem-solving strategies for coping with acquaintances who still use, offers of substances, and guilt trips.
   - *Assignment:* Continue to track thoughts, feelings, and behaviors through the functional analysis form (Box 9.1), complete the Coping with Urges to Use form (Box 9.2), and formulate a plan to handle high-risk situations.
6. Developing the coping plan
   - *Goals:* This session focuses on developing the coping plan. The coping plan includes emergency telephone numbers, safe havens, plans of when to contact services, etc.
   - *Assignment:* Continue to track thoughts, feelings, and behaviors through the functional analysis form (Box 9.1), complete the Coping

with Urges to Use form (Box 9.2), and implement the coping plan (Box 9.3).

7. Relapse prevention
   • *Goals:* This session focuses on maintaining gains made in treatment, including strategies for implementing the coping plan, and problem solving the next phase of treatment (i.e., transitioning from residential to outpatient).
   • *Assignment:* Continue to track thoughts, feelings, and behaviors through the functional analysis form (Box 9.1), complete the Coping with Urges to Use form (Box 9.2), and implement the coping plan (Box 9.3).

8. Termination
   • *Goals:* This session focuses on updating treatment plans, developing long-term goals, and reassurances that gains in treatment can be maintained.
   • *Assignment:* Continue to track thoughts, feelings, and behaviors through the functional analysis form (Box 9.1), complete the Coping with Urges to Use form (Box 9.2), and implement the coping plan (Box 9.3).

CLINICAL EFFICACY OF CBT WORKBOOKS WITH FEMALE SUBSTANCE ABUSERS

A pretest-posttest comparative experimental design was used to evaluate whether cognitive-behavioral therapy (CBT) that used workbooks extensively or a nondirective insight-oriented psychotherapy (IOP) treatment approach was more efficacious in the treatment of female substance abuse (McClanahan, 2002). Twenty-four participants were recruited, with the final sample consisting of seventeen participants who were randomly assigned to the two treatment conditions.

The cognitive-behavioral treatment in this study draws from the principles of Beck (1979), Ellis (1962, 1986), and Meichenbaum (1977). However, the CBT principles of this study (Carroll, 1998) diverge from the traditional substance abuse treatment approach by using a more client-centered and skills-building approach. The insight-oriented psychotherapy (IOP) condition of this study is based on Khantzian's (1985, 1986; Khantzian, Halliday, and McAuliffe, 1990) self-medication theory, which is a contemporary psychodynamic derivation. The self-medication model posits that when some individuals experience intrapsychic pain they turn to mood-altering substances to alleviate that pain.

BOX 9.1. Functional Analysis of Individual Patient's Cycle of Addiction

Situation (Who, What, When, Where)	Thoughts	Feelings	Behaviors	Consequences (positive and negative)
June 1, 9 a.m., woke up.	I need a drink/snort to face the day.	I was scared, feeling unsure of myself.	Went downstairs.	Positive—didn't use! Positive—felt good about myself!

BOX 9.2. Coping with Urges to Use

Date and Time	Triggers (Who, What, When, Where)	SUDS (0 to 100)	Length of Craving	Coping Mechanism
June 1, 9 a.m.	Woke up, remembered used to start the day with a drink/snort.	70	10 minutes	Went downstairs and spoke to the desk person.

BOX 9.3. High-Risk Coping Plan

Date: _____

I _____ (patient), hereby agree to not use either licit or illicit substances. If I feel the urge to use these substances, I agree to the following:

1. I will not use substances as a means of avoiding life circumstances.

2. I will leave the situation, in which case safe places that I can go include:
   _____
   _____

3. Emergency telephone numbers that I can use include:
   _____
   _____

Name: _____ Telephone: _____

Name: _____ Telephone: _____

Name: _____ Telephone: _____

4. I will remind myself of treatment gains which I have made to this point:
   _____
   _____
   _____
   _____

Participants

Participants were recruited from an outpatient, community-based, mental health clinic in urban California. Subjects were included if they were (1) female, (2) between the ages of eighteen and forty-four, and (3) had a diagnosis of substance abuse or dependence according to the *Diagnostic and Statistical Manual of Mental Disorders,* Fourth Edition (DSM-IV) (American Psychiatric Association, 1994). The participants were excluded if they were (1) male or transgender, (2) did not have a diagnosis of substance abuse or dependence according to the DSM-IV, (3) in an active state of psychosis, or (d) planning on leaving the community prior to the completion of treatment.

Demographic and psychiatric characteristics are detailed in Table 9.1. Subjects were randomly assigned to the two treatment conditions, with ten individuals initially assigned to the IOP treatment condition, and nine individuals assigned to the CBT treatment condition. Two individuals, one from each treatment condition, did not complete the study, and their data were not included in the data analysis.

Chi-square analysis revealed no statistically significant differences between the two treatment conditions for age [$\chi^2(1, n = 17) = .73, p = .12$], years of education [$\chi^2(1, n = 17) = .67, p = .19$], ethnicity [$\chi^2(1, n = 17) = .95, p = .51$], substance-related psychiatric diagnosis [$\chi^2(1, n = 17) = .86, p = .03$], or length of time since last substance use [$\chi^2(1, n = 17) = .92, p = .01$]. The fact that this was a relatively homogenous sample increases the probability that treatment effects will be caused by treatment conditions rather than by characteristics of the sample (Kazdin, 1992).

Procedure

Individuals who indicated an interest in the study were administered a brief screening interview to determine whether they met the inclusion criteria. Following this screen, they were scheduled for an intake interview, in which the informed consent process was conducted. If the recruit agreed to

TABLE 9.1. Demographic Characteristics at Intake

Variable	IOP ($n = 9$)				CBT ($n = 8$)			
	M	SD	Number	%	M	SD	Number	%
Age (years)	35.2	2.2			34.9	4.2		
Education (years)	11.9	1.8			11.8	0.9		
Months clean	4.1	2.9			3.5	1.6		
Ethnicity								
African American			8	89			5	63
Caucasian			0	0			1	13
Other			1	11			1	13
Substance related disorder								
Alcohol, current			1	11			0	0
Cocaine, current			8	89			7	88
Amphet., current			0	0			1	12

M = mean; SD = standard deviation; IOP = insight-oriented psychotherapy; CBT = cognitive-behavioral therapy participate in the study, he or she was assigned a client number, and the pretest assessment was initiated. If he or she was not interested in participating in the study, the individual was given referrals to community-based treatment programs. Participants were reimbursed after each assessment and treatment session. Posttest assessment was conducted after the completion of the treatment sessions.

Measures

Pre- and postintervention assessment included a diagnostic interview for depression (SCID; Spitzer et al., 1990) based on the DSM, and the Addiction Severity Index-F (ASI-F) (SAMHSA, 1997b).

Due to the complexity and length of training required to competently administer the SCID and the ASI-F, the principal investigator conducted each assessment interview as well as each of the treatment sessions. External raters were used to evaluate therapist adherence to theoretical principles and treatment manuals. The study was approved by the Institutional Review Board for the Protection of Human Subjects, and the patients were treated in accordance to ethical guidelines set forth by the American Psychological Association (1992).

Means and standard deviations were used to analyze variability in the data, effect sizes [$ES = (M_1 - M_2)/SD_{pooled}$] were used to determine statistical significance of the variance between sample means, and multivariate analysis of variance # (MANOVA) analyses (Tabachnick and Fidell, 1996) were conducted to determine statistical significance between groups. Table 9.2 presents the data for each treatment condition for the alcohol- and drug-status composite scores of the ASI-F.

IOP Within-Group Analysis

Within the IOP treatment condition, there was an increase in the alcohol-status composite score from pre- to posttest assessment. These scores yielded a large negative effect size ($ES = -.53$) from pretest ($M = .29$, $SD = .25$) to the posttest assessment ($M = .42$, $SD = .01$). This negative effect was a result of three individuals who relapsed during the course of treatment. Treatment yielded a small effect size ($ES = .04$) on drug status from the pretest ($M = .19$, $SD = .06$) to the posttest assessment ($M = .18$, $SD = .05$).

The IOP treatment produced virtually no change from pretest to posttest for employment status ($ES = .00$), legal status ($ES = .01$), family/social status ($ES = .00$), or psychiatric status ($ES = .00$). The lack of significant effect size

TABLE 9.2. Multivariate Test (Hotelling's T^2) for ASI-F Scales

Subscale	df	Value	sig.	p
Drug and alcohol	2	1.280	.056*	.05
Employ, legal, family, psychiatric	4	.329	.451	.025

*statistically significant
df = degrees of freedom; sig. = significance level; p = probability that the significance level is acceptable

indicates that the IOP treatment was not effective at increasing psychosocial functioning for the subjects assigned to this treatment condition.

CBT Within-Group Analysis

Subjects in the CBT group reported significant changes in both the alcohol- and drug-status composite scores from pre- to posttest assessment. Treatment yielded a large effect size (ES = .55) on alcohol status from pretest (M = .24, SD = .28) to the posttest assessment (M = .07, SD = .13). The CBT treatment also resulted in a large effect size (ES = 1.03) on drug status from the pretest (M = .22, SD = .07) to the posttest assessment (M = .13, SD = .07).

Subjects who received the CBT treatment condition yielded a small to medium effect size (ES = .10) on employment status from the pretest (M = .72, SD = .23) to the posttest assessment (M = .69, SD = .20). Treatment resulted in a small effect size (ES = .05) on legal status from the pretest (M = .21, SD = .17) to the posttest assessment (M = .19, SD = .17). A small to medium effect size (ES = .12) was observed in family/social status from the pretest (M = .41, SD = .15) to the posttest assessment (M = .39, SD = .20). Treatment yielded a medium effect size (ES = .17) in psychiatric status from the pretest (M = .29, SD = .20) to the posttest assessment (M = .25, SD = .19).

Figure 9.1 graphically represents that the CBT treatment resulted in a 71 percent reduction of mean alcohol-status composite score from the pretest (M = .24) to the posttest assessment (M = .07). This is contrasted to a 45 percent increase in mean alcohol-status composite score for the IOP treatment condition from the pretest (M = .29) to the posttest assessment (M = .42). The CBT treatment resulted in a 39 percent reduction of mean drug-status composite score from the pretest (M = .22) to the posttest assessment (M = .13). This is contrasted to a slight increase in the composite scores of the IOP condition.

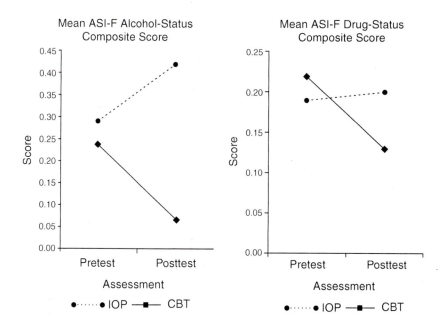

FIGURE 9.1. Mean ASI-F Alcohol- and Drug-Status Composite Scores

Between-Group Analysis

The MANOVA group effect was statistically significant for drug status, $F(1, 17) = 10.236$, $p = .013$, and for alcohol status, $F(1, 17) = 5.566$, $p = .046$. To determine which dependent variable was contributing to the overall F statistic, separate t tests were conducted for each dependent variable. Both the alcohol-status t test was statistically significant, $t(1, 17) = 2.359$, $p = .046$, as was the drug-status t test, $t(1,17) = 3.199$, $p = .013$. These results indicate that both treatment conditions contributed to the significance of the MANOVA F statistic.

A separate MANOVA was conducted to determine whether group differences were present for the employment-, legal-, family/social-, and psychiatric-status. Hotelling's T^2 $[T^2(4,17) = .329$, $p = .451]$ was not statistically significant for the psychosocial-dependent variables, thus the F statistic was not analyzed.

CONCLUSION

Statistical procedures (means, standard deviations, effect size, and MANOVA) indicated that CBT was more than ten times more effective than IOP in the reduction of alcohol use and four times more effective than IOP in the reduction of drug use in this sample.

Several explanations may account for why the cognitive-behavioral treatment condition produced statistically and clinically significant results for the participants of this study. First is that individuals in the early stages of recovery require concrete direction in learning the steps necessary to break the cycle of addiction. More specific, the cognitive-behavioral treatment condition included specific homework with sessions devoted to several relapse-prevention techniques (coping with cravings, developing the motivation to stop, and developing skills to help the user decline invitations to use substances) (Carroll, 1998). Thus, manualized treatment using homework was the causal agent of change. Another reason is that before individuals can stop using substances, they must be committed to abstinence (Buelow and Buelow, 1998). The CBT subjects may have been more committed to abstinence, or the material covered in the CBT sessions most likely taught these individuals the skills necessary for abstinence. A third reason is that cognitive-behavioral therapy is structured, goal-oriented, and focused on the immediate problems that substance abusers face in their recovery process (National Institute on Drug Abuse [NIDA], 1998). A final explanation is that problem-solving approaches are often preferred by African Americans and other ethnic groups (Clark, McClanahan, and Sees, 1998). Additional research is needed in order to determine which, if either, treatment (CBT or IOP) is efficacious in the treatment of substance abuse for individuals in the latter stages of recovery.

If the results from the original study (McClanahan, 2002) can be replicated with other substance abusing females and expanded to other psychiatric issues, it would be reasonable to extrapolate that the use of workbooks is essential to treatment in the twenty-first century. It would therefore be reasonable to assume that manualized treatment would be the treatment of choice for many psychiatric disorders.

REFERENCES

American Psychiatric Association (APA) (1994). *Diagnostic and statistical manual of mental disorders*, Fourth edition. Washington, DC: Author.
American Psychological Association (1992). *Ethical principles of psychologists*. Washington, DC: Author.

Beck, A. T. (1979). *Cognitive therapy and the emotional disorders.* New York: Meridian.

Blumenthal, S. J. (1998). Women and substance abuse: A new national focus. In C. L. Wetherington and A. B. Roman (Eds.), *Drug addiction research and the health of women* (NIH Publication No. 98-4289) (pp. 13-32). Rockville, MD: National Institute on Drug Abuse.

Buelow, G. D. and Buelow, S. A. (1998). *Psychotherapy in chemical dependence treatment: A practical and integrative approach.* Pacific Grove, CA: Brooks/ Cole.

Carroll, K. M. (1998). *A cognitive-behavioral approach: Treating cocaine addiction,* Manual 1. Therapy manuals for drug addiction. Rockville, MD: U.S. Department of Health and Human Services.

Clark, H. W., McClanahan, T. M., and Sees, K. (1998). Substance abuse services in systems of care: Linkages and issues in serving culturally diverse populations. In M. Hernandez and M. A. Isaacs (Eds.), *Promoting cultural competence in children's mental health services* (pp. 207-228). Baltimore, MD: Brookes.

Ellis, A. (1962). *Reason and emotion in psychotherapy.* New York: Lyle Stuart.

Ellis, A. (1986). *Handbook of rational-emotive therapy.* New York: Springer.

First, M. B., Gibbon, M., Spitzer, R. L., and Williams, J. B. W. (1990). *Structured clinical interview using the DSM-III, patient version (SCID-P).* New York: New York State Psychiatric Institute, Biometrics Research.

Hatsukami, D. K., Perkins, K., Lukas, S. E., Rukstalis, M., Brady, K. T., and Wetherington, C. L. (1997). Drugs of abuse and gender differences. *Problems of drug dependence 1996: Proceedings of the fifty-eighth annual scientific meeting, the College on Problems of Drug Dependence.* National Institute on Drug Abuse Research Monograph 174 (NIH Publication No. 97-4236). Washington, DC: U.S. Government Printing Office.

Kazdin, A. E. (1992). *Research design in clinical psychology,* Second edition. Needham Heights, MA: Allyn and Bacon.

Khantzian, E. J. (1985). Psychotherapeutic intervention with substance abusers: The clinical context. *Journal of Substance Abuse Treatment, 2,* 83-88.

Khantzian, E. J. (1986). A contemporary psychodynamic approach to drug abuse treatment. *American Journal of Drug and Alcohol Abuse, 12*(3), 213-222.

Khantzian, E. J., Halliday, K. S., and McAuliffe, W. E. (1990). *Addiction and the vulnerable self: Modified dynamic group therapy for substance abusers.* New York: Guilford.

Leshner, A. I. (1998). Gender matters in drug abuse research. *NIDA Notes, 13*(4), 3-4.

McClanahan, T. M. (2002). A comparative evaluation of cognitive-behavioral and insight-oriented psychotherapy in the treatment of female substance abuse. Manuscript submitted for publication.

Meichenbaum, D. (1977). *Cognitive behavior modification: An integrative approach.* New York: Plenum.

National Institute on Drug Abuse (1998). *Drug addiction research and the health of women* (NIH Publication No. 98-4289). Rockville, MD: U.S. Department of Health and Human Services.

Substance Abuse and Mental Health Services Administration (SAMHSA) (1997a). *Preliminary results from the 1996 National Household Survey on Drug Abuse* (DHHS Publication No. [SMA] 97-3149). Washington, DC: Substance Abuse and Mental Health Services Administration, Office of Applied Studies.

Substance Abuse and Mental Health Services Administration (SAMHSA) (1997b). *Supplementary administration manual for the expanded female version of the Addiction Severity Index (ASI) instrument The ASI-F* (DHHS Publication No. [SMA] 96-8056). Rockville, MD: Author.

Substance Abuse and Mental Health Services Administration (SAMHSA) (1998). *National admissions to substance abuse treatment services: The Treatment Episode Data Set (TEDS), 1992-1996* (DHHS Publication No. 98-3244). Rockville, MD: U.S. Department of Health and Human Services.

Tabachnick, B. G. and Fidell, L. S. (1996). *Using multivariate statistics,* Third edition. New York: HarperCollins.

Chapter 10

Workbooks and Psychotherapy with Incarcerated Felons: Replication of Research in Progress

Oliver McMahan
John Arias

The purpose of this chapter is to illustrate how workbooks can be utilized along with talk therapy to rehabilitate incarcerated felons. A brief rationale is presented for the use of writing and programmed distance writing (PDW) in therapy in general and then a specific rationale for their use with inmates to improve emotional control and thinking. An illustration of an intervention program conducted by the author and co-author is described. The intervention program is a replication of an earlier program conducted with felons (Reed, McMahan, and L'Abate, 2000). Combined results are analyzed. Conducting studies in correctional facilities presents special problems that limit the use of control groups and the study of long-term effects (Megargee, 1995). Similar limitations were discovered in this study, including the lack of a control group. However, this program is illustrative of how workbooks can be used to obtain what we hope are synergistic results.

BENEFITS OF WRITING
IN INTERVENTIONS WITH FELONS

Since prison populations are at record levels, structured self-report assessments and interventions based on programmed writing, as in workbooks, have the promise of being cost-effective and mass produced (Megargee, 1995). The need for improved interventions for inmates stands in light of an apparent avoidance of felons by traditional mental health programs and professionals (Milan, Chin, and Nguyen, 1999). Simon (1998) suggested that there was an "absence of interest on the part of psychologists in studying not only the criminal offender, but also the antisocial personality disorder" (p. 150). Simon (1998) further proposed that factors for improvement may be similar among offenders as well as nonoffenders: "If studied systematically, will we find out that the same nonspecific factors associated with improvement in non-offenders also predict successful outcome with offenders?" (p. 151). Simon (1998) advocated that "effective treatments should be developed and evaluated and made available to offenders motivated to undergo the difficult process of change" (p. 152).

Writing as part of a protocol of mental health interventions for prisoners makes sense both as an intervention that can be used and replicated cost-effectively in the absence of interest by the mental health profession and as an intervention that has been effective with nonoffenders. Programmed distance writing, such as in workbooks, can be administered in a manner similar to brief interventions, supplementing traditional talk therapies. Brief counseling contacts have been found to be helpful with prisoners being treated for depression (Wilson, 1990).

The written modality has been found to be reliable as an alternative to oral assessments. In a study with felons, oral and written modalities were compared in administering the Environmental Deprivation Scale (EDS). Oral responses have been traditionally used with the EDS. However, a Pearson correlation of .89 was found when comparing them with written responses. It is suggested that the oral process could be replaced with the more cost-effective written group interview process.

In a study involving 301 inmates, Weeks and Widom (1998) used written self-reports to assess the impact of childhood abuse. They found the written modality as a reliable means of assessment, correlating childhood physical abuse, sexual abuse, and neglect with criminality. Eisenberg (1989) successfully used the written modality to have felons draw life maps as part of logotherapy.

A study by Richards et al. (2000) with 400 felons in a psychiatric maximum security facility related writing to health benefits. Inmates were asked to write about traumatic events. The written intervention resulted in significantly fewer visits for health care and fewer requests for health services. Interestingly, the study found that writing was helpful for persons likely to be inhibited. Also, the experimental group expressed more negative emotions than the control group.

FELON WRITERS AND EMOTIONALITY

As found in the Richards et al. (2000) study mentioned earlier, emotionality is an important contributor to the effectiveness of PDW for felons. Felons have a demonstrable level of negative affect, higher than nonoffenders (Shaffer, Waters, and Adams, 1994). In a study involving 100 inmates, Shaffer, Waters, and Adams (1994) measured emotionality and other traits using the original Minnesota Multiphasic Personality Inventory (MMPI) and other scales. They concluded that "dangerousness can be predicted with a better-than-chance accuracy" (p. 1067). On the MMPI, inmates had higher F and 1 scores, indicating more general distress, atypicality of behavior and attitude, dissatisfaction with their state, more unhappiness with their situation, and perhaps more nonconforming approaches at coping with their unhappiness. The state and degree of felon emotionality along with the predictability of dangerousness call for interventions that address emotionality in a manner appropriate for inmates.

The at-risk condition of prisoner emotionality is compounded by the nature of incarceration. Remaining in enclosed areas increases feelings of isolation and negative affect. Prisoner emotionality is further impacted by the nature of negative affect, creating an isolation from others as well as the outside world. Talk therapy may not be as adequate as other modalities, including PDW, for the unique impact of incarceration upon prison affect and resulting symptomology. Investigating groups using traditional talk therapy (Marcus, Hamlin, and Lyons, 2001) studied the relationship between depressive negative affect and the propensity to be isolated by others. Subjects were members of twelve felon therapy groups with twelve members in each group ($N = 144$). The study confirmed that felons reporting high levels of depressive negative affect were most likely to be rejected by other members of the group.

Criminal psychopathological interventions using verbally oriented approaches may have an inherent deficit when addressing felon emotions of fearfulness. Patrick, Cuthbert, and Lang (1994) studied felon physiological responses to fear imaging. They found that responses were smaller and slower for antisocial criminal psychopaths than subjects with lower psychopathy. They noted that responses did not differ on fearfulness. The proposal of the study was that the lower response and same level of fearfulness perhaps accounts for the "reckless, impulsive life-styles of psychopaths" (p. 533). Although those with higher psychopathy were just as fearful internally, physiologically they were delayed in their responsiveness. The net result was someone who did not respond as readily to danger or consequences. Whether learned or innate, the evidence suggests a physiological reason for delayed criminal responsiveness.

Patrick, Cuthbert, and Lang (1994) further noted that their study "helps to explain why verbally oriented approaches to treatment, which rely on language-affect connections, are so notoriously ineffective with this population" (p. 533). Finally, they projected that the response deficit in psychopaths may not be specific to fearful imagery but applicable to "other forms of negative affect, such as anger" (p. 533).

In light of the benefits of PDW to the general population and to felons, noted earlier in this chapter, PDW may be an important alternative for the inmate population. Writing as an intervention modality has been found cost-effective and has demonstrated health benefits. A variety of methodologies along the spectrum of the therapeutic process, including assessment, opening up emotionally, confronting stressful events, logotherapy, cognitive process, and confronting negative affect, have used the written modality.

CONTINUING RESEARCH IN PROGRESS: REHABILITATION PROGRAM USING PROGRAMMED DISTANCE WRITING

Research has been continuing on incarcerated felons using PDW. The study is being conducted in a county justice center in the southeastern United States. This center houses approximately 120 male and female inmates, from which were drawn the respondents in this study. The research is being conducted as part of a counseling program that is an extension of graduate counseling training for a local religious seminary. These services are provided free of charge by graduate students in training, who are supervised by a faculty member, the lead author of this study.

Felons in the study received a pre- and postassessment battery that included five instruments measuring a variety of dimensions. The Anger Inventory (Schutte and Malouff, 1995) was used to measure change in negative affect. Reliability information was not available for this instrument. The Reaction Inventory was used to measure reactivity propensity and anger arousal in relationships. The instrument has a reliability measure of .95 (Evans and Strangeland, 1971). The Aggression Questionnaire was used to measure four aspects of aggression: physical aggression, verbal aggression, anger, and hostility. The overall score is presented in Table 10.1. The instrument has a reported reliability of .80 for the total score (Buss and Perry, 1992). The Irrational Belief Scale was used to assess irrational beliefs that may underlie depression and anxiety. The instrument has a reliability of .89 (Malouff, Valdenegro, and Schutte, 1987). The Automatic Thoughts Questionnaire was used to identify thoughts of individuals when they are depressed. The instrument has a reliability of .98 (Hollon and Kendall, 1980).

As an intervention to supplement face-to-face talk therapy, inmates were given PDW using assignments from L'Abate's (1992) social training workbook. This workbook includes assignments from a variety of themes, including goals and wants, mistakes, control, emotions and feelings, thinking, and other subjects. Each assignment is designed to take approximately forty-five to ninety minutes to complete. Interventions in both the pilot and

TABLE 10.1. Results of Programmed Distance Writing Along Five Measures of Affect and Cognition

Variable	Pretest mean score	Posttest mean score	Mean gain scores	t-score	SD	2-tail p
Anger inventory	58.5	48.0	−10.5	−3.30	18.5	0.003
Reaction inventory	226.5	198.2	−28.3	−2.60	61.3	0.016
Aggression questionnaire	95.8	87.6	−8.2	−3.00	15.9	0.006
Irrational belief scale	66.9	61.6	−5.3	−3.96	10.4	0.010
Automatic thoughts questionnaire	92.4	75.5	−16.9	−7.30	16.9	0.000

Note: $n = 29$ (*df* $= 28$, $p < 0.01$)

replication studies spanned a nine-month period. The format was the same in both the pilot and replication studies, using homework assignments after each session of traditional talk therapy. However, the use of writing was emphasized and the use of talk was minimized. The writing took place in the inmates' cells and in recreational break areas between talk sessions.

Table 10.1 reflects combined data for both the pilot and replication studies. Pre- and postassessments were analyzed with a paired samples test (see Table 10.1). The analysis in Table 10.1 indicates that the PDW intervention along with face-to-face therapy made a significant ($p < 0.01$) positive difference in four measures, anger, aggression, irrational belief, and automatic thoughts, through reduced gain scores. The data for reactivity indicated acceptable significance ($p = 0.05$) and positive result through reduced gain scores.

Through face-to-face feedback, inmates in general reported less depression and greater ability to control anger. They also reported fewer automatic thoughts leading to depressiveness. Anecdotal observations from face-to-face interviews reported general pleasure on the part of inmates in the homework tasks. Following are a few case studies of inmates in the replication study who used PDW. The cases represent extreme gain score responses (elevation and reduction) to the various measures. The cases are presented with the question asked in the PDW and the response of the inmate.

The first two cases represent the extreme gain measures according to the anger inventory. The first inmate had a gain score of eighteen, indicating an increase in anger during the intervention. PDW responses included the following:

QUESTION: What happens to you when you let others control your actions?

INMATE 1: (1) get into trouble, (2) get things blamed on you, (3) get your feelings hurt.

The second inmate had a gain score of –26 on the anger inventory, indicating a reduction in anger during the intervention. PDW responses included the following:

QUESTION: What happens to you when you do not stay with your feelings and instead go into action right away?

INMATE 2: Get mad and [throw] stuff around.

Q: What happens to you when you cannot split your feelings and emotions from your actions?

I2: I get real angry, get real emotional, a lot of stress.

Q: What did you learn from this lesson?

I2: It is not good to mix them [emotions and actions] all together and it's not safe.

The second inmate also showed the greatest improvement on the aggression questionnaire with a negative gain score of –34.

The next case was an inmate who scored the highest improvement on both the reactivity inventory (–137) and the irrational belief scale (–29). PDW responses included the following:

QUESTION: Describe four times when you did not think before you acted. What happened to you?

INMATE 3: Stealing, driving, misuse friends, just sometimes. Get beat up or put in jail.

Q: What is the difference between poor thinking and good thinking?

I3: Both are the same.

Q: Would you agree that good thinking helps you, while poor or bad thinking hurts you?

I3: Yes. Helps you stay out of trouble.

Q: What did you learn from this lesson about thinking?

I3: When you think good, [then] good things happen, like you get your privileges back!

Q: Why is good thinking better than bad thinking?

I3: (1) the end result, (2) helps you with life's problems.

The next case was an inmate who had the highest gain in the irrational belief scale score, indicating an increase in depressive and negative thoughts. PDW responses included:

QUESTION: List as many feelings and emotions as you can.

INMATE 4: (1) angry, frustrated, (2) sad, (3) [disgusted].

QUESTION: What happens to you when you do not stay with your feelings and instead go into action right away?

I4: I put my foot in my mouth. I'm afraid I'll hurt someone if I get into a fight with someone and I don't want to do that.

Q: Give four reasons why we must split feeling and emotions from actions.

I4: (1) Someone could get hurt, (2) regret something you do later, (3) hurt someone's feelings, (4) putting myself in danger for doing something.

CONCLUSION

PDW and other written modalities have been found to be effective and efficient methods of intervention delivery. Writing is a modality that has benefits for the offender population as well as the nonoffender population. In fact, indications suggest that problems unique to penal institutions, felons, and mental health interventions may be effectively addressed with greater use of written modalities of intervention. The emotional issues that may increase while in incarceration, the inclination to further isolate already depressive inmates, and the potential delayed physiological response to talk therapies provide ample opportunity for therapists who intervene with inmate populations to consider using written modalities as a viable supplement to current, traditional talk therapies.

The replication of continuing research presented in this chapter included data that was replicated with different inmates and therapists. The results were an increase in desired effects. All five scales indicated significant improvement in emotionality and cognition. Specifically, reductions in anger, inclination and reactivity, irrational beliefs, aggression and depressive thoughts were recorded in pre- and posttest measures. Although face-to-face intervention was used, the focus was on written PDW homework assignments. The result was an increase in the inmates' ability to think more clearly and effectively about their emotionality, negative responses, and accountability for their actions—all desired outcomes for interventions with the felon population.

REFERENCES

Buss, A.H. and Perry, M. (1992). The aggression questionnaire. *Personality Processes and Individual Differences, 63,* 452-459.

Eisenberg, M. (1989). Exposing prisoners to logotherapy. *International Forum for Logotherapy, 12,* 89-94.

Evans, D.R. and Strangeland, M. (1971). Development of the Reaction Inventory to measure anger. *Psychological Reports, 29,* 412-414.

Hollon, S.D. and Kendall, P.C. (1980). Cognitive self-statements in depression: Development of an automatic thoughts questionnaire. *Cognitive Therapy and Research, 4,* 249-383.

L'Abate, L. (1992). *Programmed writing: A self-administered approach for interventions with individuals, couples, and families.* Pacific Grove, CA: Brooks/ Cole.

Malouff, J.M., Valdenegro, J., and Schutte, N.S. (1987). Further validation of a measure of irrational belief. *Journal of Rational-Emotive and Cognitive-Behavior Therapy, 5,* 189-193.

Marcus, D.K. Hamlin, R.J., and Lyons, P.M. (2001). Negative affect and interpersonal rejection among prison inmates in a therapeutic community: A social relations analysis. *Journal of Abnormal Psychology, 110,* 544-552.

Megargee, E.I. (1995). Assessment research in correctional settings: Methodological issues and practical problems. *Psychological Assessment, 7,* 359-366.

Milan, M.A., Chin, C.E., and Nguyen, Q.K. (1999). Practicing psychology in correctional settings: Assessment, treatment, and substance abuse programs. In A.K. Hess and I.B. Weiner (Eds.), *The handbook of forensic psychology* (pp. 580-602). New York: John Wiley & Sons, Inc.

Reed, R., McMahan, O., and L'Abate, L. (2001). Workbooks and psychotherapy with incarcerated felons. In L. L'Abate (Ed.), *Distance writing and computer-assisted interventions in psychiatry and mental health* (pp. 157-167). Westport, CT: Ablex.

Richards, J.M., Beal, W.E., Seagal, J.D., and Pennebaker, J.W. (2000). Effects of disclosure of traumatic events on illness behavior among psychiatric prison inmates. *Journal of Abnormal Psychology, 109,* 156-160.

Schutte, N.S. and Malouff, J.M. (1995). *Sourcebook of adult assessment strategies.* New York: Plenum.

Simon, L. (1998). Do offender treatments work? *Applied and Preventive Psychology, 7,* 137-159.

Weeks, R. and Widom, C.S. (1998). Self-reports of early childhood victimization among incarcerated adult male felons. *Journal of Interpersonal Violence, 13,* 34-361.

Wilson, G.L. (1990). Psychotherapy with depressed incarcerated felons: A comparative evaluation of treatments. *Psychological Reports, 67,* 1027-1041.

SECTION III:
COUPLES

Chapter 11

Marriage Preparation and Maintenance

Mario Cusinato

The purpose of this chapter is to summarize a program for marriage preparation and maintenance (MPM) conducted in part through the use of workbooks. However, this program needs to be nested within a historical and cultural context to indicate how it came about because of deficits in the very area of MPM.

HISTORICAL AND CULTURAL CONTEXT FOR MARRIAGE PREPARATION AND MAINTENANCE

Marriage preparation and maintenance programs are proposed, supported, and utilized for reasons stemming from the current sociocultural context of Western civilization, but also for reasons intrinsic to conjugal couple training. "More couple and less conjugality" is a recurrent expression used in the literature to summarize the changes that affect every phase of the family life cycle—especially its early phases. It is not a question of stating the contradiction between two terms, but rather of placing more stress on one of the two sides. Indeed, "the center of conjugality is now the couple and their relationship. The partners establish rules and negotiate rights, duties and room for action" (Scabini, 1995, p. 120). Undeniably, this accentuated subjectivation has consequences that can lead to a sort of narcissistic attention to individual needs and bring about the failure of a shared project based on responsibility and reciprocity. The relationship may sometimes develop on the idealization of the couple relationship, and so disappointment and frustration are bound to emerge very soon.

Partners are called upon to build and blend conjugal identity. The developmental perspective of family relationships has highlighted specific tasks

---

This work has been implemented at the Family Center in Treviso (Italy) by the author in collaboration with a dozen professionals and about 200 volunteer couples. Since 1995 a three-year course for volunteers as family trainers has been established.

for each step (Stahmann and Salts, 1993). The first especially engages the two partners in a critical leap defined as "the transition from watch synchronization to couple timing" (Galimberti, 1985, p. 142), which needs the disenchantment that follows falling in love to build and maintain a shared commitment based on reciprocity. This is not an easy task because it depends on the ability to create a "balance between two loyalties" (Scabini, 1995, p. 123): toward one's family of origin and toward the newly acquired family.

Within this framework are placed the possibilities, urgency, and opportunities offered by marital preparation and maintenance programs as efficacious prevention opportunities (Berger and Hannah, 1999). Vis-à-vis couple relationship frailty, with all the negative consequences it has on individuals, families, and society, training initiatives are the best possible type of prevention, and it is well known that to prevent is better than to cure. For this reason, religious communities, traditionally on the front line in this (Cunningham and Scanzoni, 1993), but also other social agencies (schools and universities, educational systems, state and local governments) (Fournier and Olson, 1986; Stahmann and Salts, 1993), have long been committed to marriage preparation and maintenance.

The generally positive atmosphere of the premarital couple relationship and of the participants in enrichment programs favors the learning of communication and cooperation abilities (Cusinato and Salvo, 1998; Kieren and Doherty-Poirier, 1993). This situation is totally different from the stressful fixes experienced by married couples with difficulties who are forced to deal with relational problems that are no longer deferrable. In general terms, unmarried couples are called upon to learn that marriage is a process that needs time and energy. The two partners must become aware of and consolidate their styles, through the investment of time, energies, and money, in their marriage if they want it to be successful. The options are many. It may be sufficient to participate in some type of enrichment program or counseling session to clarify some problematic aspects of their relationship. They might become aware of the need to postpone their marriage to better define some aspects or to reach a better reciprocal acceptance. They may even realize that they are not made for each other!

Premarital educational and conjugal enrichment programs do not typically envisage explicit forms of family or couple therapy (Stahmann and Salts, 1993; Wright, 1983). Therapists are rarely approached by engaged and married couples living a normal relationship—they usually have to deal with couples and families already experiencing problems and suffering. However, something is changing in this respect and an integrated picture of training, counseling, and therapy is slowly making its way into the distinction proposed between the three levels of family-discomfort prevention (Berger and Hannah, 1999; L'Abate, 1990).

STRATEGIES FOR INTERVENTION

Educational and counseling activities that are specific to marriage preparation and the early years of marriage have long been in existence. The international literature reports multiple initiatives and proposals that are nonetheless difficult to know and evaluate in their wholeness as their sources are spread over a number of different disciplines in answer to the interdisciplinary nature of this field (Fournier and Olson, 1986). Many factors hinder the identification of their efficacy and of their differences. In short, marriage preparation programs are just as useful as conjugal enrichment programs (Giblin, Sprenkle, and Sheeham, 1985). However, most research studies on this issue underline a number of methodological problems that greatly restrict reliability of results (Bagarozzi and Rauen, 1981; Gurman and Kniskern, 1977; Hof and Miller, 1981). The most recurrent problems are

1. lack of control groups allowing to check whether the change is actually due to the program or to couples' normal maturity process;
2. evaluations include only subjective satisfaction evaluations rather than objective measures;
3. evaluations are based on a very brief period of time that may have no relation to long-term effects (however, marriage is supposed to be long term!);
4. tests are not devised with validity and reliability criteria; and
5. the research designs used do not have appropriate strategies to single out the efficacy specific to the different programs.

As a result, a twofold methodological limitation exists: in the programs, which must be improved, and in the research studies on the program themselves, so as to make the comparison between the different initiatives more reliable and to be in a position to provide indications to those who work in the field. Following this premise, our next step will be to consider what the literature indicates about the characteristics of the programs.

Intervention Programs

Programs have been classified by Schumm and Denton (1979) into four basic approaches: (1) formal marital education, (2) educational counseling, (3) enrichment programs, and (4) counseling proposals. As already said, the majority of couples do not ask for therapeutic help in the early years of marriage, and so intervention programs have the form of education, educational counseling, and enrichment.

Educational courses in family life address topics related to marriage and the family. Usually, they require a six- to twenty-week attendance. The family life programs offered in college/university settings typically use a specific textbook and follow a structured classroom educational format (Cox, 1990; Rice, 1990). Both instructors and students may find a student study guide useful (Kohl, 1990). Educational counseling usually concerns programs combining education and counseling. Couples can ask to read some booklets, see a film or a videotape, and then go on to take part in some form of couple counseling or group discussion concerning specific aspects. Enrichment programs are usually offered to functional individuals/couples who are not experiencing difficulties in their relationship and wish to develop their resources. On the other hand, counseling responds to difficulties that have already troubled the couple to some degree.

Methods of Teaching, Learning, and Changing

Considering that they are related to the type of program, didactic strategies vary according to the goals of the program. The most common is the *lecture,* which has the advantage of allowing many people to attend and the limitation of being less efficacious (Norem et al., 1980). Managing mass participation can be complicated and problematic if active didactic methods are used.

Another didactic method used is *group discussion.* Since the 1970s, the use of this modality has been widespread because it allows couples to focus on specific aspects of marital life that are relevant to them. Unlike lectures, group discussion allows first-person involvement and, even more important, reciprocal observation on how each individual manages what he or she is experiencing. Group discussion can also be a counseling modality if the group is guided by a counselor able to lead the group to elaboration of personal and relational conflictual aspects.

Another method used at times is *modeling:* it needs the active presence of an adequately trained facilitator, upon whom the participants rely during their training. Several topics are dealt with: direct positive contact, listening capacity, role exchange, overcoming conflicts, and so on. Role-play on real or fictitious couple situations is a modeling technique for focusing problems and verifying difficulties.

Some enrichment programs propose a *personal reflection.* In it, individuals and/or couples are asked to reflect on specific topics and put their ideas in order (L'Abate, 1992). Awareness of feelings and emotions experienced during specific relational events is ameliorated. Then the partners are invited to talk and communicate personal thoughts to each other, thus enriching their understanding.

Experiential techniques are another educational modality. They can include a practical training of abilities or other tasks that are implemented as opportunities to learn. They can be used as a part of the work session or as homework to create a reference frame promoting a mutual discussion on what the couple has internalized or learned. These experiential procedures, also via the use of new educational audiovisual tools, heighten awareness of reality. Sometimes, marriage preparation programs schedule training in communication and problem solving, often producing positive change (Most and Guerney, 1983).

Last, *workbooks* have to be mentioned. L'Abate (1990) distinguishes between primary and secondary prevention and allots the structured enrichment programs to the first ambit and the workbooks to the second. Going in depth, on the one side, into the function and value of writing (L'Abate, 1992; L'Abate and Platzman, 1991) and, on the other, into the prescriptive quality of evaluation tools (L'Abate, 1992, 1994), the author progressively approached the two intervention modalities and their specificity. A structured sequence of lessons can be drawn from clinically or practically derived materials or from theory-derived models or also from the phenomenally large self-help book literature. The individuals and/or the couple are asked to answer preferably in writing. In any case, the supervision of the preventer or therapist is a crucial aspect. L'Abate has offered many examples of workbooks (L'Abate, 1992, 1997, 1999; L'Abate, Johnson, and Levis, 1987).

Olson and Olson (1999) have published a manual, *Building a Strong Marriage Workbook,* with six couple exercises using the results of the Premarital Personal and Relationship Evaluation/Evaluating and Nurturing Relationship Issues, Communication, Happiness (PREPARE/ENRICH) Inventories:

1. exploring areas of relationship strength and growth;
2. strengthening couple communication skills, including assertiveness and active listening;
3. resolving couple conflict using the ten-step Conflict Resolution Model;
4. exploring family-of-origin issues using the Couple and Family Map;
5. developing a workable budget and financial plan; and
6. developing personal, couple, and family goals.

Many other authors have offered workbooks as a modality of intervention with individuals, couples, and families (Berger and Hannah, 1999).

Intervention Challenges

At the end of their review on marriage preparation programs, Fournier and Olson (1986) draft some advice that is at the same time a synthesis of study results, a sense of their long and direct commitment, and a wish for a "qualitative leap" in the area of marriage preparation:

1. Premarital preparation should be seen as a national priority to help marriages get off to a good start. The prevention of divorce begins with providing good premarital preparation.
2. Premarital couples should be encouraged to begin the process of preparation and dealing with relationship issues at least *one year* before marriage.
3. Premarital programs should prime couples to participate in enrichment programs after marriage. Programs can facilitate this by offering several sessions before marriage and several sessions six months after marriage.
4. Premarital and newlywed programs should ideally have three components: premarital inventories and couple dialogue, small-group discussion with other couples, and a communication-skill-building program.
5. Premarital couples and their parents should be encouraged to spend as much money, time, and energy in preparing for the marriage relationship as they do for the wedding ceremony. This will help ensure that they see marriage as an important investment and as a process that continues for the lives of the individuals.
6. Lay couples should be encouraged to become actively involved with premarital couples and to work with them through their first year of married life.
7. Research should be continued to find the most effective types of premarital preparation programs. It would be useful to assess the relative advantages of various types of programs to determine when each can be most appropriately and effectively offered.

A PROGRAM OF MARRIAGE PREPARATION AND MAINTENANCE

Work with couples before and after marriage started in the first half of the 1970s. A great deal of effort was applied, particularly in creating and verifying strategies for intervention that might respond to the needs of enhancement shown by the partners. Different training strategies shown in the literature were implemented and tested. At the beginning of the program, passive listening as an assignment was eliminated because it was outdated and irrelevant to the needs of the couple. An active-listening participation method was implemented using the following strategies: (1) answer to current needs by giving a formal definition of values held by individual partners; (2) a real-life, concrete consideration of abstract theoretical concept; (3) small group training about interpersonal relationships in an auditorium or traditional classroom. Indeed, careful attention to the needs of individual partners and couples brought about the elaboration of a new program that included different intervention options. Currently, couples are equipped with a specific workbook, including parts for individual in-depth study, couple dialogue, group discussion, and/or supervision work by the leader (preventer, enricher, or facilitator). Some content-concise cards are enclosed in the workbooks, usually to introduce individual work.

A Model of Developmental Couple Relationship

Couple typology has changed progressively in the past thirty years of educational work (Donati, 1997). The educational level has increased remarkably, especially for women, and so have women's career opportunities and jobs. The most apparent changes have concerned the age at which individuals get married. In the 1970s the mean age was twenty-four for women and twenty-five to twenty-six for men; in the 1990s twenty-six and twenty-nine respectively; in these early years of 2000, twenty-nine and thirty-one respectively. This demographic aspect is known in Italy, as in all the countries of the Mediterranean area, as the "long" family of the young adult (Scabini, 1995). The traditional development of the couple relationship evolves into the transformation summarized in Figure 11.1, which takes inspiration from a flow-chart of the mate selection process first offered by Adams (1979).

In addition to the initial drive to fall in love, which is overpowering and rooted in human biology, the current construction of a stable couple relationship shows a slower way in which personal, cultural, social, and fortuitous factors are affected, together with the construction of the relational self engaging all of us since our births. At least four stages with three transitions exist. Within the current trend of delaying marriage after the age of thirty, these stages are sizeable and can continue for years. Furthermore, it is not taken for granted that the triggering → conclusion → triggering again cycle is not repeated more times:

1. *Triggering attraction:* Perhaps it is not correct to call this a phase, because it is rather a form of spending time with each other that lasts over a (more or less) prolonged period. However, it is the beginning of the relationship, and in the mind of the two protagonists it remains the ideal reference point.

2. *Consolidation of attraction:* It is obviously connected to spending time together, almost its sedimentation, even if it is not an automatic and passive event. There is the commitment to become a couple, leaving an individual perspective and cultivating duality.

3. *Decision to get married:* The transition from the previous phase coincides with becoming engaged, which, according to the couple's cultural environment, can simply be a formal act (less and less these days!) but also a new way of considering each other and the relationship. In other words, an ethical element of commitment makes its way into the relationship. It is this element that leads to the "decision," although we can see "stalemate" couples, at a standstill in the engagement phase, who can sometimes become permanent living partners.

4. *Permanence in marriage:* The premise is the wedding ceremony with all of its implicit meanings: personal, social, and religious. In such permanence the project can be realized, or at least the couple should realize it, if they have enough resources to overcome obstacles and decide for the choice.

By focusing on the variables included in Figure 11.1, factors fostering the relationship are above the middle line of the figure, whereas hindering factors are below it. Fostering factors predict whether the relationship will continue either in marriage or in living together. Hindering factors predict the end of the relationship. Visually, fostering factors would mean an upward trend in the relationship. Hindering factors would mean a downward trend. Although other influencing factors may exist, the ones shown in Figure 11.1 have been formalized and verified. Let us comment on some of them.

"Personal immaturity" appears at the beginning and at the end of the process—at the beginning it hinders the triggering, at the end it causes the marriage to break up. There are different degrees of immaturity, and in any case this element may affect the couple process all along. For example, "complementariness of needs" is certainly a factor that favors attraction consolidation, but these needs can be "immaturity needs" and then the resulting fix can be anybody's guess. Each and every couple presents more or less mature objectives and needs. Scabini and Cigoli (2000) maintain, for the continuity of the bond, the need to check partners' ability to transfer

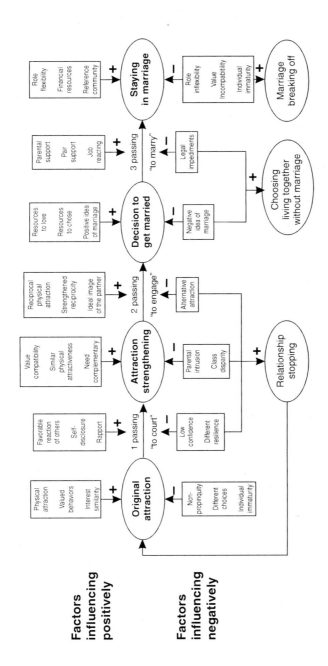

FIGURE 11.1. The Process from Falling in Love to Staying in Love

225

partner interests from initial needs to subsequent ones: this elasticity of investment would be the secret of a successful marriage.

Parental influence is remarkable throughout the process, albeit in different ways. As early as the first phase parents can favor or not favor consolidation, but they are decisive in the transition to the actual engagement. If they activate intrusive behaviors, they can provoke tensions or even lead to the breakup of the relationship. If the two protagonists react by isolating themselves from their parents, the damage they will receive in the third transition will be high, because they will obtain no help in consolidating their relationship into the family. The importance of shared values is considerable all along the process, but it is especially so in the relationship consolidation phase and then in marital life (at least in the negative sense that the couple must not show incompatible reference values).

Along this developmental process are three suitable moments in which specific educational proposals may be welcomed by interested people. The first coincides with the second transition, when the relational experience becomes somehow a project for the future and requires the partners to take the important decision of a reciprocal choice. This step, as shown by the model, specifies how the relational transition has been shaping over the past decade at the same time that the previous phase was getting more and more prolonged. The educational proposal offered to the partners involved in the permanent reciprocal choice represents a novelty in some ways, as we will specify later. The second suitable moment concerns the "third transition" to marriage, traditionally focused on by educational agencies working in marriage preparation.

Our program is implemented with different modalities corresponding to the different context situations of the people involved. The third moment concerns marriage maintenance: a progressive whole of different stages of life, each of them with peculiar developmental tasks, teachable moments and needs: couples with young children, couples with adolescent children, couples with young adult children, "empty-nest" couples.

In this perspective, with a multiplicity of supply and demand, the starting moment of the educational process becomes the discriminant point that can make the difference to efficacy and efficiency levels. It covers couple recruiting, first assessment of their needs and expectations, and a further evaluation of the same to outline and choose educational offers actually tailor made for their necessities. This set of applicational aspects is called the "welcoming step," which can be realized in different ways, but in any case always needs proper organization, ad hoc trained preventers, correct materials, and protocols.

The first meeting between the family counselor and the couple takes place in an informal atmosphere of socialization and reciprocal acquaintance with the goal of expressing needs, of making individual and/or couple resources emerge, of defining the motivations that can support the work. At the same time, it is important to expound the different programs, which vary according to how each program should be implemented. For example, partners can make various choices: (1) working in a small group format with other couples or just seeing a counselor as a couple; (2) receiving support to learn more about choosing a partner in general or committing oneself specifically to prepare for marriage; (3) preventing possible problems by using an enrichment workbook, with debriefing in a small group, or entering into individualized counseling if some symptoms or relational difficulties became prominent. This sensitive time for outlining a picture and then orienting toward a specific intervention is actually a collaboration between professionals as supervisors and volunteers as preventers.

The welcoming step ends with a training contract and forming work groups or entrusting attending couples to a suitable preventer. The contract expresses the aims, the work schedule, and the obligations undertaken over the educational moment. The creation of the work groups follows the criteria of homogeneity and differences. The basic tool for any action is a contract with thirty-one evaluation items (welcoming the two partners before marriage; the contract after marriage is similar) filled in by the counselor after the meeting on a five-point scale and concerning nine content areas: experiences in the family of origin, juvenile experiences, love experiences, interests and commitments, work experiences, relationship, religious orientation, personality issues, and acceptance level of training. In general, evaluations on high levels of the scale suggest (1) ability and willingness to attend the program with workbook exercises and (2) supervision in a small group. Middle or low scores on this evaluation suggest the opportunity to entrust the couple to a preventer (workbook and individual supervision) or to propose some counseling sessions with a professional. Any decision is made with the supervision of the professional.

The welcoming step appears as the milestone of marriage preparation and maintenance. An empirical study (Peruffo and Faccin, 1992) was realized in 1991 with 106 couples. Half attended a marriage preparation program with welcoming steps, workbooks, and small-group debriefing; the other half attended a course of lectures with speeches and discussions. The choice of subjects was performed by matching the attendees, couple by couple, on the basis of age, education, sociocultural status, length of engagement, and wedding date. At pre- and posttest couples were asked to fill out an adapted form of PREPARE (Olson, Fournier, and Druckman, 1982): Marriage Preparation (FPR) (Cusinato, 1985). Data analyses revealed a statistically significant change ($p < .05$) for three out of ten dimensions between pre- and posttest for the first subgroup and six out of ten dimensions for the second. At first sight this result could point to a higher efficacy of the second program. Nevertheless, the intergroup comparisons showed significant differences on seven dimensions in the pretest and on five dimensions in the posttest. These differences (particularly in the pretest comparison) may be explained only by the objectification work accomplished during the welcoming step on individual resources and needs, as well as on the couple construction dimensions.

Programs and Workbooks

All MPM programs follow the same basic structure: they are subdivided in sessions or lessons usually performed at one- or two-week intervals. Every session includes the introduction theme (in group or with the preventer), individual work, couple dialogue, homework check, and conclusion (in group or with the preventer). Every step is guided by a suitable workbook— the main part of it concerns individual work in which the attendee is invited to take notes of his or her feelings, thoughts, questions, and answers. This personal output is the subject of couple dialogue and also of group discussion and conclusion. Depending on the attendees' workbooks, the preventer is guided by a textbook that explains every exercise and passage, and he or she keeps a structured diary with scale evaluations and free notes.

WORKBOOKS FOR MARRIAGE PREPARATION

Four workbooks were developed—one to deal with the first transition point described earlier and three to deal with the second transition point.

1. *The Choice to Love* (Cusinato, 2001): This workbook helps attendees verify, restore, and support individuals' resources at the time of their reciprocal commitment with a plan expanding into the future. Many are the important factors, but ability to choose and ability to love appear to represent the core of this relational phase. The workbook includes three sessions on the ability to love and three sessions on the ability to choose. Individual and couple exercises are structured with reference to results obtained by the administration of the Adult Attachment Questionnaire (AAQ) (Salvo, Cusinato, and Rossetti, 1996), the Self-Other Profile Chart (Cusinato and Pastore, 2001), and the Family Emotion Scale (FES) (Cusinato, 1997). As pre- and posttests, the Relational Answers Questionnaire (RAQ) (L'Abate, in press) are applied. An empirical study in progress shows some positive changes of the dimensions of this test (Cusinato, in progress).

2. *Orienting Couples for Life* (Cusinato, 1985): This workbook requires the couple to perform an individual elaboration with written answers, a couple dialogue, and a group discussion and conclusion to verify the couple's experience and plan (that is, their past and their future) so that the couple can live in the present with more awareness and satisfaction. The program includes two parts: the first comprises fourteen weekly sessions, the second five monthly sessions. The program lasts about a year, and during that time quite a few attending couples get married. The first part includes three educational units:
   - couple identity;
   - context influence on the couple's history and project; and
   - personal and couple resources (particularly religious resources).

   Realized as an enrichment experience, it offers the opportunity to verify, learn, and/or improve couple communication particularly at the intimacy level. The second part concerns five relational categories, derived from the FPR inventory:
   - personality issues;
   - leisure activities;
   - affective and sexual relationship;
   - parental perspective; and
   - couple opening to family, friends, and community.

   It is an opportunity to verify, learn, and/or improve couple negotiation according to the flowchart shown in Figure 11.2. Since 1975 almost twenty thousand people have attended marriage preparation with this workbook.

3. *Time of Joy and Plans* (Cusinato, 1996a): This workbook shares the same structure and contents as Cusinato's (1985), but is offered to one couple at a time supported by a preventer. The two partners check their individual work and couple dialogue with the preventer and then draw their own conclusions.

4. *Love Overcomes Any Obstacle* (Cusinato, 1996b): This workbook shares the same structure as the previous two, but it is used by one individual whose partner lives in a very distant town, region, or state and cannot attend the same program. He or she is probably attending a marriage preparation course where he or she lives. The workbook suggests that the individual completes the exercises and sends the written answers to the partner, who also has the chance to communicate his or her comments. After this feedback, the attendee checks the work with the preventer and draws his or her own conclusions.

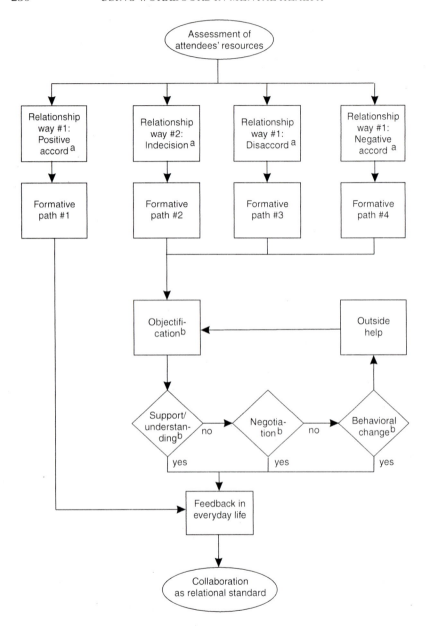

FIGURE 11.2. Path Flowchart of the Premarriage Workbook. *Sources:* [a]Olson, D.H., Fournier, D.G., Druckman, J.M. (1982); [b]Weiss, R.L. (1978).

In the last three programs, attendees are asked to answer the FPR inventory (Facco, 1999), an adapted version of PREPARE (Olson, Fournier, and Druckman, 1982), which can be used in its full version or subdivided into two parallel forms. Data elaboration is used both as pre- and posttests, and as formative assessment. At the pretest, attendees are usually asked to do the full version, whereas in the posttest they are asked to do first or second subscale. As a formative tool, the preventer receives two computerized reports, one of them shows an outline of individual and couple data, the other a comprehensive profile concerning the couple's strengths and growth areas. These data represent reference frames in which the preventer can interpret with more accuracy what couples feel and express. Every five sessions all attendees receive a computer report with information on the content considered, which they are asked to use as an input for individual work and couple dialogue. In fact, this information represents an effective support for the objectivation effort and the negotiation process.

WORKBOOKS FOR MARRIAGE MAINTENANCE

Three workbooks are specific to marriage within the marriage enrichment project. Their purpose is to support couples' identities in their many different roles, such as parents, workers, relatives, and intimate partners. They are used whenever married couples meet, which is usually once a month.

1. *The Two of Us with Others* (Cusinato, Simioni, and Simioni, 2001b): The workbook stimulates the progressive understanding (and also appreciation) of the reference of the vertical priorities in which the relationship should take bottom place among the numerous requirements, commitments, and interests within the family, in the work ambit, and in the social context. Usable tools are individual reflection, dialogue with the partner, and recurrent support of discussion and sharing with other couples going through the same phase of family life. The workbook includes five sessions concerning the values and accomplishments of intra- and intercouple communication and cooperation, and also encouragement to practice different concrete strategies in order to place the relationship at the center of interests and duties, with the trend toward intimacy fulfillment. It is an introductory program to subsequent levels of educational perspectives.
2. *The Two of Us Together with Others* (Cusinato, Simioni, and Simioni, 2001a): This workbook helps the couple to focus on different parts of personal interests and activities and choose the current "most sensible objects" (for example family events, needs of elderly parents, behav-

iors of adolescent children, work experiences and relations, and so on). In addition, it encourages a reading at the conjugal level that makes it possible to point out the correct modalities for preserving the couple's priority at the value level and at the practical level. In this way, contents are periodically focused on and chosen by the attendees. The workbook suggests the modalities of objectivation, negotiation, and fulfillment.

3. *A Plan for the Two of Us* (Cusinato, Simioni, and Simioni, 2002): The use of this workbook is recommended when partners perceive the need for a pause to find a sense in their own lives by differentiating and connecting the specific objects of love and negotiation. It includes seven sessions:
   - story of a pathway,
   - starting motivations to connect two individuals,
   - sharing joys and sorrows between welcoming and forgiveness,
   - the various directions of couple fertility,
   - past and future steps of the family life cycle with related tasks,
   - horizontal and vertical priorities,
   - living the present moment to the fullest.

Administration of these three workbooks is usually accompanied by some standardized measurements as pre- and posttests, that is to say Couple Intimacy Scales (CIS) (Cusinato, 1992) and/or Couple Negotiation Scales (CNS) (Materazzo, 1994). The former stem from the spiral model of intimacy (Cusinato and L'Abate, 1994) is operationalized in six subscales; the latter represent an adaptation of the ENRICH inventory by Olson, Fournier, and Druckman (1982) with seven subscales. The protracted use of these assessment tools pointed out that the successful application of workbooks (that is, attendees show interest and trust in the work and preventers attest positive changes of behaviors and attitudes) often records significant differences between pre- and posttest positive or negative results: posttest scores can appear higher or lower than the pretest. The meaning of the first result is more easily grasped; the second is less predictable. In this case, the intervention probably causes a higher objectification of the dimensions implied so that attendees can assess their relationships more realistically. As a consequence the pretest scores decrease.

EVALUATION OF THE EDUCATIONAL PROCESS

In addition to the tests mentioned earlier, other more or less qualitative or quantitative assessment tools follow the formative process and are worth mentioning. At the end of every session, preventers and attendees are asked to complete some five-point scales. The contents of the preventers' scales concern (1) the way in which every person/couple has used the workbook in individual work, couple dialogue, and group discussion; (2) some aspects of group experience on attendees and group leadership (for example, their own level of empathy); (3) content analysis, discussion, and assimilation. Some final notes can concern specific behaviors (for example, couples not attending the group) and the general group climate. At the end of the program, the preventer completes twenty-eight five-point scales summarizing the different aspects analytically assessed during the course. For example, Figure 11.3 shows two very different assessment patterns. The assessment on the first couple (#737) highlights a high standard of resources, motivation and

N.	Items	COUPLE #737 (very little → very much)	COUPLE #738 (very little → very much)
1	Did the couple show persevering interest?	4	3
2	Did they attend actively?	4	2
3	Did they work individually at home?	4	3
4	Did they do the dialogue work?	4	2
5	Did they learn to answer in written form?	4	2
6	Can they express themselves?	4	2 / 5
7	Can they face their couple difficulties?	3	3
8	Are they open-minded in their speech and attitudes?	5	2
9	Are they optimistic?	5	4 / 5
10	Do they have positive couple relationships?	4	2
11	Did they use the program for improving this aspect?	4	2
12	Did they have positive relationships with their families?	4	4
13	Did they use the program for improving this aspect?	4	3
14	Can they show themselves as an open couple?	5	3
15	Did they use the program for improving this aspect?	5	4
16	Are they aware of the complex aspects of their life?	5	3
17	Did they use the program for improving this aspect?	5	3
18	Did they show a religious orientation?	4	3
19	Did they use the program for improving this aspect?	4	2
20	Did they show a moral coherence?	3	3
21	Did they use the program for improving this aspect?	4	2
22	Can they combine couple life and work commitment?	5	4
23	Did they use the program for improving this aspect?	4	2
24	Did they show a parenting sense?	4	3
25	Did they use the program for improving this aspect?	4	2
26	Are they sensitive to the continuum couple education?	5	3

FIGURE 11.3. Final Assessing Scales on Two Couples Performed by the Preventer

application, the second one (#738) shows only two high points concerning the couple's general, optimistic attitude and the woman's fluency.

The assessment scales completed by the attendees concern six items:

1. individual feelings during the group meeting;
2. individual ability to express himself or herself;
3. interest level on the contents dealt with;
4. empathy level with the partner;
5. understanding level of the contents dealt with; and
6. usefulness level of the homework.

For example, Figure 11.4 shows previous couples' assessment patterns showing a similar trend and contrast indicated by the preventer.

Couple #738 did not attend one group session and the scores of the two partners are often discordant and rather low. On the other hand, the rating scores of the welcoming unit had highlighted the low fluency of the men and a limited motivation to attend the program; nevertheless the discussion of the case was in favor of offering them this educational opportunity.

Assessment of Educational Results

Remarks made on the unexpected results of workbook administration suggested a further, deeper analysis of the matter (Cusinato, 1998). In particular, the attention focused on the workbook *Orienting Couple Life,* given that it has been in use longer and with more people. In 1986 a check on its first decade of use offered the following picture:

- In ten years, 1,500 couples had attended the program, 90 percent of whom regularly attended the first part. Of these, 50 percent asked to continue with the second part of the program, and 90 percent of these couples completed the program.
- The program covered the premarital and newlywed period, helping people with their new life situation and its impact.
- Five percent of the attendees had broken off their relationship before getting married, probably becoming aware of the frailty of their relationship while following the program.
- Four percent of attendees had decided to separate, and the same number had asked for psychotherapeutic treatment.

In 1990, a further check revealed that the number of divorced couples had risen to ten, and the same number had asked for therapeutic help.

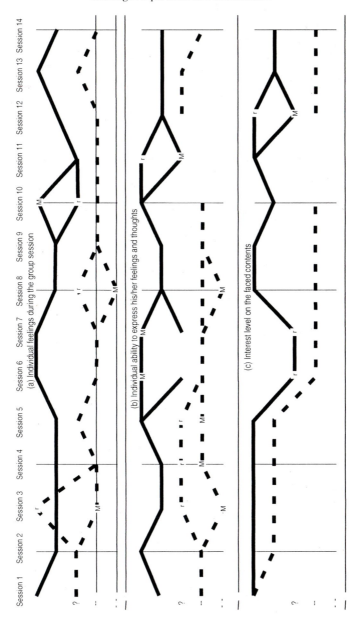

FIGURE 11.4. Self-Assessing by Couple #737 (—) and Couple 738 (····) Across the Sessions

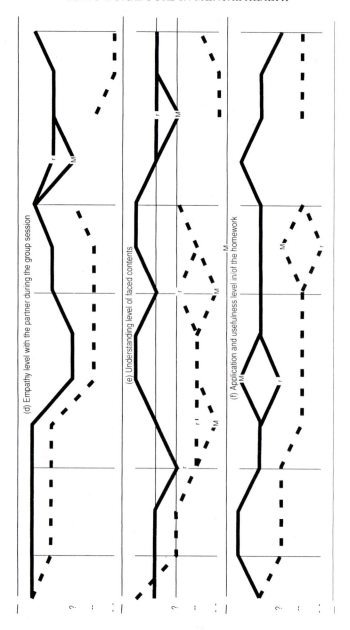

FIGURE 11.4. Self-Assessing by Couple #737 (—) and Couple 738 (····) Across the Sessions *(continued)*

During the summer of 1989, an inquiry carried out with preventers on a number of aspects required them to state the motivations attendee couples had given for their participation in the program. The answers were compared with those given by couples attending more traditional premarriage courses, mainly lessons. Results are summarized in Table 11.1.

Sometimes the program has been considered suitable only for highly educated and motivated people. However, reasons for attending the program are more varied that those for attending more traditional courses. Interestingly, item (e) (people without personal motivations, without even curiosity) registers a recovery of 50 percent—mostly likely because 90 percent of the attendees actually completed the program. As regards educational levels of attendees, the distribution is the following: elementary school 2.9 percent, middle school 33.7 percent, high school 37.0 percent, technical school 16.7 percent, and university 9.7 percent. It can therefore be concluded that the program may be attended by any couple.

Follow-up research was carried out in 1997-1998 (Cusinato, 2000). In November 1997, the help of fifty-six group preventers was asked for and obtained. They were to contact the attendees of the groups trained about five years earlier and inform them that they would soon receive a letter on "how they liked and thought useful both their marriage preparation program and their current couple/family life." Attendees were asked to take in due account this request for collaboration, answer individually, and send back the form.

Results showed that sixteen couples (2.45 percent) had split up before the wedding and nineteen (3.68 percent) after the wedding. Considering that the couples attending the program had already reached a firm reciprocal choice, 2.45 percent of couples splitting up before the wedding is not a low percentage. This shows that the program urges participants to perform a cogent check. A rate of 3.68 percent of separations can be compared with about 8 percent of separations in Italy in the first five years of marriage. In this way

TABLE 11.1. Motivations for Attending Marriage Preparation Programs

Motivation Items	Program: Orienting in Couple Life (%)	Traditional Courses (%)
a. Personal interest	20	5
b. Suggestions by friends and relatives	20	—
c. Attending is felt as recommended	20	50
d. Openly recommended by the priest	20	30
e. Openly asked by the priest	20	15

the program decreased separations by more than 50 percent. The other 373 couples were sent an explanatory letter and the questionnaire, including (1) information items on the five years and recollection of the training; (2) the Partner Quality Test (sixteen items evaluated on a five-point Likert scale [Maino and Aceti, 1996]); and (3) the Marital Satisfaction Scale (eleven items evaluated on a five-point Likert scale [Maino, 1997]). Data analysis showed different tesserae of a mosaic typical of the first steps of the family cycle (see Table 11.2), absorbed by child care, but where the couple relationship plays a primary role.

TABLE 11.2. Items on the Five-Year Family Life and Training Recollection

Information on couple/familiy life	Subjects' answers (*N*)	Percent (%)
Particularly positive events		
Wedding day	10	3.76
Couple life	52	19.55
Childbirth	194	72.93
Work success	10	3.76
Total	266	100.00
Particularly negative events		
Work trouble	39	28.47
House move	20	14.60
Health trouble	38	27.73
Death of a relative	19	13.87
Couple difficulties	21	15.33
Total	137	100.00
*Training attended in current time**		
No training	176	58.67
Individual training	14	4.66
Couple training	110	36.67
Total	300	100.00
*Contacts with trainers**		
No contacts	145	48.49
No contacts, but wished for them	88	29.44
Contacts	66	22.07
Total	299	100.00

*Classified and summarized from free questions

Some tensions emerged in regard to occupational involvement. However, the main commitment is devoted to family problems (particularly as far as negative events are concerned). It is significant that a high percentage of couples had continued their training in some ways and had also maintained relations with their preventers or at least had wished to. Tables 11.3 and 11.4 show the total usefulness assessment on premarriage preparation. It appears quite positive because more than one half allot high or very high scores and the most frequently mentioned contents concern couple identity and communication. The same aspects correlated significantly with the total usefulness assessment (together with aspects of trust, gender, and sex).

The Partner Quality Test (PQT) and SSC scale data were correlated with FPR-10 (Facco, 1999) subscales applied at the end of the program. Significant analysis results are shown in Table 11.5.

Ability of reciprocal acceptance, relational problem solving, and gender flexibility strengthened by marriage preparation and maintenance (40 percent of them mention experiences of continual education) nurtures, directly or indirectly, couple satisfaction and positive partner consideration during the subsequent five-year period.

CONCLUSION

Workbooks work well in the ambit of interventions for pre-marriage preparation and maintenance. They are received and used favorably by couples showing interest, commitment, and steadfastness. Attendees recognize the received advantages for their relationship during the programs, at the end of them, and also after a number of years. This firm belief is supported by the results of standardized tools applied as pre- and posttests, by qualitative observations and assessment of trainers/preventers during the formative process and at the end of it, and by the behavioral effects of partners on their concrete family life. Cost-effectiveness is positive, worth being always checked and made known to all people interested in these proposals.

TABLE 11.3. Total Usefulness Evaluation of the Program (on a Ten-Point Scale)

Assessment Range	Number	Percent (%)
Points 1-4	33	11.6
Points 5-6	79	27.6
Points 7-8	139	48.6
Points 9-10	35	12.2
Total	286	100.0

TABLE 11.4. Program Contents Recalled and Assessed (Ten-Point Scale)

Assessed Items	Given Points	Correlation with the Global Usefulness Assessment
Couple identity	*65 (Z = 3.76)	.39 (p < .01)
Couple communication	*66 (Z = 2.73)	.42 (p < .01)
Group discussion	29	
Faith aspects	48	.38 (p < .01)
Gender and sex	35	.57 (p < .01)
Reciprocal welcome	33	
Free time	*19 (Z = −4.74)	
Parenting	40	
Couple openness	37	.52 (p < .01)

*On log-linear analysis, these items show significant differences compared to the others.

TABLE 11.5. Correlations Between FPR Subscales and PQT and SSC Data

Couple Dimensions	PQT	SSC
Reciprocal acceptance of personality issues	.26*	.21*
Conflict resolution	—	.28*
Role flexibility	.30**	.30**

*p < .05; **p < .01

Workbooks for premarriage preparation and maintenance are working well even if they are applied with the support of volunteers committed to family prevention work. Their technical abilities may sometimes appear modest, but these limits are offset by their dedication, ideal motivation, and service flexibility.

Workbooks are not a panacea for all the difficulties linked to premarriage preparation and maintenance interventions. The welcoming of the recruited couples represents a particularly sensitive moment in which the training has to be matched to a specific program opportunity. Technical support is needed that offers a right evaluation of resources and needs of recruits, as is the supervision of a professional who assumes decision responsibility. Workbooks addressing specific aims have to be preferred to those with a large spectrum, many goals, and requiring a long time to be completed. In fact, the former are better able to answer the needs of the couples who accept attendance, taking into account their individual, relational, and actual resources, and also the current developmental tasks of their life-cycle stage. Their requirements may be many and different: enrichment, enhancement, or strengthening of their relational competencies.

Usually, the couples are informed about the precise contents of family life and relationships that may benefit from consulting competent professionals in ethics, religious matter, physics, genetics, sexual disorders, legal matters, and so on. Because of this, the use of workbooks is part of an integrated service at many levels of intervention (for example, primary, secondary, and tertiary family prevention), in plurality of competence, at different levels of responsibility (for example, volunteers or professionals), and in steps of intervention (welcome, evaluation work, group session, individual work supervision, counseling on specific aspects, etc.).

At best, the new challenges to premarriage preparation and maintenance can be gathered, understood, and answered only within a large service project. The growing number of marital or couple conflicts and problems point to the need for large-scale premarital preparation and long-term couple/marriage maintenance programs. However, we are also facing the creation of different lifestyles for couples. An ever-growing number of couples embark on a second marriage (Storm, Spremkle, and Williamson, 1986). Many couples live together before or outside the legal aspects of a formal marriage. Marriage is often delayed until the age of thirty, after the couple has lived together for many years. Consequently, transition points in the integration of a couple living together are spread out over time and are taking on different importance. Adolescence becomes more prolonged. Male and female infertility appears on the increase (Silvestrini, 1988). Assisted or artificial insemination is frequently considered, but not always with the awareness that is may undermine couple understanding. On the other side of the developmental cycle, an extension of the conjugal relationship after the parenting phase, along the third and fourth age of the life cycle exists.

Participation of volunteer couples is possible, useful, and fruitful for all people. Nevertheless, their basic preparation deserves strong commitment, yet at the same time, their continual education and the supervision of their performances have to be realized with the context of a wise service plan. In particular, volunteers have to be helped in conceptually distinguishing what promotes a welcoming attitude, a climate of socialization, and an empathetic experience from the acquisition of relational competencies that represent the understanding before and after marriage and along all the phases of the conjugal life cycle.

Finally, the perspective of combining the use of workbooks with the administration of assessment tools as an ordinary working policy that goes beyond those exceptional situations in which training falls within specific and subsidized research projects still remains open. The demand surfacing at this time requires an evaluation accompanying the everyday actions of the entire team engaging in premarriage preparation and maintenance, made possible by simple, reliable, theoretically consistent instruments, from which any preventer can derive useful support for his or her own actions. Without a doubt, any premarriage preparation and maintenance program has to be dealt with within a system perspective in which several competencies find their integration.

REFERENCES

Adams, B. N. (1979). Mate selection in the United States: A theoretical summarization. In W. R. Burr, R. Hill, F. I. Nye, and I. L. Reiss (Eds.), *Contemporary theories about the family*, Volume 1 (pp. 259-267). New York: Macmillan.

Bagarozzi, D. A. and Rauen, P. (1981). Premarital counseling: Appraisal and status. *The American Journal of Family Therapy, 9*, 13-20.

Berger, R. and Hannah, M. T. (Eds.) (1999). *Preventive approaches in couple therapy*. New York: Brunner/Mazel.

Cox, F. (1990). *Human intimacy: Marriage, the family, and its meaning*, Fifth edition. St. Paul, MN: West.

Cunningham, L. and Scanzoni, L. D. (1993). Religious and theological issues in family life education. In M. E. Arcus and J. D. Schvaneveldt (Eds.), *Handbook of family life education*, Volume 1: *Foundations of family life education* (pp. 189-228). Newbury Park, CA: Sage.

Cusinato, M. (1985). *Per orientarsi nella vita di coppia*. (Orienting couple life). Treviso, Italy: Centro della Famiglia.

Cusinato, M. (1992). *Misteriosa, non magica la nostra intimità. Programma di miglioramento dell'intimità coniugale* [(Our mysterious, not magic intimacy. Enhancement program of marital intimacy]).Treviso, Italy: Centro della Famiglia.

Cusinato, M. (1996a). *Tempo di gioia e di progetti* (Time of joy and plans). Treviso, Italy: Centro della Famiglia.

Cusinato, M. (1996b). *Un amore che non conosce ostacoil (Love overcomes any obstacle)*. Treviso, Italy: Centro della Famiglia.

Cusinato, M. (1997). *Family Emotion Scale*. Padua, Italy: Interdepartmental Center of Family Research, University of Padua.

Cusinato, M. (1998). Un programma strutturato di formazione al matrimonio (A structured program of marriage preparation). In M. Cusinato and P. Salvo (Eds.), *Lavorare con le famiglie: Programmi, interventi, valutazione* (Working with families. Programs, interventions, and evaluation) (pp. 109-142). Rome: Carrocci.

Cusinato, M. (2000). Cambiamenti relazionali nella formazione prematrimoniale: Valutazione immediata e di follow-up (Relational changes in the pre-marriage formation: Immediate evaluation and follow-up). *Età Evolutiva, 66,* 50-61.

Cusinato, M. (2001). *La scelta dell'amore* (The choice of love). Treviso, Italy: Centro della Famiglia.

Cusinato, M. (in progress). *The ERAAwC model for assessing attitude changes in pre-marriage intervention.*

Cusinato, M. and L'Abate, L. (1994). A spiral model of intimacy. In S. M. Johnson and L. S. Greenberg (Eds.), *The heart of the matter: Perspectives on emotion in marital therapy.* New York: Brunner/Mazel.

Cusinato, M. and Pastore, M. (2001). Uno strumento di valutazione dell'importanza di sé in rapporto all'altro: Analisi delle strutture tassonomiche in prospettiva evolutiva (An evaluation tool of self-importance in relation to the other: Analyses of tassonomic structures in developmental perspective). *Età Evolutiva, 69,* 5-18.

Cusinato, M. and Salvo, P. (Eds.) (1998). *Lavorare con le famiglie: Programmi, interventi, valutazione* (Working with families. Programs, interventions, and evaluation). Rome: Carrocci.

Cusinato, M., Simioni, E., and Simioni, M. (2001a). *Noi due assieme agli altri* (The two of us together with others). Treviso, Italy: Centro della Famiglia.

Cusinato, M., Simioni, E., and Simioni, M. (2001b). *Noi due con gli altri* (The two of us with others). Treviso, Italy: Centro della Famiglia.

Cusinato, M., Simioni, E., and Simioni, M. (2002). *Il progetto di noi due* (A plan for the two of us). Treviso, Italy: Centro della Famiglia.

Donati, P. (Ed.) (1997). *Uomo e donna in famiglia: Quinto rapporto CISF sulla famiglia in Italia* (Man and woman in the family: The Fifth CISF's report on the family in Italy). Cinisello Balsamo, Italy: San Paolo.

Facco, G. (1999). Revisione delle Scale FPR-10: Contributo per la messa a punto delle categorie relazionali considerate. (Revision of FPR-10 Scales: Contribution for setting up considered relational categories). *FIR, 4,* 25-48.

Fournier, D. G. and Olson, D. H. (1986). Programs for premarital and newlywed couples. In R. F. Levant (Ed.), *Psychoeducational approaches to family therapy and counseling* (pp. 174-231). New York: Springer.

Galimberti, C. (1985). Il processo di formazione della coppia (The process of couple shaping). In E. Scabini (Ed.), *L'organizzazione famiglia tra crisi e sviluppo (Family organization between crisis and development)* (pp. 131-174). Milano: Franco Angeli.

Giblin, P., Sprenkle, D. H., and Sheeham, R. (1985). Enrichment outcome research: A meta-analysis of premarital, marital, and family interventions. *Family Coordinator, 30,* 297-306.

Gurman, A. S. and Kniskern, D. P. (1977). Enriching research on marital enrichment programs. *Journal of Marriage and Family Counseling, 3,* 3-11.

Hof, L. and Miller, W. (1981). *Marriage enrichment: Philosophy, process, and program.* Bowie, MD: Brady.

Kieren, D. K. and Doherty-Poirier, M. (1993). Teaching about family communication and problem solving: Issues and future directions. In M. E. Arcus and J. D.

Schvaneveldt (Eds.), *Handbook of family life education*, Volume 2: *The practice of family life education* (pp. 155-179). Newbury Park, CA: Sage.

Kohl, J. (1990). *Study guide to accompany intimate relationships, marriage, and families*. Mountain View, CA: Mayfield.

L'Abate, L. (1990). *Building family competence. Primary and secondary prevention strategies*. Newbury Park, CA: Sage.

L'Abate, L. (1992). *Programmed writing: A self-administered approach for interventions with individuals, couples, and families*. Pacific Grove, CA: Brooks/Cole.

L'Abate, L. (1994). *A theory of personality development*. New York: Wiley.

L'Abate, L. (1997). *The self in the family: A classification of personality, criminality, and psychopathology*. New York: Wiley.

L'Abate, L. (1999). Taking the bull by the horns: Beyond talk in psychological interventions. *The Family Journal: Therapy and Counseling for Couples and Families, 7*, 206-220.

L'Abate, L. (in press). *Personality in intimate relationships: Socialization and psychopathology*. New York: Kluwer Academic.

L'Abate, L., Johnson, T. B., and Levis, M. (1987). Treatment of depression in a couple with systematic homework assignments. *Journal of Psychotherapy and the Family, 2*, 117-128.

L'Abate, L. and Platzman, (1991). The practice of programmed writing (PW) in therapy and prevention with families. *American Journal of Family Therapy, 19*, 1-10.

Maino, E. (1997). Desiderabilità sociale, atteggiamento ottimista e qualità della relazione coniugale (Social desirability, optimistic attitude, and marital relationship). Unpublished graduate thesis in psychology. Padua, Italy: University of Padua.

Maino, E. and Aceti, G. (1996). Partner Quality Test: Messa a punto di una nuova forma (Partner Quality Test: Setting up a new form). *FIR, 1*, 123-134.

Materazzo, R. (1994). Le scale di negoziazione coniugale: contributo allo studio di validità concorrente e di costrutto. (Marital negotiation scales: A contribution of concurrent and construct validity). Unpublished graduate thesis in psychology. Padua, Italy: University of Padua.

Most, R. and Guerney, P. (1983). An empirical evaluation of the training of lay volunteer leaders for premarital relationship enhancement. *Family Relations, 32*, 239-251.

Norem, R. H., Schaefer, M., Springer, J., and Olson, D. H. (1980). Effectiveness of premarital education program. Unpublished paper. Stillwater, OK: Family Study Center, Oklahoma State University.

Olson, D. H., Fournier, D. G., and Druckman, J. M. (1982). *PREPARE-ENRICH counselors manual*. Minneapolis, MN: Prepare-Enrich.

Olson, D. H. and Olson, A. K. (1999). PREPARE/ENRICH Program: Version 2000. In R. Berger and M. T. Hannah (Eds.), *Preventive approaches in couple therapy* (pp. 196-216). New York: Brunner and Mazel.

Peruffo, P. and Faccin M. L. (1992). Ricerca su due corsi di formazione al matrimonio nel Veneto (Research study on two educational programs to marriage in Veneto). *Relazioni, 11*(5), 21-24.

Rice, F. (2000). *Intimate relationships, marriage, and families.* Mountain View, CA: Mayfield.

Salvo, R., Cusinato, M., and Rossetti, N. (1996). Attaccamento e relazione di coppia (Attachment and couple relationship). *FIR, 1,* 5-16.

Scabini, E. (1995). *Psicologia sociale della famiglia: Sviluppo dei legami e trasformazioni sociali* (Family social psychology: Development of ties and social transformations). Torino: Boringhieri.

Scabini, E. and Cigoli, V. (2000). *Il famigliare: Legami, simboli e transizioni* (Family system: Bonds, symbols, and transitions). Milano: Raffaello Cortina.

Schumm, W. R. and Denton, W. (1979). Trends in premarital counseling. *Journal of Marital and Family Therapy, 22,* 23-32.

Silvestrini, L. (1998). *S.O.S. Fertilità* (S.O.S. Fertility). Rome: L'Airone.

Stahmann R. F. and Salts, C. J. (1993). Educating for marriage and intimate relationships. In M. E. Arcus and J. D. Schvaneveldt (Eds.), *Handbook of family life education,* Volume 2: *The practice of family life education* (pp. 33-63). Newbury Park, CA: Sage.

Storm, C. L., Sprenkle, D., and Williamson, W. (1986). Innovative divorce approaches developed by counselors, conciliators, mediators, and educators. In R. L. Levant (Ed.), *Psychoeducational approaches to family therapy and counseling* (pp. 166-309). New York: Springer.

Weiss, R. L. (1978). The conceptualization in a behavioral perspective. In T. Paolino and B. S. McRady (Eds.), *Marriage and marital therapy: Psychoanalytic, behavioral, and systems theory perspective* (pp. 165-239). New York: Brunner/Mazel.

Wright, H. N. (1983). *Premarital counseling.* Chicago: Moody Press.

Chapter 12

Homework in Couple Therapy: A Review and Evaluation of Available Workbooks

Krista S. Gattis
Mia Sevier
Andrew Christensen

Couples often enter therapy with entrenched interaction patterns and ways of thinking about each other that are painful and unfulfilling. They may avoid conflict at all costs or engage in nasty arguments daily. They may see each other as needy, whiny, lazy, unreliable, or worse. Both partners may be in emotional pain and may fail to recognize that they are not alone in their suffering. Fed by strong negative emotions, these thought and behavior patterns may be difficult to break. Although couple therapy can promote positive change, it is often limited by financial and time constraints. It also takes place outside of the context of couples' daily lives. Consequently, couple therapists frequently implement homework assignments designed to bridge the gap between the therapy office and a couple's regular environment.

DEFINING HOMEWORK

Although the use of homework in couple treatment is quite common, it is empirically ill defined and underresearched (Dattilio, 2002; Brooks, 2001). Indeed, what is meant even by the term *homework* varies among clinicians, theoreticians, and researchers. Homework may include everything from strict behavioral plans to unstructured journaling to assigned readings. Homework assignments for couples may be broadly defined (e.g., "write about your relationship for fifteen minutes") or highly specific (e.g., "discuss the issue of how to manage finances for ten minutes"). Moreover, the number of available workbooks with homework assignments for couples is substantial. In addition, many of the guides provide not only exercises but also copious information to help couples understand their own relationships. This bibliotherapy is useful in promoting awareness of issues in relationships, changing attitudes, and helping couples to develop new ideas about acceptable interactions (Brooks, 2001).

The goal of this chapter is to review a subset of homework resources based on empirically supported treatments for couple therapists, as well as provide a broad overview of issues in homework with couples. For the purposes of this chapter, homework is broadly defined as any prescriptive activity in which a couple engages between therapy sessions. In therapy with individuals, homework often takes the form of written exercises since treatment focuses on changing a single client's inner dynamics and behavior. However, in couple therapy, a relationship is the focus of treatment. Hence, homework sometimes takes more dyadic forms, such as structured interactions, exchanging positive behaviors, or videotaping discussions between partners. Thus, the definition of homework here has been broadened from traditional written assignments to include a variety of between-session interventions designed to strengthen couple relationships.

CLINICAL ISSUES IN HOMEWORK WITH COUPLES

Well-chosen homework can lead to therapeutic insights, increase motivation for change, and serve as much-needed practice for breaking ingrained behavior patterns. In these ways, homework in couple therapy shares many features with homework in individual therapy. However, homework for couples also has features particular to couple work.

As mentioned earlier, a primary way that couple (and family) treatment differs from individual treatment is its focus on a relationship, rather than on an individual. As a consequence, therapy goals are likely to be dyadic, and in the case of homework assignments, the focus typically turns to relationship repair and development, rather than individual growth. Dattilio (2002) has outlined several main types of homework targeting relationships, including bibliotherapy, audio- and videotaping out-of-session interactions, activity scheduling, journaling, behavioral task assignments, and cognitive restructuring through thought records.

Dyadic homework for couples may have some special advantages. For example, behavioral exchange exercises (i.e., partners agreeing to do positive things for each other) can turn the tide of negativity in a relationship. Likewise, communication exercises practiced in the comfort of a couple's own home may help them modify their interactions to be more positive and to become less sensitive to negative interactions.

In considering between session assignments, the overarching goals of each couple's therapy may inform the therapist's choice of exercises. For partners who have become estranged and distant, intimacy increasing collaborative assignments may be most productive. On the other hand, for partners who are struggling with frequent and heated conflicts, assignments that each partner completes independently may be more appropriate until partners have a more thorough understanding of their own thoughts and feelings.

Iatrogenic Effects of Homework

Although between-session assignments have the potential to help couples learn new ways of understanding each other, it is important for homework not to exacerbate existing relationship difficulties. For example, if a husband sees his wife as unreliable and irresponsible, and she neglects to comply with homework assignments, then a therapist may inadvertently support the husband's position that the wife cannot be counted on. Thus, therapists must be careful to view homework from a dyadic perspective and to evaluate its effect on the relationship, rather than simply on the individual partners. Behavioral marital therapists Lester, Beckham, and Baucom (1980) also recommend providing a "safety valve" in the early phases of therapy for homework assignments. Designed to prevent homework assignments from disintegrating into fights, the safety valve involves discontinuing any exercise after a predetermined number of destructive behaviors or statements have occurred.

Homework Resistance

As with any kind of therapy, resistance may be an issue with homework compliance in couples. Either or both partners may not complete agreed-upon readings or activities. To help generate enthusiasm for homework and increase the probability of compliance in short-term couple therapy, Halford (2001) talks with couples about the importance of the assignment, asks explicitly about partners' comprehension of the task, and asks couples whether they believe the assignment will be useful. With this process, he attempts to "draw out the partners' commitment to undertaking these tasks . . . [and] develop their sense of excitement about the possibility of change" (Halford, 2001, p. 56). Creating systematic, goal-oriented homework assignments collaboratively with couples may also increase compliance (Brooks, 2001). In addition, couple therapists should be sensitive to clients' needs for structure versus creative freedom in the development and implementation of homework assignments.

Even with a therapist's best efforts at explanation and motivation, either or both members of a couple may not complete assignments. Halford (2001) suggests a process for understanding resistance to homework completion. This three-step process includes ensuring that couples understand and have the skills to complete the task, addressing any negative thoughts about the consequences of completing the task, and understanding any environmental hurdles for compliance (e.g., one spouse refuses to participate). Dattilio (2002) notes that couples who have difficulty completing homework assignments may have difficulties working together, communicating, and coping with underlying concerns about change in the relationship. As in all kinds of therapies, homework assignments should be carefully conceived and discussed in the session to be most helpful for couples. Tasks that emphasize the importance of self-directed change and are specific to the therapeutic issues may be more likely to be completed because of their perceived relevance to relationship problems (Dattilio, 2002; Halford, 2001).

RESEARCH BASIS OF HOMEWORK WITH COUPLES

The use of homework with couples has many potential benefits. Supporters of homework in any therapeutic modality cite its potential to help clients see themselves as agents of change, to make more progress in less time, and to help generalize the improvements made in therapy to the real world (Dattilio, 2002; Glick et al., 2000; Lester, Beckham, and Baucom, 1980). Homework assignments may facilitate not only therapy, but also the initial assessment process if couples are asked to complete standardized self-report inventories of relationship functioning outside of session (Halford, 2001). Halford (2001) notes that assigning homework in the early sessions establishes an expectation for couples that their therapeutic work must be continued between sessions and that success is likely to be a function of their own efforts.

Little research has been conducted on the effects of homework in couple therapy, and no comprehensive meta-analytic research has been undertaken on what exercises or books are most effective. Although many treatment protocols involve homework, research studies often fail to include data related to homework compliance or homework-related gains, and many studies have too little power to evaluate the effects of homework (Kazantzis, Deane, and Ronan, 2000). The limited research available has shown that homework increases the gains made in therapy and that homework compliance in therapy is a predictor of therapy success (Holtzworth-Munroe et al., 1989). Although the causal direction of the relationship between homework compliance and therapy success is unclear, doing our best to actively engage couples in the therapeutic process seems to be important.

WORKBOOKS FOR USE WITH COUPLES

Introduction

In attempting to separate relationship self-help books, books of exercises aimed at couples, and books of exercises for therapists to give to couples, the waters muddy very quickly. Rather than make arbitrary distinctions among the many types of "workbooks," we decided to consider books based on empirically supported therapies that focus on couples actively working on their relationships outside of the therapist's office. The books reviewed here are primarily self-help books, which vary in their focus on insight versus behavioral exercises. This chapter was developed with the idea of working with distressed couples in a therapy situation, rather than with distress-prevention efforts for couples. (See Chapter 13 for more information on that topic.)

Three different therapies for couples have received empirical support sufficient to meet established criteria for being "efficacious" or "specific and efficacious" treatments: behavioral couples therapy, cognitive and cognitive-behavioral couple therapy, and emotionally focused couple therapy (Baucom et al., 1998; Christensen and Heavey, 1999). We are aware of no workbooks on emotion-focused therapy for couples. Therefore, this chapter focuses mainly on books that come from the cognitive-behavioral tradition. However, we also include books that espouse approaches similar to emotion-focused therapy, the behavioral approaches, and a recent integrative approach gaining empirical support. In addition, we make recommendations for a few books on special couple-related problems, such as sexual dysfunction and extramarital affairs.

To narrow the field of available workbooks to the best of the bunch, we surveyed couples therapists and researchers for their favorite books for couples. We contacted the most well-known couple researchers from a variety of theoretical orientations and communicated with many clinicians and researchers through psychology mailing lists on the Internet. Although our postings received dozens of responses, a few titles emerged again and again. Researchers and clinicians alike converged on a few selected texts. These are the texts we have chosen to review here.

We should note that we have opted not to review manuals marketed only to therapists for the purposes of treatment planning. These manuals typically focus heavily on in-session interventions and case management issues, rather than on the between-session assignments that are the focus of this chapter.

Although the workbooks in this chapter are chosen for their theoretical underpinnings, many have elements of eclecticism. For instance, some largely behavioral treatises contain elements of acceptance- or emotion-focused therapy. The books also vary in complexity and scope, and these variations are noted in the reviews. Finally, each review is annotated with any thoughts about the kinds of couples most and least likely to benefit from the work. A cautionary word: Any good assignment must be carefully screened by the therapist for its applicability to a given client. We recommend that therapists peruse potentially relevant resources themselves.

The Books

After the Fight: Using Your Disagreements to Build a Stronger Relationship (Wile, 1993)
After the Honeymoon: How Conflict Can Improve Your Relationship (Wile, 1988)

Description: These two books are based on collaborative couple therapy (Wile, 1999), which suggests that relationship difficulties arise from a lack of self-acceptance, as well as a lack of partner-acceptance. Individuals are believed to constantly experience a flowing stream of different thoughts, feelings, and reactions. When partners reproach themselves for having certain unavoidable feelings, they are unable to explore or share these internal experiences constructively with their partners and may act in a way that creates relationship conflict. As suggested by the titles, conflict is seen as inevitable and useful in relationships. Wile suggests that partners can use fights as clues to figure out important unsaid feelings that, if expressed, could lead to greater relationship intimacy and relationship satisfaction. Wile encourages readers to build a nonaccusing, nonanxious platform from which to understand themselves, their partners, and their relationship. Wile's approach bears some similarity to emotion-focused therapy and integrative behavioral couple therapy.

Practical usage: Although differing in organization, both books take a nonblaming, playful stance on relationships. Wile uses several characters in each of his books, including a wife, a husband, himself, and a skeptic. His characters demonstrate the key points of the book through internal dialogues and conversations with one another. He provides useful section subtitles to inform readers of his key points and often provides extensive lists of ideas for readers to consider. Both books could be assigned in portions or totality for couples to read. *After the Honeymoon* seems to be written primarily for use by couples. *After the Fight* seems to be written with therapists in mind, since it includes large portions explaining a hypothetical therapist's experience and contrasting differing theoretical approaches. However, it might also be used directly with couples, since much of the book deals with issues in a typical couple's experience.

Exercises: These books do not contain explicit exercises, but clearly steer readers toward a new nonreproachful understanding of relationships. A therapist working in conjunction with chapters assigned as homework could ask couples to write each week about how book ideas relate to their own inner experiences and their relationship functioning.

Brief Couples Therapy Homework Planner (Schultheis, O'Hanlon, and O'Hanlon, 1999)

Description: This text provides therapists with a host of primarily written homework assignments for individual partners and couples engaged in couple therapy. The authors come from a solution-focused theoretical tradition (Hoyt, 2002, chapter in Gurman and Jacobson, 2002), which has many similarities to the behavioral approach. Each exercise is creatively titled and includes an introductory paragraph, often using metaphors to help the client understand the goals of the task. Each exercise is also supplemented with a note to therapists about what problems may be most helped by the exercise, as well as sample debriefing questions for the couple after they have completed the assignment. The authors also provide a few informational handouts for couples about broad topics such as communication.

Practical Usage: This book contains a broad array of exercises, many of which could be completed by partners individually or jointly. The language is easy to understand and the metaphors are illuminating, although the writing style can be wordy. Each exercise is conveniently formatted on its own page for easy reproduction, and the book comes with a handy disk so that forms may be modified by clinicians.

Exercises: The exercises in this book range from broad assignments designed to orient couples toward their problem areas (and the changes they would like to make) to more specific tasks designed to help couples do things, such as manage household work and improve their sexual relationship. Many exercises involve list making, especially focusing on how partners can modify their current ways of relating to their spouses to create more satisfying interactions. Other assignments involve tracking verbal and non-verbal behaviors during conflict, experimenting with new kinds of discussions about problem areas, journaling about positive and negative feelings, and participating in behavioral experiments designed to improve both problems and intimacy.

A Couple's Guide to Communication
(Gottman et al., 1976)

Description: This is an extensive workbook of behavioral marital therapy techniques. Although it contains some research-based psychoeducational material (especially about sexual problems), the real focus of this text is skill building through communication training and behavioral exchange. This book is engaging, specific, and didactic, and contains many suggestions and exercises. The guide outlines a number of communication traps in relationships and provides more positive alternatives (including ideas such as validation, active listening, and an excellent section on how to identify the underlying issues in trivial disagreements).

A Couple's Guide to Communication was published in 1976, and it is unsurprisingly a little dated. However, the main ideas and most vignettes are current. Although this book occasionally suffers from confused organization, the chapters are generally cohesive and focused.

Practical usage: Couple therapists may find this book to be a particularly helpful adjunct to therapy since it is very readable and the chapters are self-contained enough to make good between-session assignments. Moreover, the kinds of exercises suggested in the book would make excellent fodder for discussions and problem solving in therapy sessions. The suggestions in this text may seem somewhat rigid to some couples. For example, some highly sophisticated couples may find the section on how to be polite to one's spouse somewhat off-putting in its parental tone. Nevertheless, the authors are careful to note that some ideas may be more helpful than others for a given couple, and the overall thoughtfulness of the strategies they suggest may far outweigh any concerns about rigidity.

Exercises: The activities described in the book are creative, practical, and simple, and include behavioral assignments, list making, paradoxical interventions, and suggestions for fun things to do as a couple. Examples include making a chart of feelings to help with feeling identification, creating a marital suggestion box, and writing a contract specifying behavioral changes each partner will make. There are also written self-quizzes on the ideas presented in the book, including how to label certain kinds of interactions and what a good response to certain spouse behaviors might include.

Fighting for Your Marriage: Positive Steps for Preventing Divorce and Preserving a Lasting Love (Markman, Stanley, and Blumberg, 2001)

Description: Written from a cognitive-behavioral perspective and based on the well-researched Prevention and Relationship Enhancement Program (PREP; Stanley, Blumberg, and Markman, 1998), this text is divided into four sections. The first part covers hallmarks of good relationships including an atmosphere of safety, intimacy, and responsibility. In addition, the authors explore behavioral roles, gender-based communication, and intimacy styles that are likely tied to conflict in relationships. The next section explores communication and problem solving, including perceptual filters, the speaker-listener technique, the effects of hidden issues, and the inevitability of differences between partners. The third section addresses ways to maintain friendship, fun, enjoyable sexual relations, and spirituality. The final section encourages couples to recognize unrealistic expectations, develop forgiveness, and move toward commitment to change.

Practical usage: The presentation style is easy to read, lighthearted, and enthusiastic, and the book offers very concrete and directive advice throughout. Therapists who wish to expand clients' understanding of general relationship dynamics and/or implement structured communication and problem-solving skills could easily assign chapters in conjunction with their therapeutic work. However, the authors' suggestions reflect the program's prevention focus and imply a level of collaboration and enthusiasm for the relationship that may be lacking in couples entrenched in dissatisfying relationships.

Exercises: Exercises with specific instructions appear at the end of each chapter, and are designed to help partners apply what they have read to their own relationship. Examples include quizzes for couples to identify destructive relationship patterns, problem areas, and relationship expectations, an assignment to formulate statements that could help derail arguments, and specific instructions for practicing positive communication skills and problem solving, such as the speaker-listener technique and XYZ statements. In addition, other exercises are designed to help couples build friendship and intimacy, and include making a "fun deck" to select enjoyable activities, practicing sensate-focused touching, and using provided questions to prompt discussions on spirituality.

Other books based on PREP include *A Lasting Promise: A Christian Guide to Fighting for Your Marriage* (Stanley et al., 1998), *Becoming Parents: How to Strengthen Your Marriage As Your Family Grows* (1999), *Fighting for Your Jewish Marriage* (Crohn et al., 2000), *Fighting for Your African American Marriage* (Whitfield et al., 2001), and *Fighting for Your Empty-Nest Marriage* (Arp et al., 2000).

Reconcilable Differences
(Christensen and Jacobson, 2000)

Description: Written from the perspective of integrative behavioral couple therapy (Jacobson and Christensen, 1996), and meant to be used as an adjunct to this treatment, the primary focus of this book is on building emotional acceptance in relationships.* *Acceptance* is defined as tolerating or even embracing unpleasant partner behavior because of new experiences of the partner, the self, and the relationship, which create a new context for the problematic behavior. Throughout the book, acceptance is promoted by showing readers how to view their relationships more objectively, develop a nonblaming understanding of relationship problems, and express emotions in ways that build compassion rather than conflict. Also included in this book are sections suggesting ways to improve communication and problem-solving. The concluding portion helps readers identify unacceptable relationship behavior, such as domestic violence and verbal abuse.

Practical usage: This book is directed toward couples entrenched in conflict. The authors rarely offer specific advice because of their concern that little useful advice fits all couples, and because advice giving can backfire (e.g., one partner criticizes the other for failing to implement some advice). Instead, the authors offer broad principles and new ways of viewing problems. Readers can identify with case studies and discussions of key concepts. Although readers seeking specific advice may not take to this presentation style, other readers may appreciate the opportunity to consider their relationships in juxtaposition to the concepts and principles presented in the book. Therapists could use this text to help couples expand their awareness

---

*Because one of the authors of this chapter, Christensen, was the senior author of this book, it is difficult to provide an objective evaluation. We have tried to be descriptive rather than evaluative and therefore leave evaluation to the reader. For a review of this book, see Berscheid (2001).

of common relationship dynamics and find ways to build acceptance in their relationship.

Exercises: Carefully constructed exercises at the end of each chapter invite readers to apply presented principles and perspectives to their relationships. For example, Chapter 1 concludes with an assignment instructing readers to write three perspectives on a recent argument: their own, their partner's, and an observer's view. Other written exercises encourage couples to answer questions about relationship patterns, to gain a deeper context for (and intellectual distance from) areas of incompatibility, and to provide a voice for underlying emotions. Exercises also guide partners on asking for small changes, expressing feelings using positive communication techniques, and taking constructive action in response to conflict.

The Seven Principles for Making Marriage Work (Gottman and Silver, 1999)

Description: Based broadly on a cognitive-behavioral approach and more specifically on Gottman's treatment manual (Gottman, 1999), this book touts research findings from Gottman's research on happy and unhappy couples and encourages readers to implement elements of happy relationships into their own marriages. Gottman believes that most marital therapy fails because of its focus on conflict resolution, and partners should instead focus on building intimacy and friendship in their relationships. Suggestions to couples include advice on how to get to know each other better, nurture fondness and admiration, become available and responsive to each other in small ways, and create a sense of shared meaning. Differences in expressing emotions and handling conflicts between men and women are explored, and husbands are especially encouraged to begin to accept their wives' influence. Gottman and Silver encourage readers to distinguish between solvable and unsolvable conflict and to handle each type differently.

Practical usage: Some of this text seems most applicable to couples who collaborate in their relationship, since this book is written with the expectation that partners will work through the text together. Given an early emphasis on identifying the positives (or lack thereof) in readers' relationships, it seems likely that a couple highly entrenched in conflict could end up blaming and criticizing each other. Some exercises require a level of sophistication in the reader, since they suggest that partners explore underlying issues, such as family histories, and they assume couples will be able to use the material uncovered in a constructive, nonblaming way. This text's presentation style is clearly prescriptive and includes claims that, in completing exercises, couples should expect an increase in strong, warm feelings and greater relationship intimacy.

Exercises: This book contains a multitude of exercises designed to help couples identify signs of intimacy and friendship, make concrete behavioral changes, implement alternative ways to begin to think about relationship partners, and learn ways to communicate more effectively. For example, the section on What to Do When Your Spouse Doesn't Turn Toward You instructs both spouses to fill out and then discuss questions detailing negative feelings that they have felt during the week. Partners then discuss triggers for the feelings, deeper origins for the feelings, each partner's own contribution to the problem, and how each could make the problem better in the future. Another exercise, Softened Startup, provides readers with a sample situation and an example of a harsh way to begin a conversation about it. Readers are asked to practice soft and nonblaming ways to begin a conversation about the provided topic.

Stop Blaming, Start Loving!: A Solution-Oriented Approach to Improving Your Relationship (O'Hanlon and Hudson, 1995)

Description: Based on a solution-oriented theoretical approach, this guide suggests that changing behaviors, rather than examining emotion, cognition, or personality, is the key to improving troubled relationships. Readers are encouraged to give up unhelpful blaming "stories" that they have constructed about their partners and to personally take responsibility for improving their relationships. Partners are encouraged to behave differently by taking actions, such as framing complaints in specific concrete terms and changing their own behavior in unpleasant relationship patterns. The book thoroughly and clearly addresses ways to improve intimacy and sex, healing rituals for unfinished business and reconnection, and destructive relationship patterns, such as betrayals of trust and violence.

Practical usage: A clear strength of this book is its engaging, clear, and concise presentation style. Key ideas are presented with easy-to-understand writing, to-the-point vignettes, and summary boxes. The authors, who are married, depathologize couples' struggles by using examples from their own relationship. In addition, use of this text does not require both partners' involvement.

Exercises: Numerous exercises encouraging couples to examine their relationships and begin to act more constructively are regularly interspersed throughout the chapters in boxes called Action Steps. Each is informatively titled, brief, and involves specific action. Examples include Meaningful Praise, which instructs readers to praise their partner once per day for one week when the partner does something that can be appreciated, and to write a love letter about a time when the reader felt close to the partner. Another action step, Action Requests, provides a fill-in-the-blank sentence asking partners for specific behavioral changes they would like made.

We Can Work It Out: Making Sense of Marital Conflict (Notarius and Markman, 1993)

Description: This book offers a cognitive-behavioral approach to eliminating martial conflict and increasing positive exchanges in relationships. The authors base their approach on researched differences between happy and unhappy couples, and assert that the major problems in unhappy couples are ineffective communication and poor conflict management. Hence, the primary focus of the book is to teach partners how to talk without fighting. Couples are offered a systematic approach to identify ways of thinking and behaving in their own relationships that contribute to destructive patterns, and to apply standard methods to promote positive communication and problem-solving skills. The last chapter in the text focuses on rekindling positive aspects of relationships, such as friendship, fun, and sensuality.

Practical usage: This book requires couples to be motivated and committed to making changes in their relationships. The authors expect that couples will be able to develop teamwork and come to view relationship difficulties as a common enemy, rather than view each other as enemies. A therapist wishing to help couples implement standard communication or problem-solving skills could readily use chapters of this book to educate couples about conflict.

Exercises: Every few chapters, questionnaires, exercises, and assignments are presented that are designed to help couples recognize and change interactional problems and improve communication skills. For example, one exercise encourages exploration of hidden anger that may be interfering with positive communication. Another exercise, the Floor Exercise, targets communication directly by instructing partners to take turns communicating as the "speaker" while the partner who is listening uses index cards with plus, minus, or zero signs to provide feedback to the speaker on how his or her message is being interpreted.

Why Marriages Succeed or Fail
(Gottman, 1994)

Description: This book is an educational treatise for couples, with relatively few practical suggestions and advice. Gottman's specialty is couple interaction, and the strengths of this book are its detailed descriptions and examples of communication patterns in couples. The book comes from a largely cognitive-behavioral stance, with a focus on communication styles, physiological arousal during conflict, and reciprocal interactions between spouses. Gottman does an excellent job of normalizing conflict in couples and explaining how different relationship styles may all be equally "healthy." The section on the Four Horsemen of relationships (criticism, contempt, defensiveness, and stonewalling) is articulate and ripe with good examples.

Practical usage: Gottman draws extensively, and nearly exclusively, on his own research on couples, which may be troublesome for less sophisticated and research-oriented readers. Nearly the first hundred pages are summaries of research findings, with few direct applications for couples. However, for couples with significant communication difficulties who enjoy reading, this book may be a very helpful educational adjunct to therapy. For less sophisticated couples, some of Gottman's prognostic statements may be appealing and helpful, such as the idea that happy couples have a ratio of 5:1 positive to negative interactions. For more sophisticated couples, this information may feel too general to be applicable. Nevertheless, it is an excellent resource for couples with significant communication troubles who would benefit from education about these problematic patterns.

Exercises: In terms of the provision of exercises or direct advice, this book is relatively spare. There are brief self-tests throughout the book, which are helpful for providing insight and applying typologies to individual relationships, but provide few suggestions on how to improve relationship functioning. Self-tests focus on issues such as whether partners respect each other. A section on Diagnosing Your Marriage uses the results of the self-tests to provide an overall description of the relationship. Although the diagnostic section is comprehensive and encourages couples to explore their marriage in relation to the concepts presented in the book, its structure is somewhat confusing and some couples may get bogged down in flipping between pages.

SPECIAL CONSIDERATIONS

Although reviewing books for the myriad specific problems that couples experience is beyond the scope of this chapter, it is important to note that excellent books are available for dealing with difficulties such as affairs, sexual dysfunction, and violence in relationships. *After the Affair* (Spring and Spring, 1997) is an excellent guidebook for couples navigating marriage after one partner has been unfaithful. Although the book is mostly targeted at the faithful partner, whom Spring and Spring term the "Hurt Partner," it also speaks to the experience of the "Unfaithful Partner." Spring and Spring's approach is eclectic, combining emotion and acceptance-focused strategies with more cognitive behavioral techniques, such as communication training and behavioral exchange.

For couples experiencing sexual difficulties, *For Yourself: The Fulfillment of Female Sexuality* (Barbach, 2000) and *The New Male Sexuality*, Revised Edition (Zilbergeld, 1999) are likely to be helpful adjuncts to couples therapy. These down-to-earth educational guides provide sound advice and applied exercises for addressing sexual difficulties.

For couples experiencing violence, controversies exist about how to deal with violence in the context of couples therapy, and these issues are beyond the scope of this chapter. Nevertheless, in their book *When Men Batter Women*, well-known couple violence researchers Neil Jacobson and John Gottman (1998), recommend *Getting Free* by Ginny NiCarthy (1997) as a guide for women in abusive relationships.

REFERENCES

Arp, D. H., Arp, C. S., Stanley, S. M., Markman, H. J., and Blumberg, S. L. (2000). *Fighting for your empty-nest marriage.* New York: Jossey-Bass.

Barbach, L. (2000). *For yourself: The fulfillment of female sexuality.* New York: Signet.

Baucom, D. H., Shoham, V., Meuser, K. T., Daiuto, A. D., and Stickle, T. R. (1998). Empirically supported couple and family interventions for marital distress and adult mental health problems. *Journal of Consulting and Clinical Psychology, 66,* 53-88.

Berscheid, E. (2001). Review of "Reconcilable Differences." *Contemporary Psychology: APA Review of Books, 46,* 229-232.

Brooks, M. (2001). Extending techniques from the office to home using homework. In G. R. Weeks and S. R. Treat (Eds.), *Couples in treatment,* Second edition (pp. 215-225). Philadelphia: Brunner-Routledge.

Christensen, A. and Heavey, C. L. (1999). Interventions for couples. *Annual Review of Psychology, 50,* 165-190.

Christensen, A. and Jacobson, N. S. (2000). *Reconcilable differences*. New York: Guilford Press.

Crohn, J., Markman, H. J., Blumberg, S. L., and Levine, J. R. (2000). *Fighting for your Jewish marriage*. New York: Wiley.

Dattilio, F. M. (2002). Homework assignments in couple and family therapy. *Journal of Clinical Psychology, 58,* 535-547.

Glick, I. D., Berman, E. M., Clarkin, J. F., and Rait, D. S. (2000). *Marital and family therapy,* Fourth edition. Washington, DC: American Psychiatric Press.

Gottman, J. M. (1994). *Why marriages succeed or fail*. New York: Simon and Schuster.

Gottman, J. M. (1999). *The marriage clinic: A scientifically based marital therapy*. New York: Norton.

Gottman, J. M., Notarius, C., Gonso, J., and Markman, H. (1976). *A couple's guide to communication*. Champaign, IL: Research Press.

Gottman, J. M. and Silver, N. (1999). *The seven principles for making marriage work*. New York: Crown.

Gurman, A. S. and Jacobson, N. S. (Eds.) (2002). *Clinical handbook of couple therapy,* Third edition. New York: Guilford.

Halford, W. K. (2001). *Brief therapy for couples: Helping partners help themselves*. New York: Guilford.

Holtzworth-Munroe, A., Jacobson, N. S., DeKlyen, M., and Whisman, M. A. (1989). Relationship between behavioral marital therapy outcome and process variables. *Journal of Consulting and Clinical Psychology, 57,* 658-662.

Hoyt, M. F. (2002). Solution-focused couple therapy. In A. S. Gurman and N. S. Jacobson (Eds.), *Clinical handbook of couple therapy,* Third edition. New York: Guilford.

Jacobson, N. S. and Christensen, A. (1996). *Integrative couple therapy: Promoting acceptance and change*. New York: Norton.

Jacobson, N. S. and Gottman, J. M. (1998). *When men batter women: New insights into ending abusive relationships*. New York: Simon and Schuster.

Kazantzis, N., Deane, F. P., and Ronan, K. R. (2000). Homework assignments in cognitive and behavioral therapy: A meta-analysis. *Clinical Psychology: Science and Practice, 72,* 189-202.

Lester, G. W., Beckham, E., and Baucom, D. H. (1980). Implementation of behavioral marital therapy. *Journal of Marital and Family Therapy, 6,* 189-199.

Markman, H. J., Stanley, S. M., and Blumberg, S. L. (2001). *Fighting for your marriage: Positive steps for preventing divorce and preserving a lasting love*. San Francisco: Wiley.

NiCarthy, G. (1997). *Getting free: You can end abuse and take back your life*. Seattle, WA: Seal Press.

Notarius, C. and Markman, H. (1993). *We can work it out: Making sense of marital conflict*. New York: Putnam.

O'Hanlon, B. and Hudson, P. (1995). *Stop blaming, start loving!: A solution-oriented approach to improving your relationship*. New York: Norton.

Schultheis, G. M., O'Hanlon, B., and O'Hanlon, S. (1999). *Brief couples therapy homework planner*. New York: Wiley.

Spring, J. and Spring, M. (1997). *After the affair: Healing the pain and rebuilding trust when a partner has been unfaithful.* New York: HarperCollins.

Stanley, S. M., Blumberg, S. L., and Markman, H. J. (1998). Helping couples fight for their marriage: The PREP approach. In R. Berger and M. Hannah (Eds.), *Handbook of preventive approaches in couple therapy* (pp. 279-303). New York: Brunner/Mazel.

Stanley, S. M., McCain, S., Trathen, D. W., and Bryan, B. M. (1998). *A lasting promise: A Christian guide to fighting for your marriage.* New York: Jossey-Bass.

Whitfield, K. E., Stanley, S. M., Blumberg, S. L., and Markman, H. J. (2001). *Fighting for your African American marriage.* San Francisco: Jossey-Bass.

Wile, D. B. (1988). *After the honeymoon: How conflict can improve your relationship.* San Francisco: Wiley.

Wile, D. B. (1993). *After the fight: Using your disagreements to build a stronger relationship.* New York: Guilford.

Wile, D. B. (1999). Collaborative couple therapy. In J. M. Donovan (Ed.), *Short-term couple therapy* (pp. 201-225). New York: Guilford.

Zilbergeld, B. (1999). *The new male sexuality,* Revised edition. Chicago: Bantam.

Chapter 13

Intimacy in Couples:
Evaluating a Workbook

Eleonora Maino

The present chapter describes the experimental use of an intimacy workbook within a public health agency belonging to a consortium of institutions providing family support services.

This attention for the family is justified by the fact that family plays a crucial role in every individual's life: it is the context in which relationships are first established and the individual develops and feels protected. It is therefore extremely relevant from a social point of view. However, modern society has shown the increasing weakness of a dyad that plays a fundamental role within the family: the couple.

Divorce and separation are on the increase. As stated by Andolfi (1999), what is most striking is the fact that a critical period for the development of the couple's relationship no longer exists. The couple may break up any time (e.g., after a very short period, the birth of their first child, or after twenty to thirty years of living together).

These considerations—along with the belief that the implementation of primary prevention and training is easier and less energy-consuming, as well as less costly, than remediation (L'Abate, 1990)—led me to experiment with a structured intervention plan on two small groups of couples. The present chapter reports on this approach and the associated use of an intimacy workbook.

The author wishes to thank Drs. Gisolfo Facco, Barbara Restà, and Cristiano Mangili for their valuable help. Special thanks go to Don Edoardo Algeri, coordinator of the Bergamo Family Pastoral Center, who supported the project's implementation within the Bergamo Family Support Center.

CONTEXTUAL CONSIDERATIONS

This experimental study was carried out at the Bergamo Family Support Center (northern Italy), which is a consortium of different institutions, both publicly and privately run. The center is innovative compared to the traditional organization of services for at least two reasons. First, the Family Support Center works at a preventive-promotional level and is particularly concerned with young couples. Second, it is the factual demonstration of the will to apply policies based on collaboration and integration of services to meet family needs.

Although the traditional sociosanitary services are focused not so much on the family and their needs as on the individual within the family (children, disabled people, elderly, severely ill, pregnant women, etc.), services provided by the Family Support Center are founded on the belief that promotion of the quality of life of each single individual will not be effective unless the family as a whole is considered.

Within this perspective, intervention plans are preventive in nature and focus on the couple, their parental role and the intergenerational responsibility. The Family Support Center provides training, such as vocational workshops for parents and teachers, primary prevention interventions related to the parent-child relationship and the couple's life, and legal counseling, as well as secondary prevention services, such as adoptions and family mediation. The center can also carry out tertiary prevention interventions, such as psychotherapy. In this case, clinical interventions on families with multiple problems and groups of maltreated or abused children are carried out.

Last, but not least, an office within the Family Support Center investigates and documents the organization of local services, their psychosocial intervention approaches, and the existing forms of maltreatment, abuse, and family violence.

THE EARLY COUPLE RELATIONSHIP

This section reports on a primary prevention intervention for couples who have been married for less than five years. An early intervention supporting the couple in the first stages of marriage relies on the conviction that a satisfactory, supportive, stable relationship is an important resource and positively influences the development and well-being of both partners and their children.

After all, to love and be loved is undoubtedly one of the most enriching experiences, and, as stated by L'Abate (1994, 1997), to grow up and live in a loving and caring family promotes full development of personality.

One of the most meaningful learning experiences in a person's life is the couple relationship. According to Blanck and Blanck (1968), marriage is a great opportunity for growth and development for the couple, whereas Menghi (1999) considers the relationship as an "exceptional opportunity for development for all" and "one of the main objectives of a couple relationship is promotion of the development of both partners" (pp. 42-43).

Marriage meets many different needs, such as overcoming loneliness, feeling accepted and understood, promoting the other's well-being, feeling supported, loved, and protected, being able to rely on one's partner, sharing enthusiasm for a positive event, feeling sexually satisfied, and having a family, etc. (Whitaker, 1999; Sternberg, 1986; L'Abate, 1986, 1990; Cusinato and L'Abate, 1994).

Given this background, it is quite clear how a couple relationship is loaded with many different expectations that are often linked to the individual's wish to have—either unconsciously or not—his or her needs and desires satisfied.

As stated by Scabini and Cigoli (2000), the couple relationship is not only founded on a stated alliance—which finds its social ratification in marriage and which is supported by the commitment and a common project associated to the couple's will to carry out the relationship—but also on a secret alliance. The latter is an unconscious mix of needs and expectations arising from the personal and family history of either partners.

For these reasons too, often people who are about to get married have unrealistic expectations about what marriage can offer them and what they need to do (Crosby, 1985). They expect that marriage will satisfy all their needs and will feel frustrated and angry once they realize this will not happen. According to Crosby, people often have unrealistic hopes. It is the ensuing disappointment and the decision to overcome those illusions that will enable them to grow.

In this regard, Barnett (1981) considers marriage to be a developmental process in which each partner goes through an extended period of honeymoon that ranges between five and seven years and ends with a crisis that can be coped with in three ways: (1) the partner is rejected in the hope of preserving an illusionary ideal; (2) apathy prevails, thus preventing growth and satisfaction; or (3) unrealistic thoughts are abandoned and the real self of both partners is accepted.

Being a couple is not only "a state" but a process involving different relational skills and including the ability to communicate, negotiate, and, above all, to love. In L'Abate's view (1986), the latter is linked to the ability to take care of the other and be involved, to focus on positive aspects while disregarding negative ones, be emotionally available to the self and the other, forgive the other as a sign of acceptance or toleration, and forget the needs for performance, perfection, problem solving or production while extending the concept of intimacy to include grief-sharing and the fear of being hurt (L'Abate, 1986). These abilities are not only inborn but can be learned and improved or be better expressed, and contribute to the development and strengthening of marriage (Beck, 1988).

The earlier the realization comes that not all of one's needs and expectations can be satisfied by the couple relationship, and that "being a couple" is a process which must be supported by relational skills that can be improved, the easier it is for the couple to build a stable and satisfactory relationship. It is not easy to become aware of this, especially in the first years of marriage. For example, in Italy women ages twenty-five to twenty-nine years and men ages thirty to thirty-four years are the largest group among separated couples (Francescato, 1992). These data support what has already emerged from clinical practice: the fact that the early years of marriage are characterized by harsh conflict between the partners. These conflicts are often due to the partner's difficulty to overcome differences related to their lives, family models, and personal features; the realization that the chosen partner no longer meets conscious or unconscious needs because he or she has changed or the partner has changed, but he or she has remained the same; the disappearance of some myths that are often linked to marriage, such as the conviction that time will not affect a solid couple relationship, or that the couple must share everything, or, still, the inability to overcome unrealistic expectations about this.

Further, in the early years of marriage much interference from the families of origin may prevent the couple from taking distance from them and building a separate and independent family.

RESEARCH WITH STRUCTURED INTERVENTIONS

With these assumptions, I devised a primary prevention program for young couples aimed at enhancing some relational skills that are relevant for development and maintenance of a satisfactory couple relationship.

A three-year program was thus developed that addressed intimacy issues (year one), negotiation and conflict management (year two), and parental role (year three). I adopted an approach reflecting that of structured intervention programs, because in my view, it was most appropriate to meet our needs. I needed to carry out a training-based intervention to help the participating couples understand their relationships, individually and together with the partner, but also within a small group of peers going through the same developmental stage. Further, the most effective approach was one that could involve people the most, making them feel responsible for their relationship and possible changes.

Last, this approach allowed us to make use of workbooks. Workbooks can be considered to be structured measures in that they guide reflection, either individually, in pairs, or in small groups; are ad hoc in that they meet a particular clinical or vocational purpose; and are idiographic and nomothetic, that is, they can meet the needs of the individual user but can also be generalized to people with similar needs.

In the present chapter, I report on the first-year program carried out with two groups of couples and the experimental use of an intimacy workbook (Cusinato, 1992) aimed at enhancing their capacity to love (L'Abate, 1986).

Method

Respondents

Two groups of couples living in Bergamo participated in this study. Selection of couples took place at two separate times. The first meeting was an informative meeting for all the couples that had agreed to participate in the program. On that occasion, four family-relationship psychologists presented the following: (1) the aims and the structure of the program; (2) the working methods, that is verbal communication and use of writing, personal reflection time, discussion with the partner and group discussion under the supervision of two psychologists and meetings with the psychologists, if the couple deemed it useful; (3) the tools used (self-reports and workbooks); and (4) the type of involvement requested to each participant.

The first meeting was specifically called to allow each participant to decide whether the program could meet his or her needs and expectations. Later meetings with each couple were held to learn more about them, their relational dynamics, and the reasons they had decided to participate in the program, as well as to have them complete the self-reports geared to investigate some relational aspects.

This preparatory work allowed me to select couples who showed a stable and quite satisfactory relationship in spite of some aspects they wanted to deepen. The suggested program is a primary prevention intervention aimed at enhancing and strengthening some relational abilities and not a remediation intervention.

The fifteen selected couples were divided into two groups of seven and eight couples, respectively. After the first meeting, a couple belonging to the first group and three couples from the second group abandoned the program. Therefore, Group 1 consisted of six couples and Group 2 had five couples.

The two groups can be considered identical in terms of sociodemographic features, that is, age [Group 1: range 26 to 38, mean = 31.2 years; Group 2: range 23 to 35 years, mean = 29.08 years; $F(1,20) = 1,58; p = 22$], education [$\chi^2(1.1) = .20; p = .15$], occupation [$\chi^2(1,4) = 6.54; p = .16$], duration of marriage in months [$F(1,20) = .323; p = .57$], and number of children [$\chi^2(1,1) = 1; p = .63$]. However, they can be denoted as experimental group ($n = 6$ couples) and control group ($n = 5$ couples), respectively, based on the results obtained by the analysis of variance (ANOVA) of the self-report measures that are illustrated later.

Evaluation

Our team first verified the stability of the couple relationship, excluding highly dysfunctional couples or couples at risk of breaking up so as to make sure we could work with couples needing to enhance their relationship and not requiring a remediation intervention. In addition to the clinical interview, we used the Italian version (Maino and Resta, 1999) of Stanley's Commitment Inventory (Stanley and Markman, 1992) and the Optimistic Attitude Scale (Maino, 1996a,b, 1998). These measures reveal the partners' involvement, the wish to keep their relationship stable over time, and the confidence and credit that each partner attributes to the relationship.

To measure intimacy, closeness, and emotional availability of the couple, the Couple's Intimacy Scales were used (Cusinato and L'Abate, 1994), which investigated each partner's ability to share experiences and feelings, respect the other's feelings, accept his or her limits, and value his or her potentials, forgive errors, and share grief.

Last, since several authors have stated the measures that are commonly used to assess the couple's adjustment are affected by social desirability to such an extent as to be of little significance (Kirkpatrick, 1963; Cone, 1967), and self-report scores can be considered valid only if social desirability as a variable is included in the experimental design (Chesser, Parkhurst, and Schaffer, 1979), the Couple Social Desirability Scale was administered as well (Maino, 1996a,b, 1998).

This scale is designed to detect a deliberate and conscious attempt on the part of the couple to make a good impression so as to avoid criticism about themselves and their actions.

Test: Analysis of Results

The data collected with the self-reports were used to draw a functioning profile for each couple that revealed the strengths and weaknesses of their relationship. The professionals were thus able to establish the stability of the couple relationship, and all the participating couples had a reference guiding their efforts during the program.

On the psychogram (Figure 13.1), all of the couples were in the normal range. They thus showed a good functioning profile in relation to credit, confidence, and involvement; few perspectives of breaking up and emotional detachment, and an authentic way of being not excessively influenced by the will to make a good impression.

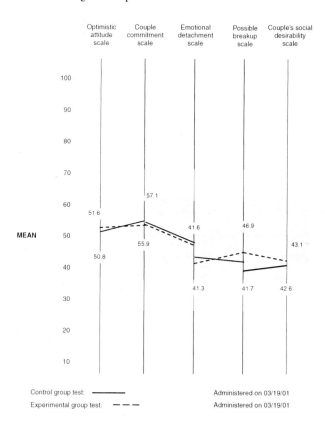

FIGURE 13.1. Psychogram of the Mean Standard Self-Report Scores on Relationship Stability and Social Desirability

The ANOVA showed that only one significant difference was found on the possible breakup scale (control group: n = 10 participants, mean = 21.7; experimental group: n = 12 participants, mean = 25; F (1,20) = 4,71; p = .042). In particular, although couples belonging to the experimental group scored in the normal range, they considered breakup to be one of the possible outcomes of their relationship should marked dissatisfaction persist or emerge.

As shown by the psychograms based on the Couple's Intimacy Scales, all of the couples were in the normal range. However, there was some variability, pointing to areas tapped by the workbook that needed some working on.

The psychogram of the mean positive agreement scores (Olson, Fournier, and Druckman, 1989) shows a clear discrepancy between the two groups. The couples from the experimental group needed to strengthen their intimacy-related areas (Figure 13.2) to a greater extent than couples from the control group.

On the Couple's Intimacy Scales, significant differences were found between the two groups. More specific, (1) the partner's capacity to express one's feelings and deeper parts of self (control group: n = 10 participants, mean = 35.5; experimental group: n = 12 participants, mean = 31.08; F = (1,20) = 6,62; p = .018); (2) the capacity to respect the partner's feelings and beliefs (control group: n = 10 participants, mean = 35.6; experimental group: n = 12 participants, mean = 31.25; F = (1,20) = 4,86; p = .039); (3) the capacity to accept the partner as is (control group: n = 10 participants, mean = 33.6; experimental group: n = 12 participants, mean = 29.75; F = (1,20) = 4,43; p = .036); (4) the capacity to value the partner's potentials (control group: n = 10 participants, mean = 36.5; experimental group: n = 12 participants, mean = 32.25; F = (1,20) = 8,05; p = .010). In contrast, no significant differences were found with regard to the deepest dimensions of Cusinato and L'Abate's (1994) intimacy model, that is, the capacity to forgive the partner's errors and share hurts, which is indicative of the fact that the couple relationship is functional. Given these findings, our team started experimenting with a structured intervention program approach. In particular, during the first year we verified the efficacy of the intimacy workbook.

INTERVENTION: AN INTIMACY WORKBOOK

The proposed workbook, *Not Magical But Mysterious . . . Our Intimacy* (Cusinato, 1992), was developed to help couples reflect on their own experiences, adopt, improve, or learn increasingly functional relational modalities, for their own and their partners' well-being.

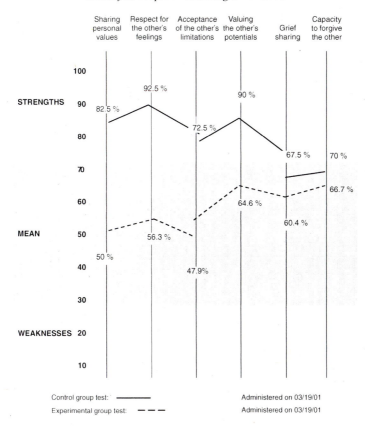

FIGURE 13.2. Psychogram of the Mean Positive Agreement Scores on the Couple's Intimacy Scales

The workbook consists of eight assignments, each with a list of questions about a certain issue that the individual or the couple is requested to answer. These assignments are based on the spiral model of intimacy developed by Cusinato and L'Abate (1994) and the Couple's Intimacy Scales that are administered as pre- and posttests. The subscales reflect the model's stages. It is thus possible to select a stage or involve the couple in those dimensions in which the test evidences a stronger need for support (Cusinato and Salvo, 1998).

The main lines of the program concern personal identity and the couple's unity: in this regard, basic prerequisites for the couple's intimacy—which is best reflected in the ability to share hurts and accept the fact that we are often hurt by the people who are closest to us—are the capacity to assert oneself as an individual with an intrinsic value, distinct and independent of others; the possibility to share our distinctive features with others; and the capacity to accept one's partner as is, valuing his or her potentials and helping him or her achieve them.

The program combines verbal communications between trainers and couples as well as writing about personal reflections, couple's discussions, and meetings with the professional. Compared to standard procedures, our intervention was slightly different. Whereas the former presuppose a monthly meeting between the professional and each couple, we opted for a monthly meeting between the professional and a small group of couples. Despite the fact that the topics dealt with were sensitive issues, in our opinion it could be important for couples going through the same stage to share experiences as a way to socialize and promote growth, both individually and as a couple.

The leaders' task was to guide the discussion and create an atmosphere as relaxed as possible, without being intrusive. Each partner was asked to do some homework related to each issue, either individually or in pairs, but they were not expected to tell the group the details. They had to share with the rest of the group the feelings, discoveries, positive aspects, or the disappointment revealed by the homework. Within the group, specific considerations and differences between partners were disclosed and accepted somewhat carelessly. On several occasions, the group became a tool to tell the partner what had not been told, explained, or understood during the couple discussion.

Sometimes participants felt reassured by the fact that other group members shared their thoughts, needs, and wishes which the partner might not understand. Couples showing particular difficulties or disagreement with what had been dealt with were offered a chance to have meetings with the professionals to discuss these issues.

Retest: Analysis of Results

Once the eight units of the workbook had been completed, all couples again received the measures used at the beginning of the program to assess possible pre- and posttest differences and the efficacy of the intervention.

As occurred at baseline, the psychogram of each couple showed scores in the normal range on the following scales: credit, confidence, and involvement; possible breakup; emotional detachment and an authentic way of being, not excessively influenced by the will to make a good impression. Figure 13.3 shows mean standard scores.

ANOVA revealed only one significant difference on the possible breakup scale (control group: $n = 10$ participants, mean = 22,2; experimental group:

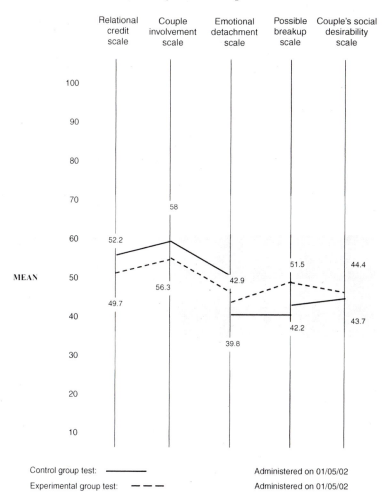

FIGURE 13.3. Psychogram of the Mean Standard Scores of the Retest

$n = 12$ participants, mean = 27,67; F (1,20) = 13,23; $p = .002$). Once again, although couples belonging to the experimental group scored in the normal range, they considered breakup to be one of the possible outcomes of their relationship, should marked insatisfaction persist or emerge.

In this perspective, it seems that the proposed intervention did not have a significant impact on these dimensions. All of the couples show mean positive agreement scores on the Intimacy Scales. However, a comparison of mean values of positive agreement (Olson, Fournier, and Druckman, 1989) and initial scores shows a lower discrepancy between the two groups of couples (Figure 13.4).

ANOVA shows only one significant difference, precisely on the scale indicating the capacity of the partner to communicate his/her own feelings and deepest aspects of self (control group): $n = 10$ participants, mean = 35.4; experimental group: $n = 12$ participants, mean = 31.83; $F (1,20) = 8.35$; $p = .009$).

From this point of view, the program had a strong impact on the variables of the Couple's Intimacy Scales on which the workbook was structured. Further, the analysis of variance on the test-retest scores did not reveal any significant differences for any of the scales within each group.

This outcome means that fluctuations of scores are not so significant as to dramatically change the degree of intimacy within the couple. However, the fluctuations allow us to consider the two groups as homogeneous, that is, belonging to the same population, on the retest for all variables related to intimacy, except for communication.

DISCUSSION AND SUMMARY

The goal of this chapter was to illustrate the experimentation that was carried out on structured intervention programs and the use of a couple intimacy workbook within a public health service. In particular, we wanted to verify whether the program structure and the contents of the workbook, of writing and the work to be done individually, in pairs and within a small group led by professionals, could impact on some dimensions of the couples' intimacy.

This intervention gave rise to some qualitative and quantitative considerations. From a qualitative point of view, the feedback received by participants underlined how the structure of the workbook and use of writing were not considered to be disruptive by the couples. In contrast, they were valued and used by all of them.

The structure of the program led the couples to agree to devote some time exclusively to their relationships, thus avoiding the trap of thinking that their relationships did not need to be cherished to remain satisfactory. Writing was seen as an efficacious tool in that it helped the couples obtain a clearer understanding of their relationships and the associated emotions, feelings, and the opinions, sometimes not shared, of their partners.

With regard to the specific contents of the workbook, we found that they tapped relevant aspects of the couple relationship.

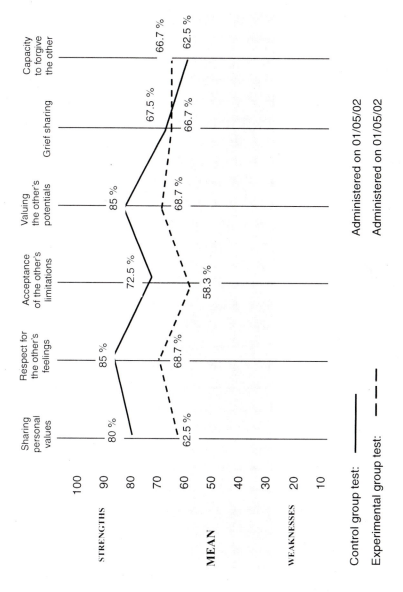

FIGURE 13.4. Psychogram of the Mean Positive Agreement Scores on the Couple's Intimacy Scales

278USING WORKBOOKS IN MENTAL HEALTH

Last, the individual, couple, and group work was favorably judged, both
by the couples and professionals alike. On one hand, the work carried out individually helped the couples stay focused on personal identity, thus oppos-
ing the myth that couples must share everything. On the other hand, the
work the partners did together helped them start a common project involving them on equal footing. Group work was a chance for them to share experiences, difficulties, points of satisfaction, and establish significant social
relations.

This possibility was supported by the results of an evaluation checklist
that the couples were asked to complete at the end of each meeting. This
checklist was rated on a Likert five-point scale (1 = very little; 2 = little; 3 =
enough; 4 = much; 5 = very much) and investigated

1. the level of interest for each unit;
2. the difficulty experienced in personal work and usefulness of the contents of each unit;
3. the perceived usefulness of the work carried out together with the
partner;
4. the extent to which both partners had succeeded in opening up to the
other;
5. the usefulness of group discussion;
6. the extent to which some freedom of expression had been perceived; and
7. how well professionals had led the group.

Results revealed that the contents of each single unit were considered to
be very interesting and involving by 77.38 percent of participants and useful
by 70.2 percent; 73.8 percent of them did not find any difficulties in doing
written assignments guiding personal reflection; 50 percent of them found it
very useful to work with the partner versus 16.6 percent who considered
it useless; 48 percent of participants were quite satisfied with the way they
had opened up to their partner (compared to 16.6 percent who were little satisfied); 85.71 percent of them found group discussion very interesting and
involving; 71.42 percent considered discussion very useful; and 91.6 percent of participants judged the way the professionals had led the group very
positively.

In conclusion, at a quantitative level, the analysis of variance made on the
test-retest scores confirmed the significance, impact, and efficacy of the
program and the associated workbook. These findings encourage us to persevere in our efforts to make this approach available to a larger number of
couples to help them enhance their well-being.

REFERENCES

Andolfi, M. (Ed.) (1999). *La crisi della coppia*. Milano: Raffaello Cortina Editore.
Barnett, J.E. (1981). The natural history of a marriage. *Pilgrimage, 9*, 5-19.
Blanck, R. and Blanck, G. (1968). *Marriage and personal development*. New York: Columbia University Press.
Chesser, B.J., Parkhurst, A.M., and Shaffer, D.L. (1979). Marital adjustment: Controlling the tendency to distort evaluations. *Home Economics Research Journal, 8*, 27-36.
Cone, J.D. (1967). Social desirability and marital happiness. *Psychological Reports, 21*, 770-772.
Crosby, J.F. (1985). *Illusion and disillusion: The self in love and marriage*. Belmont, CA: Wadsworth.
Cusinato, M. (1992). *Misteriosa non magica la nostra intimità* (Not magical but mysterious . . . our intimacy). Treviso: Centro della Famiglia.
Cusinato, M. and L'Abate, L. (1994). A spiral model of intimacy. In S.M. Johnson and L.S. Greenberg (Eds.), *The heart of the matter: Perspectives on emotion in marital therapy* (pp. 108-123). New York: Brunner/Mazel.
Cusinato, M. and Salvo, P. (1998). *Lavorare con le famiglie* (Working with families). Roma: Carrocci Editore.
Francescato, D. (1992). *Quando l'amore finisce* (When love ends). Bologna: il Mulino.
Kirkpatrick, C. (1963). *The family as process and institution*. New York: The Ronald Press Company.
L'Abate, L. (1986). *Systematic family therapy*. New York: Brunner/Mazel.
L'Abate, L. (1990). *Building family competence: Strategies of primary and secondary prevention*. Thousand Oaks, CA: Sage.
L'Abate, L. (1994). *A theory of personality development*. New York: Wiley.
L'Abate, L. (1997). *The self in the family: A classification of personality, criminality, and psychopathology*. New York: Wiley.
Maino, E. (1996a). Desiderabilità sociale, atteggiamento ottimista e qualità della relazione coniugale (Social desirability, optimistic attitude, and quality of conjugal relationship). Unpublished doctoral dissertation. Padova: Università degli Studi, Facoltà di Psicologia.
Maino, E. (1996b). Desiderabilità sociale in ambito coniugale: definizioni e strumenti (Social desirability in the conjugal context: Definitions and instrumentation). *Famiglia, Interdisciplinarietà, Ricerca, 1*, 179-193.
Maino, E. (1998). Desiderabilità sociale e atteggiamento ottimista: Contributo alla costruzione di due scale in ambito coniugale (Social desirability and optimistic attitude: Contribution to the construction of two scales for couples). *Bollettino di Psicologia Applicata, 227-228*, 65-76.
Maino, E. and Resta, B. (1999). Operazionalizzazione del costrutto di impegno nella relazione di coppia: Validazione dello Stanley's Commitment Inventory (Operationalization of the construct of commitment in couple relationship: Vali-

dation of Stanley's Commitment Inventory). *Famiglia, Interdiscliplinarietà, Ricerca, 4*, 5-23.

Menghi, P. (1999). La coppia utile (The useful couple). In M. Andolfi (Ed.), *La crisi della coppia* (The crisis of the couple) (pp. 41-54). Milano: Raffaello Cortina Editore.

Olson, D.H., Fournier, D.G., and Druckman, J.M. (1989). *Prepare and Enrich Manual*. Minneapolis, MN: Prepare/Enrich.

Scabini, E. and Cigoli, V. (2000). *Il famigliare* (The family context). Milano: Raffaello Cortina Editore.

Stanley S.M., and Markman H.J. (1992). Assessing commitment in personal relationships. *Journal of Marriage and the Family, 54*, 595-608.

Sternberg, R.J. (1986). A triangular theory of love. *Psychological Review, 93* (2), 119-135.

Whitaker, C.A. (1999). Le funzioni del matrimonio (The functions of marriage). In M. Andolfi (Ed.), *La crisi della coppia* (The crisis of the couple) (pp. 3-12). Milano: Raffaello Cortina Editore.

SECTION IV:
FAMILIES

Chapter 14

Manualized Treatment for School-Refusal Behavior in Youth

Christopher A. Kearney
Krisann M. Alvarez

The publication of manuals and workbooks to help clinicians address mental health problems has burgeoned tremendously in recent years. Many of these treatment packages have been geared toward adults, but more are being targeted toward child-based problems (e.g., anxiety). In addition, most manuals and workbooks have been designed for formal psychological disorders (e.g., depression), but others have been designed for amorphous or less well-defined areas. This chapter discusses one such area, school-refusal behavior, and examines a therapist guide and parent workbook that have been created to address this problem.

School-refusal behavior refers to a child's refusal to attend school and/or difficulties remaining in classes for an entire day (Kearney, 2001). The behavior generally refers to youth with complete or partial absences from school, severe morning misbehaviors designed to induce nonattendance, and/or extreme dread about school that precipitates pleas for future nonattendance. School-refusal behavior is a heterogeneous phenomenon marked by various internalizing and externalizing behavior problems. Common internalizing problems include general and social anxiety, somatic complaints, fear, fatigue, depression, and worry, among others. Common externalizing behavior problems include defiance, noncompliance, aggression, running away from school or home, tantrums, and clinging, among others. In many cases of school-refusal behavior, a combination of these behavior problems is present.

School-refusal behavior may also lead to many short-term and long-term problems if left unaddressed. Common short-term problems include deteriorating academic performance and grades, family conflict, legal difficulties, social alienation, and psychological disorders. Common long-term problems include delinquency, school dropout, and later occupational and marital difficulties. School-refusal behavior is thought to be present in some form in about 5 to 28 percent of school-age children, and is seen fairly equally among boys and girls.

RATIONALE FOR THE CREATION AND DEVELOPMENT OF A THERAPIST GUIDE AND PARENT WORKBOOK

Theoretical Reasons

A key problem for clinicians who address youth with school-refusal behavior has been disarray in the literature. During the past century, many terms for school absenteeism have been propogated, including *school phobia, separation anxiety, school refusal,* and *truancy.* Unfortunately, each term has its own original meaning and contemporary authors often use their own definition of each term. Even more confusing is the fact that many mental health professionals use these terms interchangeably. The result has been considerable disagreement about the classification, assessment, and treatment of this population.

To address this situation, Kearney and colleagues (Kearney, 2001; Kearney and Silverman, 1990, 1999) devised a functional model of school-refusal behavior. This model is based more on the function of school-refusal behavior, or why youth refuse school, than on the myriad internalizing and externalizing forms of the behavior. Specifically, youth are thought to refuse school for one or more of the following reasons:

1. to avoid school-related stimuli that provoke a sense of general negative affectivity and somatic complaints;
2. to escape aversive social and/or evaluative situations (e.g., peer interactions, tests, athletic performances);
3. to obtain attention from significant others; and
4. to obtain tangible reinforcement outside of school (e.g., sleeping late, watching television, being with friends).

The first two functional conditions refer to youth who refuse school for negative reinforcement or to stay away from something aversive at school. The latter two functional conditions refer to youth who refuse school for positive reinforcement or to approach more palatable rewards outside of school. Many youth also refuse school for a combination of these reasons.

The functional model was designed as a fresh approach to classifying school-refusal behavior and was meant to embrace historical concepts in the area. For example, youth who are specifically fearful of school (i.e., school phobia) are incorporated into the first functional condition. Similarly, youth classified as truant (i.e., missing school without parental knowledge) are often part of the fourth functional condition. One advantage of the functional model is that it organizes the school-refusal behavior population more succinctly and more completely than past attempts. The system is also linked to specific and practical assessment and treatment strategies outlined in a therapist guide and a parent workbook.

Practical Reasons

A key practical reason for designing a therapist guide and parent workbook for school-refusal behavior, in addition to the treatment strategies to be discussed, was to delineate a clear assessment strategy for this population. Although many ancillary measures (e.g., for anxiety) are used to evaluate youth with school-refusal behavior, almost no instruments have been designed specifically for this population and no formal assessment strategy has been outlined. The treatment manual for school-refusal behavior offers a step-by-step assessment strategy based on functional analysis as well as copies of one instrument designed specifically for this purpose: the School Refusal Assessment Scale (SRAS).

The SRAS was designed to measure the relative strength of the four functions as they pertain to a particular case. The scale has sixteen items that have been shown to display good reliability and validity (Kearney and Silverman, 1993). A revised version of the scale contains twenty-four items and also has good reliability and validity (Kearney, 2002a). Factor analysis of items indicates the presence of three main factors: negative reinforcement, attention seeking, and pursuit of tangible reinforcement. The publication of the therapist guide allows clinicians to access and use the SRAS to help make informed decisions about prescriptive treatments, which are described next.

DESCRIPTION OF THE THERAPIST GUIDE
AND PARENT WORKBOOK

Title and Content

The therapist guide discussed here is titled *When Children Refuse School: A Cognitive-Behavioral Therapy Approach/Therapist's Guide* (Kearney and Albano, 2000b) and is published by the Psychological Corporation (www. psychcorp.com). The accompanying parent workbook, *When Children Refuse School: A Cognitive-Behavioral Therapy Approach/Parent Workbook*, is also published by the Psychological Corporation (Kearney and Albano, 2000b).

The therapist guide and parent workbook each contain eight chapters in addition to a plethora of accompanying figures, tables, references, and forms that a clinician can use when addressing a particular case. Chapter 1 is an introduction to the guide and workbook and covers several areas regarding school-refusal behavior, including its definition, prevalence, major characteristics, functions, and traditional treatments. An introduction to the functional model is also made and is followed by a summary of the structure of the guide/workbook and important caveats for their use.

Chapter 2 covers assessment, including the importance of assessing this population thoroughly and via functional analysis. Recommendations are made with respect to screening potential clients over the telephone, methods of assessing major behavior problems and maintaining variables of school-refusal behavior, monitoring attendance and other behaviors on a daily basis, and contacting school officials and medical professionals. A sample case of assessment and assigning treatment is also provided.

Chapter 3 covers the consultation session as well as general treatment session procedures. In particular, the therapist and client are informed about pertinent discussions at this time, including events of the past week, daily logbook ratings, assessment results, and rationales for specific treatment packages. For therapists, pretreatment considerations are also discussed, including child, parent, school, and other variables that could mediate treatment. In addition, several issues relevant to each treatment condition are covered to increase the flexibility of the manual. These issues include, among others, addressing difficult clients, scheduling future sessions, developmental considerations, between-session work, and decisions about guiding therapy toward termination. Chapters 4 to 7, to be discussed at greater length later, reflect prescriptive treatment approaches for each functional condition. Chapter 8 covers methods of preventing slips and relapse, as well as recommendations for addressing youth with chronic or very severe school-refusal behavior.

Function 1: Avoidance of Objects or Situations That Cause General Distress/Negative Affectivity

Therapist Manual

The therapist manual provides specific guidelines for practitioners who address youth who refuse school to avoid objects or situations that cause negative affectivity. Treatment for this functional condition is composed mainly of psychoeducation, building an anxiety and avoidance hierarchy, somatic control exercises, imaginal and in vivo desensitization, processing exposures, and completing daily logbooks and homework assignments. The therapist guide provides specific examples for teaching children about the three response components of anxiety (physiological, cognitive, behavioral) and how each of these components occurs sequentially for that individual. For example, illustrations are made of how each response set can be identified and linked. As such, the child is helped to understand the nature and process of anxiety. The therapist guide is also helpful for building an anxiety and avoidance hierarchy for various school-related items that cause inordinate distress. This hierarchy involves five to ten items that are rated on a zero to eight scale for strength of anxiety and avoidance. Common examples include walking into a classroom by oneself, increased time in a classroom, walking down a hallway, and separating from parents, among others. The hierarchy is arranged from items that are least to most anxiety- or avoidance-provoking in nature. Hierarchy examples are provided in the therapist guide.

Somatic control exercises refer to those techniques taught to youth with difficulty controlling physical symptoms of anxiety. Tension-release relaxation exercises for different muscle groups are used in addition to breathing retraining, which involves slow and deep inhalation though the nose and slow exhalation through the mouth. These are designed as portable exercises that a youth can use in any anxiety-provoking situation and may be useful for interrupting or thwarting the next stages of anxiety. In the therapist guide, scripts are included for each of these somatic control exercises so that the practitioner can simply read from the manual in session as the client follows along.

The heart of this therapy approach, however, is gradual exposure to those events that provoke anxiety. The child is required, first via imagination and then in real-life situations, to enter into circumstances that would typically generate much distress. A common exposure is to have the child attend one or two classes or spend much of his or her time in school in the library. Gradually, increasingly more time at school is required in addition to specific tasks, such as moving between classes or asking a teacher for help. In the therapist guide, several features are evident to assist the development and administration of these exposures. These features include examples of therapist-client dialogue and imaginal scenes, scales to track anxiety during an exposure, recommendations for conducting and processing the exposures, and illustrations of habituation curves that may be shared with the client after an exposure.

Interoceptive exposures may also be conducted for paniclike symptoms. These exposures are processed with the therapist who examines patterns of anxiety ratings during each event. It is hoped that a pattern of habituation will occur over time and the child will realize that avoidance is unnecessary for anxiety to diminish. In the therapist guide, several examples are given of interoceptive exercises and appropriate techniques that can be matched to a client's needs. In addition, tables are available for specific recommendations regarding the removal of safety signals, or objects or persons that one relies on to feel better in an anxiety-provoking situation.

Parent Workbook

The parent workbook regarding this function provides information about what the therapist will likely do in a given session. In this way, the client is not surprised by the techniques that are used and has a better grasp of the rationale for their use (in conjunction with therapist feedback). Examples include the illustrations, tables, scripts, and recommendations listed previously. Clients may work out of the book by writing examples of hierarchy items in the appropriate table and showing it to the therapist, reading specific scripts or examples that are relevant to their case, and identifying which habituation curve most applied to them. In addition, of course, the parent workbook contains the daily logbooks and homework assignments that are associated with each session. At the beginning of each session, therefore, children are expected to show the therapist their daily emotional ratings and outline how they responded to each homework assignment (e.g., identify which exposure they engaged in that week).

Function 2: Escape from Aversive Social and/or Evaluative Situations

Therapist Guide

The therapist manual also provides specific guidelines for practitioners who address youth who refuse school to escape aversive social and/or evaluative situations. Treatment for this functional condition is similar to Function 1 in several ways (i.e., psychoeducation, hierarchy development, behavioral exposures). In this treatment package, however, the exposures tend to be targeted more toward specific social and/or evaluative situations. Common exposures in this group, for example, include tests, athletic or musical performances, writing or speaking before others, peer conversations, speaking on the telephone, and eating in the lunchroom. As with Function 1, children in this group are required to gradually increase their level of school attendance as well. This may be done initially with help (i.e., with a friend, parent, therapist), but increased independence over time is a key goal. The therapist manual contains specific illustrations for linking anxiety-based response components, building social/evaluative hierarchies, and administering and processing exposures.

Because youth in this functional condition tend to be older than those in Function 1, cognitive restructuring is instituted as well. Cognitive restructuring focuses on the irrational thought patterns a youth may have in given situations. For example, many youth engage in absolutist thinking, overgeneralizations, mind reading, catastrophizing, and disqualification of positive information. Others may be perfectionists who believe that mistakes will result in terrible and long-standing consequences. Cognitive restructuring is designed to help youth challenge and modify unreasonable thoughts that may prevent appropriate exposures or school attendance. The therapist guide assists clinicians in this regard by listing specific cognitive distortions, providing illustrations for how the therapist and significant others can help a child challenge these thoughts, offering detailed therapist-client dialogue to show how cognitive restructuring is done, and outlining dispute handles or specific questions that children can ask themselves to challenge an unrealistic thought.

Parent Workbook

As before, the parent workbook regarding this function provides information about what the therapist will likely do in a given session. In this way, the client is better prepared for certain techniques, such as cognitive restructuring. Illustrations, tables, scripts, and recommendations are available so that the psychoeducation, hierarchy development, and exposure processes can be facilitated. Clients may also work out of the book by logging their unrealistic thoughts during the week and comparing them to the list of cognitive distortions found in the workbook. In this way, they can gain a quicker and better grasp of their thinking patterns and what changes are needed. In addition, clients can access the dispute handles in the parent workbook to help themselves modify their thoughts between sessions. Common obstacles (and their solutions) to cognitive restructuring are also included in the workbook for clients who become frustrated. Specific examples of commonly avoided scenarios (e.g., test, physical education anxiety) and how to handle them are also included. In addition, of course, the parent workbook contains the daily logbooks and homework assignments that are associated with each session. At the beginning of each session, therefore, children are expected to show the therapist their daily emotional ratings and outline how they responded to each homework assignment (e.g., identify how they modified cognitive distortions during that week).

Function 3: Pursuit of Attention from Significant Others

Therapist Guide

The therapist manual also provides specific guidelines for practitioners who address youth who refuse school for attention from significant others. Treatment for this function is not as child based as the first two functions but focuses more on parent-based contingency management. Specifically, this involves modifying parent commands; establishing regular morning, daytime, and evening routines; setting up attention-based rewards for attendance and punishments for nonattendance; engaging in forced school attendance under certain circumstances; and addressing excessive reassurance-seeking behavior. The therapist guide provides explicit examples of parent commands that are most common and most unhelpful in this population. Therapists are encouraged to require parents to list commands given to their child and modify the commands toward greater clarity and succinctness. The therapist guide contains a list of common errors that parents make (e.g., lecturing, criticism, questioning) which may be used to dissect each command on the parents' list. Recommendations for modifying the command are also given.

Another common technique for this group is establishing daily routines. A set but not rigid routine is planned for the morning so the child has enough time to rise from bed and prepare for school. Input from the child may be helpful in this regard, although the parents and therapist should have the final say. Should the child remain home from school, a strict and supervised daytime routine is implemented with an emphasis on academic work. Appropriate and inappropriate behaviors are followed-up immediately and during the evening. The therapist guide provides examples of time lines for morning routines, suggestions for what parents should do if the child stays home from school, and how to structure evening routines.

In some cases, forced school attendance is used. This is saved, however, as a last resort and for cases in which the child is missing most school days and only refusing school for attention (i.e., no anxiety is present). The therapist guide provides specific criteria for when forced school attendance should be used. Excessive reassurance-seeking behavior is also addressed by shaping the child's behavior (e.g., answering a repeated question only once per hour) and providing limits and consequences (e.g., for excessive calls from school). The therapist guide lists specific examples of questions that are employed by children and how parents should respond to these questions. Therapist-client dialogue is also included so practitioners have an idea of how these procedures may be conveyed to clients.

Parent Workbook

The parent workbook regarding this function allows parents to work very closely with the therapist in modifying parent commands and establishing regular routines throughout the day. In addition, the parent workbook provides guidelines for how parents can develop appropriate incentives for their child to attend school and appropriate punishments for their child when he or she misses school. The parent workbook, for example, lists many different rewards and punishments that parents can consider and implement during the week. Progress regarding these consequences and how they could be tailored to an individual child can then be raised with the therapist. Specific recommendations for forced school attendance and addressing excessive reassurance seeking are also provided. In addition, of course, the parent workbook contains the daily logbooks and homework assignments that are associated with each session. At the beginning of each session, therefore, children are expected to show the therapist their daily emotional ratings and parents must outline how they responded to each homework assignment (e.g., implement routines).

Function 4: Pursuit of Tangible Rewards Outside of School

Therapist Guide

The therapist manual also provides specific guidelines for practitioners who address youth who refuse school for tangible rewards outside of school. Treatment for this functional condition is more family based, and the goal is to increase incentives for school attendance and decrease incentives for nonattendance. The core of this approach is contingency contracting, in which family members, with a therapist's help, devise written agreements that list specific requirements and accompanying rewards and punishments. A common base for a contract, for example, would be to require a youth to attend a certain amount of school in exchange for the opportunity to complete chores at home for payment. Failure to attend school might result in loss of payment and grounding. Increased supervision of the child during the day, possibly even escorting him or her from class to class, may be necessary as well. Initial contracts are simple and under the therapist's direction, although later contracts are more complex and developed more independently by family members.

The therapist guide outlines specific recommendations for defining a behavior problem and designing and implementing contracts. Several sample contracts are provided so that therapists have a good idea as to what to include. Sample contracts include those based on household responsibilities, school preparation behaviors, and school attendance behaviors. A blank contract form is also provided so therapists can enter listings for privileges and responsibilities at general and specific levels.

In addition to contracts, other procedures for this functional condition include communication skills training and peer-refusal-skills training. Communication skills training is useful because conflict characterizes many of these families. Such training involves reducing negative or harmful interactions and building positive ones. Peer-refusal-skills training involves providing youth with skills to repel temptations to miss school, such as offers from friends. The therapist guide provides specific recommendations for each of these techniques, therapist-client dialogue, and tables that list common communication problems, alternative communication patterns, and selected interventions for sleep-related problems—a common occurrence in this group.

Parent Workbook

The parent workbook regarding this function allows family members to work very closely with the therapist in designing and implementing contracts and practicing new skills for communicating and refusing offers to miss school. In particular, the parent workbook outlines specific recommendations for conducting home-based meetings that family members can refer to when gathering to discuss problems. Examples include rules for speaking and the contents of the discussions. In addition, parents and other relevant adults are provided with guidelines for escorting a youth to school should he or she have continuing difficulty following though on contracts. Adults may use these guidelines to induce school attendance and allow a youth to gain rewards for such attendance. In addition, of course, the parent workbook contains the daily logbooks and homework assignments that are associated with each session. At the beginning of each session, therefore, children are expected to show the therapist their daily emotional ratings and family members must outline how they responded to each homework assignment (e.g., implement contracts).

Forms

Various forms are made available that can be copied from the therapist guide and parent workbook during treatment. These include instructions and recording sheets for behavioral observations, versions of the School Refusal Assessment Scale, child and parent logbooks, a feelings thermometer for measuring anxiety or other emotions, an anxiety and avoidance hierarchy sheet, and a blank exposure record form and contract.

RESEARCH EVIDENCE

Completed Research

The procedures in the therapist guide and parent workbook represent cognitive-behavioral family-systems-oriented techniques that have been shown to be highly effective. A summary of supporting evidence for these individual techniques is available elsewhere (Kearney, 2001). A key advantage of the therapist guide and parent workbook is that they organize treatment packages that best fit the individual needs of a particular client.

This method of prescribing individualized treatment for youth with school-refusal behavior based on function has been tested in preliminary studies. Because the therapist guide is so new, large-scale studies have not yet been done. However, Kearney and Silverman (1990, 1999) conducted two studies that show the procedures within this model to be effective. Kearney and Silverman (1990) examined seven youth with acute school-refusal behavior and assigned prescriptive treatment on the basis of their main function of nonattendance. Daily ratings of internalizing behavior, as well as pre- and posttreatment measures of school attendance and other behaviors, were obtained. The School Refusal Assessment Scale (SRAS) was used to determine each youth's primary function. Prescriptive treatment lasted three to nine weeks. Six youth met criteria for positive end-state functioning (90 percent school attendance or 75 percent reduction in distress) by posttreatment and six-month follow-up, and one youth experienced no change in attendance but a substantial reduction in distress.

Similarly, Kearney and Silverman (1999) conducted a controlled study of prescriptive and nonprescriptive treatment in eight youth with acute school-refusal behavior. Similar dependent measures were used, and the SRAS was used to derive primary functions of school-refusal behavior. Four participants in the experimental group received individualized prescriptive treatment based on the highest-rated functional condition from parent and child SRAS scores. Four other participants in the control group received individualized nonprescriptive treatment based on the lowest-rated functional condition from parent and child SRAS scores. All participants who received prescriptive treatment successfully returned to full-time school attendance within ten treatment sessions. In addition, posttreatment measures of distress were greatly improved. However, participants who received nonprescriptive treatment experienced worsened school attendance by the end of the control period. Following prescriptive treatment for this group, however, full-time school attendance for each was nearly reached (4.25 percent absenteeism compared to 49.75 percent at pretreatment and 58.25 percent at the end of the control period). All gains were maintained at the six-month follow-up.

Other case data have also supported the use of the functional model in prescribing treatment for youth with school-refusal behavior (Chorpita et al., 1996). In fact, the model has been shown to be effective as well for youth with mixed functional profiles or those who refuse school for multiple reasons (Kearney, 2002a; Kearney, Pursell, and Alvarez, 2001). Taken together, these data provide strong preliminary evidence that the treatment techniques described and organized in the therapist guide and parent workbook are effective for youth with school-refusal behavior. Following are two recent cases from our clinic that illustrate the use of these procedures in more detail.

CASE STUDIES

Successful Case: Brian

Brian was a thirteen-year-old male referred to a specialized university clinic for school-refusal behavior. Brian had missed approximately thirty-five days of school at the time of his assessment in November, and had missed all of the past four weeks of school. At the time of his evaluation, Brian was spending nearly all of his time at home reading, watching television, playing with his dog, and sleeping. He was not completing any academic work and was considerably behind his peers who were attending eighth grade.

During the interview, Brian reported three main reasons for his absenteeism. First, several classmates reportedly had called him names, although Brian could not remember what names were used. Second, he complained of the amount of schoolwork that was given him, but admitted that much of this was makeup work due to his lack of attendance. Finally, he stated that recent family changes had deprived him of much time with his mother. His absenteeism from school forced his mother to miss work to stay home and supervise him.

Brian's mother confirmed this report and said that her recent marriage to Brian's stepfather had created a lot of instability within the family. Particularly problematic was the unclear role that Brian's stepfather had with respect to disciplining the children. As a result, only Brian's mother was available to do so, and Brian seemed to be exploiting this situation. Brian's mother, Mrs. B., reported that her son had had problems attending school at the end of the previous year, but she had hoped these problems would fade over the summer. She described Brian as a generally well-behaved youth except with respect to school attendance. She also expressed considerable dismay over the situation and indicated that the resulting pressures on her family were enormous.

The assessment consisted of a structured diagnostic interview and several child self-report and parent/teacher report questionnaires (see Kearney, 2001, and Kearney and Albano, 2000b, for a full description of a recommended assessment protocol for youth with school-refusal behavior). Among the latter was the School Refusal Assessment Scale (Kearney, 2002b; Kearney and Silverman, 1993), the instrument designed to measure the relative strength of the four functional conditions described earlier for school-refusal behavior. Versions of the SRAS were administered to Brian and his mother and stepfather. Results indicated that Brian was primarily refusing school for attention and for tangible reinforcement outside of school.

In this type of case, in which two functional conditions primarily maintain school-refusal behavior, prescriptive treatment involves components of each relevant package. In Brian's case, therefore, treatment consisted of (1) contingency management with a special focus on creating morning routines and initial partial attendance, and (2) oral contracts and family communication and problem-solving training to increase rewards for school attendance, decrease rewards for nonattendance, and help the family resolve many of the issues that prompted conflict and absenteeism in the first place.

Initial treatment focused mainly on establishing a clear morning routine, modifying parent commands to increase clarity, and requiring Brian to attend two classes of his choosing. The morning routine included specific times for waking, rising from bed, preparing for school as if going to first period class, and entering the car. Parent commands were changed from lecturing and criticism to clear, succinct commands that were followed with rewards and punishments for compliance and noncompliance, respectively. Finally, Brian chose two of his favorite classes, band and science, to go to on a regular basis. His selection was fortuitous because the classes were back to back, meaning that his mother needed to make only one dropoff and one pickup per day. School officials were also contacted to ensure that the partial attendance schedule was acceptable.

During this process, the therapist and parents worked together using the therapist guide and parent workbook. For example, the morning routine was modeled after the one provided in the workbook, commands were logged and then modified as Brian's parents matched their commands to those listed in the workbook, and rewards and punishments were derived following their reading of the workbook's guidelines. The therapist also consulted the guide before discussions with school officials, since many recommendations are provided about the kind of information that should be sought.

Initial therapy in this direction was successful—Brian attended the classes without difficulty and did not encounter any problems with peers or teachers. This initial success greatly energized the family, and two additional classes were added to the schedule following the next treatment session. Recognizing that subsequent classes would be more difficult, however, the therapist employed techniques from the guide to improve family communication and, more specifically, to establish periods in which Brian could spend time alone with his mother (e.g., evening walks, movies). Strong consequences were also established for refusing to attend school, including loss of time with his mother, loss of television and computer privileges, and grounding. Brian was also told that any ongoing failure to attend class would be met with a formal escort by his father and stepfather.

Following occasional slips, Brian achieved full-time school attendance within three weeks. Ongoing therapy was needed to clarify parent roles within the family, ensure that all makeup work was completed, and address new somatic complaints made by Brian. Long-term follow-up indicated that Brian was able to complete the academic year and advance to ninth grade. In addition, he was able to rebuild his peer relationships and join some extracurricular activities.

Unsuccessful Case: Sadie

Sadie was a fifteen-year-old female also referred to a specialized university clinic for youth with school-refusal behavior. At the time of her assessment in January of the academic year, she had already missed 90 percent of school days and had not been in school since mid-September. School officials had recently informed Sadie's mother, Mrs. S., that her daughter had failed the first semester, was in violation of the school's attendance policy, and was being referred to juvenile court for truancy and educational neglect. They also indicated that they were willing to work with Sadie to help her salvage the year and earn at least partial credit during tenth grade.

During the assessment session, Sadie indicated that she had overwhelming anxiety about attending school. She complained of paniclike symptoms whenever she walked into class, strolled down hallways, or performed before others. In particular, she stated that she became short of breath, that her heart would race, and that she had fears of losing control and running out of the school. Sadie said these symptoms had begun at the end of ninth grade but that she had endured them to finish the school year. This year, however, had brought such unbearable distress that she was not able to attend. She did indicate a desire to go back to school and address her anxiety, but also inquired extensively about home schooling.

Sadie's mother echoed her daughter's report in most areas. She agreed that Sadie had overwhelming anxiety and could not attend school at this time. Mrs. S. also stated, however, that Sadie greatly enjoyed spending time with her during the day and felt independent as a result of not going to school. Mrs. S. also conceded that she had a long history of acquiescing to Sadie since her divorce several years ago. With respect to school attendance in particular, Mrs. S. said that she deferred to Sadie's judgment as to whether she could attend school and was likely to continue to do so. A conversation with Sadie's school counselor also confirmed the presence of some anxiety, but the counselor was adamant that Mrs. S.'s acquiescence to her daughter was primarily the cause of Sadie's absenteeism.

The assessment process mirrored that of Brian and revealed that Sadie did have severe general and social anxiety. On the School Refusal Assessment Scale, Sadie scored high on each functional condition, indicating that she was refusing school to decrease anxiety, get attention from her mother, and enjoy the many amenities of staying home from school. When confronted with these data, both Sadie and her mother admitted that it was an accurate assessment.

Treatment for Sadie's case was initially designed to reduce her anxiety symptoms. The first therapy session concentrated on educating Sadie and her mother about the three response systems of anxiety (cognitive, physiological, behavioral) and how these systems occurred in sequence. In Sadie's case, for example, worries about catastrophic events at school would usually trigger physical panic symptoms and subsequent avoidance of school. The therapist and Sadie covered many different examples of this sequence to illustrate that control of Sadie's irrational cognitions could interrupt the panic process and make school attendance easier. The first session also led to an agreement that Sadie would attend her favorite class, art, and supply ratings of anxiety for each ten-minute period she was in class.

In doing so, the therapist and Sadie utilized the therapist guide and parent workbook to design drawings that illustrated her anxiety sequence. The therapist also located the cognitive distortions section and compared Sadie's recent thoughts with those in the workbook. Thus, Sadie could see that many of her thoughts were common for people with anxiety disorders but also irrational in nature and in need of alteration. Recommendations from the workbook were also used to identify which class Sadie would attend first.

At the second therapy session, Sadie reported that she had successfully attended the art class for three of the last five days. Her anxiety ratings were as her therapist had predicted: high in the early stages of the class but diminishing over time. This provided evidence to Sadie that she could eventually habituate to anxiety-provoking situations and that avoidance was unnecessary. Much of the second session was also devoted to dissecting and modifying Sadie's thoughts during class, such as her fear that everyone would look at her strangely and that she would trip and fall. Sadie came to understand that these were low-probability events, especially now that she was back in class and no one was asking her questions about her prior absence.

Unfortunately, the initial success shown by Sadie devolved into stagnation. Although Sadie continued to attend her art class, she reneged on several agreements over the next three therapy sessions (and between-session telephone conversations) to attend two other classes. Attempts at compromise, such as attending only part of one class, also failed. Interestingly, Sadie reported that her anxiety was not high but she insisted that she was unable to attend any more classes. In addition, she repeated her desire for home schooling.

Treatment then shifted more to Mrs. S. and the commands and consequences she administered to Sadie regarding school attendance. Repeated attempts to have Mrs. S. follow through on consequences for Sadie's nonattendance failed because Mrs. S. was concerned that her daughter would suffer psychological damage from having to go to school. She was re-informed of the purpose of exposure-based treatment but seemed unresponsive. Further pressure from the school also had no effect. In cases such as these, common predictors of poor prognosis include poor parental support, single-parent family, chronic course of symptoms, multiple functions of school-refusal behavior, and treatment noncompliance. Sadie and Mrs. S. eventually discontinued the treatment process without significant advancement.

PREDICTIONS ABOUT THE FUTURE OF MANUALS AND WORKBOOKS IN MENTAL HEALTH INTERVENTIONS

The explosion of manualized treatments upon the marketplace is certainly a reflection of the extensive empirical support that psychosocial therapies have received in recent years. Such treatments have the advantages of helping professionals coalesce valuable techniques and address larger numbers of clients with a particular problem. However, manuals have also been criticized for being too technique-oriented, inflexible, developmentally insensitive, and dismissive of individual client characteristics that necessitate changes in a treatment plan. In addition, the issue of treatment noncompliance is not often covered.

Future manuals and workbooks for mental health interventions will clearly have to address these concerns. Future works will likely include, for example, more description of the process of therapy and how clinicians may act during a session to increase therapeutic effectiveness. In addition, it may be the case, especially for youth, that multiple manuals or sections for a particular disorder will be separately devoted to young children, older children, and adolescents to account for developmental changes (e.g., cognitive) that demand different therapy approaches. Similarly, manuals will likely pay closer attention to unique client and family characteristics (e.g., level of comorbidity) in certain cases that could affect treatment outcome. Finally, more detailed recommendations must be made to address noncompliance and dropout in therapy. The therapist guide and parent workbook described in this chapter contain suggestions for each of these issues, but future editions will likely include more detailed information.

CONCLUSION

The publication of manuals and workbooks to help clinicians address psychological disorders is relatively new and has significant advantages and potential drawbacks. As such, it may be best to view these initial works as we do with new computer programs: interesting, useful, progressive, and having some bugs. During the next generation of manual development, one should expect to see more diversity in content and a better fit with the complex cases seen by most clinicians.

REFERENCES

Chorpita, B.F., Albano, A.M., Heimberg, R.G., and Barlow, D.H. (1996). A systematic replication of the prescriptive treatment of school refusal behavior in a single subject. *Journal of Behavior Therapy and Experimental Psychiatry, 27,* 281-290.

Kearney, C.A. (2001). *School refusal behavior in youth: A functional approach to assessment and treatment.* Washington, DC: American Psychological Association.

Kearney, C.A. (2002a). Case study of the assessment and treatment of a youth with multifunction school refusal behavior. *Clinical Case Studies, 1,* 67-80.

Kearney, C.A. (2002b). Identifying the function of school refusal behavior: A revision of the School Refusal Assessment Scale. *Journal of Psychopathology and Behavioral Assessment, 24,* 235-245.

Kearney, C.A. and Albano, A.M. (2000a). *When children refuse school: A cognitive-behavioral therapy approach—Parent workbook.* San Antonio, TX: The Psychological Corporation.

Kearney, C.A. and Albano, A.M. (2000b). *When children refuse school: A cognitive-behavioral therapy approach—Therapist's guide.* San Antonio, TX: The Psychological Corporation.

Kearney, C.A., Pursell, C., and Alvarez, K. (2001). Treatment of school refusal behavior in children with mixed functional profiles. *Cognitive and Behavioral Practice, 8,* 3-11.

Kearney, C.A. and Silverman, W.K. (1990). A preliminary analysis of a functional model of assessment and treatment for school refusal behavior. *Behavior Modification, 14,* 344-360.

Kearney, C.A. and Silverman, W.K. (1993). Measuring the function of school refusal behavior: The School Refusal Assessment Scale. *Journal of Clinical Child Psychology, 22,* 85-96.

Kearney, C.A. and Silverman, W.K. (1999). Functionally based prescriptive and nonprescriptive treatment for children and adolescents with school refusal behavior. *Behavior Therapy, 30,* 673-695.

Chapter 15

A Review of Workbooks and Related Literature on Eating Disorders

Katherine J. Miller

INTRODUCTION

Workbooks for recovery from eating disorders have been used extensively in psychotherapy, especially cognitive-behavioral models tested in randomized clinical trials (RCTs). In the past decade researchers have attempted to discover whether using these workbooks in a self-help format is effective for some portion of the population. These books, often called guides or manuals, meet the criteria for L'Abate's definition of a workbook (see Chapter 1)—they contain written homework assignments on specific topics and stepwise, written instructions on when and how to do them. This chapter reviews published workbooks supported by research-based evidence of outcomes that are used in psychotherapy or self-help for anorexia nervosa (AN), bulimia nervosa (BN), or binge-eating disorder (BED).

Outcome research on eating disorders has focused on RCTs, many more on BN than AN, and methods used for bulimia are being adapted for the newest diagnosis of BED. Although the field has made great progress in the past three decades, many patients are not helped by the current treatments, and a high rate of relapse exists. Mitchell and colleagues (1997) have demonstrated that RCTs screen out some of the BN patients most difficult to treat (e.g., overweight, unsuccessfully medicated, substance abusing, or high suicide risk). Researchers are seeking new methods to treat refractory cases, predictors of success, active ingredients of treatment, and better relapse prevention.

These lines of research are occurring within a context of managed care and limited resources. One approach to limited resources is the stepped care model. This model requires that the least invasive and expensive form of treatment be used, followed by more intensive forms for nonresponders (Haaga, 2000). In the modified form, clinicians select the least intensive form that they judge will succeed. However, we do not yet have reliable predictors of who will benefit from which level of care, nor do we know when to switch levels (Kaplan et al., 2001; Wilson, Vitousek, and Loeb, 2000).

Recently, attention has been given to developing self-help models that are low-cost, easy to disseminate, and effective for a significant number of people. This is in part a response to the high costs of service delivery within traditional services (Garvin and Striegel-Moore, 2001). In addition, relatively few psychotherapists are trained in the specialized treatment models with demonstrated efficacy (Wilson, Vitousek, and Loeb, 2000), and many persons suffering from eating disorders do not have access to specialized services. These factors make the use of workbooks in a self-help format more attractive.

Unlike self-help in the 1960s, which advocated sharing of information, mutual support, political awareness, and egalitarian group process, self-help is now conducted by professionals who define the problem and recommend solutions (Garvin et al., 2001). Self-help methods based on researched treatments for eating disorders have been implemented after professional assessment. "Pure" or "unguided" self-help means giving the eating-disordered person a book of information and specific steps for recovery, with later professional follow-up. In guided self-help, a professional or lay therapist provides periodic support, but the sessions are briefer and/or fewer than traditional methods.

Self-help can be empowering and nonstigmatizing and can overcome barriers to care, such as distance, cost, scheduling problems, and unwillingness to attend treatment (Rosen, 1987). It can encourage further help seeking (Garvin, Striegel-Moore, and Wells, 1998), but failure may discourage the client from going on to more intensive treatment or may decrease the sense of self-efficacy (Wilson, Vitousek, and Loeb, 2000).

Some of the workbooks reviewed here are intended for use in the context of psychotherapy only (Apple and Agras, 1997; NRI, 1998a,b,c,e), whereas others (Cooper, 1995; Fairburn, 1995; NRI, 1998d; Schmidt and Treasure, 1993) have been used both in psychotherapy and self-help. The sole workbook for anorexics (Crisp et al., 1996) uses self-help in conjunction with psychotherapy.

The eight workbooks meeting the criteria for this review will be considered in order of publication, with a description of the book and related research. Table 15.1 lists writing assignment topics that are explicitly given in each book. Others are addressed but without writing assignments. Table 15.2 provides basic information about each study. Most studies include female participants only, and more than 95 percent are Caucasian. A wider range of socioeconomic and educational levels is represented.

TABLE 15.1. Writing Assignment Topics in Eating Disorder Workbooks

Topic	Workbooks							
	1	2	3	4	5	6	7	8
Food log	X	X	X	X	X	X	X	X
Binge/purge behaviors	X	X	X	X	X	X	X	X
Weekly weigh-ins		X	X	X	X			
Exercise	X	X	X		X	X	X	X
Diary				X				
Eating disorder self-assessment	X				X			
Cost-benefit analysis of ED	X		X	X	X	X	X	X
Choosing a support person	X							
Motivational enhancement	X							
Alternative behaviors	X	X	X	X	X	X		
Weight and shape concerns	X	X			X	X	X	X
Body image	X			X	X	X	X	X
Food avoidance and dieting	X	X	X		X	X	X	X
Identifying binge triggers	X		X		X	X	X	X
Problem solving	X	X	X		X	X	X	X
Challenging beliefs and distortions	X	X			X	X	X	X
Avoided situations	X	X				X	X	X
Handling lapses, relapse prevention	X	X	X		X	X	X	X
Planning meal times	X	X	X	X		X	X	X
Planning menus	X	X	X	X		X	X	X
Childhood experiences	X			X		X	X	X
Sexual abuse	X							
Assertiveness	X			X		X	X	X
Self-destructive behaviors	X							
Relationships	X			X	X			
Work issues	X			X				
Family issues	X			X		X	X	X
Sexual issues	X			X				
Knowledge self-assessment					X			
Summary sheets of progress			X	X	X	X	X	X

Sources: (1) Schmidt and Treasure, 1993; (2) Cooper, 1995; (3) Fairburn, 1995; (4) Crisp, 1995a,b; (5) Apple and Agras, 1997; (6) NRI, 1998b; (7) NRI, 1998d; (8) NRI, 1998a.

TABLE 15.2. Characteristics and Cessation Data of Studies on BN and BED by Eating Disorder Workbook

Author, Year	n	Dx	Modality	Duration	Sessions No.	Sessions Length	Percent Completers	Follow-Up Time (%)	% Cessation, Post Binge	% Cessation, Post Purge	% Cessation, Post Both	% Cessation, Follow-Up Binge	% Cessation, Follow-Up Purge	% Cessation, Follow-Up Both
Schmidt and Treasure, 1993														
Schmidt, Tiller, and Treasure 1993	28	BN[a]	USH	4-6 wk	0	–	92.9	–	–	–	57.7[b]	–	–	–
Treasure et al. 1994	110	BN	USH	8 wk	0	–	73.6	–	31.0	24.0	22.0	–	–	–
			CBT	8 wk	8	*			35.0	29.0	24.0	–	–	–
			WL	8 wk	0	–			17.0	15.0	11.0	–	–	–
Treasure et al. 1996	110	BN	USH/CBT	16 wk	0-8	*	78.2	18 mo (58.2)	–	–	30.0	–	–	40.0
			CBT	16 wk	16	*			–	–	30.0	–	–	41.0
Thiels et al. 1998	62	BN	GSH/CBT	16 wk	8	50-60 min	79.0	6-24 mo (77.0)	16.1	25.8	12.9	69.6	60.9	60.9
			CBT	16 wk	16	50-60 min			61.3	54.8	54.8	54.8	70.8	70.8
Cooper, 1993														
Cooper, Coker, and Fleming, 1994	18	BN	GSH	4-6 mo	8	20-30 min	100.0	–	–	–	50.0	–	–	–
Cooper, Coker, and Fleming, 1996	82	BN	GSH	4-6 mo	8	20-30 min	81.7	1 yr (61.0)	50.7	44.8	32.8	72.0	74.0	64.0
Fairburn, 1995														
Grave, 1998	17	BN	GSH	16 wk	6				35.3					
Wells et al., 1997	9	BED	GSH	3 mo	8	30 min	88.9	–	42.9					
Carter and Fairburn, 1998	72	BED	GSH	12 wk	6-8	25 min	88.0	6 mo (85.0)	50.0[c]	–	–	50.0[c]	–	–
			USH	12 wk	0	–			43.0[c]	–	–	40.0[c]	–	–
			WL	12 wk	0	–			8.0[c]	–	–	–	–	–
Loeb et al., 2000	40	BED[d]	GSH	12 wk	6	30 min	67.5	6 mo (45.0)	69.0[e]	–	–	69.0[e]	–	–
			USH	12 wk	0	–			46.0[e]	–	–	46.0[e]	–	–
Agras et al., 2000	220	BN	CBT	20 wk	19	50 min.	58.6[f]	1 yr (58.6)	–	–	45.0[c,f]	–	–	40.0
			IPT	20 wk	19	50 min			–	–	8.0[c,f]	–	–	27.0

Author, Year	n	Dx	Modality	Dura-tion	Sessions No.	Sessions Length	Percent Completers	Follow-Up Time (%)	% Cessation, Post Binge	Purge	Both	% Cessation, Follow-Up Binge	Purge	Both
Apple and Agras, 1997														
Agras et al., 1989	77	BN	CBT	4 mo	14	60 min	87.0	6 mo	–	56.3	56.0	–	59.0	–
			CBT+RP	4 mo	14	60 min			–	31.2	–	–	20.0	–
			SM	4 mo	14	60 min			–	23.5	–	–	18.0	–
			WL	4 mo	0	–			–	5.8	–	–	–	–
Agras et al., 1992, 1994	71	BN	CBT+med	16 wk	18	50 min	93.0[f]	1 yr (86.0)	65.0[g]	64.0[g]	64.0[f]	–	–	40.0
			CBT+med	24 wk	18	50 min			65.0[g]	64.0[g]	70.0[f]	–	–	78.0
			CBT	16 wk	18	50 min			50.0[g]	48.0[g]	55.0[f]	–	–	54.0
			Med	16 wk	0	–			35.0[g]	33.0[g]	40.0[f]	–	–	18.0
			Med	24 wk	0	–			35.0[g]	33.0[g]	42.0[f]	–	–	67.0
Telch et al., 1990	44	BED	Grp CBT	10 wk	10	90 min	90.9	10 wk (72.7)	79.0	–	–	32.6	–	–
			WL	–	–	–			0.0	–	–	–	–	–
			Replication	10 wk	10	90 min			52.4	–	–	–	–	–
Wilfley et al., 1993	56	BED	Grp CBT	16 wk	16	90 min	85.7	1 yr (89.3)	28.0[c]	–	–	*	–	–
			GRP IPT	16 wk	16	90 min			44.0[c]	–	–	*	–	–
			WL	16 wk	0	–			0.0	–	–	8		
Agras, Telch, et al., 1994	108	BED	Grp Wt Loss	36 wk	30	90 min	77.8	3 mo (64.8)	19.0	–	–	14.0	–	–
			Grp CBT+Wt Loss	36 wk	12+18	90 min			37.0	–	–	28.0	–	–
			Grp CBT+Wt Loss	36 wk	12+18	90 min[b]			41.0	–	–	32.0	–	–
Agras et al., 1997	93	BED	Grp CBT+Wt Loss	36 wk	12+18	90 min	–	1 yr (82.0)	41.0	–	–	33.0	–	–
NRI, 1998b														
Mitchell et al., 1990, and Pyle et al., 1990	171	BN	Grp CBT+placebo	12 wk	24	1.5-3 hr	73.1	6 mo (36.7)[h]	–	–	51.0	–	–	62.0
			Grp CBT+med	12 wk	24	1.5-3 hr			–	–	*	–	–	47.1
			Med	12 wk	0	–			–	–	16.0	–	–	33.0
			Placebo	12 wk	0	–			–	–	*	–	–	–

TABLE 15.2 (continued)

Author, Year	n	Dx	Modality	Dura-tion	Sessions No.	Sessions Length	Percent Completers	Follow-Up Time (%)	% Cessation, Post Binge	% Cessation, Post Purge	% Cessation, Post Both	% Cessation, Follow-Up Binge	% Cessation, Follow-Up Purge	% Cessation, Follow-Up Both
Mitchell et al., 1993	143	BN	Grp CBT—A1	12 wk	24	45.0 hr total	86.0	–	69.7[f]	72.7[i]	63.6[i]	–	–	–
			Grp CBT—A2	12 wk	16	22.5 hr total			73.2[i]	70.7[i]	68.3[i]	–	–	–
			Grp CBT—A3	12 wk	24	45.0 hr total			70.6[i]	76.5[i]	67.6[i]	–	–	–
			Grp CBT—A4	12 wk	12	22.5 hr total			32.4[i]	29.4[i]	20.6[i]	–	–	–
NRI, 1998d														
Mitchell et al., 2001	91	BN	Med	16 wk	0	–	97.8	–	16.0	–	–	–	–	–
			Placebo	16 wk	0	–			*	–	–	–	–	–
			Med+USH	16 wk	0	–			26.0	–	–	–	–	–
			Pla-cebo+USH	16 wk	0	–			24.0	–	–	–	–	–
NRI, 1998a														
Peterson et al., 1998, 2001	61	BED	Grp—TL	8 wk	14	1 hr	84.0	1 yr (86.2)	68.8[e]	–	–	50.0[e]	–	–
			Grp—PSH	8 wk	14	1 hr			68.4[e]	–	–	61.5[e]	–	–
			Grp—SSH	8 wk	14	1 hr			86.7[e]	–	–	66.7[e]	–	–
			WL	8 wk	0	–			12.5[e]	–	–	–	–	–

Note: All cessation percentages have been calculated in terms of completers only, unless otherwise noted. "–" indicates cell is not applicable. "*" means the information was not reported. Abbreviations: BN = bulimia nervosa, BED = binge-eating disorder, USH = unguided or pure self-help, GSH = guided self-help, CBT = cognitive-behavioral therapy, Grp = group, WL = wait list, RP = response prevention, med = medication, SM = self-monitoring, IPT = interpersonal psychotherapy, WtLoss = weight loss, NRI = Neuropsychiatric Research Institute, TL = therapist-led, PSH = partial self-help, SSH = structured self-help.

a Nineteen had ICD-10 BN; four of these also had ICD-10 AN; nine had atypical BN.
b 53.6 percent of the sample ceased either bingeing or purging, not both.
c Percentages based on intent to treat.
d 82.5 percent of sample were BED; others were subthreshold BED (7.5 percent) or BN (10 percent).
e Percent abstinent from objective binges, although some had subjective binges.
f Measured at thirty-two weeks.
g Measured at sixteen weeks.
h Only participants who had responded to treatment (n = 68) were followed up by maintenance and then evaluated (n = 61).
i End-point analysis used the last rating available for all participants.

DESCRIPTIONS OF WORKBOOKS
AND RELATED RESEARCH

Ulrike Schmidt and Janet Treasure (1993)

One of the earliest workbooks for persons with eating disorders (Schmidt and Treasure, 1993) came out of the work of Ulrike Schmidt and Janet Treasure at the Eating Disorders Unit of the Maudsley Hospital in London under Professor Gerald Russell. Their methods were translated into a self-help book for use, with or without professional care, by those with BN or BED.

The workbook first discusses the processes of change and helps the reader conduct a self-assessment. Two exercises are available to enhance motivation—a balance sheet evaluating reasons for giving up bulimia or not, and two letters to a friend in five years, one as if still bulimic and one assuming recovery. A support questionnaire helps the reader choose a support person for the recovery process.

Chapters 2 through 6 of the workbook address unhealthy eating habits, and Chapters 8 through 14 relate the eating disorders to other life issues. A therapeutic diary is the daily vehicle for processing thoughts and feelings in relation to behaviors and needs; the diary includes food records and binge/purge behaviors in an ABC (antecedents, behavior, consequences) format. As each issue is presented, behavioral and writing exercises are incorporated, including reactions to questions in the text, monitoring, and planning. Family work includes exercises such as drawing a family tree with everyone's weight and height, drawing self and family, and writing one's life story. Problem solving, examining self-defeating thoughts, and practicing assertiveness are used for skill development. Significant attention is paid to body image, sexual abuse issues, relationship issues, and relapse prevention. Chapters cover weight, impulsiveness, and addictions.

A clinician's guide (Treasure and Schmidt, 1997) describes in depth how to use motivational enhancement therapy for BN, using principles developed by Miller and Rollnick (1991) for substance abusers. Evidence that poor compliance accounted for much of the poor outcome in self-help formats (Troop et al., 1996) led Treasure and Schmidt to enhance the motivational aspect of treatment. They include case examples and worksheets to increase readiness for the action stage of therapeutic work.

A pilot study, a controlled outcome study, and two follow-up studies have been conducted on self-help using the workbook by Schmidt and Treasure (1993). In the pilot study (Schmidt, Tiller, and Treasure, 1993), twenty-eight bulimic women were given the book and told to work through it in the four to six weeks before their next visit. They improved significantly on all clinician-rated measures except body-shape concerns, with 46 percent of completers much or very much improved, 31 percent somewhat improved, and 23 percent unchanged. The only significant change on the self-report scales were improvement on the bulimia severity scale—no changes were seen on the bulimic symptom score, associated eating disorder pathology, depression, or self-concept. Patients felt positive about the book's promoting motivation and change.

In 1994, Treasure et al. reported a controlled trial of the manual for BN that compared eight weeks of pure self-help (PSH), cognitive-behavior therapy (CBT), and a wait-list condition (WL). PSH clients received the same treatment as in the previous study, but in addition they were offered eight sessions of CBT if they had not made progress by the eight-week assessment. After the first eight weeks, full remission from bingeing and purging was observed in 22 percent of the PSH group, 24 percent with CBT, and 11 percent of the WL group (a nonsignificant difference). PSH and CBT groups showed similar decreases in binge frequency, weight control behaviors except vomiting, weight/shape concern, distress, clinician-rated overall severity, and global symptoms. The CBT group improved more in abnormal dietary pattern, vomiting frequency, and degree of dietary restraint.

Treasure et al. (1996) extended and followed up on the 1994 study. The CBT group continued therapy for sixteen weeks, and the 80 percent of the PSH group not recovered at eight weeks were offered eight CBT sessions. Of those who accepted, the median number of sessions was three. At sixteen weeks 30 percent in each group were symptom-free, and after eighteen months remission rates were 40 percent for PSH/CBT and 41 percent for CBT.

Thiels et al. (1998) translated the Schmidt and Treasure (1993) handbook into German to compare guided self-change (GSC) to sixteen sessions of standard CBT. In the German culture a self-help model seemed unlikely to gain compliance, so the GSC group saw trained clinicians for eight bi-weekly sessions (fifty to sixty minutes) over sixteen weeks. The first four sessions focused on Chapters 1 to 6 of the manual and the last four focused on the most relevant additional chapters. By the end of treatment, 54.8 percent of CBT and 12.9 percent of the sequential group had not binged or vomited in the previous week. At follow-up, a significant increase was observed in cessation of bingeing and vomiting: 60.9 percent in the sequential group and 70.8 percent in the CBT group. Although knowledge about eating disorders improved faster in the sequential group and depression improved faster in the CBT group, both reached similar levels at follow-up.

Since compliance with the self-care manual had been predictive of outcome, Troop et al. (1996) studied predictors for this variable using data for the fifty-five women in the sequential condition in Treasure et al. (1994).

They devised a compliance scale by adding scores from three factors: amount read, exercises completed, and the degree to which the manual had been shared with someone, as recommended in the text. Overall compliance score best predicted full remission. Those who were more distressed read less, and those who were most concerned about their weight completed fewer exercises and had a lower overall compliance score. Those with a longer duration of illness were more likely to comply.

Turnbull and colleagues (1997) studied predictors of global outcome in the study by Treasure et al. (1996). Longer duration of illness and lower severity of bingeing at the beginning of treatment predicted better outcome posttreatment and at an eighteen-month follow-up. In separate analyses for the two groups, duration of illness was a significant predictor of outcome for CBT posttreatment but not follow-up, whereas binge frequency was the only predictor for the sequential group both at posttreatment and follow-up.

In summary, unguided self-help reduced bingeing and purging and led to abstinence in about 20 percent of completers. Adding eight CBT sessions matched outcome at follow-up to that of sixteen CBT sessions, although CBT worked faster and had some added benefits. Compliance was correlated with remission and was predicted by less distress and weight concern and longer duration of bulimia. Binge frequency at baseline was also a predictor of outcome.

Peter J. Cooper (1993, 1995)

Cooper's (1993) workbook was based on the cognitive-behavioral treatment for bulimia nervosa refined at Cambridge Eating Disorders Unit in collaboration with Christopher Fairburn, first described by Fairburn in 1981. The book was revised to include binge-eating disorder in 1995. It provides a highly structured program designed to give the minimum requirements for normalizing eating habits and attitudes toward weight and shape. The book is appropriate for self-help or psychotherapy except for those with any of the following characteristics: rigid, grossly disturbed eating habits; completely socially isolated; too demoralized to have the energy to change; anorexia nervosa; comorbid disorders requiring more help, e.g., problems with alcohol or self-harm; or a significant medical condition or pregnancy.

Part One (Cooper, 1995) is introduced by a first-person account of one day in the life of a bulimic woman, and the text throughout has generous quotes from many sufferers of BN and BED. The first six chapters of the book give basic information about the eating disorders, their etiology and effects, and the basic treatment model. Part Two is a self-help manual that gives a step-by-step guide to recovery. The major writing assignment is daily monitoring of food intake, time and place, compensatory behaviors, and the context in which these occur. A weekly review is recommended to identify patterns and set goals for the following week. The goal is to regularize eating, so the second step is planning meal times and menus. The third step is to plan alternate activities to replace binging, and the reader develops and refines a list that works for her or him. Fourth, a problem-solving method is taught and practiced in writing, linking eating-disordered behaviors with daily life problems. The fifth step is eliminating dieting, and writing hierarchies of difficult foods and situations helps the reader overcome his or her fears in an organized way. In the sixth and last step, cognitions about weight and shape are addressed, beginning with an exercise of listing valued qualities in friends and then considering applying the same values to the self. Cognitive distortions and underlying beliefs are explained, primarily perfectionism and all-or-nothing thinking, with the daily monitoring sheets again being the vehicle to record them. Relapse prevention is addressed very briefly.

Two studies have been conducted using the 1993 version of Cooper's handbook. In 1994, Cooper, Coker, and Fleming reported on use of the book for self-help with eighteen women with BN. Participants were evaluated, given the manual, and supervised by a social worker with no specialist training about eating disorders. The modal number of twenty- to thirty-minute sessions was eight over four to six months. Half of the women had stopped bingeing and purging by the end of the study, and binge/purge frequency lessened 85 percent and 88 percent respectively. Dissatisfaction with body shape and dietary restraint improved significantly, but not attitudes toward weight and shape. Patients reported liking the intervention, feeling that it let them be in control.

Cooper, Coker, and Fleming (1996) studied a larger sample of BN patients using guided self-help in the same format as the previous study, but adding evaluation instruments as pre- and posttests plus a one-year follow-up. Of the completers, 62 percent had a favorable outcome, meaning at least a 75 percent reduction in binge frequency. At posttest, about one-fourth of the whole sample and a third of completers had ceased bingeing and purging. In addition, substantial improvements were seen in weight and shape concern, associated eating-disorder pathology, and depression. At follow-up, 72 percent had ceased binging, 74 percent had ceased vomiting, and 64 percent did neither. Dropouts were more likely to have a personality disorder or history of AN.

Cooper's studies offered professional guidance while participants were using the self-help book, as did Thiels and colleagues (1998), but sessions were half as long, the number was flexible, and the work was spread over a longer time period. Results of the two studies after treatment were very discrepant, but the remission at follow-up for both was almost two-thirds of completers.

Christopher Fairburn (1995)

Fairburn's 1995 book is based on the CBT model developed with Cooper and others and similarly can be used for guided or unguided self-help or psychotherapy. The same populations are addressed and the same six steps are described, with introductory chapters giving current scientific information. The book is somewhat more comprehensive than Cooper's (1995), such as describing more research findings and incorporating more information that is specifically about binge-eating disorder. In addition to the daily monitoring form, Fairburn has a weekly summary sheet for listing weigh-ins, binges, compensatory behaviors, number of "good days" (those on which the planned steps were being followed), and special events. The reader completes a cost-benefit analysis before beginning the six steps, and the criteria for moving on to the next step are very thorough, with comprehensive checklists at the end of each chapter.

Fairburn and Wilson (1993) edited a comprehensive book for professionals about the nature, assessment, and treatment of binge eating. The final chapter (Fairburn, Marcus, and Wilson, 1993) describes in detail the CBT treatment for BN and BED on which the later workbook is based.

Three outcome studies have evaluated the use of Fairburn's book for BED and two for BN. Wells et al. (1997) used guided self-help with nine women with BED. Participants were given the book and eight thirty-minute telephone sessions over three months with a lay therapist (psychology graduate student), the first four sessions weekly and the last four biweekly. They showed significant decrease in overall eating-disorder symptoms, binge frequency, and general psychiatric symptoms. Three achieved abstinence from bingeing, two made clinically significant decreases, one made no change, and one had a slight increase. The authors concluded that four to six months should be allowed for this self-help method.

A second study of the same sample by Garvin, Striegel-Moore, and Wells (1998) evaluated qualitative feedback about the program. They found that participants developed a sense of relationship not only with the therapist on the phone but also with the author of the book, the manual itself, the people portrayed in clinical vignettes, and the structure of the program. Many developed a more positive attitude about seeking help. Varied reactions to the book related to differences in symptoms, knowledge, and personality style, but the program's flexible structure allowed for tailoring it to individual needs. In terms of coping skills, participants reported the most benefit from

daily monitoring, structuring time, and decreasing their all-or-nothing attitude—they felt a lack of help with weight and shape concerns. Successful
completers felt empowered and an increase in self-esteem, and some without symptom reduction felt less alone and ashamed and more supported.
Others blamed themselves or the program for ineffectiveness.

Carter and Fairburn (1998) used Fairburn's (1995) book to compare three
groups with BED: guided self-help (GSH), pure self-help, and wait-list control. The interventions were designed as they might be used in primary care
or the community. The GSH group received the book and six to eight individual, twenty-five-minute sessions with facilitators who had no formal clinical qualifications. Facilitators were given brief training but no ongoing supervision, and they provided support in the use of the book. The book was
mailed to the PSH group with the request to read and follow the program
over the next twelve weeks. Unlike other PSH studies, participants were not
told that therapists would review their records. The WL group received only
the assessment before and after twelve weeks, and then they were assigned
to PSH or GSH. Only the treatment groups made significant improvements
in objective binge frequency, associated eating pathology, general psychiatric symptoms, and knowledge of the book's educational content. Compliance was significantly better in the GSH condition, with significantly better
outcome than PSH on binge frequency at all time points and on dietary restraint at twelve weeks. Half of the GSH group had stopped bingeing at
twelve weeks, and 43 percent of PSH and 8 percent of WL, and this was
maintained at six-month follow-up.

Loeb and colleagues (2000) also compared guided self-help and unguided self-help (USH) for binge eaters using Fairburn's (1995) book. Six
thirty-minute sessions with a trained clinician were provided over twelve
weeks, corresponding to the six steps of the program, and therapists were
given weekly supervision by a senior clinician. The therapists facilitated use
of the manual by clarifying content, encouraging and praising, and using
cognitive restructuring to challenge problematic thoughts that were barriers
to success. The USH group was given a suggested schedule for following
the handbook for ten weeks, with an appointment set up for the twelve-week
point. Patients were given prepared envelopes to mail in their food records
weekly, and they were invited to call if serious problems arose. They were
also told that an investigator would call if anything of concern were observed on the self-monitoring sheets. Cessation of bingeing was 30 percent
for the USH group and 50 percent for GSH in the intent-to-treat sample, but
46 and 69 percent respectively for completers. GSH was superior to USH in
binge frequency and number of days, eating concern, restraint, overall
eatng pathology, and interpersonal sensitivity, but not weight and shape
concerns. The overall sample improved significantly on self-reports of eat-

ing-disorder pathology, psychiatric symptoms (except for paranoia), depression, and self-esteem.

Two studies have used Fairburn's (1995) book to treat BN. Grave (1998) studied a small BN sample using guided self-help over four months, and by the end of treatment more than one-third abstained from bingeing and purging. Agras et al. (2000) used Fairburn's book in the CBT condition in comparing individual CBT and interpersonal psychotherapy (IPT). CBT results were superior for completers posttreatment (45 versus 8 percent abstinence) but not after one year (45 versus 40 percent).

In summary, guided self-help achieved a 33 to 50 percent abstinence rate in four studies, whereas unguided self-help led to 30 to 43 percent abstinence in two studies. Changes held up well in the two follow-up studies. This compared favorably with the outcome of a randomized clinical trial with 45 percent of CBT completers abstinent after treatment and 40 percent at one-year follow-up.

Arthur H. Crisp, Neil Joughin, Christine Halek, and Carol Bowyer (1996)

Crisp and colleagues (1996) wrote a workbook for sufferers of AN, based on a treatment model developed at St. George's Hospital in London (Crisp et al., 1989). The authors recommend the book for self-help in the sense of a commitment to change, along with the help of therapists, family, and friends. The theory behind the model is developmental and psychodynamic, incorporating the behavior changes needed for a return to health. Crisp published a logbook (Crisp, 1995b) to use with the workbook, and a full explanation of Crisp's treatment philosophy can be found in a third volume (Crisp, 1995a).

The thirty-step program requires ongoing writing exercises. The first is keeping a diary about emotions in general and patterns of thoughts, feelings, and behaviors related to binge eating, purging, and overexercising. The first nine steps focus on how to discover what underlies the eating disorder, and include exploratory exercises that are focused on familial and interpersonal topics, to be done both alone and with parents, such as a life map, weight biography, family tree, and imagining how others would describe oneself. The pros and cons of recovery are discussed, and the reader completes a cost-benefit analysis leading to a choice—to stop losing weight, to recover, or to continue in the same way.

Steps ten to fifteen focus on how to stop losing weight by very slowly working toward regular meals and decreasing purging behaviors and overexercising. For those who wish to gain weight to an adult level, steps sixteen to twenty-one address coming to terms with what it would mean to grow in every area of life. Using the logbook (Crisp, 1995b) is recommended here. It has space to write weekly about sixteen headings, e.g., "the meaning of my shape to me," "my family relationships, then and now," and "why I approach others in the way that I do." A monthly self-assessment grid is used for twenty-four areas of functioning and to identify resources; a chart for weekly weigh-ins is recommended. Steps twenty-two through twenty-six cover how to gain weight by using meal planning and monitoring, and steps twenty-seven through thirty focus on how to maintain a normal weight.

In a 1991 study, Crisp and colleagues compared four groups of combined adolescents and adults over one year of treatment: (1) several months of inpatient treatment followed by twelve outpatient sessions; (2) twelve individual and family outpatient sessions spread over ten months; (3) ten group psychotherapy sessions for anorexics and ten separate sessions for parents, both addressing themes in the inpatient logbook; and (4) evaluation only. The two outpatient groups also received four sessions with the dietician who covered the approach to weight gain in Crisp et al.'s (1996) self-help book. Outcomes for the three treatment groups significantly surpassed those of the control group, even though 70 percent of the control group sought some type of treatment during the year. Weight gain at its highest point was significantly higher in the inpatient group than the others and took less time to achieve, but after one year the three groups were comparable. All three groups on average surpassed prepubertal thresholds but did not attain normal adult weights.

Gowers and colleagues (1994) followed up the progress of Group 2, treated with an active form of psychodynamic individual and family therapy, in comparison with the control group. After two years Group 2 had a significantly better outcome than the untreated group in weight gain (94.5 versus 83.0 percent of matched mean population weight) and body mass index (BMI = 20.08 versus 17.83), and showed significant improvements in physical, psychological, social, sexual, and general functioning. Sixty percent in the treated group compared with 20 percent of the control group were evaluated as being well or nearly well.

This course of research used approaches far less intensive than Crisp's standard treatment model. For example, Group 1 would normally have had weekly outpatient sessions for two years after several months of hospitalization. Nevertheless, progress was decidedly better than with no treatment, and follow-up of one of the groups showed continuing improvement over the next two years.

Robin Apple and W. Stewart Agras (1997)

The workbook by Apple and Agras (1997) was developed for BN and BED through clinical trials at Stanford University and multicenter studies, originally based on Fairburn's (1981) model. It is derived from manual-based CBT for use with therapy with a qualified professional, not self-help, and includes eighteen to twenty fifty-minute individual sessions, or ninety-minute group sessions combined with three individual sessions, over six months. The workbook is introduced at the first session—the client is asked to do reading before each session and review it afterward. A self-assessment after each chapter evaluates knowledge gained.

The first chapter describes BN and BED and provides a checklist for the reader to evaluate his or her own symptoms. A cost-benefit analysis helps the client decide whether to embark on treatment. From Chapter 3 on, the client completes daily records of food intake, binge/purge behaviors, and exercise, with a summary sheet to record the numbers of binge or purge episodes each week. Other writing exercises include listing pleasurable alternatives to bingeing, feared and problem foods, and binge triggers; practicing the problem-solving method; challenging problem thoughts; listing valued personal characteristics and physical attributes unrelated to weight or shape; and identifying mood and interpersonal binge triggers and planning how to manage them. Forms are provided to summarize progress at the middle and end of treatment, and a relapse prevention and maintenance plan is composed at the end.

The accompanying guide for therapists (Agras and Apple, 1997) describes the CBT method and cites the related research. The book recommends an assessment protocol and cautions the therapist against use of this method for those with AN, substance abuse disorders, or severe depression. The workbook is appropriate for persons with full syndrome or subclinical BN or BED. The guide outlines each session and offers clinical approaches for each step of the way.

Two outcome studies on CBT for BN have used earlier versions of Apple and Agras's (1997) workbook. Agras et al. (1989) compared self-monitoring of caloric intake and purging behaviors, individual CBT, CBT plus response prevention of vomiting, and wait-list controls. All treatment groups showed significant improvement in frequency of purging, with the CBT group significantly better in reducing purging and fostering improvement on psychological variables.

Agras and colleagues (1992) conducted a controlled comparison for BN of fifteen individual sessions of CBT, desipramine hydrochloride for sixteen or twenty-four weeks, and combined treatment for sixteen or twenty-four weeks. At thirty-two weeks the twenty-four-week combined treatment was superior to sixteen weeks of medication for purging, and superior to sixteen or twenty-four weeks of medication for bingeing. At the one-year follow-up (Agras, Rossiter, et al., 1994), both CBT and the combined twenty-four-week treatment proved significantly better than 16 weeks of medication. In the twenty-four-week combined group, 78 percent had recovered, 18 percent in the sixteen-week desipramine group, with the others in between.

Three studies using group CBT for BED have also used precursors to the Apple and Agras (1997) workbook. Group CBT for binge eaters was evaluated by Telch et al. (1990) in comparison to wait-list controls. At the end of ten weekly ninety-minute group sessions, 79 percent of participants reported abstinence from binge eating with none of the wait-listed subjects succeeding in this regard. The latter group then received treatment, resulting in a 73 percent abstinence rate. A later study (Wilfley et al., 1993) compared group CBT with group IPT for binge eaters, with wait-list controls. Only the two treatment groups showed significant change posttreatment and at the six- and twelve-month follow-up.

Agras, Telch, et al. (1994) used an additive design to study weight loss and binge eating in overweight participants with BED. Twelve group CBT sessions followed by eighteen group weight loss sessions led to significant improvement in binge eating but not weight loss, whereas thirty weeks of weight loss group achieved its goal but did not significantly reduce binge-eating. Adding desipramine to the CBT/WL treatment was successful for both goals. A one-year follow-up (Agras et al., 1997) was conducted with participants who had been treated during one of three studies of overweight binge eaters with group CBT followed by weight loss treatment. Results showed that those who had stopped binge eating lost weight, whereas those who continued bingeing gained weight.

In summary, the workbook by Apple and Agras (1997) has evolved through use in a large program of research using CBT. It has played a role in seeking the best combination of treatments for bulimics and for normal weight and overweight binge eaters.

Neuropsychiatric Research Institute, 1998b

The Neuropsychiatric Research Institute affiliated with the University of North Dakota has published programs for treating BN and BED, in conjunction with the Eating Disorders Institute and the University of Minnesota Eating Disorders Program. The programs include workbooks for individual treatment (NRI, 1998c) and group treatment (NRI, 1998b), self-help (NRI, 1998d) for BN, and a professionals guide (NRI, 1998f). Another workbook is for group therapy for BED (NRI, 1998a), with a separate handbook (NRI, 1998e) on the meal planning system, accompanied by a professional's guide (Boutacoff, Zollman, and Mitchell, 1998). No studies have examined using the workbook for individual treatment of BN. The group treatment workbook will be described first, and the BN self-help book and group treatment workbook for BED will follow.

The workbook for group treatment for BN is designed for nineteen sessions over twelve weeks: sixteen with a therapist and three with a dietician. In the preparation phase (two therapy sessions and three dietician sessions) clients learn the meal planning system, begin eating three meals/day, learn more about bulimia, evaluate pros and cons of recovery, and sign a contract committing themselves to change. The goals of the interruption phase (ten sessions) are to stop all bulimic behavior, eat three meals/day, and identify and change unhealthy thoughts. Patients plan meals daily and keep a food log and eating-behaviors chart. Many exercises are devoted to evaluating and changing cues, consequences, and automatic and maladaptive thoughts. Clients diagram their behavior chains and identify places to intervene. The workbook includes a large section on body image, including a body inventory and body image journal. In the stabilization phase (four sessions), a thorough relapse prevention plan is designed, including a plan for a healthy lifestyle.

A separate guide for professionals (NRI, 1998f) explains the theory behind the treatment model for BN and provides information about the exchange system used in meal planning. Instructions are included for each unit in the group and individual therapy workbooks. Clients in group therapy for BN also use a book on healthy eating (NRI, 1998e) that addresses typical concerns of people with eating disorders. It explains nutritional needs and individualized meal patterns, teaches meal planning, and suggests ways to be successful in eating a healthy diet. A guide for professionals (Boutacoff, Zollman, and Mitchell, 1998) outlines the change process for healthy eating, with practical information about typical ways in which people with eating disorders think. The client workbook is included as well as guidelines for special needs related to diabetes mellitus or MAO inhibitors.

The first study using this workbook (Mitchell et al., 1990) compared four groups: group therapy with and without imipramine, imipramine only, and placebo. Those who received group therapy had significantly more improvement than imipramine or placebo groups on number of binge eating episodes, number of vomiting episodes, hours spent binge eating, depression, and anxiety. Imipramine treatment was significantly better than placebo on eating behavior, anxiety, and depression. Augmenting group therapy with imipramine added nothing on self-reports of eating behavior and clinician-rated overall severity, but it did make a positive difference on depression, anxiety, and clinician global improvement ratings. More participants on imipramine dropped out of the study than those without. Pyle et al. (1990) conducted a six-month follow-up of the sixty-one participants who had responded to the initial treatment and were given four months of maintenance treatment (support groups and/or medication). Thirty percent relapsed—a lower relapse rate occurred among those who had initially received group therapy than among the imipramine-only group.

Mitchell et al. (1993) conducted a randomized study comparing four models of twelve-week group psychotherapy: (1) high intensity (forty-five hours) with high emphasis on early interruption of eating symptoms; (2) high intensity with no emphasis on early interruption; (3) low intensity (22.5 hours) with high emphasis on early interruption; and (4) low intensity with no emphasis on early interruption. In the first three groups about two-thirds were free of bingeing, vomiting, and laxative use at the end of treatment, whereas one in five of the low intensity/low interruption group were abstinent. It is notable that only the latter model met once per week. All others had two or three sessions per week, either toward the beginning or throughout treatment.

Neuropsychiatric Research Institute, 1998d

The NPI self-help book for BN is written for adults, primarily females of normal body weight, and it is not appropriate for those with severe depression or active substance abuse problems. As with the BN group workbook, it covers meal planning and normalizing eating patterns, behavioral strategies to avoid binge eating, cognitive restructuring, body-image issues, and relapse-prevention strategies. It is significantly shorter than the individual treatment workbook and does not include daily monitoring of binges and compensatory behaviors, listing of alternative behaviors, or a summary of progress at the end.

Mitchell and colleagues (2001) compared four treatments for BN: fluoxetine, placebo, fluoxetine with self-help manual, and placebo with self-help manual. Participants in the self-help conditions were given fourteen assignments that would take one hour each evening and told to follow them as best they could. At the end of sixteen weeks all but the placebo group had significant reduction in vomiting episodes, with a nonsignificant decrease in binge eating. About one-fourth of participants in the self-help groups had stopped bingeing and purging, and 16 percent of the fluoxetine group were abstinent. Both fluoxetine and self-help groups had greater reduction in binge/purge episodes than those without, indicating an additive rather than interactive effect for these two treatment components. No significant effects of treatment on general eating-disorder pathology, other compensatory behaviors, or depression were observed.

Neuropsychiatric Research Institute, 1998a

The NRI workbook for group therapy of BED follows the BN group therapy, with essentially the same exercises except for adding a segment on weight loss. It recommends fourteen sessions over sixteen weeks, with weekly meetings for twelve weeks and two-week gaps before the last two sessions. Peterson and Mitchell (1996) have published an excellent case example illustrating an individual's progress through the group process.

Peterson et al. (1998) evaluated three different models of group CBT for binge eaters. The time frame was altered to an eight-week program, with one-hour twice-weekly sessions for the first six weeks, then weekly meetings for the last two weeks. In the therapist-led group (TL), a psychologist gave psychoeducational information for the first half-hour, then led a discussion and homework review for an additional half-hour. In the partial self-help condition, participants watched videotaped segments of the same therapist presentations and then a therapist led the half-hour discussion. Participants in the third group, structured self-help (SSH), watched the same videos and led their own discussion. They were given a detailed list of discussion topics for each session, members were assigned to facilitate the discussions, and staff collected forms and turned on the videotape each time. Participants were evaluated before and after treatment and one, six, and twelve months later (Peterson et al., 2001). The number of objective binges and hours of bingeing significantly decreased for all groups from baseline to all later times: all groups made significant improvement on eating behavior, depression, self-esteem, and body satisfaction. At the twelve-month follow-up, the criteria for BED were absent for a fourth of the TL and SSH groups and more than half of the PSH group.

In summary, the NRI research program has demonstrated success in studies using patient workbooks in group treatment for BN and BED as well as self-help for BN.

CONCLUSION

These workbooks for the treatment of eating disorders have demonstrated effectiveness in use by psychotherapists, and most have proven useful in some form of self-help. The books written for the popular press have avoided many past errors of self-help books (Rosen, 1987; Ellis, 1993) by not making exaggerated claims, by giving evidence of effectiveness, and by providing clear diagnostic criteria. They also identify warning signs that professional help is needed. The workbooks for psychotherapy have been used in major outcome studies that have demonstrated the efficacy of standard and newer treatments for eating disorders. Table 15.2 summarizes the various characteristics of assignments in the workbooks reviewed in this chapter. Let the interested readers reach her or his own conclusions.

We have no way of knowing the effectiveness of pure self-help—how much these books help someone purchasing them at a bookstore and proceeding to have a dialogue only with the author. The studies necessarily involve contact with and monitoring by researchers, and it appears that these interactions may have something to do with compliance (Garvin, Striegel-Moore, and Wells, 1998). Unguided self-help appears to be sufficient for at least one-fifth of users in terms of abstinence rates in these studies, ranging from 13 to 58 percent (Carter and Fairburn, 1998; Loeb et al., 2000; Mitchell et al., 2001; Schmidt, Tiller, and Treasure, 1993; Treasure et al., 1994; Treasure et al., 1996). Guided self-help has resulted in abstinence rates of 13 to 69 percent posttreatment (Carter and Fairburn, 1998; Cooper, Coker, and Fleming, 1994, 1996; Grave, 1998; Loeb et al., 2000; Wells et al., 1997; Thiels et al., 1998). Gains from both kinds of self-help have generally been maintained (Carter and Fairburn, 1998; Loeb et al., 2000) or surpassed (Cooper, Coker, and Fleming, 1996; Thiels et al., 1998; Treasure et al., 1996) on follow-up. Although standard CBT worked faster than guided self-help in one study (Thiels et al., 1998), it was not the case in others (Treasure et al., 1994, 1996), and the longer-term results were about the same (Thiels et al., 1998; Treasure et al., 1996).

Lack of success with self-help may relate to noncompliance (Thiels et al., 2001); greater weight/shape concerns or distress; shorter duration of BN (Troop et al., 1996); more knowledge or self-esteem (Carter and Fairburn, 1998); binge frequency (Thiels et al., 2000; Turnbull et al., 1997); history of AN; or personality disorder (Cooper, Coker, and Fleming, 1996).

In addition to self-help, workbooks are regularly used in randomized clinical trials for CBT. However, since workbooks are not always mentioned in journal articles this chapter does not provide an exhaustive list. Studies included here have used workbooks with individual CBT and medication regimens (Agras et al., 1992; Agras, Rossiter, et al., 1994; Mitchell et al., 1990, 2001; Pyle et al., 1990) and with different group treatment models for BED (Agras et al., 1997; Agras, Telch et al., 1994; Peterson et al., 1998, 2001; Wilfley et al., 1993) and BN (Mitchell et al., 1990, 1993; Pyle et al., 1990).

Other resources for the treatment of eating disorders, although beyond the scope of this chapter, deserve mention. Bakke et al. (2001) have used

CBT with a workbook for two rural bulimic clients via telecommunication with positive results. Group interventions for classroom and internet use show promise for lowering the risk of eating disorders (Celio et al., 2000, 2002; Springer et al., 1999; Winzelberg et al., 1998, 2000; Zabinski et al., 2001). Since some workbooks attend little to body image, adding interventions targeted to body image may improve outcome. For example, Cash (1991) has produced audiotapes with exercises for use in psychotherapy, and a self-help book (Cash, 1997), based on his extensive research. Lastly, workbooks by persons recovered from eating disorders may inspire sufferers with their personal stories (e.g., Goodman and Villapiano, 2001; Hall and Cohn, 1999; LoBue and Marcus, 1999; Villapiano and Goodman, 2000).

In conclusion, eating-disorder clinicians are seeking new treatment methods for those who cannot be helped by the standard models. At the same time, more minimal interventions, such as self-help workbooks, are being developed, partly motivated by demands for cost-effectiveness. The workbooks reviewed here have an established place in both of these endeavors.

REFERENCES

Agras, W. S. and Apple, R. F. (1997). *Overcoming eating disorders: A cognitive-behavioral treatment for bulimia nervosa and binge-eating disorder—Therapist guide*. San Antonio, TX: The Psychological Corporation.

Agras, W. S., Rossiter, E. M., Arnow, B., Schneider, J. A., Telch, C. F., Raeburn, S. D., Bruce, B., Perl, M., and Koran, L. M. (1992). Pharmacologic and cognitive-behavioral treatment for bulimia nervosa: A controlled comparison. *American Journal of Psychiatry, 149,* 82-87.

Agras, W. S., Rossiter, E. M., Arnow, B., Telch, C. F., Raeburn, S. D., Bruce, B., and Koran, L. M. (1994). One-year follow-up of psychosocial and pharmacologic treatments for bulimia nervosa. *Journal of Clinical Psychiatry, 55,* 179-183.

Agras, W. S., Schneider, J. A., Arnow, B., Raeburn, S. D., and Telch, C. F. (1989). Cognitive-behavioral and response-prevention treatments for bulimia nervosa. *Journal of Consulting and Clinical Psychology, 59,* 215-221.

Agras, W. S., Telch, C. F., Arnow, B., Eldredge, K., and Marnell, M. (1997). One-year follow-up of cognitive-behavioral therapy for obese individuals with binge eating disorder. *Journal of Consulting and Clinical Psychology, 65,* 343-347.

Agras, W. S., Telch, C. F., Arnow, B., Eldredge, K., Wilfley, D. E., Raeburn, S. D., Henderson, J., and Marnell, M. (1994). Weight loss, cognitive-behavioral, and desipramine treatments in binge eating disorder: An additive design. *Behavior Therapy, 25,* 225-238.

Agras, W. S., Walsh, B. T., Fairburn, C. G., Wilson, G. T., and Kraemer, H. C. (2000). A multicenter comparison of cognitive-behavioral therapy and interpersonal psychotherapy for bulimia nervosa. *Archives of General Psychiatry, 57,* 459-466.

Apple, R. F. and Agras, W. S. (1997). *Overcoming eating disorders: A cognitive-behavioral treatment for bulmia nervosa and binge-eating disorder—Client workbook.* San Antonio, TX: The Psychological Corporation.

Bakke, B., Mitchell, J., Wonderlich, S., and Erickson, R. (2001). Administering cognitive-behavioral therapy for bulimia nervosa via telemedicine in rural settings. *International Journal of Eating Disorders, 30,* 454-457.

Boutacoff, L. I., Zollman, M. R., and Mitchell, J. E. (1998). *Professional's guide to healthy eating: A meal planning system.* Fargo, ND: Neuropsychiatric Research Institute.

Carter, J. and Fairburn, C. (1998). Cognitive behavioral self-help for binge eating disorder: A controlled effectiveness study. *Journal of Counseling and Clinical Psychology, 66,* 616-623.

Cash, T. (1991). *Body-image therapy: A program for self-directed change.* New York: Guilford Press.

Cash, T. (1997). *The body image workbook.* Oakland, CA: New Harbinger.

Celio, A. A., Winzelberg, A. J., Dev, P., and Taylor, C. B. (2002). Improving compliance in on-line, structured self-help programs: Evaluation of an eating disorder prevention program. *Journal of Psychiatric Practice, 8,* 14-20.

Celio, A. A., Winzelberg, A. J., Taylor, C. B., Wilfley, D. E., Eppstein-Herald, D., Springer, E. A., and Dev, P. (2000). Reducing risk factors for eating disorders: Comparison of an internet- and a classroom-delivered psychoeducational program. *Journal of Consulting and Clinical Psychology, 68,* 650-657.

Cooper, P. J. (1993). *Bulimia nervosa: A guide to recovery.* London: Robinson.

Cooper, P. J. (1995). *Bulimia nervosa and binge-eating: A guide to recovery.* New York: New York University Press.

Cooper, P. J., Coker, S., and Fleming, C. (1994). Self-help for bulimia nervosa: A preliminary report. *International Journal of Eating Disorders, 16,* 401-404.

Cooper, P. J., Coker, S., and Fleming, C. (1996). An evaluation of the efficacy of supervised cognitive behavioral self-help for bulimia nervosa. *Journal of Psychosomatic Research, 40,* 281-287.

Crisp, A. H. (1995a). *Anorexia nervosa: Let me be.* Hove, UK: Lawrence Erlbaum Associates.

Crisp, A. H. (1995b). *Anorexia nervosa: Patient's log book.* Hove, UK: Lawrence Erlbaum Associates.

Crisp, A. H., Joughin, N., Halek, C., and Bowyer, C. (1989). *Anorexia nervosa and the wish to change: Self-help and discovery, the thirty steps.* London: St. George's Hospital Medical School.

Crisp, A. H., Joughin, N., Halek, C., and Bowyer, C. (1996). *Anorexia nervosa: The wish to change: Self-help and discovery, the thirty steps* (Second edition). Hove, UK: Psychology Press.

Crisp, A. H., Norton, K., Gowers, S., Hale, K. C., Boyer, C., Yeldham, D., Levett, G., and Bhat, A. (1991). A controlled study of the effect of therapies aimed at adolescent and family psychopathology in anorexia nervosa. *British Journal of Psychiatry, 159,* 325-333.

Ellis, A. (1993). The advantages and disadvantages of self-help therapy materials. *Professional Psychology: Research and Practice, 24,* 335-339.

Fairburn, C. G. (1981). A cognitive behavioural approach to the management of bulimia. *Psychological Medicine, 11,* 707-711.

Fairburn, C. G. (1995). *Overcoming binge eating.* New York: Guilford Press.

Fairburn, C. G., Marcus, M. D., and Wilson, G. T. (1993). Cognitive-behavioral therapy for binge eating and bulimia nervosa: A comprehensive treatment manual. In C. G. Fairburn and G. T. Wilson (Eds.), *Binge eating: Nature, assessment, and treatment* (pp. 361-404). New York: Guilford Press.

Fairburn, C. G. and Wilson, G. T. (Eds.) (1993). *Binge eating: Nature, assessment, and treatment.* New York: Guilford Press.

Garvin, V. and Striegel-Moore, R. H. (2001). Health services research for eating disorders in the United States: A status report and a call to action. In R. H. Striegel-Moore and L. Smolak, *Eating disorders: Innovative directions in research and practice* (pp. 135-152). Washington, DC: American Psychological Association.

Garvin, V., Striegel-Moore, R. H., Kaplan, A., and Wonderlich, S. (2001). The potential of professionally developed self-help interventions for the treatment of eating disorders. In R. H. Striegel-Moore and L. Smolak (Eds.), *Eating disorders: Innovative directions in research and practice* (pp. 153-172). Washington, DC: American Psychological Association.

Garvin, V., Striegel-Moore, R. H., and Wells, A. (1998). Participant reactions to a cognitive-behavioral guided self-help program for binge eating: Developing criteria for program evaluation. *Journal of Psychosomatic Research, 44,* 407-412.

Goodman, L. J. and Villapiano, M. (2001). *Eating disorders: Journey to recovery workbook.* Philadelphia: Brunner-Routledge.

Gowers, S., Norton, K., Halek, C., and Crisp, A. H. (1994). Outcome of outpatient psychotherapy in a random allocation treatment study of anorexia nervosa. *International Journal of Eating Disorders, 15,* 165-177.

Grave, R. (1998). Guided self-help for bulimia nervosa in a specialist setting: A pilot study. *Eating and Weight Disorders, 2,* 169-172.

Haaga, D. A. F. (2000). Introduction to the special section on stepped care models in psychotherapy. *Journal of Consulting and Clinical Psychology, 68,* 547-548.

Hall, L. and Cohn, L. (1999). *Bulimia: A guide to recovery,* Fifth edition. Carlsbad, CA: Gürze Books.

Kaplan, A. S., Olmsted, M. P., Carter, J. C., and Woodside, B. (2001). Matching patient variables to treatment intensity: The continuum of care. *Psychiatric Clinics of North America, 24,* 281-292.

LoBue, A. and Marcus, M. (1999). *The don't diet, live-it! workbook: Healing food, weight and body issues.* Carlsbad, CA: Gurze Books.

Loeb, K. L., Wilson, G. T., Gilbert, J. S., and Labouvie, E. (2000). Guided and unguided self-help for binge-eating. *Behaviour Research and Therapy, 38,* 259-272.

Miller, W. R. and Rollnick, S. (1991). *Motivational interviewing: Preparing people for change.* New York: Guilford Press.

Mitchell, J. E., Fletcher, L., Hanson, K., Mussell, M. P., Seim, H., Crosley, R., and Al-Banna, M. (2001).The relative efficacy of fluoxetine and manual-based self-help in the treatment of outpatients with bulimia nervosa. *Journal of Clinical Psychopharmacology, 21,* 298-304.

Mitchell, J. E., Maki, D. D., Adson, D. E., Ruskin, B. S., and Crow, S. (1997). The selectivity of inclusion and exclusion criteria in bulimia nervosa treatment studies. *International Journal of Eating Disorders, 22,* 243-252.

Mitchell, J. E., Pyle, R. L., Eckert, E. D., Hatsukami, D., Pomeroy, C., and Zimmerman, R. (1990). A comparison study of antidepressants and structured intensive group psychotherapy in the treatment of bulimia nervosa. *Archives of General Psychiatry, 47,* 149-157.

Mitchell, J. E., Pyle, R. L., Pomeroy, C., Zollman, M., Crosby, R., Seim, H., Eckert, E. D., and Zimmerman, R. (1993). Cognitive-behavioral group psychotherapy of bulimia nervosa: Importance of logistical variables. *International Journal of Eating Disorders, 14,* 277-287.

Neuropsychiatric Research Institute (NRI) (1998a). *Binge eating disorder group treatment: Patient workbook.* Fargo, ND: Author.

Neuropsychiatric Research Institute (NRI) (1998b). *Bulimia nervosa group treatment: Patient workbook.* Fargo, ND: Author.

Neuropsychiatric Research Institute (NRI) (1998c). *Bulimia nervosa individual treatment: Patient workbook.* Fargo, ND: Author.

Neuropsychiatric Research Institute (NRI) (1998d). *Bulimia nervosa self-help manual.* Fargo, ND: Author.

Neuropsychiatric Research Institute (NRI) (1998e). *Healthy eating: A meal planning system.* Fargo, ND: Author.

Neuropsychiatric Research Institute (NRI) (1998f). *Professionals guide to bulimia nervosa.* Fargo, ND: Author.

Peterson, C. B., and Mitchell, J. E. (1996). Treatment of binge-eating disorder in group cognitive-behavioral therapy. In J. Werne (Ed.), *Treating eating disorders* (pp. 143-186). San Francisco: Jossey-Bass.

Peterson, C. B., Mitchell, J. E., Engbloom, S., Nugent, S., Mussell, M. P., Crow, S. J., and Thuras, P. (2001). Self-help versus therapist-led group cognitive-behavioral treatment of binge eating disorder at follow-up. *International Journal of Eating Disorders, 30,* 363-374.

Peterson, C. B., Mitchell, J. E., Engbloom, S., Nugent, S., Mussell, M. P., and Miller, J. P. (1998). Group cognitive-behavioral treatment of binge eating disorder: A comparison of therapist-led versus self-help formats. *International Journal of Eating Disorders, 24,* 125 -136.

Pyle, R. L., Mitchell, J. E., Eckert, E. D., Hatsukami, D., Pomeroy, C., and Zimmerman, R. (1990). Maintenance treatment and 6-month outcome for bulimia patients who respond to initial treatment. *American Journal of Psychiatry, 147,* 871-875.

Rosen, G. (1987). Self-help treatment books and the commercialization of psychotherapy. *American Psychologist, 42,* 46-51.

Schmidt, U., Tiller, J., and Treasure, J. (1993). Self-treatment for bulimia nervosa: A pilot study. *International Journal of Eating Disorders, 13,* 273-277.

Schmidt, U. and Treasure, J. (1993). *Getting better bit(e) by bit(e): A survival kit for sufferers of bulimia nervosa and binge eating disorders*. Hove, UK, and Philadelphia, PA: Brunner-Routledge.

Springer, E. A., Winzelberg, A. J., Perkins, R., and Taylor, C. B. (1999). Effects of a body image curriculum for college students on improved body image. *International Journal of Eating Disorders, 26*, 13-20.

Telch, C. F., Agras, W. S., Rossiter, E. M., Wilfley, D., and Kenardy, J. (1990). Group cognitive-behavioral treatment for the nonpurging bulimic: An initial evaluation. *Journal of Consulting and Clinical Psychology, 58*, 629-635.

Thiels, C., Schmidt, U., Treasure, J., Garthe, R., and Troop, N. (1998). Guided self-change for bulimia nervosa incorporating use of a self-care manual. *American Journal of Psychiatry, 155*, 947-953.

Thiels, C., Schmidt, U., Troop, N., Treasure, J., and Garthe, R. (2000). Binge frequency predicts outcome in guided self-care treatment of bulimia nervosa. *European Eating Disorders Review, 8*, 272-278.

Thiels, C., Schmidt, U., Troop, N., Treasure, J., and Garthe, R. (2001). Compliance with a self-care manual in guided self-change for bulimia nervosa. *European Eating Disorders Review, 9*, 115-122.

Treasure, J. and Schmidt, U. (1997). *Clinician's guide to getting better bit(e) by bit(e): A survival kit for sufferers of bulimia nervosa and binge eating disorders*. Hove, UK: Psychology Press.

Treasure, J., Schmidt, U., Troop, N., Tiller, J., Todd, G., Keilen, M., and Dodge, E. (1994). First step in managing bulimia nervosa: Controlled trial of a therapeutic manual. *British Medical Journal, 308*, 686-689.

Treasure, J., Schmidt, U., Troop, N., Tiller, J., Todd, G., and Turnbull, S. (1996). Sequential treatment for bulimia nervosa incorporating a self-care manual. *British Journal of Psychiatry, 168*, 94-98.

Troop, N., Schmidt, U., Tiller, J., Todd, G., Keilen, M., and Treasure, J. (1996). Compliance with a self-care manual for bulimia nervosa: Predictors and outcome. *British Journal of Clinical Psychology, 35*, 435-438.

Turnbull, S., Schmidt, U., Troop, N., Tiller, J., Todd, G., and Treasure, J. (1997). Predictors of outcome for two treatments for bulimia nervosa: Short and long term. *International Journal of Eating Disorders, 21*, 17-22.

Villapiano, Monica and Goodman, Laura J. (2000). *Eating disorders: Time for change—Plans, strategies, and worksheets*. Philadelphia: Brunner-Routledge.

Wells, A., Garvin, V., Dohm, F., and Striegel-Moore, R. H. (1997). Telephone-based guided self-help for binge eating disorder: A feasibility study. *International Journal of Eating Disorders, 21*, 341-346.

Wilfley, D. E., Agras, W. S., Telch, C. F., Rossiter, E. M., Schneider, J. A., Cole, A. G., Sifford, L. A., and Raeburn, S. D. (1993). Group cognitive-behavioral therapy and group interpersonal psychotherapy for the nonpurging bulimic individual: A controlled comparison. *Journal of Consulting and Clinical Psychology, 61*, 296-305.

Wilson, G. T., Vitousek, K. M., and Loeb, K. (2000). Stepped care treatment for eating disorders. *Journal of Consulting and Clinical Psychology, 68*, 564-572.

Winzelberg, A. J., Eppstein, D., Eldredge, K. L.,Wilfley, D. E., Dasmahapatra, R., Taylor, C. B., and Dev, P. (2000). Effectiveness of an internet-based program for reducing risk factors for eating disorders. *Journal of Consulting and Clinical Psychology, 68,* 346-350.

Winzelberg, A. J., Taylor, C. B., Sharpe, T., Eldredge, K. L., Dev, P., and Constantinou, P. S. (1998). Evaluation of a computer-mediated eating disorder intervention. *International Journal of Eating Disorders, 24,* 339-349.

Zabinski, M. F., Pung, M. A., Wilfley, D. E., Eppstein, D. L., Winzelberg, A. J., Celio, A., and Taylor, C. B. (2001). Reducing risk factors for eating disorders: Targeting at-risk women with a computerized psychoeducational program. *International Journal of Eating Disorders, 29,* 401-408.

Chapter 16

Couples with a Handicapped Child: Experiencing Intimacy

Eleonora Maino
Silvia Pasinato
Donatella Fara
Umberto Talpone
Massimo Molteni

The purpose of this chapter is to introdude a study that was carried out with an intimacy workbook in a health facility providing psychological and rehabilitation services for disabled children and their families. The decision to test the efficacy of such a workbook rests on two main reasons. First, some considerations were born from our daily clinical practice and the results of an empirical study made about parents of children with a malformation syndrome or infantile cerebral palsy. This study led us to investigate more accurately the needs and resources of families we support and verify whether our intervention practice, that is psychoeducational counseling, can indeed fully meet our patients' needs, or a more effective and efficient intervention is available.

The second reason is of a practical nature. Over the past few years requests for psychological support have increased. What we needed was thus an intervention plan that could be specific yet structured, namely a methodology that could take into account the peculiarities of each single case and, at the same time, be generalizable and applied to a wide number of clients in similar cases. Hence, a methodology that was cost-effective—able to reduce costs related to therapy sessions and the specific training of professionals—but also efficacious, that is, able to produce positive changes. Since workbooks seemed to meet these needs, we decided to carried out a study under controlled conditions.

CONTEXTUAL CONSIDERATIONS

We will report on this study carried out in northern Italy at the scientific institute "Eugenio Medea." Our institute not only provides for diagnosis, treatment, and rehabilitation of disabled children but also family support. We mainly support children and adolescents (age range zero to eighteen years) with organic pathologies (genetic diseases, rare syndromes, mental retardation, neuromotor pathologies, brain injuries, and infantile brain tumors) and psychopathologies.

Our priorities include the development of knowledge and abilities for daily clinical practice as well as prevention and rehabilitation services, both physical and psychoeducational, for the family and in the patient's social context. We not only provide medical care to disabled children but also support them in their life contexts, above all in the family environment. We assume that the family is a child's basic potential resource, and as such it should be fully recognized and exploited.

The Family Psychology Service of our institute carries out assessments of family dynamics, provides counseling and family therapy, and is also involved in research that is closely related to our clinical practice.

This is something innovative, because in Italy, the Health Service has always focused on clinical interventions, often only on the disease or the affected body part, disregarding one basic variable, that is, the family and familial relations, especially in the case of child and adolescent patients.

As a theoretical perspective we adopted the systemic-relational approach proposed by Selvini Palazzoli and colleagues (Selvini Palazzoli et al., 1975; Selvini, 1985; Selvini Palazzoli et al., 1988, 1998). In our opinion, the systemic-relational approach is the most compatible with our perspective since it takes into account the individual, his or her needs, intentions, purposes, and the significant relational systems he or she belongs to.

This theoretical approach integrates the systemic-relational patterns and individual patterns (interpreted by way of the intrapsychic functioning model suggested by authors such as Bowlby [1988], Kohut [1989], Miller [1981], Fairbairn [1952]) and the current family structure (the triad) and family history (across three generations).

CLINICAL CONSIDERATIONS:
FAMILY RESOURCES AND THE IMPACT OF DISABILITY

Disability is a highly stressful and potentially traumatic event. However, in a different way and with a different intensity, disability hurts individuals, families, and every social context that is founded on essential values such as solidarity and a sense of belonging (Scabini, 1995).

We also realized that the extent of a trauma such as having a disabled child and the ensuing depression cannot be defined if the "when" and "where" are not established, that is the family context and its resources.

On these assumptions, it is clear this "hurt" can have different manifestations, be of different severity and affect the lives of many individuals and their families.

In this perspective, given a neonatal diagnosis of severe pathology, a single parent who is emotionally and socially isolated will have completely different needs from those of an emotionally-stable family with close social ties that gradually becomes fully aware of their child's mental retardation.

Our perception is that the extent of the psychological trauma and the support the family needs are not defined by the clinical severity/complexity of disability and its prognosis, but by the presence/absence and fluidity/crystallization of individual emotional, family, and social resources. In this regard, Sloper et al. (1991) observed how socioeconomic factors, along with family relations and coping strategies, are significantly correlated to stress perception and global satisfaction with life.

Our daily clinical experience has confirmed that the couple is a fundamental resource for prevention, processing and spontaneous healing of traumatic events. Byrne and Cunningham (1985) underlined how the quality of the couple's relationship is fundamental to predict the successful application of coping strategies.

On the other hand, the couple must necessarily show sufficient coherence and intimacy to cope with one of the most significant tasks of a couple's life: the ability to share hurt feelings. At the same time, coherence and intimacy must be present across many emotional dimensions: that of nuclear families, of the extended family, of friends and the community one belongs to. Only if both coherence and intimacy are present in the couple, either the couple or the single parent will benefit spontaneously from the emotional support provided from external sources or professionals. Otherwise, the couple or a single parent will need to acquire both coherence and intimacy in working with a professional before obtaining it from external sources.

INTERVENTION MODALITY: PSYCHOEDUCATIONAL COUNSELING AND WORKBOOKS

In general terms, families receiving traditional family psychoeducational counseling at our institute have potentially sufficient resources to process possibly current or residual depression states, and neither the disabled child nor any other member of the family shows evident symptoms of psychopathology. These families do not need any therapy nor are they experiencing a crisis. Most of the time they want to access a support service to cope with needs that, at least initially, relate to care and education of their most problematic child.

In this case, psychoeducational counseling helps them discipline, reorganize, and draw on the couple's resources, family resources, educational and social resources as well, however disorganized and little integrated they can be.

Yet a large subgroup of families exists in which resources, motivations, and expectations are lacking—sometimes they are distorted and at other times none are left. These families are most at risk and show some redundant and significant relational features: a reduced attitude to the couple's intimacy, poor or nonexistent experience of hurt-sharing within the couple, and/or a prevailing inability to recognize depression in the partner and one's own depression.

The usual advice and psychoeducational strategies in these families are little effective in solving the behavioral problems of the disabled child. These problems may not be severe, but are bound to become chronic. In these cases, the psychopathological intervention, either individually or in pair, must specifically address old and deep depressive states that are closely related to the child's disability and have gone unexpressed for too long.

A middle-of-the-road intervention (based both on psychoeducational counseling and psychotherapy) would thus be necessary to help parents find an answer to their question as to "What to do with a disabled child?" on the one hand, and process relational dynamics and emotional states on the other.

Establishing what the correct intervention may be is not an easy task for two reasons: it is difficult to know exactly where an intervention stops and the other begins, as well as to define a precise methodology for counseling, establishing its stages and objectives, making it generalizable, and verifying its efficacy.

Today the term *counseling* still subsumes a wide set of often undefined intervention modalities. Different professionals may use the same term to define different intervention modalities that frequently tap into psychotherapy. Clearly, this does not allow verification of the clinical and economic effectiveness of this type of intervention.

The only aspect, at least at the theoretical level, on which general consensus exists is the fact that counseling was meant initially to be an alternative to, and different from, psychotherapy. At a time when psychotherapy was synonymous with verbal communication, intrapsychic exploration, transfer and consciousness as prerequisites for change, counseling set out to requalify the wide and long-ignored field of nonverbal communication, considering analogic/pragmatic communication as an important therapeutical resource, along with geography and chronology of relations, collaboration, and experimentation of pragmatic tasks as prerequisites for any real cognitive and behavioral change.

It thus seems that at least from a historic point of view, the qualifying aspect of counseling is the privileged attention paid to analogical, contextual, and nonverbal therapeutical resources. At the outset of the systemic movement, stressing the importance of the family, this change in perspective was considered to be revolutionary and provocative compared to the prevailing psychological culture.

Today, many studies (Guidano and Liotti, 1983; Guidano, 1987; Guidano, 1991; Liotti, 1999; Liotti, 2001) support two fundamental theories that can be summarized as follows: behaviors precede and shape consciousness (and not vice versa), and knowledge of the other precedes and favors knowledge of the self.

To support these theories and put into perspective their apparent revolutionary aspect, one can recall what has always been a trivial perception: no manuals, guides, or even verbal instructions exist that can help us learn how to ride a bicycle. Only after having personally tried (possibly under an adult's monitoring) will we be able to verbally describe the skills, difficulties, and emotions we experienced and felt.

In sum, our clinical experience suggests that the originality and efficacy of counseling does not rest so much on verbally communicated contents as in operational proposals to carry out collaborative experimentations. Conversely, its weakness is the easiness with which the analogical/pragmatic/nonverbal component is diluted or lost completely.

The reason for this is probably related to another historical feature of counseling, namely the absence of precise indications as to how to operate and the lack of a clear structure. How can we remedy this? An efficacious answer is provided by structured intervention programs that, in our opinion, meet the so-called "middle-of-the-road" requirement.

Many studies (Hoopes, Fisher, and Barlow, 1984; L'Abate and Milan, 1985; Donnelly and Murray, 1991; L'Abate, 1990, 1992, 2001; Cusinato and Salvo, 1998; Smyth, 1998; Esterling et al., 1999) have shown the efficacy of this methodology in a psychological intervention perspective. This is based on the use of verbal communication and direct meetings with the professional, writing at a distance, and above all, programmed writing; the possibility to intervene with individuals, couples, and families along a continuum ranging from functionality to dysfunctionality; assessment pre- and postintervention; and the use of specific workbooks for a given situation that must be structured enough to be generalizable and able to be replicated in similar situations.

These prerequisites, along with others, make this intervention attractive for extremely different contexts: a professional's practice focused on psychotherapy, and centers, either public or private, providing therapeutical and rehabilitative intervention programs as well as training and qualification programs (Johnston, Levis, and L'Abate, 1987; L'Abate, 1991; Cusinato, 1992; Jordan, 1998; Reed, McMahan, and L'Abate, 2001).

RESEARCH WITH STRUCTURED INTERVENTIONS

Given these considerations about the functioning of families with a disabled child and intervention modalities, we set out to verify empirically what we kept observing in clinical practice—the couple's inner dynamics—and to experiment with a more structured intervention plan that takes into account the pragmatic operational aspects by use of writing. This study was funded by the Italian Health Department to compare relational dynamics—particularly those related to the couple's intimacy and their ability to share hurts—in families with a child with mental retardation and malformation syndrome, families with a child with mental retardation and infantile cerebral palsy, and families with healthy children.

The focus of our study was to verify how the child's disability, either of genetic type or due to a pregnancy-related accident, could impact on the couple's relationship and intimacy, the latter being equal to the capacity to share hurt feelings and be emotionally available to the self and other.

Method

Respondents

Three groups of couples, mostly from Lombardy (90 percent), a region in the northwest of Italy, participated in the study. The groups consisted of:

1. forty couples with children one to sixteen years of age with a diagnosis of malformation syndrome and mental retardation. The children's diagnosis was very heterogeneous, with a prevalence of Williams syndrome (eleven children), Cornelia de Lange syndrome (six), and Wolf's syndrome (four).
2. fifteen couples with children one to sixteen years of age with mental retardation and a nongenetic diagnosis (infantile cerebral palsy [ICP]).

3. forty couples with healthy children, of whom at least one was in the one to sixteen years age group. The last group was selected from a wider sample of 247 couples. Only couples with the same sociodemographic features as the other two groups were chosen.

The three groups were identical except for the presence/absence of disability in a child and type of disability: genetic factor versus nongenetic factor.

Evaluation

All of the couples received some self-reports investigating the couple's relationships. In particular, to verify the stability of the relationship and trust within the couple as well as the credit that each partner attributed to self, the Italian adaptation (Maino and Resta, 1999) of the Stanley's Commitment Inventory (Stanley and Markman, 1992) and the Optimistic Attitude Scale (Maino, 1996a,b, 1998) were used, whereas affective and emotional intimacy was investigated by the Couple's Intimacy Scales (Cusinato and L'Abate, 1994), which focus on the partner's ability to share experiences and feelings, to respect the other's feelings, to accept his or her limits and value his or her potentials, to forgive errors and share hurt feelings.

Analysis of Results

These measures allowed us to quantitatively process the data thus collected, revealing significant differences across the three groups. If requested, each couple received a couple's functioning profile evidencing the resources and weaknesses of their relationship against the investigated variables. Further, we tested the efficacy of a structured intervention program based on the same dimensions investigated by the Couple's Intimacy Scales (Cusinato and L'Abate, 1994) in a small group of families with a child with malformation syndrome.

All of the data were entered into an ANOVA design. Parents of children with malformation syndromes versus control parents showed a greater capacity to share experiences, feelings and grief, and to forgive errors. Further, a multiple regression analysis showed that the main protective factor for stability of the relationship in couples with a child with a malformation syndrome is the capacity to value the other. This may be seen as an attempt to counteract the fact that parents are directly involved in their child's disability.

The multiple regression analysis also underlined the importance of hurt-sharing as a protective factor for stability of the relationship in families with a malformation syndrome and, especially for families with a child with infantile cerebral palsy, the negative impact of this variable on the global positive view that control couples have of their relationship. In our opinion, this factor indicates a greater fear of a deeper and more involving intimacy on the part of controls.

These results support both previous studies and clinical practice. Very often, parents of a child with a disability can exploit available resources and thus functionally reorganize family relations (Perry et al., 1992; Beresford, 1994).

Therefore, as stressed by some authors (Sorrentino, 1987; Tesio, 2000) we verified that it is neither always necessary nor advisable to provide support or psychotherapeutical services. An early preventive intervention aimed at exploiting, increasing, and reorganizing available resources is more effective. This intervention for preventive purposes will require involvement of professionals that are less skilled than those involved in psychotherapy, and will therefore be more cost-effective and able to reach a large number of clients at risk or with psychological stress but with no evident relational dysfunction.

These considerations strengthened our resolve to evaluate the efficacy of a structured intervention plan on a small group of parents with a child with malformation syndrome.

INTERVENTION: AN INTIMACY WORKBOOK

The program that was proposed is titled "Mysterious but not magical our intimacy" (Cusinato, 1992) and was developed to help the couple reflect on their own experiences, adopt, improve or learn increasingly functional relational modalities, for their own and their partner's well-being.

The program consists of eight units, each with a list of questions about a certain issue that the individual or the couple are requested to answer. These units are based on the spiral model of intimacy developed by Cusinato and L'Abate (1994) and the Couple's Intimacy Scales that are administered as pre- and posttest (see Figure 16.1). The subscales reflect the program's stages. It is thus possible to select a stage or involve the couple in those dimensions where the test evidences a stronger need for support (Cusinato and Salvo, 1998).

The main lines of the program concern personal identity and the couple's cohesion. In this regard, basic prerequisites for the couple's intimacy—which is best reflected in the ability to share hurt and accept to be hurt by the people that are closest to us—are the capacity to assert oneself as an individual with an intrinsic value, distinct and independent of others, the possibility

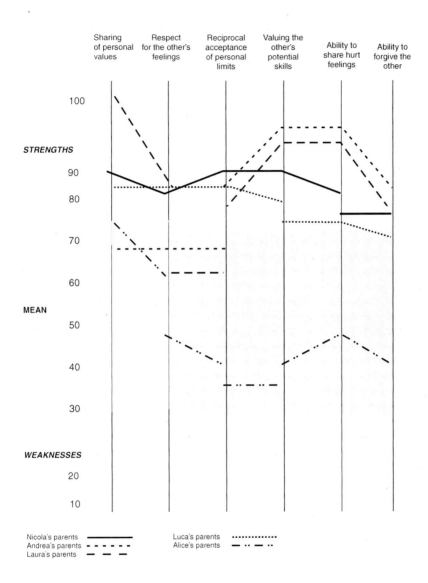

FIGURE 16.1. Psychogram of Positive Agreement on the Couple's Intimacy Scales

to share distinctive features with others, and the capacity to accept one's partner as is, valuing his or her potentials and helping him or her achieve them. The program uses verbal communication as well as programmed writing, personal reflections, couple's discussions, and meetings with the professional.

REPRESENTATIVE CASE STUDIES

Five couples with children with a genetic diagnosis were selected whose profile did not evidence a dysfunctional couple's relationship but highlighted some aspects that could be strengthened.

We decided to focus on genetic pathologies versus other pathologies of organic cause for three main reasons: in the literature many authors underlined the risk factors and the many psychological implications, both for the patient and his or her family, of a hereditary pathology (Boyce et al., 1991; Foster and Berger, 1985; Frude, 1991) and the need for as early an intervention as possible with support being provided to families; our clinical experience in relation to counseling with these families; and the increasing requests made by referring professionals that stress the need for psychological support to parents, especially upon communication of the diagnosis.

Among the five couples that were selected, two could participate only in the first meeting for two different reasons: geographical distance from our institute (Alice's parents) and the child's concurrent frequent admissions to other hospitals (Luca's parents). Laura's parents discontinued about halfway through because of a high level of conflict within the couple, whereas the other two couples attended meetings regularly and showed involvement.

All of the couples who were selected to participate show personal histories and couple's histories that are highly heterogeneous. Similarly, the children's pathologies are very different in terms of severity and impairment. The families' cultural levels and economic status, as well as the type of social involvement (extended family and community), are extremely different also.

Following is a description of the couples' characteristics, their expectations about the structured intervention plan, and the way they used it, with particular attention to writing and the impact of the program on the couple's relationship.

Nicola

We met Nicola's parents first. The father is a forty-two-year-old painter, and the mother is a forty-three-year-old housewife. Both left school early (primary school), their economic status is in the middle range, and from a social point of view they are well integrated within their community, with many friends and good relations with their own families, both individually and as a couple.

They met when they were very young, and were married seventeen years ago, after a long engagement. They have two children, Nicola (age seventeen) and Marta (age nine). Nicola is affected with Smith-Lemli-Opitz syndrome (SLOS), a genetic pathology, which is extremely severe and is due to a neomutation. Smith-Lemli-Opitz syndrome has a series of highly invalidating organic and functional dysfunctions as correlates (severe mental retardation, severe lordoscoliosis, cryptorchidism, poor visus, expressive language disorder). The diagnosis of SLOS was made soon after the child was born.

Nicola has always been supported by our center as far as rehabilitation is concerned (physiotherapy, psychomotor therapy, special education), while he underwent surgery in other hospitals located in northern Italy.

We first met Nicola's parents when we administered our research questionnaires. On that occasion, the couple asked us for a copy of their couple's profile.

The psychogram (Figure 16.2) considering the percentage of positive agreement between parents on the Couple's Intimacy Scales showed good communication between the couple, with both partners available to listen to each other and share their intimate thoughts. Although some improvement is possible, they also showed respect for the other's perspectives and thoughts and, especially at difficult times, they could relate to the other without playing on each other's weaknesses.

They are able to value each other and, although these aspects can be improved, can accept and forgive the other's errors and share hurt, difficulties, and negative experiences. During the second meeting with Nicola's parents we discussed their profile. Both conceded that the profile was truthful and agreed that they were content with their relationship, which was supported by the ongoing involvement of both.

However, during the meeting they expressed the need to reflect and critically consider the dimensions tapped by the Couple's Intimacy Scales and to find some time for themselves as a couple without focusing on work and social commitments, their children, and/or household-related tasks.

For this reason, we invited them to participate in our program to improve intimacy. To do this, they had to sign a contract, use a workbook, and devote some time to reflection in three structured situations: personal reflection, discussion, and the couple's discussion with the professional.

The couple attended several meetings regularly and, despite some initial reservations concerning writing—especially from Nicola's mother, given her education level and tendency to use verbal communication—they complied

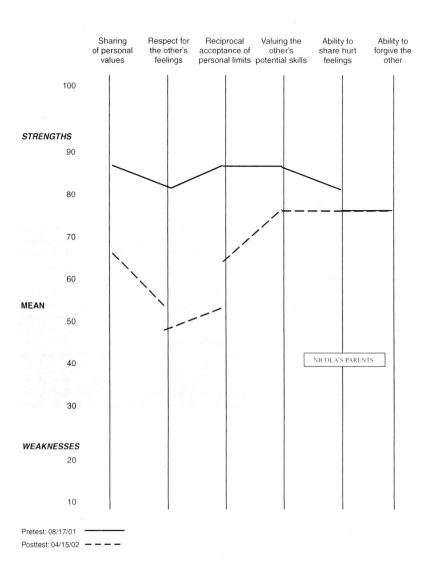

FIGURE 16.2. Psychogram of Positive Agreement on the Couple's Intimacy Scales

with the methodology and structure of the program. At the end of the program, the couple was given the Couple's Intimacy Scales again and a new couple's profile emerged, which, as can be seen in Figure 16.2, shows lower positive agreement on almost all the dimensions investigated by the program.

This outcome did not surprise us, and we did not attribute it to a negative effect of the program. It is evidence of a greater awareness on the part of the couple of their intimacy and their relationship. In our opinion, this greater awareness was due to the two qualifying aspects of the program, that is, an active involvement and use of writing, which help people become more conscious of themselves and their relations. As they attended meetings, Nicola's parents showed

1. an increasingly greater awareness of themselves, which led them, on the one hand, to provide written reassurances of mutual esteem and, on the other, to consider the difficulties in balancing different individual features, relational aspects associated to their children's education, and some aspects of their social and family life;
2. the progressively acquired ability to show the other one's way of being even through conflict, along with the desire to have one's needs recognized and satisfied; and
3. a greater capacity to consider some aspects of their relationship related to intimacy in a critical, yet constructive, way.

In our opinion, this is also reflected in the agreement on the "ability to share hurt feelings" and "ability to forgive errors," which remained unchanged. On these scales, Nicola's parents have always shown greater critical thinking and sharing of hurt feelings for two reasons. First, they both believe they shared the greatest hurt of all, that is, the fears and difficulties related to the care and treatment Nicola needed and the need for taking decisions that could have threatened his life. Second, they both realized that forgiving the other's errors, trusting the partner, and giving him or her credit is difficult but essential for the stability of the relationship.

The efficacy of the workbook was also shown by the couple's qualitative assessment. Both recognized its efficacy as the workbook led them to reflect on some aspects of their relationship that they took for granted but have never paid sufficient attention to, and the way the program is organized along with written homework helped them find time for themselves as a couple.

Despite some initial reservations, they also judged positively the written part of the program, since written communication was more effective than verbal communication in helping them define, recognize, and focus on ideas, feelings, and experiences.

Andrea

Andrea's parents were the second couple participating in the structured program. The father is forty-five years old, has a high level of education (he has a graduate degree), and is a banker. The mother is forty-six years old, has a degree in language and literature, and taught until the second child was born. Then, she stayed at home to raise the children and manage the house. Andrea's parents have a high sociocultural level and a high economic status. They have many interests and are always looking for new stimuli to share with their children. They have very good social relations and are extremely dynamic.

They met when they were thirty and got married two years later. That was about fifteen years ago. They have two children: Alessandro, thirteen, and Andrea, ten. Andrea is affected with Costello's syndrome. Costello's syndrome is a genetic disease due to a neomutation. Andrea shows mild mental retardation, expressive language delay, hypotonia, and mild facial dysmorphism. The child is supported by our center and attends speech therapy as well as psychomotor therapy sessions.

Andrea's parents accessed the structured intervention program in the same way as Nicola's parents: they received the Couple's Intimacy Scales, and a couple's profile was completed. Their needs and our considerations led us to invite them to participate in the program.

On their couple's profile (Figure 16.3), they showed a good ability to talk and listen to the partner, respect the other's peculiarities, and accept the other's values and weaknesses, although these skills could be slightly improved. Both parents value the other's potentials, with a very good ability to share hurt. However, the ability to accept and forgive errors could be improved.

During the initial meeting Andrea's parents conceded that their relationship was as described by the profile and that they were content with it. However, they wanted to reflect on some aspects of their relationship more accurately and find some time for themselves as a couple. Both agreed that struggling to ensure a good relationship and feeling close to the other and supported was fundamental at times when they had to cope with difficult or painful events. They thus deemed it important to improve their relationship.

Given their needs, we invited them to participate in the study of the structured intervention program on intimacy. From our viewpoint, it was interesting to verify the effects of the whole program and the workbook with a couple that, unlike Nicola's parents, seemed to have a more realistic view of their relationship and had a higher education and economic status.

Andrea's parents showed interest in the program, were motivated, and complied with the instructions and the methodology. At the end of the program, the couple received the Couple's Intimacy Scales again, and a new couple's profile emerged, which, as can be seen in Figure 16.3, shows higher positive agreement on almost all the scales.

We explained this result in terms of the attitude that the couple showed as they carried out the program. Our perception is that they both kept expressing positive, yet realistic, views of the relationship, even in writing, continuously reinforcing them, thus adding to what Gottman (1999) calls the "emotional bank deposit."

During this process, they kept restating and reinforcing the mutual respect and the possibility to confess, with no fears, one's weaknesses in the awareness that the partner would nonetheless accept them. In this way, the most fragile area of their relationship, the ability to forgive errors and trust the

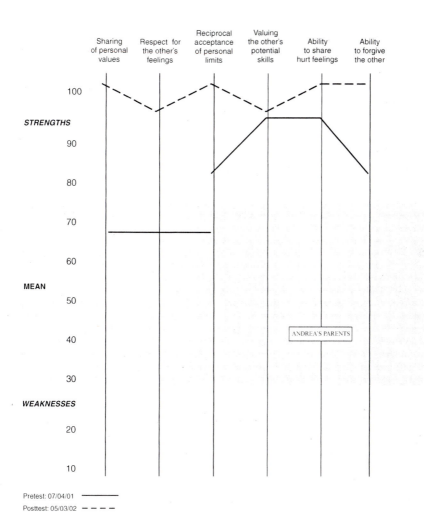

FIGURE 16.3. Psychogram of Positive Agreement on the Couple's Intimacy Scales

other—which is also the last and deepest aspect of the spiral model of intimacy (Cusinato and L'Abate, 1994)—was reinforced.

Andrea's parents, as with Nicola's, recognized the efficacy of the program, both in terms of contents and the way it was organized. In their opinion, the selected contents were crucial to consolidate a couple's relationship. They also expressed a positive view of the workbook, since it was easy to use, more direct than verbal communication, less time-consuming and more efficacious (i.e., it helped them get a clearer picture of their thoughts, experiences, feelings, and values and convey them to the partner).

Laura

The other couple that participated in the intervention program was Laura's parents. They met when they were very young and got married after living together for two years. The father is thirty-seven and is a worker. The mother is thirty-four and is a housewife, but she is looking for a part-time job.

Their sociocultural level is very low and they show poor and inadequate abilities and social relations. Both do not have good relations with their families of origin, which strongly impacts their couple's relationship and make it precarious.

They have only one child, Laura, age nine, who is affected by Cogan's syndrome, a dominant autosomal disease. Laura shows moderate mental retardation, mild facial dysmorphism, low vision, gross and fine motor clumsiness, muscle hypotonia, and mild microcephaly. At present she attends primary school at our center where she also receives psychomotor therapy and speech and language therapy.

Their couple's profile (Figure 16.1) based on positive agreement on the Couple's Intimacy Scales shows good communication and good agreement in valuing the potential skills of the partner and sharing hurt feelings. Some aspects need to be improved, such as the capacity to accept the other's weaknesses, respect his or her views, feelings, and thoughts, as well as to accept and forgive errors.

During the first meeting we were struck by the fact that the couple acknowledged their profile and recalled frequent episodes characterized by high conflict. The couple also conceded that their decision to get married was more a way to escape their families of origin than a reasoned choice. This confession led us to invite them to take part in the study. It was not clear whether they wanted to make a good impression or had a completely idealized view of their relationship.

We wanted to verify how the program could impact their own perceptions of the relationship, investigate to what extent the program could help Laura's parents to be more fully aware of their relationship, and to attempt to achieve a more realistic couple satisfaction.

At first, they fully complied with the program but progressively became more detached as they went on and addressed deep aspects of their relationship. Eventually they (the husband first and then the wife) gave up writing and working on their own and together.

Furthermore, the meetings with the professionals were characterized by conflict and mutual reproach. Laura's parents took the issues dealt with in the various meetings as an opportunity to discuss personal difficulties, such as the difficulty to manage daily life aspects related to home or work, difficulties within the couple and associated to a lack of mutual recognition and the inability to understand and recognize the partner's needs, and difficult family and social relations concerning conflicting relations with their families of origin, the lack of consistency in Laura's education, and the absence of a supporting social network and friends.

We soon realized that the couple could not carry out the program. On one hand, we had verified that the couple had needs that could not be met by our structured intervention program. On the other, their mistaken view of themselves as a couple was a defense mechanism they had adopted to avoid becoming aware of the inadequacies that would add up to their individual inadequacies.

We thus discontinued the program. The couple promptly accepted this decision because they felt that the program was the cause of conflict in their relationship. We offered them socioeducational support that took into account their social background and met their needs that were associated to management of the child, work, and home.

DISCUSSION AND SUMMARY

The goal of this chapter was to illustrate the study we carried out with the help of a couples intimacy workbook with parents of children affected by a malformation syndrome. The study was designed to verify the efficacy of a more structured and standard intervention than the psychoeducational counseling that is generally applied in our working context.

On the one hand, we verified that in clinical practice counseling is not always efficacious in meeting the needs of families, and perhaps psychotherapy would not be successful either. On the other, a more cost-effective and standard intervention can meet the increasing requests for support and reach more people.

In addition, our findings also encouraged us to carry out this study. If, on the one hand, the findings confirmed our hypothesis that these families have inner resources they draw on to cope with a stressful and potentially dramatic event, such as having a disabled child, on the other we found empirical evidence that a good couple's relationship is a fundamental resource to help parents cope with that event. Hence, our decision to conduct a study on a couples intimacy workbook.

Although our study concerned only a few couples, and our considerations can be seen from a qualitative perspective and not quantitative, it has nonetheless revealed some significant elements with regard to the methodology of the structured intervention plan and the contents of the workbook.

In particular, the way the program is organized and use of writing were not considered to be disruptive factors. On the contrary, they were valued and used by all of the couples, regardless of their education.

The contents and the duration of the program allowed the couple to attempt and find some time to devote to their relationship. We noticed that this highly pragmatic and structured aspect, that is, not dependent on the contents of the program, impacted their relationship and the possibility to reflect on it.

Despite some initial reservations, writing became a natural process once the assignments and the need to do them according to instructions had been clarified. The couple had been reassured that this was not an exercise in good writing but helped them to better convey their ideas, writing too became a natural process.

Regarding the contents of the program we verified that it actually tapped crucial aspects of a couple's relationship. Reflecting on them helped Nicola's parents to look at their relationship more realistically and feel a greater satisfaction with it, Andrea's parents to enrich and improve it, and revealed the problem issues in the relationship of Laura's parents.

Last, we noticed that this type of enrichment program meets one need that has been expressed repeatedly by parents: finding an efficacious way to help them improve their relationship. A strong relationship does not always help parents find the necessary resources for sharing the load of care of a disabled child, but also contributes to a positive family context in which all members, including the disabled child, benefit from it.

This conclusion is most encouraging and leads us to persevere in our attempt to make this intervention plan generalizable to a larger number of couples and be more context-specific.

REFERENCES

Beresford, B. A. (1994). Resources and strategies: How parents cope with the care of a disabled child. *Journal of Child Psychology and Psychiatry and Allied Disciplines, 83,* 171-200.

Bowlby, J. (1988). *Una base sicura* (A secure base). Tr. it. Milano: Raffaello Cortina Editore.

Boyce, G. C., Behl, D., Mortensen, L., and Akers, J. (1991). Child characteristic, family demographics, and family processes: Their effects on the stress experiences by families of children with disabilities. *Counselling Psychology Quarterly, 4,* 273-288.

Byrne, E. A. and Cunningham, C. C. (1985). The effects of mentally handicapped children on families: A conceptual review. *Journal of Child Psychology and Psychiatry, 26,* 847-864.

Cusinato, M. (1992). *Misteriosa non magica la nostra intimità* (Mysterious but not magical our intimacy). Treviso: Centro della Famiglia.

Cusinato, M. and L'Abate, L. (1994). A spiral model of intimacy. In S. M. Johnson and L. S. Greenberg (Eds.), *The heart of the matter: Perspectives on emotion in marital therapy* (pp. 108-123). New York: Brunnel/Mazel.

Cusinato, M. and Salvo, P. (1998). *Lavorare con le famiglie* (Working with families). Roma: Carrocci Editore.

Donnelly, D. A. and Murray, E. J. (1991). Cognitive and emotional changes in written essays and therapy interviews. *Journal of Social and Clinical Psychology, 10,* 334-350.

Esterling, B. A., L'Abate, L., Murray, E. J., and Pennebaker, J. W. (1999). Empirical foundations for writing in prevention and psychotherapy: Mental and physical health outcomes. *Clinical Psychology Review, 19,* 79-96

Fairbairn, W. R. D. (1952). *An object-relations theory of the personality.* New York: Basic Books.

Foster, M. and Berger, M. (1985). Research with families with handicapped children: A multilevel systemic perspective. In L. L'Abate (Ed.), *The handbook of family psychology and therapy* (pp. 741-780). Chicago: Dorsey.

Frude N. (1991). *Understanding family problems. A psychological approach.* New York: Wiley.

Gottman, J. (1999). *Intelligenza emotiva per la coppia* (Emotional intelligence for couples). Milano: Rizzoli.

Guidano, V. F. (1987). *Complexity of the self.* New York: Guilford.

Guidano, V. F. (1991). *The self in process: Toward a post-rationalist cognitive therapy.* New York: Guilford.

Guidano, V. F. and Liotti, G. (1983). *Cognitive processes and emotional disorder.* New York: Guilford.

Hoopes, M. H., Fisher, B. L., and Barlow, S. H. (1984). *Structured family facilitations programs: Enrichment, educations, and treatment.* Rockville, MD: Aspen System Publications.

Johnston, T. B., Levis, M. M., and L'Abate, L. (1987). Treatment of depression in a couple with systematic homework assignments. *Journal of Psychotherapy, 49,* 225-236.

Jordan, K. (1998). Programmed writing and therapy with conflictual couples. *Journal of Family Psychotherapy, 9,* 27-39.

Kohut, H. (1989). *Seminari* (Seminars). Tr. it. Roma: Astrolabio.

L'Abate, L. (1990). *Building family competence: Strategies of primary and secondary prevention.* Thousand Oaks, CA: Sage.

L'Abate, L. (1991). The use of writing in psychotherapy. *American Journal of Psychotherapy, 45,* 87-98.

L'Abate, L. (1992). *Programmed writing: A self-administration approach for interventions with individuals, couples, and families.* Pacific Grove, CA: Brooks/Cole.

L'Abate, L. (Ed.) (2001). *Distance writing and computer-assisted interventions in psychiatry and mental health.* London: Ablex Publishing.

L'Abate, L. and Milan, M. (Eds.) (1985). *Handbook of social skills training and research.* New York: Wiley.

Liotti, G. (1999). *Le discontinuità della coscienza* (The discontinuity of the conscience). Milano: Franco Angeli.

Liotti, G. (2001). *Le opere della coscienza* (The works of the conscience). Milano: Raffaello Cortina Editore.

Maino, E. (1996a). Desiderabilità sociale, atteggiamento ottimista e qualità della relazione coniugale (Social desirability, optimistic attitude, and quality of conjugal relationship). Unpublished doctoral dissertation. Padova: Università degli Studi, Facoltà di Psicologia.

Maino, E. (1996b). Desiderabilità sociale in ambito coniugale: Definizioni e strumenti (Social desirability within the conjugal context: Definitions and instruments). *Famiglia, Interdisciplinarietà, Ricerca, 1,* 179-193.

Maino, E. (1998). Desiderabilità sociale e atteggiamento ottimista: Contributo alla costruzione di due scale in ambito coniugale (Social desirability and optimistic attitude: Contribution to the construction of two scales within the conjugal context). *Bollettino di Psicologia Applicata,* 227-228, 65-76.

Maino, E. and Resta, B. (1999). Operazionalizzazione del costrutto di impegno nella relazione di coppia: Validazione dello Stanley's Commitment Inventory (Operationalization of the commitment construct in couple relationship: Validation of Stanley's Commitment Inventory). *Famiglia, Interdiscliplinarietà, Ricerca, 4,* 5-23.

Miller, A. (1981). *Il bambino inascoltato* (Social psychology of the family: Development of ties and social transformation). Tr. it. Torino: Bollati Boringhieri.

Perry, A., Sarlo, M. C., Garvey, N., and Factor, D. C. (1992). Stress and family functioning in parents of girls with Rett Syndrome. *Journal of Autism and Developmental Disorders, 22,* 235-248.

Reed, R., McMahan, O., and L'Abate, L. (2001). Workbooks and psychotherapy with incarcerated felons: Research in progress. In L. L'Abate (Ed.), *Distance writing and computer-assisted interventions in psychiatry and mental health* (pp. 157-171). London: Ablex Publishing.

Scabini, E. (1995). *Psicologia sociale della Famiglia: Sviluppo dei legami e trasformazioni sociali.* Torino: Bollati Boringhieri.

Selvini, M. (1985). *Cronaca di una ricerca: L'evoluzione della terapia familiare nelle opere di Mara Selvini Palazzoli* (Chronology of a research: Evolution of family therapy in the works of Mara Selvini Palazzoli). Roma: La nuova Italia Scientifica.

Selvini Palazzoli, M., Boscolo, L., Cecchin, G. F., and Prata, G. (1975). *Paradosso e controparadosso* (Paradox and counterparadox). Milano: Feltrinelli.

Selvini Palazzoli, M., Cirillo, S., Selvini, M., and Sorrentino, A. M. (1988). *I giochi psicotici nella famiglia* (Family psychotic games). Milano: Raffaello Cortina Editore.

Selvini Palazzoli, M., Cirillo, S., Selvini, M., and Sorrentino, A. M. (1998). *Ragazze anoressiche e bulimiche* (Anorexic and bulimic girls). Milano: Raffaello Cortina Editore.

Sloper, P., Knussen, C., Turner, S., and Cunningham, C. C. (1991). Factors related to stress and satisfaction with life in families of children with Down Syndrome. *Journal of Child Psychology and Psychiatry, 32,* 655-676.

Smyth, J. M. (1998). Written emotional expression: Effect sizes, outcome types, and moderating variables. *Journal of Consulting and Clinical Psychology, 66,* 174-178.

Sorrentino, A. M. (1987). *Handicap e riabilitazione: Una bussola sistemica nell'universo relazionale del bambino handicappato* (Handicap and rehabilitation: A systemic compass in the relational world of the handicapped child). Roma: Nuova Italia Scientifica.

Stanley, S. M. and Markman, H. J. (1992). Assessing commitment in personal relationships. *Journal of Marriage and the Family, 54,* 595-608.

Tesio, E. (Ed.) (2000). *L'uovo fuori dal cesto* (The egg outside the nest). Torino: Utet.

SECTION V:
CONCLUSION

Chapter 17

The Status and Future of Workbooks in Mental Health: Concluding Commentary

Luciano L'Abate
Lorna L. Hecker

People have a tendency to say things online they would never have the courage to say to someone's face. In cyberspace, people share intimate details, hopes, and fears with friends they have never seen—precisely because they are unseen. (Ainsworth, 2002, p. 195)

People express themselves differently when communicating with voice, text, and visuals. Unique aspects of identity and self emerge in these different modalities. Moving from one modality to another sometimes proves to be a very important event in the therapy. For these reasons, clinicians must design treatment plans involving combinations of different channels of communication or transitions between different channels. (Fenichel et al., 2002, p. 484)

INTRODUCTION

To summarize what has been presented in the pages of this book, distance writing, and especially programmed distance writing available in self-help mental health workbooks, can fill a void in the delivery of traditional mental health services. When transmitted and administered via the Internet, these workbooks may become the first line of defense (or attack!) in prevention, psychotherapy, and rehabilitation in the delivery of mental health services. Workbooks and structured computer-assisted interventions (SCAI) are two approaches that might qualify as being cost-effective and mass-oriented, besides being versatile. They can be used in parallel as an adjutant or as an alternative to professional interventions requiring face-to-face relationships based on talk (Esterling et al., 1999). For instance, research by Greist et al.

351

(2000) in an early clinical trial, integrated interactive voice response, self-help booklets, and videotapes, significantly reducing reports of depression.

According to a Harris Poll, 24 million people have sought mental health treatment online (Blair, 2001). Because of advances in technology, the way people conduct their personal lives is changing drastically. Convenience of services is a major attraction for those with busy lives, and in an era when privacy is shrinking, anonymity is also valued (Manhal-Baugus, 2001). The Internet offers both advantages in mental health treatment.

According to a report on mental health by the surgeon general (USDHHS, 1999), the cost of mental illness in the United States alone is approximately $200 billion annually and roughly $10 billion per year is spent on 100 million outpatient visits to physicians and mental health personnel. The prevalence of mental and emotional disorders is much greater than indicated by these already high numbers. Only 10 to 25 percent of those suffering from such disorders seek and receive treatment. Hence, any new mass-oriented technological intervention that has the preventive potential to lower costs of treatment while maintaining or increasing efficacy will have a large economic impact on the health industry and also make treatment more affordable for affected individuals.

Yet even in this comprehensive source no mention was made of alternative possibilities through distance writing, computers, and the Internet. Even more crucial was the absence of any mentions about the mental health personnel that will be required to treat literally millions of victims. It is not clear how these patients are going to be screened, identified, and treated— and by whom. Perhaps, what has been suggested in the pages of this book may provide an alternative choice, if not a solution.

Combinations of workbooks, computers, and Internet technologies may amount to a paradigmatic shift that could revolutionize how mental health services and psychological interventions, especially psychotherapy, will be delivered in this century (Mahrer, 2000; Norcross, 2000). If that is the case, two things are certain: (1) there will be a great deal of resistance to change from the present status quo (L'Abate, 1997), and (2) it will take a great deal of time for this change to take place.

One is reminded of what happened in Italy during World War I (Helprin, 1991). At the beginning of the war, copies of messages to various branches of the defense forces were written by hand by literally thousands of scribes. Thousands of personnel hours were spent in transcription of these messages in at least six copies needed for the different branches of the defense forces. As a result, many messages were either transcribed with errors or sent to the wrong address or both, to the point that distribution of materials to the front lines was frequently erroneous. If ammunition was needed, blankets were received instead. If food or medicines were needed, ammunition was received instead.

This state of affairs was changed suddenly with the introduction of a machine that made five to six copies contemporaneously. It was called the "typewriter." It cut down to just one-fifth the number of necessary scribes, decreasing substantially the number of errors in the messages as well. Only those scribes who were willing and able to learn the technical intricacies of this machine were able to retain their jobs. Those who could not, in spite of strikes and public demonstrations, had to find other jobs.

Of course, not all revolutions take place overnight, especially when we are dealing with hundreds of thousands of mental health personnel affecting millions and millions of people who need help. The most significant barrier in regard to changing the traditional mode of how mental health prevention and treatment is dispensed is funding. Funding for mental health services has long been an area of contention among mental health disciplines. At present, reimbursement requirements set by the Health Care Financing Administration (HCFA) require face-to-face psychotherapy (Nickelson, 1998). Offering multiple modes of therapy in addition to face-to-face therapy makes intuitive sense, since people learn differently and probably vary in the mode of therapy best suited for them as individuals. Mental health funding, however, has been truncated to one mode of therapy for all people. Based on the small amount of the population who actually seek face-to-face therapy, it would behoove the mental health establishment to offer services in varying modes.

Too many people in need of mental health help cannot be reached through the spoken word alone. We need all three media of intervention (nonverbal, verbal, and written) to reach as many people in need of help as we possibly can. Among these three media, distance writing (DW) and SCAI are by far the cheapest to administer in terms of professional time required. In the long run, they may be even the most cost-effective (Esterling et al., 1999). It seems as if the timing of interventions would be important too. Most people may not go to premarital education, but might attend prenatal sessions regarding their relationship. This seems to be an investment point. What are the investment points that could be utilized for workbooks?

Although talk is infinite in its unlimited expressions, writing can be programmed toward a finite, limited topic. This specification allows evaluation to be linked with treatment. Through programmed writing (i.e., workbooks) this link can be achieved much more specifically and effectively than through talk. With the skyrocketing costs of health and mental health care unlikely to show any decline, there is no question that workbooks are and will become increasingly an important, cost-effective, paratherapeutic and parapreventive way of helping people in need of mental health assistance. Workbooks cover most possible and clinically relevant topics, obviating the need to enumerate them here (L'Abate, 1996, 2004).

When transmitted and administered through the Internet, workbooks may become the first line of defense or attack in prevention, psychotherapy, and rehabilitation in the delivery of mental health services. Workbooks and structured computer-assisted interventions are two approaches that might qualify as being cost-effective and mass-oriented. They can be used in parallel as an adjutant or as an alternative to professional interventions requiring face-to-face relationships based on talk.

Workbooks can be made isomorphic with specific theoretical models, a feature that is absent in less structured forms of distance writing, like expressive writing (Pennebaker, 1997, 2001), or, for that matter, talk-based psychotherapy (L'Abate, 2001). Electronic therapy can offer multiple types of therapeutic relationships with several types of communication (Fenichel et al., 2002; Suler, 2001). In addition to challenges for electronic and other forms of therapy that do not involve face-to-face contact, there are additional concerns. When using the Internet, confidentiality concerns remain even with encryption technologies. Privacy must be ensured—recent computer viruses have been programmed to send e-mails to all those on one's address list or to random addresses. All information should be digitally encrypted with high power encryption, such as secure sockets layer (SSL) 128-bit encryption (Derrig-Palumbo, 2002). Password protection is a must for this type of work. Confidentiality no longer lies solely in the ethics and values of the therapist, but also is reliant on their technical prowess, or those they hire to secure treatment data. Another important barrier to electronic therapy is that technology has outpaced regulations with no state licensure or governing laws on how to conduct online therapy (Leslie, 2002; McCarty and Clancy, 2002). Without proper legal guidelines, therapists travel at their own risk into the cyberfrontier.

Hence, it is expected that it will take time to change attitudes, working habits, and overall perspective on how to work at a distance from needy people without face-to-face contact. In addition to funding changes, change will occur when most students are trained in these new techniques (Jordan, 2001) and start practicing under supervision what they will be doing for the rest of their working lives.

UNSTRUCTURED VERSUS STRUCTURED INTERVENTIONS

The major issue with focused and programmed writing deals with the nature of interventions. Are unstructured, nonspecific interventions, as most psychotherapeutic techniques are, more cost-effective and efficient than structured interventions? L'Abate (1976) has argued for the last quarter of a century that structure in and by itself, including evaluation, is therapeutic. If this argument is valid, the specific structure provided by workbooks would provide possible benefits in respondents by offering specific times and places for homework assignments by appointment and a predictable direction for the intervention by matching assignments with referral questions. The latter benefit would be concrete enough for respondents to understand in ways that would be difficult to understand using talk alone.

One important issue in workbook administration is respondents' resistance to this approach. One way to solve this controversial issue, in L'Abate's eighteen-year experience with workbooks, was to make treatment contingent on signing an informed consent form, matching one hour of face-to-face therapy with one hour of written homework assignments. In the informed consent form, prospective respondents agreed to cooperate in this fashion. Otherwise, they would be better off seeking professional help elsewhere. They would be accepted for treatment anyway if they had adequate financial resources or good insurance, or liked the therapists a great deal (L'Abate, L'Abate, and Maino, 2003).

QUESTIONS ABOUT PROGRAMMED DISTANCE WRITING

The arguments mentioned earlier and in the chapters included in this work raise at least four questions.

Do we need face-to-face verbal contact to establish a therapeutic alliance?

The answer is an emphatic no! In addition to the evidence reported in Chapter 2, admittedly with undergraduates, professional relationships using unstructured interventions are developed over the Internet every day. These interventions still mimic online what happens face-to-face (Fenichel et al., 2002; Hsiung, 2002; Occhetti, 2002). Just as in face-to-face contacts, they lack specificity and are usually unable to match treatment with the referral question or diagnosis, because of the inadequacies inherent in the spoken medium. Whether these online relationships are therapeutic remains to be seen. Likely, many nonprofessional relationships established online are opportunistic rather than therapeutic. Nonetheless, they are witnesses to the inevitable and inexorable fact that it is indeed possible to establish close working or even intimate relationships at a distance without face-to-face contact provided there is communality or similarity of interests, goals, and expectations (Ainsworth, 2002). As Ainsworth (2002) contends, it is possible that distance interventions may promote more openness than face-to-face, talk-based interventions.

Some argue that online relationships diminish the biases of the offline world. Gender, physical appearances, age, and so on are eliminated online, thus increasing the ability for emotional connection to occur (Merkle and Richardson, 2000). The perception of anonymity decreases discomfort, eases embarrassment, and erases the stigma to disclosing one's inner world. This ability to discuss deep personal concerns more quickly is an advantage unavailable in face-to-face therapy (Finfgeld, 1999; Manhal-Baugus, 2001).

This conclusion is even more relevant in many professional relationships. The editor of this book has never met face-to-face many of the contributors or other colleagues similarly inclined. Yet, cooperation and collaboration was established and maintained online. Furthermore, establishment of a professional relationship led to the opening up and sharing of painful, personal experiences, as ilustrated by Chapter 3.

***Can change for the better be achieved at a distance
without face-to-face personal and verbal contact
between a professional and troubled people?***

The answer to this question is an overwhelming yes! As the work of Pennebaker and others reviewed in Chapter 1, as well as the research reviewed in Chapter 2 and other chapters, amply demonstrated, people can change as a result of writing about past traumatic experiences or in completing workbooks. Admittedly, a great deal of this research was based on functional and semi-functional respondents. The jury is still out about the use of writing, in its four structures, with many severe psychopathologies and psychiatric conditions (Lepore and Smyth, 2002), even though Gould (2001), and De Giacomo (De Giacomo and DeNigris, 2001; L'Abate and De Giacomo, 2003), have successfully applied structured writing approaches to many psychiatric conditions. The importance of using writing with incarcerated felons, as suggested by McMahan and Arias in Chapter 10, suggests that this is a completely open area ripe for exploration.

Is writing more cost-effective than talking?

The answer to this question is a qualified yes, but depending on the circumstances. Certainly, a great deal of information can be gathered by computer-assisted evaluations obtained online. By the same token, a great deal of information can be gathered through structured autobiographical questionnaires (McMahan and L'Abate, 2001). Workbooks themselves can be used as structured, face-to-face interviews to guarantee that clinical operations and interventions, even when administered verbally, are equivalent from one respondent to another as well as from one clinical setting to another. But then, why waste valuable professional time to administer interventions that could be answered in writing directly from respondents themselves?

Will writing supplant talk completely?

The answer here is no. There will always be need to talk, if nothing else to communicate interest and personal involvement (Ainsworth, 2002). On the other hand, one could argue that talk can be counterproductive and even countertherapeutic, as in the case of many felons who use talk to make a good impression and con professionals in the process, as shown by Reed, McMahan, and L'Abate (2001) and in Chapter 10 by McMahan and Arias.

EPIDEMIOLOGICAL IMPLICATIONS OF WORKBOOKS

As already suggested in Chapter 1, workbooks can be used in primary prevention programs universally administered to functional respondents. Workbooks can be used in secondary prevention programs with targeted, semifunctional populations that are not yet clinical, chronic, or in crisis, but that could use combinations of talk-based and computer-assisted interventions, such as adult children of alcoholics, for example. In tertiary prevention, or psychotherapy, workbooks can be combined with crisis interventions, medication, and other interventions for clearly dysfunctional individuals, couples, and families. The mentally ill and their relatives, who are now swamping hospital emergency rooms, might need to work on them while they are waiting for hours to be seen by a professional who at best will administer medication.

What about all the traumas of September 11? What about all the people who suffered from posttraumatic stress disorder (PTSD)? Who and how are they going to be reached? Millions of Americans need treatment for psychological wounds suffered on September 11. Those events are not something a person just gets over in a flash. Untreated PTSD can become a life-shattering chronic illness on both emotional and physical health levels. In the Adverse Childhood Experiences Study (ACES) by Felitti et al. (1998), a sample of 9,508 patients who were recently medically evaluated completed surveys about seven categories of childhood trauma (adverse childhood experiences). Patients with four or more ACES, compared to persons with no ACES, were 4.6 times more likely to suffer depression, 12.2 times more likely to have attempted suicide, and 10.3 times more likely to have injected drugs. They were 2.2 times more likely to have ischemic heart disease, 1.9 times more likely to have cancer, 2.4 times more likely to have a stroke, in addition to generally being 2.2 times more likely to be in poor health among other problems. The costs of unresolved traumas to both mental and physical health are staggering.

One small study by Lange et al. (2000) utilized online standardized treatment of posttraumatic stress and pathological grief administered via the Internet. Twenty students with PTSD symptomatology participated in the study with a treatment that consisted of ten writing sessions (forty-five minutes each), with computer-mediated communication between therapist and participants, during a period of five weeks. The therapeutic procedure included completing questionnaires, writing essays, and reading instructions for the next stage. Assessment occurred pretreatment, posttreatment, and six weeks follow-up. Significant improvement occurred in reducing posttraumatic stress symptomatology and pathological grief symptoms. It appears that as technology increases more of these types of studies and intervention may be able to both ameliorate PTSD as well as aid in prevention of it.

PTSD may begin as an acute stress reaction from living through or witnessing a life-threatening event. This trauma obviously was worst for those who survived the September 11 attacks, for the families of those who lost their lives, and for rescue workers. Even so, those who watched the horrifying events unfold on television went through a real trauma—particularly those who watched them replayed over and over again. What is totally unique about this situation is that the trauma for most people involved television images. The images were so traumatic and so compelling that they are burned into our memories the same way a traumatic event is burned into the memory of a victim of violence. At least one in ten people exposed to a traumatic event will develop PTSD. If the condition affects only a much smaller fraction of those exposed via TV, the number of cases will still be staggering.

Women seem to be twice as vulnerable to PTSD as men. A recent traumatic event—or a past trauma that remains unhealed—increases that vulnerability because women in the past have been traumatized more often than men, thus predisposing them to PTSD as a result. People who are depressed or who suffer other untreated psychiatric conditions also are at increased risk. Traumas directly impact hypothalamic-pituitary-adrenal (HPA) axis causing glucocorticoid hypersecretion. This hypersecretion affects hippocampal function and can impact PTSD symptomology and a host of other health-related problems. Hyperactivity of the HPA axis has also been seen in suicide victims (Lopez et al., 1997). The negative impact of traumas on the hypothalamic-pituitary-adrenal axis could possibly be regulated by focused, expressive writing à la Pennebaker or completing one of the many emotionality-workbooks developed by the first writer (L'Abate, 1996).

The question is how do we determine what represents the beginning of psychological disorder and what is normal? When one adds similarly traumatized victims of sexual, physical, and verbal abuse there is no way in which face-to-face verbal contact is going to be available to all who have experienced past and present traumas. We need mass-distributed, cost-effective ways to help so many people in need of help and the old, face-to-face, verbal paradigm is not going to cut it. Workbooks will fulfill those two functions. However, they are still in need of continuous research. Technologies such as television and personal digital assistants (PDAs) can and will allow a much wider distribution of workbooks than face-to-face, talk-based interventions or even the Internet.

A RESEARCH AGENDA FOR WORKBOOKS

A great deal of research needs to be accomplished in the future. Interested researchers can carry out some of the following proposals.

Hemispheric Dominance in Affective Speaking and Writing

Sufficient information exists about hemispheric dominance in relation to language and talking (Greenfield, 2000; Iaccino, 1993; Kolb and Whishaw, 1985; Lenneberg, 1967; Ornstein, 1997). However, scant information is available on the role of hemispheric dominance in writing (Levy and Ransdell, 1996; Sharp, 1988). A great deal is known about cerebral dominance in language and talking, possibly related to the left hemisphere. (Borbely et al., 1999; Meador et al., 1999; Sharp, 1988; Wang, 1996). The problem is compounded when a dimension of painful-pleasurable feelings is considered (Borod, 2000). Current neuropsychological and cognitive neuroscience have focused on the roles of the amygdala and prefrontal cortex (PFC), and particularly the ventromedial PFC. In addition, Broca's area seems impeded in cases of trauma, especially childhood trauma. It makes sense that writing, either expressive or programmed, may help restore some physiological functions.

Provisionally, it is hypothesized that the left hemisphere is relatively dominant for thinking and talk, whereas the right hemisphere is relatively dominant for movements and writing. However, certain variables need to be taken into consideration: (1) sex differences; (2) nature of the task, whether in writing or talking, that is, expressive (traumatic experiences) versus programmed writing or talking, that is, answering detailed questions about traumatic experiences; and (3) level of emotionality—traumatic versus neutral versus pleasurable. For example, expressive writing about one's traumatic experiences may rely more on the right hemisphere than on the left hemisphere. By the same token, programmed writing about one's traumas or hurts may rely more on the left than on the right hemisphere because of its reliance on more cognitive functions.

This hypothesis is proposed on the basis of the following observations:

1. More recently, the right hemisphere is being considered as relatively more dominant for talk than for writing, especially as far feelings and emotions are concerned (Greenfield, 2000; Iaccino, 1993; Kolb and Whishaw, 1985; Ornstein, 1997; Schore, 2003).

2. Usually, the left hemisphere is considered relatively more dominant for thinking. Consequently, if thinking is more related to writing (Grabowski, 1996; Hayes, 1996; Hayes and Nash, 1996), then it should be more related to the left hemisphere than to the right one. However, this dominance needs to be qualified by the nature of both writing and talking tasks. For instance, writing about deeply emotional events, such as past or present traumatic experiences might come under the dominance of the right hemisphere (Greenfield, 2000), as would be the case of talking about the same type of experiences.

3. Criminals and acting-out, impulsive individuals show greater dominance in the right hemisphere over the left. Eye-hand coordination and performance is usually higher than ears-mouth functions, as a review of the literature on cerebral dominance in criminality (Reed, McMahan, and L'Abate, 2001) uniformly concludes. The supposed seat of thinking, the left hemisphere, is less dominant than the right hemisphere in individuals who act without thinking about the possible consequences of their impulsive behavior, as in the case of criminals.

4. Feelings and emotions are also usually considered under the relative dominance of the right hemisphere than the left (Dalgleish and Power, 1999; Schore, 2003). Consequently, psychotherapy, which supposedly involves language and emotions, would be more a function of the right than of the left hemisphere. If that is the case, and writing is more related to thinking, then the left hemisphere would be more dominant in writing than in talking, depending, of course, on the nature of the task. Writing could be programmed, as in workbooks and systematically written homework assignments (L'Abate, 2002). If programmed writing is devoted to either traumatic, neutral, or pleasurable experiences just as expressive writing, which is a less structured and, therefore, more open-ended type of writing. By the same token, which

hemisphere would be more dominant? When the dimension of trauma and painfulness is introduced (Lepore and Smyth, 2002), which hemisphere will be more dominant, the left or the right? No information about these questions is available in the extant literature (Levy and Randsdell, 1996).

5. None of the references already cited (Greenfield, 2000; Iaccino, 1993; Kolb and Whishaw, 1985; Ornstein, 1997) cover writing, but they do cover language as far as cerebral dominance is concerned. Rapp and Caramazza (1995) discuss Broca's original hypothesis that language stems from left hemispheric functions. However, this hypothesis has been questioned by Iaccino (1993) and Ornstein (1997). Rapp and Caramazza (1995) were the main source of information about the relationship between "orthographic," i.e., writing, and "phonological" forms (pp. 903-905). Two alternative hypotheses were proposed:

Hypothesis A views the semantic system as composed of two separate output lexicons: the phonological and the orthographic.

Hypothesis B views the phonological system as mediating the relationship between the semantic system and the orthographic output lexicon. Rapp and Caramazza conclude their chapter thusly:

> The results we have described also have important implications for theories of the functional organization of the human brain. The patterns of performance we have described suggest that distinct neural mechanisms are responsible for the representation and processing of the meanings and the orthographic and phonological forms of words. (p. 911)

Neither these nor other sources obtained from a literature search on this topic* gave any specific information about the relationship between cerebral dominance and writing, which in this case would qualify as "complex writing," rather than writing simple letters, as performed in past studies. The only study about cerebral dominance and writing, groundbreaking, but unpublished, was performed by Sharp (1988) under the direction of James W. Pennebaker. Sharp explored hemispheric activity in frontal and parietal lobes during inhibition (writing about neutral, trivial topics) and confrontation (writing about painful experiences). She predicted that greater congruence in brainwave activity between hemispheres for alpha and beta frequency would be associated with confronting as opposed to inhibiting writing, as measured by an electroencephalogram (EEG). She used twenty-

---

*Thanks to Gerald Sutin, PhD, for his help with a literature search in the biology of writing.

four right-handed undergraduates as respondents. Analyses of EEGs within subjects for the two writings found higher cortical congruence when respondents wrote about emotionally laden experiences as opposed to trivial ones. In addition to these measures, skin conductance levels measured during writing served also as indicators of inhibition. Using this variable for internal analysis of individual differences in level of disclosure, further evidence was found to support the hypothesis that cortical congruence is associated with less inhibition. Clearly, this is the kind of study that needs replication in its various implications, including a control condition of no writing (baseline), and also writing about pleasant and pleasurable experiences.

6. Recently, Sadoski and Paivio (2001) have provided a dual coding theory about two separate information coding systems: one for verbal representations and the other for nonverbal presentations. Apparently, according to this theory, there are two separate information processing systems: one for words and one for pictures. How these systems deal with visual versus auditory stimuli remains an open question. Nonetheless, these two coding systems need to deal with emotional versus cognitive information processing as possibly related to the reticular ascending (RAS) and reticular discending systems (RDS) (Power and Dalgleish, 1997). Schore (2003) goes as far as to relate affect regulation, attachment, and mental health to the regulation of the right hemisphere.

7. The introduction of writing as a "cure" (Lepore and Smyth, 2002) makes this issue even more relevant, since, up to now, no reference can be found about the relative role of cerebral dominance in writing of any kind. If one writes about emotional experiences, will this process be more governed by the right or by the left hemisphere or other neural pathways? By the same token, if one were to write about neutral experiences, will this process be more governed by which hemisphere? Furthermore, if one were to either write or talk about pleasurable experiences, which hemisphere will be more involved?

8. The issue of sex differences in cerebral dominance is omnipresent and cannot be avoided. Hence, an equal number of respondents from each sex should be included in an experimental design.

Group Design

Assuming that hemispheric dominance can be measured via EEG or MRI, or any other up-to-date method, the experimental task would involve randomly assigned subjects who will talk about their traumatic experiences, never disclosed with anyone before, in a microphone connected to a tape-recorder (the Pennebaker paradigm, Lepore and Smyth, 2002) for fifteen minutes a day for four consecutive days. A second experimental group would write accordingly about traumatic experiences, following the same routine of fifteen minutes a day for four consecutive days. A third and fourth group would either write or speak in a microphone about funny, hilarious, or very pleasant experiences in their lives, including jokes for fifteen minutes a day for four consecutive days.

Two control groups of respondents would either write or talk for the same amount of time in a taperecorder about neutral topics, such as listing: (1) all the objects in one's room one day, (2) all of the meeting places in one's life, (3) one's methods of transportation since childhood to adulthood, starting with tricycle to skates, to bicycle, to motorcycle, and eventually cars, (4) places one has visited in one's lifetime, etc.

The experimental design for this type of study would consist of the following.
- Independent variables
- Length of talking or writing: constant for everybody, regardless of task
- Topics: Pleasant, Unpleasant, Neutral (three groups)
- Sex differences: Men versus women (two groups)
- Writing (expressive versus programmed) versus (expressive versus programmed) talking (2×2 Factorial Analysis: $3 \times 2 \times 2 \times 2$)
Dependent Variables: EEG or MRI tracings.

Single-Subject Design

Instead of a group design, which would be quite complex and very likely unyielding from the viewpoint of analysis, a single-subject design may be more feasible in terms of analysis.

Expressive Writing. Begin a proposed research project on affectivity in speaking and writing in cerebral dominance by using a pilot single-subject design using (paid?) volunteers, thusly:

1. Take baseline readings under neutral conditions, that is, writing and speaking about neutral topics:
   - After writing about neutral topics for fifteen minutes, once a baseline has been established, a respondent reads aloud what has been written;
   - a respondent can then write about traumatic experiences for another fifteen minutes;

- after writing, respondent can read aloud what has been written for another fifteen minutes.

2. To counteract and control for serial effects, the experimental condition should be reversed after establishing a baseline, that is, talking aloud first and writing second, rather than writing first and talking second about neutral topics. In this condition, talking should be recorded into a tape recorder, so that respondents can then write what has been said aloud. The same sequence should be applied to speaking in a tape-recorder for fifteen minutes about traumatic experiences and then writing from what has been said.

3. The same procedure can be followed for joyful, pleasurable, and pleasant experiences.

4. Use respondents from both sexes for each condition.

Programmed Writing. One criticism about expressive writing and disclosure from a relational viewpoint (L'Abate and De Giacomo, 2003) lies in its being completely internal, intrapsychic, and nonrelational. Although it may help individuals improve their intimate relationships, no evidence exists, as far as these authors know, about such improvements. Hence, it is necessary to add a second dimension of disclosure, and that is, sharing hurts with those we love and who love us. Since this disclosure and sharing are very difficult to achieve, especially in clinical relationships, it will be crucial to include programmed writing about one's hurts to encourage relational disclosure and intimacy with loved ones. Consequently, to match the programmed equivalent of expressive writing, one could use one section of the intimacy workbook (L'Abate, 1996) devoted entirely to encourage individuals to share their hurts with loved ones. Since this section consists of three assignments, the last assignment could be repeated to match the four sessions required by expressive writing. The same experimental procedure outlined earlier should be followed. However, instead of expressive writing, respondents would answer questions in systematically written homework assignments either in writing or by speaking aloud.

Implications

This proposal, if valid, would contribute to theoretical as well as practical implications.

Theoretically, it is just as important to know more about the relative influence of cerebral dominance in writing, as in the case with talking. We know a great deal about the former, but we know precious little about the latter. Practically, if writing assumes greater and greater applicability in prevention and psychotherapy (L'Abate, 2002; L'Abate and De Giacomo, 2003; Lepore and Smyth, 2002), it will become increasingly crucial to discover under what conditions each modality is useful and under what conditions it is not. Are there individual differences in writing (Levy and Randsdell, 1996)? Are there individual differences between expressive and programmed writing? What are the cerebral functions underlying each type of writing? How about sex and gender differences? If we do not know more about cerebral dominance and affective writing and talking, how are we going to rehabilitate individuals affected by cerebral dysfunctions?

PSYCHOTHERAPY AND WORKBOOK-BASED INTERVENTIONS

This area is completely open to comparative evaluation. One step in this direction has been taken by L'Abate, L'Abate, and Maino (2002). They compared the number of sessions in ten years of part-time private practice without workbooks versus fifteen years of the same practice using workbooks. The results are still under statistical analysis.

Cost-effectiveness of Workbooks

Of course, this is a crucial area to evaluate. Indeed, one would argue that the whole issue of cost-effectiveness is a basic one to the whole enterprise of workbook-based interventions. One needs to compare respondents from the same population who receive either face-to-face verbal therapy with respondents matched on various independent variables (diagnosis, age, sex, socioeconomic status, education) who receive only workbook-based interventions.

Workbooks and Manuals

Therapeutic manuals have been trumpeted for years as the solution to the many ills of psychotherapy, to the point that so-called empirically based interventions have become synonymous with manuals. Past and recent controversies about the use of manuals, as already reviewed in Chapter 1, have not solved many issues relating to their applications in psychotherapy. One could argue against their use (L'Abate, 2002). Because of their reliance on face-to-face talk, manuals are helping to maintain the status quo in psychotherapy. Consequently, manuals are destined to be used by a handful of researchers (with grant money), but will not reach the majority of therapists who are not interested in research applications or findings, as argued in

Chapter 1. In brief, manuals (1) leave the burden of responsibility solely on the shoulders of psychotherapists, (2) avoid involvement on the part of respondents in the process of change, (3) are expensive to record, transcribe, and code, and (4) are no more researchable or cost-efficient than psychotherapy without manuals. Workbooks, on the other hand, do not share these disadvantages and should be compared with manuals to see which is more cost-effective and efficient.

Online Administration of Mental Health Workbooks

The costs of treating depression (Rost et al., 1998), let alone anxiety and work performance and procrastination, both on inpatient and outpatient bases, averaged $631 (in 1994 dollars) with an average of about twelve outpatient visits per year. More than 75 percent of the sample used in that study (336 patients) visited a general physician only, whereas 17.2 percent visited both physicians and mental health professionals. About 7 percent visited a mental health practitioner only. The surgeon general's report on mental health (USDHHS, 1999) estimated that one out of five Americans suffered from some kind of mental or emotional disorder. There are not enough mental health practitioners to treat so many handicapped people through face-to-face, verbal psychotherapy. With the seemingly rising rate of major behavioral and mental disorders, it is important to consider cost-effective, mass-oriented, parapreventive, and paratherapeutic methods of treatment for depression and similar disorders, such as anxiety and panic attacks, that reduce the work performance in the general adult population and increase procrastination (Ferrari, Johnson, and McCown, 1995).

Anxiety, depression, work performance, and procrastination disorders are extremely widespread in the general population. Most people suffering from these disorders do not receive treatment, primarily because traditional therapeutic approaches are both time consuming and expensive (USDHHS, 1999). In contrast, computer-assisted, online interventions require only a minimal investment in already available computers. Homework assignments can be appropriately administered automatically and can be monitored by an assistant, without the direct participation of a qualified, supervising clinician. This approach provides significant economic benefits to both clinicians and respondents.

Up to the present, workbooks have been used successfully with undergraduates who admitted to being depressed or anxious, as reviewed in Chapter 2. However, no information exists on whether these workbooks will be effective with a self-referred adult population, outside of an academic setting. The major goal of the proposed research is to determine whether these workbooks are useful in lowering levels of anxiety, depression, and work procrastination when administered online to adults who volunteer for this project on an experimental basis.

The previous arguments support the use of workbooks as additions or as alternatives in preventive, psychotherapeutic, and rehabilitative practices, making them ancillary as well as independent methods of intervention. It would behoove practitioners using them to include informed consent and pre- and postobjective evaluations as standard operating procedures because of still unresolved professional issues facing this approach (Foxhall, 2001; L'Abate, 2002). If it can be demonstrated that workbooks do produce (statistically) significant changes in respondents over time, then the whole approach can and will be added to already existing online therapists who are mimicking the same unstructured approaches used in talk-based psychotherapy.

Through workbooks, online professionals will be able to reach people who may not need psychotherapy but who could use a structured approach that matches specifically their needs. In addition to anxiety, depression, and work performance, whole new populations of potential respondents will be able to receive help online: shut-ins, handicapped, missionary and military couples, rural residents, families, Peace Corps volunteers, etc. Functional and semifunctional people, without a diagnosed condition, who are not in crisis, will be able to use workbooks instead of having to rely on the spoken work to receive help. Through workbooks it will be possible to conduct prevention in a much more cost-effective and mass-oriented fashion than is possible through talk.

Hence, it would be relevant to determine whether workbooks as cost-effective additions or alternatives to face-to-face psychotherapy might decrease levels of anxiety and depression, and improve work performance and procrastination to reach a higher level of adjustment. Respondents may learn positive ways of dealing with these conditions at a distance from professionals.

The purpose of this proposed research is to explore the feasibility and cost-effectiveness of administering online workbooks for treating anxiety, depression, work performance, and procrastination in the general population.

Specific Aims

The purpose of this proposal would be to explore the feasibility and cost-effectiveness of workbooks transmitted on the Internet for treating anxiety, depression, and work performance and procrastination in an adult population. Up to the present, in research reviewed in Chapter 2, workbooks have been used successfully with undergraduates who admitted to being depressed. However, no information is available about whether these workbooks will be effective with a self-referred adult population, outside of an academic setting and online.

This proposal aims at exploring feasibility and cost-effectiveness of workbooks transmitted on the Internet for treating anxiety, depression, and work performance and procrastination in an adult population. These three conditions account for the majority of dysfunctions in the U.S. population (USDHHS, 1999).

The overriding goal of this proposal would be to test the feasibility of administering workbooks for the effective treatment of mental disorders (e.g., anxiety, depression, work performance, and procrastination) through the Internet. Would any reductions in anxiety, depression, and procrastination scores be still present at a six-month follow-up? The impact of workbooks could be assessed by evaluating changes in test scores after completion of retest and on a six-month follow-up.

Research Plan

The design could include three experimental groups (anxiety, depression, and work performance), and two control groups, one on a waiting list, without any intervention, and the other writing about neutral, innocuous subjects (cars, clothes, houses, hang-outs, etc.). Both control groups will be given the option to choose one of the three workbooks used by the experimental groups after completing and fulfilling their control functions.

Analysis of variance (ANOVA) and analysis of covariance (ANCOVA) could be used to evaluate whether mean change scores in the three experimental groups will be significantly greater that those of the two control groups. In addition, correlation coefficients among the pre-post measures of anxiety, depression, and work performance, as well as personality propensities, self-criticism and overdependency would allow to find whether workbooks performance in change scores is related to any of these independent variables. It would be important to determine what factors in the historical background of respondents will relate to their scores on pre- and post measures, and whether they predict workbook improvements or not.

Participation in the study would be recruited on a strictly voluntary basis—informed consent would be required of all participants before being allowed to complete the evaluation/screening battery. They will be admitted to either the experimental group with a workbook of their choice or one of the two control groups. Participants will undergo an extensive evaluation battery, described earlier, to ensure that they are not suffering from extreme, clinical conditions requiring medical and psychiatric treatment. Extreme cases would be informed that they do not quality for this study and will be referred to appropriate treatment settings.

Potential Risks and Dangers

Although some potential risks are associated with distance and programmed writing (Fenichel et al., 2002; Foxhall, 2001; L'Abate, 2002; Leslie, 2002; Occhetti, 2002), definite steps need to be taken to minimize these risks. Respondents at risk for psychological harm are primarily those who suffer from panic attacks, those with serious medical problems, such as heart disease or epilepsy, and those who are (or have recently been) taking drugs with major physiological or psychological efficacy. As delineated earlier, the screening process is designed to exclude persons with these characteristics from the project. In case of significant physical or psychological distress, both respondents and monitoring experimenters should have the ability to terminate quickly any writing sessions. Given these safeguards, and the fact that only one respondent reported being extremely depressed in twenty-five years of previous research (despite the use of less stringent screening procedures), we understand that in dealing with the general public and disturbed individuals, definite problems will arise.

CONCLUSION

Consequently, the usefulness of workbooks for large-scale, mass-oriented, cost-effective purposes needs to be explored further. Up to the present, empirical efforts have been oriented toward demonstrating the usefulness of workbooks with undergraduates. They can now be used to help people at risk for possible breakdown and in need of preventive or paratherapeutic assistance. It is questionable at this time whether and how workbooks can be used in helping people in crisis. However, the incredulous question of whether we can help people at a distance can be laid to rest. People indeed can be helped at a distance, provided we use responsible and sensitive safeguards and guidelines, such as informed consent, stringent evaluation and screening, and professional availability if and when crises develop. Studies and research summarized in this book and proposed in this chapter support the use of workbooks with nonclinical and clinical populations offline and online.

REFERENCES

Ainsworth, M. (2002). My life as an e-patient. In R. C. Hsiung (Ed.), *E-therapy: Case studies, guiding principles, and the clinical potential of the Internet* (pp. 194-215). New York: Norton.

Blair, R. (2001). Psychotherapy online. *Health Management Technology, 22,* 24-27.

Borbely, K., Balogh, A., Donauer, N., and Nyary, I. (1999). Speech activation SPECT measurements in the determination of hemispheric dominance. *Orszagos Idegsebeszeti Tudomanyos, Intezet, 140,* 2805-2809.

Borod, J. C. (2000). *The neuropsychology of emotions.* New York: Oxford University Press.

Dalgleish, T. and Power, M. (1999). *Handbook of cognition and emotion.* Chichester, UK: Wiley.

De Giacomo, P. and DeNigris, S. (2001). Computer workbooks in psychotherapy with psychiatric patients. In L. L'Abate (Ed.), *Distance writing and computer-assisted interventions in psychiatry and mental health* (pp. 114-132). Westport, CT: Ablex.

Derrig-Palumbo, K. (2002). Online therapy: The marriage between technology and a healing art. *Family Therapy Magazine* (September/October), 20-23.

Esterling, B. A., L'Abate, L., Murray, E., and Pennebaker, J. M. (1999). Empirical foundations for writing in prevention and psychotherapy: Mental and physical outcomes. *Clinical Psychology Review, 19,* 79-96.

Felitti, V. J., Anda, R. F., Nordenberg, D., Williamson, D. F., Spitz, A. M., Edwards, V., Koss, M. P., and Marks, J. S. (1998). Relationship of childhood abuse and household dysfunction to many of the leading causes of death in adults: The Adverse Childhood Experiences (ACE) study. *American Journal of Preventive Medicine, 14,* 245-258.

Fenichel, M., Suler, J., Barak, A., Zelvin, E., Jones, G., Munro, K., Meunier, V., and Walker-Schmucker, W. (2002). Myths and realities of online clinical work. *CyberPsychology and Behavior, 5,* 481-497.

Ferrari, J. R., Johnson, J. L., and McCown, W. G. (1995). *Procrastinaton and task avoidance: Theory, research, and treatment.* New York: Plenum.

Finfgeld, D. L. (1999). Psychotherapy in cyberspace. *Journal of the American Psychiatric Nurses Association, 5,* 105-110.

Foxhall, K. (2001). HIPAA rules begin to take shape. *Monitor on Psychology* (July/August), 40-42.

Gould, R. L. (2001). A feedback-driven computer program for outpatient training. In L. L'Abate (Ed.), *Distance writing and computer-assisted interventions in psychiatry and mental health* (pp. 93-111). Westport, CT: Ablex.

Grabowski, J. (1996). Writing and speaking: Common grounds and differences toward a regulation theory of writing language production. In C. M. Levy and S. Randsdell (Eds.), *The science of writing: Theories, methods, individual differences, and applications* (pp. 73-91). Mahwah, NJ: Earlbaum.

Greenfield, S. (2000). *The private life of the brain: Emotions, consciousness, and the secret of the self.* New York: Wiley.

Greist, J. H., Osgood-Hynes, D. J., Baer, L., and Marks, I. M. (2000). Technology-based advances in the management of depression: Focus on the COPE program. *Disease Management and Health Outcomes, 7,* 193-200.

Hayes, J. R. (1996). A new framework for understanding cognition and affect in writing. In C. M. Levy and S. Randsdell (Eds.), *The science of writing: Theories, methods, individual differences, and applications* (pp. 1-27). Mahwah, NJ: Earlbaum.

Hayes, J. R. and Nash, J. G. (1996). On the nature of planning in writing. In C. M. Levy and S. Randsdell (Eds.), *The science of writing: Theories, methods, individual differences, and applications* (pp. 29-55). Mahwah, NJ: LEA.

Helprin, M. (1991). *A soldier of the great war.* New York: Harcourt and Brace.

Hsiung, R. C. (Ed.) (2002). *E-therapy: Case studies, guiding principles, and the clinical potential of the Internet.* New York: Norton.

Iaccino, J. F. (1993). *Left-brain right-brain differences: Inquiries, evidence, and new approaches.* Mahwah, NJ: Earlbaum.

Jacobs, M. K., Christensen, A., Snibbe, J. R., Dolezal-Wood, S., Huber, A., and Polterok, A. (2001). A comparison of computer-based versus traditional individual psychotherapy. *Professional Psychology: Research and Practice, 32,* 92-96.

Jordan, K. B. (2001). Teaching psychotherapy through workbooks. In L. L'Abate (Ed.), *Distance writing and computer-assisted interventions in psychiatry and mental health* (pp. 171-190). Westport, CT: Ablex.

Kolb, B. and Whishaw, I. Q. (1985). *Fundamentals of human neuropsychology.* New York: Freeman.

L'Abate, L. (1976). *Understanding and helping the individual in the family.* New York: Grune & Stratton.

L'Abate, L. (1996). Workbooks for better living. Available at <www.mentalhealthhelp.com>.

L'Abate, L. (1997). The paradox of change: Better them than us! In R. S. Sauber (Ed.), *Managed mental health care: Major diagnostic and treatment approaches* (pp. 40-66). Bristol, PA: Brunner/Mazel.

L'Abate, L. (Ed.) (2001). *Distance writing and computer-assisted interventions in psychiatry and mental health.* Westport, CT: Ablex.

L'Abate, L. (2004). *A guide to self-help workbooks for clinicians and researchers.* Binghamton, NY: The Haworth Press.

L'Abate, L. (in press). *Personality in intimate relationships: Socialization and psychopathology.* New York: Kluwer Academic.

L'Abate, L. and De Giacomo, P. (2003). *Intimate relationships and how to improve them: Integrating theoretical models with preventive and psychotherapeutic applications.* Westport, CT: Praeger.

L'Abate, L., L'Abate, B. L., and Maino, E. (2003). Reviewing 25 years of professional practice: Written homework assignments and length of therapy. Manuscript submitted for publication.

Lange, A., Schrieken, B., van de Ven, J-P, Bredeweg, B., and Emmelkamp, P. M. G. (2000). "Interapy": The effects of a short protocolled treatment of post-traumatic stress and pathological grief through the Internet. *Behavior and Cognitive Psychology, 28,* 175-192.

Lenneberg, E. H. (1967). Biological foundations of language. New York: Wiley.

Lepore, S. J. and Smyth, J. M. (Eds.) (2002). *The writing cure: How expressive writing promotes health and emotional well-being.* Washington, DC: American Psychological Association.

Leslie, R. S. (2002). Practicing therapy via the Internet: The legal view. *Family Therapy Magazine, 1,* 39-41.

Levy, C. M. and Ransdell, S. (Eds.) (1996). *The science of writing: Theories, methods, individual differences, and applications.* Mahwah, NJ: Earlbaum.

Lopez, J. F., Vazquez, D. M., Chalmer, D. T., and Watson, S. J. (1997). Regulation of 5-HT receptors and the hypothalamic-pituitary-adrenal axis: Implications for the neurobiology of suicide. *Annals of the New York Academy of Sciences, 836:* 106-134.

Mahrer, A. R. (2000). What is the next big revolution in the field of psychotherapy? *Psychotherapy, 37,* 254-358.

Manhal-Baugus, M. (2001). E-therapy: Practical, ethical, and legal issues. *Cyberpsychology and Behavior, 4,* 551-563.

McCarty, D. and Clancy, C. (2002). Telehealth: Implications for social work practice. *Social Work, 47,* 153-162.

McMahan, O. and L'Abate, L. (2001) Programmed distance writing with seminarian couples. In L. L'Abate (Ed.), *Distance writing and computer-assisted interventions in psychiatry and mental heath* (pp. 137-156). Westport, CT: Ablex.

Meador, K. J., Loring, D. W., Lee, K., Hughes, M., Lee, G., Nichols, M., and Heilman, K. M. (1999). Cerebral lateralization: Relationship of language and ideomotor praxis. *Neurology, 53,* 2028-2031.

Merkle, E. R. and Richardson, R. A. (2000). Digital dating and virtual relating: Conceptualizing computer-mediated romantic relationships. *Family Relations, 49,* 187-192.

Nickelson, D. W. (1998). Telehealth and the evolving health care system: Strategic opportunities for professional psychology. *Professional Psychology: Research and Practice, 29,* 527-535.

Norcross, J. C. (2000). Here comes the self-help revolution in mental health. *Psychotherapy, 37,* 370-377.

Occhetti, D. R. (2002). E-communication: The pros and cons. *Family Therapy Magazine, 1,* 28-31.

Ornstein, R. (1997). *The right mind: Making sense of the hemisphere.* New York: Harcourt and Brace.

Pennebaker, J. M. (1997). *Opening up: The healing power of expressing emotions.* New York: Guilford.

Pennebaker, J. M. (2001). Explorations into the health benefits of disclosure: Inhibitory, cognitive, and social processes. In L. L'Abate (Ed.), *Distance writing and computer-assisted interventions in psychiatry and mental health* (pp. 34-44). Westport, CT: Ablex.

Power, M. and Dalgleish, T. (1997). *Cognition and emotion: From order to disorder.* East Sussex, UK: Psychology Press.

Rapp, B. C. and Caramazza, A. (1995). Disorders of lexical processing and the lexicon. In M. S. Gazzaniga (Ed.), *The cognitive neurosciences* (pp. 901-911). Cambridge, MA: MIT Press.

Reed, R., McMahan, O., and L'Abate, L. (2001). Workbooks and psychotherapy with incarcerated felons: Research in progress. In L. L'Abate (Ed.), *Distance writing and computer-assisted interventions in psychiatry and mental health* (pp. 157-167). Westport, CT: Ablex.

Rost, K., Zhong, M., Fortney, M., Smith, J., and Smith, G. R. (1998). The cost of treating depression. *American Journal of Psychiatry, 155,* 883-888.

Sadoski, M. and Paivio, A. (2001). *Imagery and text: A dual coding theory of reading and writing.* Mahwah, NJ: LEA.

Schore, A. N. (2003). *Affect dysregulation and disorders of the self.* New York: W. W. Norton.

Sharp, L. K. (1988). Inhibition, hemispheric symmetry in frontal and parietal lobes. Master Thesis, Southern Methodist University, Dallas, Texas.

Suler, J. (2001). Assessing personal suitability for online therapy: The ISMHO clinical case study group. *Cyberpsychology and Behavior, 4,* 675-679.

U. S. Department of Health and Human Services (USDHHS) (1999). *Mental health: A report of the surgeon general.* Rockville, MD: National Institute of Mental Health.

Wang, Y. (1996). Relations between the sides of linguistic cerebral dominance and manuality in Chinese aphasics. *Chinese Medicine, 109,* 572-575.

Appendix

Survey Questionnaire:
Participant Satisfaction with Workbooks

Dear Participant:

This questionnaire is sent to you because you have answered homework assignments (handouts, lessons, or exercises) administered to you in a self-help workbook. We would like your frank opinion about the usefulness of those assignments. We would like to know whether workbooks in general provide a useful avenue of service delivery in mental health. Your opinion is important to us and we welcome it, guaranteeing complete confidentiality and anonymity. Your answers will be coded and only group norms will be used.

1. Title of workbook (an approximate title will suffice): _____
_____

2. Author of workbook (if known): _____

3. How many assignments did you finish in this workbook? Please check the answer which best reflects your experience:
   a. All of them _____
   b. Most of them _____
   c. Some of them _____
   d. None of them _____
   e. Write the approximate number of assignments to the best of your recollection _____

This questionnaire was developed with the help of Rubin Battino, Mario Cusinato, Dennis Dailey, Lorna Hecker, and Eleonora Maino.

4. How were assignments (handouts, lessons, exercises, homework) from the workbook given to you?
    a. From professional helper(s) at the end of a therapy/counseling/or training session _____
    b. Through the mail _____
    c. Through faxes _____
    d. Through the Internet _____
        ☐ As e-mail messages
        ☐ As attachments to e-mails
    e. Other _____

5. How often were these assignments given to you?
    a. Daily _____
    b. Twice each week _____
    c. Weekly _____
    d. Once every two weeks _____
    e. Once a month _____
    f. As needed _____
    g. Other times (please specify) _____

6. Where did you complete your assignments? Give percentages if necessary:
    a. Always at home _____
    b. Mostly at home _____
    c. In my car _____
    d. In my office _____
    e. In a restaurant _____
    f. Somewhere else _____

7. How helpful was this workbook in your recovery from whatever concern distressed you initially?
    a. Very helpful _____
    b. Helpful _____
    c. Somewhat helpful _____
    d. Not helpful at all _____

8. How much helpful information did you learn about your concerns/difficulties or problem(s) from using this workbook? Please check which answer applies best to you:
    a. A great deal _____
    b. A lot _____

    c. Some _____
    d. None _____

9. How helpful was this workbook in learning coping strategies in dealing with your concern(s)?
    a. Very helpful _____
    b. Helpful _____
    c. Somewhat helpful _____
    d. Not helpful at all _____

10. Whether it was useful or not, tell us why you answered the way you just did. Your specific comments would be helpful to us. _____

_____
_____
_____
_____
_____
_____

11. How much did this workbook contribute to your well-being and welfare? On a scale from 0 to 100 percent, circle the percentage of how much this workbook contributed to your well-being. (0 = not at all; 100 = a great deal):

    0 10 20 30 40 50 60 70 80 90 100

12. The following question may be difficult to answer. In comparison to other help or treatments, how much of your well-being was due to using assignments in the workbook and how much was due to other interventions? Please, give us your best estimate. Write in percentages of how much the professional help you received affected your well-being. Your answers in this part, together with the percentage circled above, should total 100 percent.
    a. _____ Crisis intervention: This is help given during or immediately after a breakdown or crisis. It means seeing a mental health professional for just a few face-to-face sessions.
    b. _____ Prevention: This type of help takes place to *avoid* breakdowns and crisis, as well as more serious and expensive interventions. Frequently, it takes place in groups of individuals, couples, or families.
    c. _____ Psychotherapy: This type of help means talking with a professional face-to-face for one or more sessions. Circle which type(s) of help applies to you:

☐ Individual
☐ Couple
☐ Family
☐ Group

d. _____ Rehabilitation: This intervention usually takes place after hospitalization or incarceration.

e. _____ Medication

f. _____ Hospitalization

g. _____ Incarceration

h. _____ Any other intervention? Please describe in your own words:_____

_____

_____

_____

_____

_____

Total = Answers in this part and part 11 equal 100 percent

13. We are interested in your open and frank opinions about the use of workbooks in the delivery of mental health or substance abuse services. Please tell us what you think and feel about them as an alternative or additional way to help people at risk, in need, or in distress: _____

_____

_____

_____

_____

_____

_____

_____

_____

_____

14. To understand fully the effect the workbook has had on your well-being, general demographic information is needed. Again, rest assured that this information cannot and will not be traced back to you and that complete anonymity is guaranteed.

a. Age: _____

b. Gender: F _____ M _____

c. Marital Status: Single _____ Married _____ Divorced _____
Separated _____ Widowed _____ Living with partner _____

    d. Education: Check the choice that applies to you:
        ☐ Below high school
        ☐ High school
        ☐ Some college
        ☐ Completed college or equivalent degree
        ☐ Master's degree or equivalent diploma
        ☐ Doctorate or equivalent diploma
        ☐ Postgraduate specialization
    e. What *types* of concern(s) were you getting help for (for example, mood, anxiety, eating, substance abuse disorder, marital or family problem, etc.)? Please describe briefly these concern(s) in your own words:_____

_____

_____

_____

_____

    f. In what setting did the treatment take place? (For example, private professional office, public mental health clinic, inpatient, outpatient, hospital, substance abuse center, partial hospitalization, jail):

_____

_____

15. Feel free to share/write any additional comments:_____

_____

_____

_____

_____

_____

_____

_____

_____

_____

_____

Please mail back the completed questionnaire in the enclosed addressed and stamped envelope.

Thank you very much for your help!

Index

3SI (stage-specific schema inventory), 132-133
3SWB. *See* Stage-specific schema workbook

AAQ (Adult Attachment Questionnaire), 228
Abuse. *See Healing the Trauma of Abuse: A Women's Workbook*
Acceptance, defined, 256
ACES (Adverse Childhood Experiences Study), 357-358
Adams, B. N., 223
Addiction Severity Index-F (ASI-F), 199
Addictions
  alcohol, 160, 164
  drugs. *See* Drug abuse
  gambling. *See* Gambling
  smoking, 165
Administration
  effectiveness of distance writing versus talking, 32-33
  evaluation and informed consent, 50-51
  Healing the Trauma of Abuse: A Women's Workbook, 146-147
  matching evaluation with interventions, 32
  online workbooks, 366-369
  overview, 31-32
  stage-specific schema workbook, 131-132
Adson, D. E., 301
Adult Attachment Questionnaire (AAQ), 228
Advantages of workbooks
  cost-effectiveness, 44-45
  overview, 39, 40

Advantages of workbooks *(continued)*
  specificity, explicitness, and interactivity, 39-42
  verifiability, 45
  versatility, 40, 42-44
Adverse Childhood Experiences Study (ACES), 357-358
After the Affair, 261
After the Fight: Using Your Disagreements to Build a Stronger Relationship, 252-253
After the Honeymoon: How Conflict Can Improve Your Relationship, 252-253
Aggression Questionnaire, 208
Agras, W. S., 313, 315-316
Ainsworth, M., 355-356
Al-Banna, M., 318
Alcohol abuse, 160, 164
Allen, A., 96
Alpert, J. L., 20
Alternative psychotherapy, 11
Alvarez, Krisann M., 283
Alzheimer Society of Edmonton (ASE), 114
American Association for Marriage and Family Therapy, 17
American Psychological Association, 71, 199
Amundsen, M. J., 49
AN. *See* Anorexia nervosa
Analysis of covariance (ANCOVA)
  online versus no intervention, 368-369
  SWHA research, 81, 87, 88, 90
Analysis of variance (ANOVA)
  breakup scale, 274-275
  handicapped child research, 333
  intimacy in couples, 270, 272, 276

Analysis of variance (ANOVA)
      (continued)
   online versus no intervention,
      368-369
   SWHA research, 79, 80-81, 83
   Wheel of Wisdom, 178-179, 184
ANCOVA. See Analysis of covariance
Anda, R. F., 357
Anderson, C. W., 10
Andolfi, M., 265
Anecdotal evidence to support
      workbooks, 49
Anger Inventory, 208
Anorexia nervosa (AN). See also
      Eating disorders
   overview, 301
   workbooks and related research,
      302, 313-314
ANOVA. See Analysis of variance
Anxiety
   online workbook administration,
      366-367
   SWHA research, 86-87
Apple, R. F., 316
Arendorf, A., 49
Arguing and fighting program, 37-38
Arias, John, 205
Arledge, Ellen, 141
Arnow, B., 315-316
Asay, T. P., 3, 4
ASE (Alzheimer Society of Edmonton),
      114
ASI-F (Addiction Severity Index-F),
      199
Assessment
   eating disorders self-assessment,
      307
   gambling self-assessment, 165
   marriage preparation and
      maintenance, 239-240
   marriage self-assessment, 235-236
   Personality Assessment Inventory,
      37, 70
   School Refusal Assessment Scale,
      285, 293-294
AT (autogenic training), 15, 19-20
Autogenic training (AT), 15, 19-20
Automatic Thoughts Questionnaire,
      208

Bacon, Roger, 25
Baer, L., 351-352
Bakke, B., 320-321
Bari University Hospital, Wheel of
      Wisdom, 173, 176. See also
      Wheel of Wisdom
Barlow, D. H., 12, 35, 36
Barnett, J. E., 267
Barsfield, Joselyn Y., 141
Bartlett method, 179
Basic Personality Inventory (BPI), 105
Battered women, 261
Battino, Rubin, 115, 116
Baucom, D. H., 249
BDI. See Beck Depression Inventory
Beal, W. E., 206
Beck, A. T., 191, 194
Beck Anxiety and Depression
      Inventories, 69-70
Beck Depression Inventory (BDI)
   SWHA research, 84-87, 89-90
   use in bridging the semantic gap, 74
   workbook development, 36
   workbook series, 37
Beck test, 179-180, 182, 184-185
Beckham, E., 249
BED. See Binge-eating disorder
Behavioral couples therapy, 251
Behavioral exchange exercises, 248
Beliefs, assignment from 3SWB,
      135-138
Bergamo Family Support Center, 266,
      269
Bergin, A. E., 146
Big Five Factors model, 70
Binge-eating disorder (BED). See also
      Eating disorders
   overview, 301
   workbooks and related research,
      307-313, 315-319
Bipolar disorder, 176, 187. See also
      Depression
Bird, G., 87-88, 91
Blanck, G., 267
Blanck, R., 267
Blatt, S. J., 88-90, 96
Blumberg, S. L., 255-256
BN. See Bulimia nervosa
Body awareness and abuse, 144
Bohart, A. C., 94

Boscolo, L., 328
Bowlby, J., 328
Bowyer, Carol, 313-314
BPI (Basic Personality Inventory), 105
Brain, hemispheric dominance, 359-362
Bredeweg, B., 358
Brief Couples Therapy Homework Planner, 253-254
Brief Psychiatric Rating Scale, 70
Broca's area, 359, 361
Broodiness and depression, 110, 113
Bruce, B., 315-316
Building a Strong Marriage Workbook, 221
Bulimia nervosa (BN). *See also* Eating disorders
  overview, 301
  workbooks and related research, 307-313, 315-319
Burns, J. A., 49
Bynum, J., 146
Byrne, E. A., 329

CAI. *See* Computer-assisted interventions
Calhoon, S., 146
Caramazza, A., 361
Caregivers
  implications and conclusions, 127
  survey results, 125
  workbook, 120-123
Carrieri, Giovanni, 173
Carroll, K. M., 191, 192
Carter, J., 312
Case studies
  bias, 49
  intimacy with handicapped children, 336-337, 339-340, 342-343
  life-challenging conditions, 126
  school-refusal behavior, 294-298
Cash, T., 321
Cassirer, E., 24-25
Cautela, J. R., 17
CBRS (Communication Behaviors Rating Scale), 77
CBT. *See* Cognitive-behavioral therapy
Cecchin, G. F., 328

Center for Epidemiological Studies-Depression scale (CES-D), 84-87, 89-90
CES-D (Center for Epidemiological Studies-Depression scale), 84-87, 89-90
Change loop, 44
Charlie Brown Exceptional Patient Support Group, 115
Chevron, E. S., 88-90, 96
Chi-square analysis
  substance abuse in women, 198
  SWHA research, 80
The Choice to Love workbook, 228
Chorpita, B. F., 49
Christensen, Andrew, 247, 256-257
Cigoli, V., 224, 267
Circular intervention, 79
CIS. *See* Couple Intimacy Scales
Clark, D., 77-78
Classifications
  workbook, 35-38
  writing, 33-35
Clients Satisfaction Survey, 135
Clinical experience, in development of workbooks, 69
Clinical practice versus research, 21-27
Clinical trials
  eating disorders, 301
  gambling, 166-170
CNS (Couple Negotiation Scales), 232
Cochrane Review clinical trial results, 159
Cogan's syndrome, 342
Cognitive restructuring, 289
Cognitive-behavioral therapy (CBT)
  for couples, 251
  eating disorders, 308
  homework, 29
  manualized. *See* Manualized cognitive-behavioral protocol
  stage-specific schema workbook, 133-134
  systematically written homework assignments, 66
Coker, S., 310
Comedies, way of thinking, 175
Communication
  clinical practice versus research, 24
  A Couple's Guide to Communication, 254-255

Communication *(continued)*
  gap, 72
  school-refusal behavior, 292
  talking problems and status of
    mental health needs, 8
Communication Behaviors Rating
    Scale (CBRS), 77
Communication Reaction Form (CRF),
    79, 80-83
Community Connections
  clients' comments on workbooks,
    147-150
  prison groups, 156
  tertiary prevention, 154
  use of *Healing the Trauma of
    Abuse: A Women's Workbook,*
    142, 146
Comorbid conditions, 43
Comparative testing, 35-36
Complex writing, 361
Computer-assisted interventions (CAI)
  criteria, 15
  evidence to support workbooks,
    49-50
  future delivery of services, 65
  improvements with time, 44
Computers. *See also* Internet
  combination with distance writing,
    6-7
  openness of participants, 351-352
  The Tape of the Mind program, 177
  treatment for criminals, 27-28
  vehicle of service delivery, 4, 5-6
Confidentiality, 22, 46, 354
Conjugal identity, 217-218
Contingency contract, 291-292
Cooper, P. J., 309-311
Coping Resources Inventory for Stress
    (CRIS), 87-88
Coping skills, SWHA research, 87-88
Copyright material for workbooks,
    70-72
Cornelia de Lange syndrome, 332
Costello's syndrome, 340
Costs
  3SWB, 135
  CAI cost-effectiveness, 18
  distance writing versus talking, 33
  effectiveness of workbooks, 40, 365
  efficiency of workbooks, 354

Costs *(continued)*
  formalization options, 19
  HCFA funding, 353
  Internet workbooks, 44-45
  managed care. *See* Managed care
  mental illness in the United States,
    352
  programmed distance writing, 135
  programmed distance writing versus
    talking, 356-357
  psychotherapy, 156
  workbooks versus health care,
    353-354
  writing interventions with felons,
    205-206
Counseling, defined, 330
Counseling versus psychotherapy,
    330-331
Couple Intimacy Scales (CIS)
  couples with handicapped children,
    333, 334, 335, 337-341
  marriage preparation and
    maintenance, 232
  workbook evaluation, 270, 272, 273,
    275-276
Couple Negotiation Scales (CNS), 232
Couple Social Desirability Scale, 270
A Couple's Guide to Communication,
    254-255
Couples therapy
  American Association for Marriage
    and Family Therapy, 17
  arguing and fighting program, 37-38
  clinical issues, 248-250
  defining homework, 247-248
  early intervention, 266-268
  history, 10
  homework resistance, 249-250
  iatrogenic effects, 249
  intimacy. *See* Intimacy in couples
  metafunctions of workbooks, 46
  research basis of homework,
    250-251
  special considerations, 261
  SWHA research, 75-84, 90-91
  workbooks listing, 251-260
Craske, M. G., 35
Creating life changes, healing from
    abuse, 145-146
Creation of workbooks, 65-68

CRF (Communication Reaction Form), 79, 80-83
Criminals. *See* Felons
CRIS (Coping Resources Inventory for Stress), 87-88
Crisis intervention, 130
Crisp, A. H., 313-314
Crosby, R., 318
Crosley, R., 318
Crow, S., 301
Crying and depression, 110
Cunningham, C. C., 329
Cusinato, Mario, 217, 272, 334

Dangers of distance and programmed writing, 39, 41, 46-47, 369
DAS (Dyadic Adjustment Scale), 16, 83-84
Dattilio, F. M., 29, 248, 250
Day, J. P., 26
De Giacomo, Andrea, 173
De Giacomo, Piero, 173
Deacon, S. A., 17
Deane, F. P., 11
Dementia and depression, 109, 113-114
Demonstrative versus dialectic methods, 23
Denton, W., 219
Depression
    online workbook administration, 366-367
    personal assignments, 109-113
    personal odyssey, 106-114
    subthreshold, 51
    survey of patients, 72
    SWHA research, 84-87, 88-90, 96
    symptoms, 109-111
    Wheel of Wisdom. *See* Wheel of Wisdom
    workbooks for, 41
Depression Experiences Questionnaire (DEQ), 89-90
DEQ (Depression Experiences Questionnaire), 89-90
Derivative works, 71
Descartes, René, 25
Development of workbooks, 65-68
Dewey, J., 26

Diagnostic Statistical Manual of Mental Disorders, Fourth Edition (DSM-IV)
    gamblers, 160
    substance abuse in women, 197, 199
    SWHA research, 84-85
    workbook source of information, 69
Diagnostic Statistical Manual of Mental Disorders, Third Edition (DSM-III-R), 86-87
Dialectic versus demonstrative methods, 23
Didactic strategies, 220-222
Dies, R. R., 50-51
DiMatteo, M. R., 50
Dineen, T., 9, 11
Disability. *See* Handicapped children
Disadvantages of workbooks, 39, 41, 46-47
Discovery versus justification, 21-22
Disruptive technology, 11
Dissuasions, 164
Distance writing (DW)
    combination with computers and Internet, 6-7
    future delivery of services, 65
    history, 66
    openness of participants, 351
    purpose, 4
    reconciliation of practitioners and researchers, 26-27
    reluctance of use, 11
Documentation of treatment plans, 43
Dodge, E., 308-309
Dohm, F., 311
Donkervoet, J. C., 49
Dreams for the future, way of thinking, 176, 187
Druckman, J. M., 232
Drug abuse
    gamblers and, 160
    treatment for women. *See* Manualized cognitive-behavioral protocol
DSM-III-R (*Diagnostic Statistical Manual of Mental Disorders,* Third Edition), 86-87
DSM-IV. *See Diagnostic Statistical Manual of Mental Disorders,* Fourth Edition

DW. *See* Distance writing
Dyadic Adjustment Scale (DAS), 16,
    83-84
Dyadic homework for couples, 248-249

Eating disorders
    anorexia nervosa, 301, 302, 313-314
    bulimia workbooks and related
        research, 307-313, 315-319
    conclusions, 319-321
    overview, 301-302
    research, 304-306
    self-help workbooks, 302
    workbooks and related research,
        307-319
    writing assignment topics, 303
Eckert, E. D., 318
EDS (Environmental Deprivation
    Scale), 206
Educational counseling
    marriage preparation and
        maintenance, 220, 232-239
    psychoeducational counseling,
        329-332
Edwards, V., 357
EEG (electroencephalogram), 361-362
Effect sizes, 80, 90
Effectiveness of workbooks, 50, 92-93
Efficacy of psychotherapy, 10
Eisenberg, M., 206
Eisman, E. J., 50-51
Eisner, D. A., 9
Electroencephalogram (EEG), 361-362
Electronic therapy, 354. *See also*
        Internet
Ellis, A., 191, 194
EMDR (eye movement desensitization
    and reprogramming), 15,
    19-20
Emmelkamp, P. M. G., 358
Emotionality
    of felons, 206-208, 212
    rationality versus, 24
Emotion-focused therapy for couples,
    251
Empirical knowledge, 70
Empirically supported treatments
    (ESTs), 28

Empowerment for trauma recovery,
    142, 143-144
Engbloom, S., 319
ENRICH inventory, 221, 227, 231, 232
Enrichment programs
    marriage, 220
    SWHA couples research, 76-80
    SWHA research, 75
    workbook source of information, 67
Environmental Deprivation Scale
    (EDS), 206
Epidemiological implications of
    workbooks, 357-359
Erickson, R., 320-321
Erikson, E., 129-130
Esonis, S., 17
Esterling, B. A., 68, 86
ESTs (empirically supported
    treatments), 28
Ethical standards for workbook
    information, 71
Eugenio Medea, 328
Evaluation
    comparisons of workbooks, 50
    formalization, 16-17
    matching with interventions, 32
    pre- and posttreatment outcomes,
        49-50
    qualitative versus quantitative, 23
    SWHAs, 93
    workbook administration, 50-51
Evidence
    clinical practice versus research, 23
    support for workbooks, 49
Experiential techniques, 221
Explicitness, 39-41
Expressive writing, 363-364
Externalization, 8, 95, 283
Eyde, L. D., 50-51
Eye movement desensitization and
        reprogramming (EMDR), 15,
        19-20

Fair use laws, 71
Fairbairn, W. R. D., 328
Fairburn, C., 309, 311, 312, 313, 315
Family Emotion Scale (FES), 228
Family Environment Scale, 16

Family Information Rating Scale (FIRS), 77
Family therapy
American Association for Marriage and Family Therapy, 17
history, 10
marriage, 220. *See also* Marriage preparation and maintenance
metafunctions of workbooks, 46
school-refusal behavior, 291-292
workbooks, 38
Fara, Donatella, 327
Feedback loop, 7, 44, 45-46
Felitti, V. J., 357
Felons
benefits of writing interventions, 205-206
combination psychotherapy and social training workbook, 91
distance writing treatment, 27-28
emotionality and, 206-208, 212
impulse control prevention program, 105
measures of affect and cognition, 209-210
programmed distance writing, 205, 211-212
rehabilitation using programmed distance writing, 208-211
women's trauma groups, 156
FES (Family Emotion Scale), 228
Fighting for Your Marriage: Positive Steps for Preventing Divorce and Preserving a Lasting Love, 255-256
Finley, J. R., 18
Finn, S. E., 50-51
FIRS (Family Information Rating Scale), 77
Five-factor personality model, 37, 70
Five-year family life and training recollection, 238
Flanagan, T. J., 28
Fleming, C., 310
Fletcher, L., 318
Floor Exercise, 259-260
Flowcharts
falling in love to staying in love, 225
premarriage workbook, 230

For Yourself: The Fulfillment of Female Sexuality, 261
Form, *Webster's* definition, 13-14
Formal, *Webster's* definition, 13-14
Formalization of psychological interventions
defined, 13-14
evaluation, 16-17
implications of trends, 19-21
manuals, 17
overview, 12-16
planners, 18
SCAI Internet applications, 15, 18-19
Forms Book, 17
Fostering factors, 224
Fournier, D. G., 222, 232
FPR (Marriage Preparation), 227, 229, 231, 239, 240
Frankl, Viktor, 115
Freeman, A., 29, 129, 130
Fusco, G., 29
Future of workbooks
epidemiological implications, 357-359
group design, 362-363
hemispheric dominance, 359-362
overview, 351-354
psychotherapy and workbook-based interventions, 365-369
research agenda, 359-365
single-subject design, 363-364
unstructured versus structured interventions, 354-355

GA (Gamblers Anonymous), 159, 160, 167
Gaes, G. G., 28
Galileo, 25
Gallope, R. H., 79
Gamblers Anonymous (GA), 159, 160, 167
Gambling
background of recovery, 160-161
clinical trial, 166-170
natural versus treatment-assisted recovery, 161-162
overview, 159, 170
self-help workbooks, 164-165

Gambling *(continued)*
    stepped care model, 162-164
    workbook contents, 165
Ganahl, G. F., 80-83, 96
Garthe, R., 308, 310-311
Garvin, V., 311
Gattis, Krista S., 247
Geographic convenience
    of workbooks, 134
Getting Free, 261
Gilbert, J. S., 312
Glucocorticoid hypersecretion, 358
Goals
    Healing the Trauma of Abuse: A
        Women's Workbook, 143-146
    manualized cognitive-behavioral
        protocol, 192-194
    setting of, 165
Goldstein, Demián F., 129
Goldstein, G. J., 45
Gonso, J., 254-255
Gorman, Everett, 105
Gottman, John, 48, 254-255, 257-258,
    260, 261, 340
Gowers, S., 314
Grave, R., 313
Greist, J. H., 351-352
Grieving
    implications and conclusions, 127
    online treatment, 358
    survey results, 125-126
    workbook, 123-124
Group design, 362-363
Group discussion teaching method, 220
GSC (guided self-change), 308
GSH (guided self-help), 311-313
Guided self-change (GSC), 308
Guided self-help (GSH), 311-313

Halek, C., 313-314
Haley, J., 9-10
Halford, W. K., 249, 250
Hamilton's Anxiety and Depression
    Inventories, 70
Hamilton's Depression Scale, 36
Handicapped children
    background of study, 328
    case studies, 336-337, 339-340,
        342-343

Handicapped children *(continued)*
    discussion and summary, 343-344
    family resources and impact of
        disability, 328-329
    intervention workbook, 334, 336
    overview, 327
    psychoeducational counseling and
        workbooks, 329-332
    research, 332-334
Hanson, K., 318
Hanson, N. R., 26
Hardin, S., 79
Hare's Psychopathic Behavior scale, 70
Harway, Michele, 96
Hatsukami, D., 318
HCFA (Health Care Financing
    Administration), 353
Healing the Trauma of Abuse: A
        Women's Workbook
    administration, 146-147
    client's comments, 147-151
    core assumptions, 142
    development, 141-142
    format, 142
    goals, 143-146
    overview, 141, 156-157
    prevention goals, 153
    restoration of functioning, 155-156
    role in prevention, 151-153
    session structure and content,
        142-143
    tertiary prevention, 153, 154-155
    use in practice, 156
Health Care Financing Administration
    (HCFA), 353
Hecker, Lorna L., 17, 351
Hedges's Unbiased Effect Sizes, 90
Hegel, G., 25-26
Hemispheric dominance, 359-362
Hemispheric functions, hypothetical
    dominance, 24
Heyman, R., 18
Hippocampal function, impact of
    glucocorticoid hypersecretion,
    358
History
    couples therapy, 10
    distance writing, 66
    marriage preparation and
        maintenance, 217-219

History *(continued)*
    psychotherapy, 31-32
    typewriter, 353
    Wheel of Wisdom, 173
Hodgins, David C., 159
Holy Grail of clinical psychology, 16, 32
Homework
    administration through workbooks, 4-5
    defined, 247-248
    resistance, 11, 249-250, 355
Homework-based treatment. *See* Systematically written homework assignments
Hopelessness and depression, 110, 112-113
HPA (hypothalamic-pituitary-adrenal) axis, 358-359
Hudson, P., 258-259
Hughes, J. P., 34
Hyper-criticalness, 89
Hypothalamic-pituitary-adrenal (HPA) axis, 358-359

Iaccino, J. F., 361
Iatrogenic effects of homework, 249
ICF (informed consent form), 46-47, 50-51, 355
ICP (infantile cerebral palsy), 332, 334
Idiographic workbooks, 38, 43, 74
Immaturity for marriage, 224, 226
Impulse control, 105
Incarcerated felons. *See* Felons
Independence in clinical practice, 22-23
Indeterminism, 22
Infantile cerebral palsy (ICP), 332, 334
Informed consent form (ICF), 46-47, 50-51, 355
Insight-oriented psychotherapy (IOP), 194, 199-200, 202
Instrumental tasks, way of thinking, 175-176, 187
Intentional coping mechanism, 146
Interactivity, 39-41
Internalization, 8, 95, 283

Internet. *See also* Computers
    combination with distance writing, 6-7
    confidentiality, 354
    cost-effectiveness of workbooks, 44-45
    posttraumatic treatment, 358
    SCAI applications, 15, 18-19
    vehicle of service delivery, 5-6
    verifiability, 45
    workbook administration, 366-369
    workbook transmission, 354
Interoceptive exposure, 287-288
Interpersonal psychotherapy (IPT), 313
Interventions
    formalization, 12-19
    models, 5
Interviews, structured, 42
Intimacy in couples
    conclusions, 276, 278
    early relationship, 266-268
    with handicapped children. *See* Handicapped children
    intervention research, 268-272
    Not Magical But Mysterious...Our Intimacy workbook, 272-276
    overview, 265-266
    retest, 274-276
IOP (insight-oriented psychotherapy), 194, 199-200, 202
IPT (interpersonal psychotherapy), 313
Irrational Belief Scale, 208
Isomorphic workbooks, 89, 90, 354

Jackson, Y., 10
Jacobson, N. S., 256-257
Jacobson, Neil, 261
Johnson, J. L., 105
Jongsma, A. E. Jr., 18
Joughin, Neil, 313-314
Justification versus discovery, 21-22

Karoly, P., 10
Kay, G. G., 50-51
Kazantzis, N., 4-5, 11
Kearney, Christopher A., 283, 284, 293
Keen, E., 10

Keilen, M., 308-309
Kenardy, J., 316
Kendall, P. C., 29
Khantzian, E. J., 194
Kinneavy, J. L., 25, 34
Knussen, C., 329
Kohut, H., 328
Kolmogorov-Smirnov method, 179
Koran, L. M., 315-316
Koss, M. P., 357
Kraemer, H. C., 313
Kubiszyn, T. W., 50-51
Kuhn, T. S., 26

L'Abate, B. L., 40, 96, 365
L'Abate, Luciano
   administration, 40
   classification of workbooks, 35, 36
   clinical practice versus research, 26
   comparisons of workbooks, 50
   couples intimacy, 267-268, 272
   depression and dementia, 105, 106,
      108, 109, 113
   future of workbooks in mental
      health, 351, 355, 357, 365
   handicapped child, 334
   homework-based treatment, 65-66,
      68, 76-80, 83-87, 89-91, 92,
      94, 96
   inadequate specificity, 9, 10
   life-challenging conditions,
      115-116, 130, 131
   marriage, 221
   role of workbooks, 3, 11, 28
   selfhood model, 89-90
   structured evaluation, 17
   SWHA research, 89
   workbooks for criminals, 208
Laboratory method of evaluation
     and treatment, 66, 68
Labouvie, E., 312
Lambert, M. J., 3, 4, 146
Lambert, R. G., 89
Lampropoulos, G. K., 4-5
Lange, A., 358
Language
   3SWB in English and Spanish, 134
   metalanguage versus, 34

Laws concerning Internet information,
   354
Lecture teaching method, 220
Lenz, B. S., 18
Lepore, S. J., 68, 363
LeShan, L., 116
Lester, G. W., 249
Life-challenging conditions
   caregiver workbooks, 120-123
   case study, 126
   grieving workbooks, 123-124
   implications and conclusions, 127
   overview, 115-116
   patient workbooks, 117-120
   survey results, 124-126
   workbook description, 116-117
Linear intervention, 79
Literature, current workbooks, 27-31
Locke-Wallace Short Marital
     Adjustment Test, 80-83
Lockridge, J., 79
Loeb, K. L., 312
Love Overcomes Any Obstacle
     workbook, 229, 231

Maheu, M., 96
Maino, Eleonora, 40, 96, 265, 327, 365
Maintenance
   gamblers, 165
   marriage. *See* Marriage preparation
     and maintenance
   therapeutic step, 131
Maki, D. D., 301
Managed care
   CAI cost-effectiveness, 18
   reconciliation of practitioners and
     researchers, 26
   required use of manuals, 43
MANOVA, 86, 201
Manualized cognitive-behavioral
     protocol (CBT)
   cognitive-behavioral therapy,
     200-201, 202
   conclusions, 202
   coping with urges to use, 196
   cycle of addiction analysis, 195
   efficacy of workbooks, 194-201
   high-risk coping plan, 197

Manualized cognitive-behavioral
    protocol (CBT) *(continued)*
  insight-oriented psychotherapy, 194,
    199-200, 202
  overview, 191-192
  program description, 192-194
Manuals
  CBT. *See* Manualized cognitive-
    behavioral protocol
  DSM. *See Diagnostic Statistical
    Manual of Mental Disorders*
  formalization of psychological
    intervention, 17
  future of, 365-366
  managed care requirements, 43
  outcomes of psychotherapy, 10
  school-refusal behavior. *See* School-
    refusal behavior
  survey of use, 42-43
Marital Adjustment Test (MAT), 77,
    80-83
Marital Happiness Scale (MHS), 75-76,
    77, 80-83
Marital Issues Questionnaire (MIQ),
    83-84
Marital Progress Sheet (MPS), 75-76,
    79, 80-83
Marital Satisfaction Scale, 238
Marital therapy, SWHA research,
    75-84. *See also* Couples
    therapy
Markman, H., 254-255, 255-256,
    259-260
Marks, I. M., 351-352
Marks, J. S., 357
Marriage
  American Association for Marriage
    and Family Therapy, 17
  intimacy. *See* Intimacy in couples
  MPM. *See* Marriage preparation
    and maintenance
Marriage Preparation (FPR), 227, 229,
    231, 239, 240
Marriage preparation and maintenance
    (MPM)
  conclusions, 239-242
  cultural context, 217-219
  developmental couple relationship
    model, 223-228
  educational process, 232-239

Marriage preparation and maintenance
    (MPM) *(continued)*
  falling in love flowchart, 225
  five-year family life and training
    recollection, 238
  historical context, 217-219
  intervention problems, 219, 222
  intervention programs, 219-220
  maintenance workbooks, 231-232
  motivation for attending programs,
    237-238
  premarriage workbook flowchart,
    230
  preparation workbooks, 228-232
  program methods, 220-223
  welcoming step, 226-228
MAT (Marital Adjustment Test), 77,
    80-83
McClanahan, Terry Michael, 191
McCown, W., 105
McDonald, C., 88-90, 96
McGee, C., 49
McLaughlin, C. J., 96
McMahan, Oliver, 28, 90-91, 205, 357
Meal planning for BN and BED,
    316-318
Medication
  desipramine for binge-eating
    disorder, 316
  fluoxetine for bulimia nervosa,
    318-319
  imipramine for BN and BED,
    317-318
  MAO inhibitors and BN and BED,
    317
  reason for status of mental health
    needs, 8
  scriptotherapy and, 174
  Wheel of Wisdom and, 186
Meichenbaum, D., 191, 194
Mele, Odilia, 173
Memories, way of thinking, 176
Menghi, P., 267
Mental health status in the United
    States, 7-9
Mental health therapy workbooks, 29
Meta-analysis
  gambling interventions, 164
  studies, 50
  workbook effectiveness, 92-93

Metafunctions, 45-46
Metalanguage versus language, 34
Meyer, G. J., 50-51
MHS (Marital Happiness Scale), 75-76, 77, 80-83
Middle-of-the-road intervention, 330, 331
Miklowitz, D. J., 45
Milano group, 67, 79
Milholland, K., 96
Miller, A., 328
Miller, J. P., 319
Miller, Katherine J., 301
Miller, W. R., 307
Minnesota Multiphasic Personality Inventory-2 (MMPI-2)
    measuring felon writers, 207
    SWHA research, 84-87, 91
    workbook series, 37, 38
    workbook source of information, 70
MIQ (Marital Issues Questionnaire), 83-84
Mitchell, Caroline L., 141
Mitchell, J., 301, 318, 319, 320-321
MMPI-2. *See* Minnesota Multiphasic Personality Inventory-2
Modeling teaching method, 220
Molteni, Massimo, 327
Moody, Emily, 141
Moreland, K. L., 50-51
Morelli, P., 49
Morreale, Massimiliano, 173
Motiuk, L. L., 28
MPM. *See* Marriage preparation and maintenance
MPS (Marital Progress Sheet), 75-76, 79, 80-83
Multiple regression analysis, 333-334
Murray, E., 68, 86
Mussell, M. P., 318, 319
Myers-Briggs Inventory, 71
"Mysterious but not magical our intimacy," 334
Myths, 24-25, 42

National Depressive and Manic-Depressive Association, 72
Negative affectivity, school-refusal behavior, 286-288

Negotiation and intimacy workbook research, 83-84
Nelson, Portia, 151-153
NEO (Neuroticism, Extraversion, and Openness) workbooks, 37
Neuropsychiatric Research Institute, 316-319
Neuroticism, Extraversion, and Openness (NEO) workbooks, 37
The New Male Sexuality, 261
Newman, R., 3
Newton, Sir Isaac, 25
NiCarthy, Ginny, 261
Nomothetic workbooks, 38, 43, 73-74
Nonverbal communication
    change in healing methods, 7
    formalization, 13
    SWHAs, 93-94
Nordenberg, D., 357
Norton, K., 314
Not Magical But Mysterious...Our Intimacy workbook, 272-276
Notarius, C., 254-255, 259-260
Nugent, S., 319

Offenders. *See* Felons
O'Hanlon, B., 18, 253-254, 258-259
O'Hanlon, S., 18, 253-254
Okazaki, S., 45
O'Leary, K. D., 18
Olson, A. K., 221
Olson, D. H., 221, 222, 232
Optimistic Attitude Scale, 270, 333
Options for therapy, 20
Orienting Couple Life workbook, 234
Orienting Couples for Life workbook, 229, 231
Ornstein, R., 361
Orthographic versus phonological in cerebral dominance, 361
Osgood-Hynes, D. J., 351-352
Outcomes of psychotherapy
    therapy manuals, 10
    workbooks and, 4-5
Overdependency, 89
Overprotection as abuse, 155-156

PAI (Personality Assessment
Inventory), 37, 70
Paivio, A., 362
Pantheoretical method of
scriptotherapy, 174
Paper-and-pencil self-report, 67, 69-70,
75-76
Parental influence on marriage, 226
Partner Quality Test (PQT), 238, 239,
240
Pasinato, Silvia, 327
Passive recipients of diagnostic label,
73
Password protection, 354
PCI (Primary Communication
Inventory), 77, 80-84
PDAs (personal digital assistants) for
workbook distribution, 359
PDW. *See* Programmed distance
writing
Peer-refusal skills training for school-
refusal behavior, 292
Pennebaker, J. M., 68, 86, 91
Pennebaker, James W., 206, 361
Perfectionists and school-refusal
behavior, 289
Perkinson, R. R., 18
Perl, M., 315-316
Personal Crisis Plan, 155
Personal digital assistants (PDAs) for
workbook distribution, 359
Personal reflection teaching method,
220-221
Personality Assessment Inventory
(PAI), 37, 70
Peterson, C. B., 319
Phonological versus orthographic in
cerebral dominance, 361
PI (programmed instruction), 66
Pierce, C. S., 26
A Plan for the Two of Us workbook,
232
Planners, 18
Plato, 25
Pomeroy, C., 318
Post-traumatic stress disorder (PTSD),
27, 357-359
PQT (Partner Quality Test), 238, 239,
240
Prata, G., 328

PREP (Prevention and Relationship
Enhancement Program), 255,
256
PREPARE/ENRICH Inventories, 221,
227, 231, 232
Preventers, 16-17
Prevention
goals, 153
history of therapy, 32
role of workbooks, 151-153
tertiary, 153, 154-155
use by therapists, 11-12
Prevention and Relationship
Enhancement Program
(PREP), 255, 256
Primary Communication Inventory
(PCI), 77, 80-84
Prisoners. *See* Felons
Privacy, 22, 46, 354
Prochaska, J. O., 29-30, 31
Procrastination disorders, 366-368
Professional implications, SWHAs,
93-96
Professional standards for workbook
information, 70-71
Programmed distance writing (PDW)
classification of workbooks, 37
cost-effectiveness, 356-357
costs, 135
couples therapy, 38
effectiveness of, 355-356
for felons, 205-212
overview, 35
risks and dangers, 369
use with talk, 357
Programmed instruction (PI), 66
Programmed writing, 364
PSH (pure self-help), 308, 311-313
Psychoeducational counseling, 329-332
Psychogram
Couple's Intimacy Scales, 273, 277,
335, 338, 341
relationship stability and social
desirability, 271-272
retest, 275
Psychology industry, 9
Psychopathology, 8
Psychotherapy
counseling versus, 330-331

Psychotherapy *(continued)*
　　future of workbook-based
　　　　interventions, 365-369
　　status of, 9-12
PTSD (post-traumatic stress disorder),
　　27, 357-359
Pure self-help (PSH), 308, 311-313
Purpose of workbooks, 3-4, 52
Pyle, R. L., 318

Quality, community versus agency,
　　23-24
Quesada, Carolina J., 141
Questionnaire, participant satisfaction
　　with workbooks, 375-379
Quinlan, D. M., 88-90, 96

Raeburn, S. D., 315-316
Randomized clinical trials (RCTs), 301
Rapp, B. C., 361
RAQ (Relational Answers
　　Questionnaire), 228
RAS (reticular ascending system), 362
Rating sheets, 67, 69-70
Rationality versus emotionality, 24
RCTs (randomized clinical trials), 301
RDS (reticular discending system), 362
Rea, M., 45
Reaction Inventory, 208
Reconcilable Differences, 256-257
Reed, G. M., 50-51, 96
Reed, R., 28, 91, 357
Relapse prevention, 131
Relational Answers Questionnaire
　　(RAQ), 228
Relationship skills and SWHAs, 94
Reliving traumatic experiences,
　　144-145
Repetition of workbook administration,
　　6
Replicability
　　in research, 23
　　SWHAs, 94-95
Research
　　clinical practice versus, 21-27
　　couples homework, 250-251
　　eating disorders, 304-306, 307-319

Research *(continued)*
　　future of workbooks, 359-365
　　interventions for handicapped
　　　　children, 332-334
　　programmed distance writing for
　　　　felons, 208-211
　　school-refusal behavior, 293-294
　　structured couples interventions,
　　　　268-272
　　SWHAs, 75-92
Resistance to workbooks, 11, 249-250,
　　355
Reticular ascending system (RAS), 362
Reticular discending system (RDS),
　　362
Revised Marital Happiness Scale
　　(RMHS), 75-76, 79, 80-83
Richards, J. M., 206
Risks of distance and programmed
　　writing, 369
RMHS (Revised Marital Happiness
　　Scale), 75-76, 79, 80-83
Roberts, M. C., 10
Rollnick, S., 307
Ronan, K. R., 11
Rosenthal, R., 50
Rossiter, E. M., 315-316
Rupp, David, 69
Ruppell, Howard, 49
Ruskin, B. S., 301
Russell, Gerald, 307
Rychlak, J. F., 26

Sadoski, M., 362
Safety valve in couples therapy, 249
Satcher, D., 7-8
Satisfaction with workbooks
　　questionnaire, 375-379
Scabini, E., 224, 267
SCAI (systematically structured
　　computer-assisted
　　interventions), 15, 18-19
Schema-focused cognitive therapy.
　　See Stage-specific schema
　　workbook
Schmidt, U., 307-309, 310-311
Schneider, J. A., 315-316
School Refusal Assessment Scale
　　(SRAS), 285, 293-294

School-refusal behavior
case studies, 294-298
escape from aversive
social/evaluative situations,
288-290
forms, 293
future of manuals and workbooks,
298-299
negative affectivity, 286-288
overview, 283-284
parent workbook, 285-286, 288,
289-290, 291, 292
pursuit of attention, 290-291
pursuit of rewards outside of school,
291-292
rationale for workbook
development, 284-285
reasons, 284
research, 293-294
therapist manual, 285-292
workbook title and content, 285-286
Schore, A. N., 362
Schrieken, B., 358
Schultheis, G., 18, 253-254
Schumm, W. R., 219
Science of writing, 68
Scogin, F., 146
Scriptotherapy, 174, 188
SE (Structured Enrichment), 17
Seagal, J. D., 206
Secure sockets layer (SSL), 354
Seim, H., 318
Self-assessment. *See also* Assessment
eating disorders, 307
gambling, 165
married couples, 235-236
Self-criticism and depression, 88-89
Self-disclosure, SWHA research, 87-88
Self-esteem, SWHA research, 87-88
Self-help books
eating disorders, 302
gambling addiction, 164-165
intentional coping mechanism from
abuse, 146
Self-help books, as workbook source of
information, 70
Selfhood model, 89-90, 108
Self-Other Profile Chart (SOPC)
marriage preparation, 228
SWHA research, 87-88, 89-90

Self-report
couples intimacy, 271
SWHA research, 75-76
workbook source of information, 67,
69-70
Seligman, M. E. P., 73
Selvini Palazzoli, M., 328
Semantic gap, 72-74
Semantic reconditioning, 69
September 11 events, 357, 358
Serrano, A., 49
*The Seven Principles for Making
Marriage Work*, 257-258
Sevier, Mia, 247
Sharing of Hurts Scale (SOH), 83-84
Sharp, L. K., 361
Shure, M. B., 105
Siegel, B., 115
Silver, M., 257-258
Silverman, W. K., 293
Simon, L., 205, 206
Single-subject design, 363-364
Sisyphus, 106
Skills and SWHAs, 94-95
Sleep-related problems and school-
refusal behavior, 292
Sloan, S., 79
Sloper, P., 329
SLOS (Smith-Lemli-Opitz syndrome),
337
Smith-Lemli-Opitz syndrome (SLOS),
337
Smoking, goal of changing behavior, 165
Smyth, J., 50, 68, 92, 363
SOGS (South Oaks Gambling Screen),
160, 165, 169-170
SOH (Sharing of Hurts Scale), 83-84
Somatic control exercises, 287
SOPC. *See* Self-Other Profile Chart
Sources of information for workbook
development, 69-72
South Oaks Gambling Screen (SOGS),
160, 165, 169-170
Specialization trends, 20-21
Specificity
advantages of workbooks, 39-41
formalization trends, 20
inadequate, 9-10
prevention techniques, 12
talk psychotherapy, 73

Spitz, A. M., 357
SRAS (School Refusal Assessment
    Scale), 285, 293-294
SSC scale, 239, 240
SSL (secure sockets layer), 354
Stage-specific schema inventory (3SI),
    132-133
Stage-specific schema workbook
    (3SWB)
  administration of workbook,
      131-132
  description of workbook, 131
  development of workbook, 129-131
  implications of workbook
      interventions, 134-135
  overview, 129
  role in cognitive-behavioral therapy,
      133-134
  sample assignment, 135-138
STAI (State-Trait Anxiety Inventory),
    86-87
Stanley, S. M., 255-256
Stanley's Commitment Inventory, 270,
    333
State-Trait Anxiety Inventory (STAI),
    86-87
Status
  individual psychotherapy, 9-12
  mental health needs, 7-9
Stepped care model for gamblers,
    162-164
Stepped treatments, 12, 51-53
Stevens, G., 146
Stewart, L., 28
Stop Blaming, Start Loving!: A
    Solution-Oriented Approach
    to Improving Your
    Relationship, 258-259
Storelli, Marco, 173
Striegel-Moore, R. H., 311
Structured Enrichment (SE), 17
Structured interventions, 75, 354-355
Successive sieves, 12, 51-53
Suicide
  depression and, 110-111
  impact of HPA hyperactivity, 358
Support evidence for workbook
    interventions, 49-50

Support groups, Charlie Brown
    Exceptional Patient Support
    Group, 115
Surgeon General Report on Mental
    Health, 5-6, 7-8
Surveys
  Clients Satisfaction Survey, 135
  consumer satisfaction, 49
  life-challenging conditions, 124-126
  participant satisfaction with
      workbooks, 375-379
  use of manuals, 42-43
SWHAs. See Systematically written
    homework assignments
Sykes, C. J., 9
Symptom Scale 77, 37
Systematically structured computer-
    assisted interventions (SCAI),
    15, 18-19
Systematically written homework
    assignments (SWHAs)
  antecedents, 65-68
  contents of workbooks, 4
  meta-analysis of workbook
      effectiveness, 92-93
  overview, 65, 96-97
  professional implications, 93-96
  research, 75-92
  semantic gap, 72-74
  sources of information, 69-72

TA (trainer-assisted) groups, 83-84
Talk
  disadvantages of, 41-42
  ineffectiveness for felons, 207
  matching evaluation and
      intervention, 41
  overreliance by therapists, 11
  reason for status of mental health
      needs, 8
  semantic gap, 72-73
  trends in therapies, 16
  use with programmed distance
      writing, 357
Tallman, K., 94
Talpone, Umberto, 327
The Tape of the Mind computer
    program, 177

"The Tape of the Mind Workbook,"
174
Tape recordings
measuring hemispheric dominance,
362-363
SWHA research and, 77-78
Tarquinio, Caterina, 173
TC (trainer-conducted) groups, 83-84
Teaching machines, 66
Telch, C. F., 315-316
Telehealth, 96
Television
trauma of September 11, 358
for workbook distribution, 359
Tennessee Self-Concept Scale (TSCS),
87-88
Tension-release relaxation exercises,
287
Terminology, mental health, 72
Terms and definitions to bridge the
semantic gap, 74
Test instruments, 68
Testing theories, 47-49
Theoretical models or books, as
workbook source of
information, 70
Theory testing, 47-49
Thiels, C., 308, 310-311
Tiller, J., 308-309
Time of Joy and Plans workbook, 229
T-K (Tukey-Kramer) test, 179, 184
Todd, G., 308-309
Tompson, M. C., 45
Tragedies, way of thinking, 175, 187
Trainer-assisted (TA) groups, 83-84
Trainer-conducted (TC) groups, 83-84
Trauma of abuse. *See Healing the
Trauma of Abuse: A Women's
Workbook*
Trauma Recovery and Empowerment
(TREM), 142, 143-145
Treasure, J., 307-309, 310-311
Treatment proper therapeutic step, 131
TREM (Trauma Recovery and
Empowerment), 142, 143-145
Trends
formalization of psychological
interventions, 13, 14-15
implications of formalization, 19-21

Trends *(continued)*
talk therapies, 16
textbook focus on specific
conditions, 12-13
Triumphs, way of thinking, 176
Troop, N., 308-309, 310-311
TSCS (Tennessee Self-Concept Scale),
87-88
T-test, 105
Tucker-Ladd, C. E., 147
Tukey-HSD, SWHA research, 85, 87,
90
Tukey-Kramer (T-K) test, 179, 184
Turnbull, S., 309
Turner, S., 329
The Two of Us Together with Others
workbook, 231-232
The Two of Us with Others workbook,
231
Typewriter, 353

Unguided self-help (USH), 311-313
Unhappiness and depression, 110
Unstructured versus structured
interventions, 75, 354-355
USH (unguided self-help), 311-313

Vaira, Francesco, 173
Value systems of indeterminism, 22
van de Ven, J-P., 358
Verifiability of workbooks, 40, 45
Vernberg, E. M., 10
Versatility of workbooks, 40, 42-44
Virtual reality therapy, 15
Visual imagery, 15
VRT, cost-effectiveness, 19

Wagner, V., 76-77, 79, 80
Wait-list condition (WL), 308, 312
Walsh, B. T., 313
Wampold, B. R., 10
Waters, 207
*We Can Work It Out: Making Sense of
Marital Conflict*, 259-260
Weeks, G., 79-80

Weeks, R., 206
Weintraub, M. D., 33, 66
Weisman, A., 45
Weissman, M. M., 35-36
Welcoming step, 226-228
Wellness Recovery Action Plan, 155
Wells, A., 311
Wheel of Wisdom
   administration procedure, 176-177
   analysis of results, 178-186
   Beck test, 179-180, 182, 184-185
   conclusions, 186-188
   constructions, 175-176
   illustrated, 178
   objectives and research hypothesis,
      174
   overview, 173
   sample analysis, 177-178
   scriptotherapy, 174, 188
   technique, 175-176
   Zung test, 179, 181, 183-186
*When Children Refuse School: A
      Cognitive-Behavioral
      Therapy Approach*, 285-286
When Men Batter Women, 261
Whitten, P., 96
Why Marriages Succeed or Fail, 260
Widom, C. S., 206
Wiger, D. E., 18
Wildman, R. W. II, 75-76, 80
Wile, D. B., 252-253
Wilfley, D. E., 316
Williams syndrome, 332
Williamson, D. F., 357
Wilson, G. T., 311, 312, 313

Wincze, J. P., 36
WL (wait-list condition), 308, 312
Wolf's syndrome, 332
Women
   substance abuse. *See* Manualized
      cognitive-behavioral protocol
   When Men Batter Women book, 261
   workbook. *See Healing the Trauma
      of Abuse: A Women's
      Workbook*
Wonderlich, S., 320-321
Work performance disorders, 366-368
World War I messages, 352-353
Writing
   change in healing methods, 7
   classifications, 33-35
   complex, 361
   DW. *See* Distance writing
   expressive, 363-364
   PDW. *See* Programmed distance
      writing
   programmed, 364
   science of, 68
Written treatment plans, 42

Yates, A., 49
Yim, L. M., 49

Zimmerman, R., 318
Zollman, M., 318
Zung test, 179, 181, 183-186
Zuroff, D., 88-90, 96

Order a copy of this book with this form or online at:
http://www.haworthpress.com/store/product.asp?sku=5063

USING WORKBOOKS IN MENTAL HEALTH

Resources in Prevention, Psychotherapy, and Rehabilitation for Clinicians and Researchers

_____ in hardbound at $69.95 ((ISBN: 0-7890-1593-5)

_____ in softbound at $49.95 (ISBN: 0-7890-1594-3)

Or order online and use special offer code HEC25 in the shopping cart.

COST OF BOOKS_____

☐ **BILL ME LATER:** (Bill-me option is good on US/Canada/Mexico orders only; not good to jobbers, wholesalers, or subscription agencies.)

☐ Check here if billing address is different from shipping address and attach purchase order and billing address information.

POSTAGE & HANDLING_____
(US: $4.00 for first book & $1.50 for each additional book)
(Outside US: $5.00 for first book & $2.00 for each additional book)

Signature_____

SUBTOTAL_____

IN CANADA: ADD 7% GST_____

☐ **PAYMENT ENCLOSED:** $_____

☐ **PLEASE CHARGE TO MY CREDIT CARD.**

STATE TAX_____
(NY, OH, MN, CA, IL, IN, & SD residents, add appropriate local sales tax)

☐ Visa ☐ MasterCard ☐ AmEx ☐ Discover
☐ Diner's Club ☐ Eurocard ☐ JCB

Account # _____

FINAL TOTAL_____
(If paying in Canadian funds, convert using the current exchange rate, UNESCO coupons welcome)

Exp. Date_____

Signature_____

Prices in US dollars and subject to change without notice.

NAME_____

INSTITUTION_____

ADDRESS_____

CITY_____

STATE/ZIP_____

COUNTRY_____ COUNTY (NY residents only)_____

TEL_____ FAX_____

E-MAIL_____

May we use your e-mail address for confirmations and other types of information? ☐Yes ☐ No We appreciate receiving your e-mail address and fax number. Haworth would like to e-mail or fax special discount offers to you, as a preferred customer. **We will never share, rent, or exchange your e-mail address or fax number.** We regard such actions as an invasion of your privacy.

Order From Your Local Bookstore or Directly From

The Haworth Press, Inc.

10 Alice Street, Binghamton, New York 13904-1580 • USA
TELEPHONE: 1-800-HAWORTH (1-800-429-6784) / Outside US/Canada: (607) 722-5857
FAX: 1-800-895-0582 / Outside US/Canada: (607) 771-0012
E-mailto: orders@haworthpress.com

For orders outside US and Canada, you may wish to order through your local
sales representative, distributor, or bookseller.
For information, see http://haworthpress.com/distributors

(Discounts are available for individual orders in US and Canada only, not booksellers/distributors.)

PLEASE PHOTOCOPY THIS FORM FOR YOUR PERSONAL USE.